KT-119-123

UNDERSTANDING POLITICAL CHANGE

The British Voter 1964–1987

Anthony Heath, Roger Jowell,
John Curtice, Geoff Evans,
Julia Field and
Sharon Witherspoon

PERGAMON PRESS

Member of Maxwell Macmillan Pergamon Publishing Corporation

OXFORD · NEW YORK · BEIJING · FRANKFURT
SÃO PAULO · SYDNEY · TOKYO · TORONTO

U.K.	Pergamon Press plc, Headington Hill Hall, Oxford OX3 0BW, England
U.S.A.	Pergamon Press, Inc., Maxwell House, Fairview Park, Elmsford, New York 10523, U.S.A.
PEOPLE'S REPUBLIC OF CHINA	Pergamon Press, Room 4037, Qianmen Hotel, Beijing, People's Republic of China
FEDERAL REPUBLIC OF GERMANY	Pergamon Press GmbH, Hammerweg 6, D-6242 Kronberg, Federal Republic of Germany
BRAZIL	Pergamon Editora Ltda, Rua Eça de Queiros, 346, CEP 04011, Paraiso, São Paulo, Brazil
AUSTRALIA	Pergamon Press Australia Pty Ltd., P.O. Box 544, Potts Point, N.S.W. 2011, Australia
JAPAN	Pergamon Press, 5th Floor, Matsuoka Central Building, 1-7-1 Nishishinjuku, Shinjuku-ku, Tokyo 160, Japan
CANADA	Pergamon Press Canada Ltd, Suite No. 271, 253 College Street, Toronto, Ontario, Canada M5T 1R5

First edition 1991

Library of Congress Cataloging-in-Publication Data
Understanding political change: The British voter
1964-1987/Anthony Heath ... [et al.]. — 1st ed.
p. cm.
Includes index.
1. Elections—Great Britain. 2. Voting—Great Britain.
3. Great Britain—Politics; and government—1945-
I. Heath, A. F. (Anthony Francis)
JN956.U53   1990   324.941′085—dc20   90-48282

British Library Cataloguing in Publication Data
Understanding political change: The British voter
1964–1987.
1. Great Britain. Electorate
I. Heath, Anthony
324.62

ISBN 0-08-037255-4 Hardcover
ISBN 0-08-037256-2 Flexicover

Printed in Great Britain by BPCC Wheatons Ltd, Exeter

Contents

List of Tables and Diagrams

Tables labelled "N" appear in the footnotes within each chapter

Acknowledgements

We are particularly indebted to the Sainsbury Family Charitable Trusts, the ESRC, and Pergamon Press for funding this study. The Sainsbury Trusts generously allowed us to combine the British Social Attitudes Survey and the British Election Survey in 1987. We are also deeply indebted to the previous investigators—David Butler, Donald Stokes, Ivor Crewe, Bo Sarlvik, James Alt and David Robertson—for initiating and maintaining the series of British Election Studies which have made our study possible, and to the ESRC Data Archive at the University of Essex for providing the data for the earlier studies.

Our academic debts are many. We would like to mention in particular Andrew Adonis, Vernon Bogdanor, Andy Brown, David Butler, Bruno Cautres, Peter Clifford, David Cox, Duncan Gallie, J Gershuny, Geoff Garrett, Nan Dirk de Graaf, John Goldthorpe, Michelle Kiang, Denise Lievesley, Sarah-K McDonald, Bruno Paulson, Clive Payne, Jane Pearce, Chris Rootes, Byron Shafer, Peter Taylor-Gooby, Richard Topf, John Vickers, Jennifer Waterton and the members of ESRC Advisory Committee—Bob Bennett, Hugh Berrington, Peter Kellner, Glyn Matthias, Howard Newby, Geraint Parry and Hugh de Quetteville.

This book would not have been produced without the help of Elaine Herman, Shirley Parker, Jane Roberts and Joan Senior at Oxford and of numerous colleagues in various departments at SCPR. We are very grateful to all of them.

The author wishes to acknowledge the following sources for permission to use their material:

Her Majesty's Stationery Office for extracts from *Economic Trends* No. 422, December 1988.

Croom Helm for extracts from Crewe, "Great Britain" in *Electoral Change in Western Democracies*, Crewe and Denver (eds.), 1985.

Gower Publishing Company Ltd for extracts from Davis, "British and American Attitudes" in *British Social Attitudes: The 1986 Report*, 1986.

Basil Blackwell Ltd for extracts from Heath and McDonald, "Social change and the future of the Left," *Political Quarterly*, Vol. 58 (1987).

The Macmillan Press Ltd for extracts from Price and Bain "The Labour Force" in *British Social Trends since 1900*, Halsey (ed.), 1988.

The MIT Press for extracts from Vickers and Yarrow, *Privatization: An Economic Analysis*, 1988.

Polity Press for extracts from Abercrombie, Warde et al, *Contemporary British Society*, 1988.

Chapter 1

Social and Political Change

Our central concern in this book is to explore the social and political sources of electoral change in Britain. We intend to examine how the British electorate has changed and with what political consequences. Has the electorate become more volatile, less loyal to particular classes or parties but more inclined to switch votes on the basis of the government's record, personal self-interest and the issues of the day? Has there been the emergence of new structural or ideological cleavages which have taken the place of the old ones based on social class? Have the Conservative government's interventions to shape the social structure, whether deliberate as in the case of the extension of popular capitalism or inadvertent, had measurable electoral consequences? And how much room for manoeuvre do the political parties have in shaping public attitudes?

In answering these questions our main sources of data are the series of British election studies carried out after each General Election since 1964. These are academic sample surveys of representative cross-sections of the electorate in Great Britain (excluding Northern Ireland and Scotland north of the Caledonian Canal). They are a unique resource for understanding social and political change in Britain. (Further details of the surveys are contained in the Appendices.)

The postwar period has seen marked changes both in the electorate and in the fortunes of the political parties. In 1951, for example, Labour received 49.4% of the votes cast in Great Britain, and Labour and Conservative between them received 97.1% of the total number of votes cast, compared with a meagre 31.5% for Labour and 74.8% for the two main parties in 1987. 1951 marked the high point of Labour's fortunes and of the two-party system, and the subsequent years have seen a marked, albeit unsteady, decline of Labour at the polls, the rise of the Liberals and, briefly, of their Alliance with the SDP, and more recently the successes of the Greens in the Euro-elections of 1989 where they won 15% of the votes. In contrast the Conservatives have been able to hold their share of the vote fairly steady.

The trends have not been smooth ones. The General Election results have fluctuated quite widely, and by choosing alternative starting and finishing points for one's trends, one can modify the picture quite considerably. There are always bound to be considerable fluctuations due to transitory events such as the pre-election boom of 1966 or the miner's strike and three-day week of 1974. But the long-run direction of change has been clear enough, and it has not been an encouraging one for Labour. Thus between 1945 and 1970, Labour did not once fall below 40% of the vote; since 1970 it has only once, and then only barely, exceeded 40%.

TABLE 1.1 Share of the Vote in Great Britain 1945–87

	Conservative	Labour	Liberal/SDP	Other	
1945	39.3	48.8	9.2	2.6	99.9%
1950	43.0	46.8	9.3	0.9	100.0%
1951	47.8	49.4	2.6	0.3	100.1%
1955	49.3	47.3	2.8	0.6	100.0%
1959	48.8	44.6	6.0	0.6	100.0%
1964	42.9	44.8	11.4	0.9	100.0%
1966	41.4	48.9	8.6	1.1	100.0%
1970	46.2	43.9	7.6	2.3	100.0%
February 1974	38.8	38.0	19.8	3.4	100.0%
October 1974	36.7	40.2	18.8	4.3	100.0%
1979	44.9	37.8	14.1	3.2	100.0%
1983	43.5	28.3	26.0	2.2	100.0%
1987	43.3	31.5	23.1	2.1	100.0%

Sources: Craig (1981, 1988)

At the same time, there has been a transformation of the electorate; it has become more middle class, more educated, more prosperous, owning their own houses and shares. In 1951 65% of the labour force were in manual jobs, but by 1981 this had fallen to 50% and has almost certainly continued to fall since then (see table 13.1). In 1951 31% of the housing stock was owner-occupied, but by 1986 this had risen to 63%, and was still rising (see table 13.5). In the early 1950s around four-fifths of school-leavers left without any academic qualifications, but by 1986/87 only 11% left with no qualifications and 55% left with O-levels or higher qualifications (Social Trends 1989). If we set real Gross Domestic Product (per capita) to 100 in 1951, then the figure for 1987 was 195, and again was still rising (Butler 1989).

It is not implausible to link these social and political trends and to suppose that the social changes can at least in part explain the decline of the Labour party and success of the Conservative and centre parties, including the Greens. The Labour party has traditionally been the party of the (shrinking) working class, of the council estates, and of the trade unions. The centre parties and now the Greens tend in contrast to be rather stronger among the middle-class and educated voters, while the Conservatives have (in the twentieth century) been the party of business. Thus it is the middle class parties that have thrived while the working-class party has declined. Since there is no sign of these social trends abating or changing their direction, the long-run outlook for the Labour party does not initially appear cheerful.

There has however been considerable controversy over the nature of the causal links between social structure and political behaviour. The most radical thesis is that the causal connection between class and voting behaviour has tended to wither away, leaving behind an open and volatile electorate (see in particular Crewe 1984, Robertson 1984, Franklin 1985, Rose and McAllister 1986). There has been, it is claimed, a move from "closed-class to open elections". As Rose and McAllister put it:

> "The electorate today is wide open to change; three-quarters of voters are no longer anchored by a stable party loyalty determined by family and class ... The question facing many voters today is not whether to maintain an established party loyalty. It is: which of the parties supported in the past should I vote for next time?" (1986 : 1)

This view, if correct, is much more cheering for the Labour party. If class is no longer an important determinant of how people vote, then the declining size of the working class need not be of any great electoral significance. The long-run direction of political change can no longer be read off from the long-run social changes. By suitably adapting its appeals, the Labour party or indeed any party can hope to win more votes and regain power. The open electorate essentially means that the electoral future is open to any of the political contenders.

Writers who support this kind of view point to the decline of cohesive working-class communities centred on the old heavy industries like steel and shipbuilding and their replacement by more mixed neighbourhoods; to the increase in social mobility; to the extension of affluence within the working class thus eroding traditional values; to the increased education of the electorate making it politically more sophisticated; and to the increased availability of political information through the mass media and television in particular.

Thus in place of the traditional worker who identified with his social class and identified with Labour because "it is for the working class" (described by Butler and Stokes 1969 on the basis of the 1964 and 1966 election studies), these contemporary writers describe a more instrumental voter who is not anchored to any social grouping but is at the centre of numerous cross-pressures and more likely to vote on the basis of issues, personalities, or his personal standard of living than on class loyalty.

There is indeed substantial evidence that voters are no longer so strongly attached to their parties. In the 1960s 44% of electors said they were very strongly Conservative, Labour or Liberal, but this collapsed to 30% after the February 1974 election, and has since fallen even further to 19%. In this sense, if in no other, contemporary voters are less attached to their parties than they were before. As Ivor Crewe has summarised it: "the committed electorate has begun to make way for the hesitant electorate" (Crewe 1984:203–4).

On the other hand, we shall see in chapter 2 that electoral volatility has not in fact changed all that much. Voters' behaviour in General Elections, which after all represents the bottom line, was not much more fickle in the 1980s than it was twenty-five years earlier. Nor is it entirely clear that class has declined all that much in causal importance. In *How Britain Votes* (Heath, Jowell and Curtice 1985) we argued that Labour's decline in 1983 was general, not class-specific, that the dominant impression since 1964 was one of "trendless fluctuation" rather than steady dealignment, and that "Faced with these short-run fluctuations the political scientist does better to search for political sources of the parties' success and failure than to blame long-run changes in the character of the classes" (Heath, Jowell and Curtice 1985 : 35). This has been a somewhat controversial thesis, although it has since been supported by other investigators (Marshall, Newby, Rose and Vogler 1988; Weakliem 1989).

The theses of a shift from "closed-class to open elections" (Rose and McAllister 1986), of "the decline of class and the rise of issue voting" (Franklin 1985), of "class secularization" (Robertson 1984), or of "class and partisan dealignment" (Crewe 1984) may therefore be somewhat exaggerated. It may well be that many of these writers have fallen prey to what Marshall, in an analysis of similar arguments in sociology, has called "dualistic historical thinking". As Marshall and his colleagues have put it:

"These arguments are the probable consequence of a tendency towards dualistic historical thinking whereby a communitarian and solidaristic proletariat of some bygone heyday of class antagonism is set against the atomized and consumer-oriented working class of today. Not only is it the case that historical data suggest a less romantic reality: sectionalism, privatism, and instrumentalism have always been close to the surface of working-class life. It is also true that, conversely, class solidarities retain an importance that undermines many contemporary accounts of late capitalist societies in which sociability and altruism are reputed to have given way entirely to a 'one-dimensional' and atomized consumerism" (Marshall et al 1988:206).

These theses of dealignment, the open electorate, and so on, are in essence theses about the destruction of the earlier (and perhaps mythological) electorate divided into distinct and cohesive social classes and its replacement by a socially amorphous and more homogenous electorate. As Rose and McAllister suggested "We're all Alliance nowadays" (Rose and McAllister 1986:143). There are however alternative theses which suggest that there may be *new* lines of cleavage which divide the society rather than an absence of cleavages. On these interpretations, Britain is still divided into groups with opposing interests and ideologies but the boundaries between them are now radically different.

One of these alternative interpretations, while agreeing that social class has become less important, suggests that new social cleavages based on "sectoral locations" have come to take its place. Dunleavy and Husbands for example talk of a "polarization of consumption patterns between a commercial, commodity mode and a public service mode" particularly in the areas of housing and transport (Dunleavy and Husbands 1985:22). They suggest that there is a conflict of interest between people dependent on state provision of housing or on public transport and those who have access to the private housing market or private transport, a conflict which is particularly marked in the working class since the great majority of the middle class have long had access to both private cars and private housing. Furthermore, they suggest, these conflicts have become more politicized in recent years so that they are now tending to supplant class itself as a basis of political behaviour.

Other new sources of cleavage are believed to divide the middle classes too. Thus a number of writers (including Dunleavy and Husbands) have suggested that there is a major conflict of interest within the middle class between those employed in the private sector and those in the public sector. Thus it has been suggested that the new middle class of white-collar employees in the public sector has an interest in expanding government intervention and will accordingly favour political parties that support such government intervention. As McAdams puts the argument:

"Expansion of existing public sector agencies provides job security and opportunities for upward mobility for those already in the agencies, and the creation of new agencies provide opportunities for lateral mobility. Also, the expansion of government probably provides psychic rewards for those in government, in much the same way that increased regulation of business imposes psychic costs on executives, independent of any material costs" (McAdams 1987:25).

On the face of it this proposition seems so self-evidently true that social scientists are in danger of being accused of discovering the obvious and platitudinous. The proposition was not however supported by McAdams' American data.

A somewhat different line of argument focuses not on the distinctive interests of the new middle class but on their distinctive ideology and values. Inglehart and Rabier (1986) for example have talked of a shift from "class-based politics to quality-of-life politics". The essential ideas here are that the economic success of industrialized nations like Britain and the widespread affluence and security that they enjoy mean that some members of the electorate can turn their attention to new higher-order values to do with individual freedom, self-expression, the quality of the environment and so on. There is thus, it is held, a shift from the Old Politics of economic growth, public order and traditional life-styles to a New Politics concerned with the quality of life (Inglehart 1971, 1981; Dalton 1988). These new "postmateri-alist" values as they have been called are widely seen as a source of the rise of the Greens in Germany and they may perhaps be related to their rise in Britain too.

So while the thesis of the open electorate implies a relatively amorphous and homogeneous set of voters, the New Politics imply a divided electorate, albeit one divided along rather different lines from before. Once again, this means that the parties' electoral fortunes cannot be read off from the changes in the size of the social classes. Instead, we have to attend to the changes in patterns of employment and consumption, or to the changing value orientations of the electorate. Some of these interpretations remain fairly pessimistic for Labour since the new cleavages surrounding housing and transport are also ones where the numbers of potential Labour supporters are in decline as home and car ownership continue to rise, and so this view is one which dooms Labour even more to electoral extinction than does the original formulation based on social class.

More cheerful for the Left, perhaps, are the theories of new postmaterialist values. They at least point to the possibility of a growing radical group in the middle class that might in theory compensate for the declining numbers of traditional Labour voters in the working class. Whereas the old materialist left was based in the working class, the new post-materialist left is held to be a phenomenon of the educated middle classes, brought up in affluent environments and without the pressing material concerns of the traditional working class. The growing middle class of the late twentieth century might thus not presage continued Conservative dominance after all but rather provide a growing source of radicalism.

However, most writers are inclined to see the New Politics more as a source of new parties than as a rescue line for the old ones. The danger to the established left-wing parties is that, by espousing the new agenda of quality-of-life issues, they run the risk of losing their traditional supporters in the working class even faster than they might otherwise have done. The old and new value orientations, it is claimed, largely cross-cut and the parties thus face crucial trade-offs. For example, if the Labour party espouses nuclear disarmament, it may gain middle-class converts but it may also alienate its traditional working-class supporters who retain their beliefs in traditional social values. (Dalton 1988, Lipset 1981, cf Przeworski and Sprague 1986.)

All these views take rather a passive view of the role of the political parties themselves. They tend to see parties as the passive beneficiaries or victims of social change. Parties have to adapt to the new social realities. If there is a shift from a closed-class to an open electorate choosing on the basis of individual policy preferences, then the logical outcome is that the parties must either converge on the same centrist position, since this is where the bulk of the electorate lies, or must go down to certain electoral defeat (Downs 1957). There may be a future for the Labour party but not for a socialist party. Or if there is a shift from class-based politics to quality of life politics, then there may be hope for a radical programme aimed at improving the environment, increasing democratic participation, or extending civil rights to minorities, but it still offers little hope to the Old Left objectives of the redistribution of income and wealth.

However, it would in our view be wrong to see the political parties as wholly prisoners of social change. Although many changes such as the transformation of the class structure seem to continue more or less unchecked whichever party is in power, social change may nonetheless not be wholly independent of the political process. The present Conservative government, for example, has tried to shape social change through its policies of council house purchase and wider share ownership. Over one million council houses, approximately 5% of the total housing stock, were sold to their tenants between 1980 and 1987 (Social Trends 1989, table 8.9). Participation in the government's privatization of publicly-owned corporations was even more extensive. The programme of sales more than tripled the number of share owners to a fifth of the population (Social Trends 1989). This extension of popular capitalism, as it has been termed, was thus a major government initiative which was almost certainly intended, inter alia, to extend the Conservatives' social base. As Norris has suggested:

" . . . the radical impetus of Thatcherism is not simply to appeal to voters' 'hearts and minds', but a more ambitious strategy directly to change the 'ratchet of socialism' by tilting the electorate permanently in a Conservative direction" (Norris, 1990:66).

Our evidence in chapter 8 (and that of Norris) suggests that this may not have been altogether successful, at least in the short run, since purchasers were already relatively Conservative-inclined, but these measures may still have had the effect of consolidating Conservative support.

Secondly, other economic policies pursued by the two Conservative administrations of 1979–87 may have had unintended social and political consequences. Most obviously the government's anti-inflationary measures probably led to a rapid increase in unemployment in the early 1980s and have maintained it at a high level ever since. Unemployment at the time of the 1987 election was over double its level when the Conservatives took office in 1979, although there could be some argument over the precise extent of the government's culpability in this.

Paradoxically the rise in unemployment may have benefited the government electorally rather than damaged it: most previous research suggests that unemployment leads to political apathy, as the unemployed are removed from their participation in the more politicized world of the shop floor, not to political radicalism (Schlozman and Verba 1979). Certainly, the rise in the level of unemployment has not had the dire effects on government popularity that was once predicted by Goodhart and Bhansali (1970) who claimed that "for every increase in unemployment of 10,000 the government loses nearly 1 per cent of its popular lead" and "a governing party which allows the level of unemployment to exceed 450,000 six months before the election is likely to lose" (1970:64).

There has also been a marked decline in trade union membership since the Conservatives took office in 1979, falling from its peak of 13.3 million members in 1979 to 10.5 million in 1986 (Social Trends 1989). Again, it is not possible to determine how far this was due to government policies, such as their repeal of Labour's closed shop legislation, to unintended consequences of their economic policies (for example the anti-inflation policies that led to the rise in unemployment) or simply to long-run shifts in the British economy away from traditional heavy industries to newer, small-scale and high-tech industries, changes that might have occurred under any government. Nevertheless, on the by no means uncontentious assumption that union membership is causally linked to Labour voting, the decline of union membership represents a further contraction of the Labour party's social base.

Economic inequality has also increased greatly under Mrs Thatcher (Bean and Symons 1990, Layard and Nickell 1989). "While there may have been real gains under the Thatcher regime, they have so far not been shared widely, for the Thatcher years have coincided with a remarkable widening of the income distribution in the UK, reversing a long-established trend" (Bean and Symons 1990:46). In part this is due to the fact that the Conservative governments have made the tax system very much less progressive; in part to the increased numbers of people on social security (a consequence of higher numbers of long-term unemployed); and in part to the increased demand for high-skilled workers rather than low-skilled, a shift that probably has little to do with Mrs Thatcher.

As with the extension of popular capitalism and the rise in unemployment, the electoral consequences are not entirely obvious. But an electorate that is more unequal economically may also become a more polarized electorate politically.

There have, then, been substantial changes under Mrs Thatcher in popular capitalism, in unemployment, in economic inequality and, it should perhaps be added in economic growth (although the Conservatives' economic miracle seems to have been somewhat exaggerated: as Layard and Nickell succinctly put it "Opinion formers are well disposed to believe in the Thatcher miracle because it has been pretty miraculous for them" (1989:2). We doubt if these changes are wholly due to the deliberate policies of the government, but equally we doubt if they can be ascribed wholly to exogenous forces that would have occurred under any government.

Quite aside from these social and economic interventions, there is another means by which governments, and perhaps opposition parties, can help to shape the electorate. Thus by their rhetoric and their packaging of policies (both the contents and the presentation of the package) parties may have some influence over public opinion.

Stuart Hall for example has talked of the Conservatives' Great Moving Right Show and of the "authoritarian populism" espoused by Mrs Thatcher:

> "[Thatcherism] is a rich mix because of the resonant traditional themes—nation, family, duty, authority, standards, self-reliance—which have been effectively condensed into it. Here elements from many traditional ideologies . . . have been inserted into and woven together to make a set of discourses which are then harnessed to the practices of the radical right and the class forces they now aspire to represent" (Hall 1979:17).

The implication is that Mrs Thatcher's authoritarian populism carried at least some sections of the electorate with it.

The evidence that popular attitudes actually did shift to the right is not at all strong (see Curtice 1986; Crewe and Searing 1988), but the idea that parties may shape attitudes, rather than having to respond passively to them, is not without merit. Even in the new world of the open-minded, volatile voter, attitudes and values do not materialize out of thin air, and even in the old world of class loyalty it is unlikely that manual work automatically led to left-wing attitudes.

It may be that the Great Moving Right Show failed to move public attitudes because attitudes towards nation, family and authority were already well entrenched. The very fact that they are "resonant traditional themes" may make them resistant to political manipulation. But other, newer, themes that are not so rooted in existing social institutions may prove more malleable. This may apply particularly to new issues like the environment which have yet to become deeply rooted through processes of political socialization.

There is nothing particularly novel about this view. The old, although now unfashionable theory of party identification theory held that, if the political parties come to adopt visible and distinctive positions on an issue, they will tend to carry their identifiers with them (Belknap and Campbell 1952).

But it is a view which seems to have been neglected recently. In place of the older theory of party identification, theories of the instrumental voter choosing rationally between political parties on the basis of his or her preferences like a consumer in the marketplace have come into prominence (for example Himmelweit et al 1985). And like firms in the marketplace, the assumption is that political parties must respond to public demand, or lack of demand, for their products. We doubt if matters are quite this simple. Dualistic theoretical thinking may be as inappropriate as dualistic historical thinking.

Chapter 2

Electoral Volatility

One of the most important claims about the British electorate over the last twenty-five years is that it has become more open and more volatile, less inclined to vote on the basis of class loyalty and more inclined to vote on the basis of the issues of the day, the government's record, the personalities of the leaders, and so on. Ivor Crewe has provided the clearest and most cogent statement of this thesis although similar views have been expressed by many other writers. In 1984 he wrote:

> "As partisan and class ardour cooled, however, considerations other than habitual party and class loyalties began to influence the voting decision of more and more electors. In particular, campaign-specific factors—the outgoing government's record, the major issues of the day, the party leaders' personal qualities, specific and perhaps quite trivial incidents—took on a greater significance. Judging from the opinion polls, the three-to-four week campaign has had a stronger impact in recent years . . . Moreover, even the votes of those adhering to their usual party in the campaign are prone to waver more. Between 1964 and 1979 the proportion of voters who left their final voting decision until the campaign jumped from 17 per cent to 28 per cent, and the proportion claiming to have thought seriously of voting differently in the course of the campaign rose from 24 per cent to 31 per cent. The committed electorate has begun to make way for the hesitant electorate." (Crewe 1984:203-4)

What we have here is a theory about the changing social psychology of the voter. Whereas, it is claimed, people used to vote on the basis of habitual party loyalty, their commitment has declined and they are now open to a much wider range of influences. Instead of having a general bond with their parties, today's voters are influenced by a host of specific factors. Crewe and his colleagues have used the phrase "secularization of party choice" to refer to this process (Crewe, Sarlvik and Alt 1977:185). Traditional loyalty has given way to rational action.

Linked to, and explaining, this thesis of the voters' changing social psychology is a thesis about the changing character of the social environment in which the voter operates, and in particular a thesis about the declining cohesion of the social classes. Robertson for example has used the parallel phrase "class secularization" to describe this process (Robertson 1984:86).

In this chapter (and in the two which immediately follow) we shall concentrate on the social psychological thesis about the secularization of party choice. We shall then move on in chapter 5 to the sociological thesis of class secularization.

Attachment to the parties

One of the major pieces of evidence for the "secularization of party choice" is that there are fewer electors nowadays than there used to be who identify with any of the political parties and, even more strikingly, fewer with a very strong identification.

Throughout the series of British Election Studies respondents have been asked (with only minor wording changes):

"Generally speaking, do you usually think of yourself as Conservative, Labour, Liberal, or what?"
"[If accepts party affiliation] how strongly (chosen party) do you generally feel—very strongly, fairly strongly, or not very strongly?" (BES 1964).

Answers to these questions have been interpreted as measures of the electors' "partisan self-image" (Butler and Stokes 1969:37) or "party identification" (Belknap and Campbell 1952) and as indicating something about voters' attachments to their political party.

Butler and Stokes' work (both their survey questions and their theories) drew heavily on the American theory of party identification. The theory was developed during the 1950s and 1960s as evidence emerged that ordinary voters in America showed low levels of political information, knowledge or interest, did not have stable attitudes towards political issues, and exhibited low levels of ideological sophistication (Belknap and Campbell 1952, Campbell et al 1960, Converse 1964).[1] It appeared however that voters did have stable attachments to specific political parties and the term party identification was coined to refer to these attachments.

It was argued that these attachments performed the psychological function of helping the voter cope with political information and the complexities of politics. Voters would, for example, tend to adopt the same stances on the issues of the day as their party did. Furthermore, these attachments performed the political function of anchoring the electors to their parties and thus reducing the risk of political instability—something that particularly worried American writers in the aftermath of the politically unstable 1920s and 1930s.

> "Few factors are of greater importance for our national elections than the lasting attachments of tens of millions of Americans to one of the parties. These loyalties establish a basic division of electoral strength within which the competition of particular campaigns takes place. And they are an important factor in assuring the stability of the party system itself" (Campbell et al, 1964:67).

After the two British General Elections of February and October 1974 Crewe and his colleagues discovered that the strength of party identification had crumbled (Crewe, Sarlvik and Alt 1977). Not unreasonably, the popularity of party identification theory has never been the same since in Britain (see in particular Budge, Crewe and Farlie 1976), and it has been replaced by a variety of theories of the rational, instrumental voter who votes not out of loyalty to his or her party but rather on the basis of the government's record (Fiorina 1981) or the issues of the day (Himmelweit et al 1985).

And just as the earlier writers saw party identification as a source of electoral stability, so the crumbling of party identification has led to expectations of instability. Rose and McAllister, for example, have concluded that "Instability is certain to characterize the electorate for the whole of the 1980s" (1986:160). (See also Crewe 1985; Dalton, Beck, and Flanagan 1984.)

TABLE 2.1 Trends in Party Identification

	Conservative	Labour	Liberal/SDP	Other	None	N
1964	39	42	12	1	7	101% (1757)
1966	36	45	10	1	9	101% (1860)
1970	40	43	8	1	8	100% (1796)
February 1974	35	40	13	2	10	100% (2460)
October 1974	34	40	14	2	10	100% (2356)
1979	38	36	12	1	13	100% (1868)
1983	36	31	17	2	14	100% (3923)
1987	37	30	16	2	14	99% (3788)

Source: British Election Study cross-section surveys

Table 2.1 brings up to date the trends in partisanship.[2] As can be seen, there is a steady albeit slow decline in the proportion of the electorate who identified with a political party. Whereas in the first election study of 1964 only 7% of respondents rejected a party identification, by 1987 14% did so.[3] Much more dramatic have been the trends in strength of party identification. Table 2.2 looks at the people who identified with a party and shows that there was a decline from 48% to 23% in the proportion with a very strong identification.[4] The major change occurred in 1974, but the trend has continued on its downward path since then.[5]

TABLE 2.2 Trends in Strength of Party Identification A

	very strongly	fairly strongly	not very strongly		N
1964	48	40	12	100%	(1623)
1966	48	42	11	101%	(1688)
1970	47	41	13	101%	(1651)
February 1974	33	48	19	100%	(2162)
October 1974	29	52	19	100%	(2063)
1979	25	53	23	101%	(1621)
1983	25	47	28	100%	(3231)
1987	23	48	29	100%	(3134)

% of identifiers who felt ......

Source: British Election Study cross-section surveys

If we focus exclusively on the proportion with a very strong identification, we shall probably exaggerate the implications of the changes. Very strong and fairly strong identifiers happen to be rather similar to each other in their behaviour. For example the 1983–87 panel study showed that 79% of very strong identifiers cast their votes in the same way at the two elections, compared with 75% of fairly strong identifiers but only 59% of not very strong identifiers. It would probably be sensible to combine the first two categories, giving a decline from 88% to 71% in the proportion with a strong identification.

The trends have affected all the main parties alike, although, as table 2.3 shows, the fall has been relatively modest among Conservatives and Labour but much more substantial among the Liberals. At the beginning of our period the Liberal identifiers were not all that different from Labour or Conservative in their strength of support for their party. Not perhaps surprisingly, however, the subsequent growth of the Liberals has seen the recruitment of rather weak identifers. People who have recently defected from another party are hardly like to identify with their new party as strongly as its long-standing supporters do.

All the same, we should note that, even in 1987, it was still a majority of the respondents to our survey who said they were very, or fairly strongly, Conservative, Labour, Liberal or SDP. If we combine the results of tables 2.1 and 2.2 we find that 61% of all respondents reported a strong identification with their party in 1987. So, although there has been change, this evidence does not suggest an electorate that is altogether rootless. On this measure, attachment has declined but it has by no means disappeared.

Nevertheless, tables 2.1 and 2.2 provide rather convincing evidence of change. Something important seems to have been going on. However, other evidence does not give nearly such a clear picture of a committed electorate giving way to a hesitant electorate. No clear-cut trend appears when we look

TABLE 2.3 Trends in Strength of Party Identification B

	% who identified with their party very or fairly strongly		
	Conservative identifiers	Labour identifiers	Liberal/SDP identifiers
1964	89	89	82
1966	88	90	89
1970	90	87	79
February 1974	82	84	66
October 1974	81	85	71
1979	78	80	64
1983	77	72	61
1987	77	73	55

Source: British Election Study cross-section surveys

at the proportions who wavered or who left their decision how to vote until the campaign.

Throughout the election studies, voters have been asked when they made up their minds. Unfortunately, a major methodological discontinuity occurred in 1974. In the first three studies conducted by Butler and Stokes, respondents were asked: "How long ago did you decide to vote that way?" (BES 1964). It appears that this was an open-ended question. In the February 1974 election study (and the subsequent ones) it was replaced with a closed question, namely:

"How long ago did you decide that you would definitely vote the way you did—a long time ago, sometime this year, or during the campaign?" (BES February 1974; underlining as in the interview schedules).

These questions were of course asked only of voters. Nonvoters are therefore excluded from the results.

The first column of table 2.4 shows the trends over time, and there is indeed a major change in the figures in February 1974. However, the change in format from open to closed, and the introduction of the word definitely, mean that we can draw no firm conclusions from the jump of eleven points in late deciders. There is a serious danger that the change is artifactual. All we can be sure of is that there was no trend between 1964 and 1970, and no systematic trend between 1974 and 1987. Apart from the rather surprisingly high figure of 28% in 1979, the other figures are pretty constant. Crewe's conclusions were of course drawn after the 1979 election but before the 1983 figures became available. In 1979 one might reasonably have surmised that more and more people were leaving their decisions until the campaign, but the subsequent figures demonstrate how hazardous it is to extrapolate from

TABLE 2.4 Trends in Hesitancy

	% of voters who decided during the campaign	% of voters who thought of voting for another party	N
1964	12	25	(1504)
1966	11	23	(1517)
1970	12	21	(1431)
February 1974	23	25	(2071)
October 1974	22	(21)	(2008)
1979	28	31	(1597)
1983	22	25	(3293)
1987	21	28	(3280)

Notes: The Ns are the numbers answering the question on when the vote was decided.
The percentage in brackets is of doubtful validity (see footnote 6).
Source: British Election Study cross-section surveys

short-run trends. The 1979 figure proves in hindsight to have been a freak and the trend vanishes when the figures are updated to 1987.

Another piece of evidence comes from the question which immediately followed that on the timing of the vote decision. In the Butler and Stokes surveys respondents were asked "Did you think of voting for any other party?" (BES 1964). But again, unfortunately, there was a change of practice in February 1974 (and beyond). This time respondents were asked:

"Was there any time during the election campaign when you seriously thought you might vote for another party?" (BES February 1974; underlining as in the interview schedules)

The second column of table 2.4 shows the trends over time, or rather the lack of any smooth trend.[6] The picture is rather higgledy-piggledy and is quite different from the smooth trends of party identification. Again, 1979 is marked by a relatively large number of waverers, and in general recent elections have seen slightly more waverers than earlier ones, although the methodological changes make this verdict an unsafe one.

The picture, then, is not quite as clear as it initially appeared to be. The methodological difficulties mean that we can say nothing very useful about the changes in timing or wavering in 1974, but even if we concentrate on the period since 1974 the different pieces of evidence do not tell a consistent story. Partisanship has continued to decline, but there is no sign of any change in the timing of voters' decisions, and little sign of change in whether voters seriously considered voting for a different party.

Trends in net volatility

The general assumption made by political scientists is that, as voters' strength of attachment to their parties has weakened, so they will have become more volatile in their behaviour. And as we noted above, there is certainly evidence that voters who are less strongly attached to their parties are also more volatile.

Volatility, moreover, is ultimately the acid test of these debates about voters' attachment to the parties. Whatever voters may claim about their decisions or their strength of support, we are likely to be more impressed by what they actually do in the polling booth.

In looking at voters' behaviour, an important and useful distinction is that between net volatility and overall volatility (Crewe 1985:9). Net volatility refers to the change in the distribution of the vote between two elections, and was of course rather low between 1983 and 1987 as the parties' shares of the vote scarcely changed. Overall volatility, on the other hand, refers to the total amount of vote-switching that has taken place. The crucial point is that a great number of people change their votes at successive elections, although in most cases these changes simply cancel out: switches from Labour to Conservative, for example, are matched by switches in the reverse direction. As Crewe explained:

"In a period of dealignment the pool of relatively unattached electors swells: more voters are 'up for grabs'. But this does not necessarily undermine the established two-party system, let alone realign it in a predictable direction. The two parties may take voters from each other. If they do it simultaneously, turbulence in the electorate can still produce a stable outcome (stable dealignment)" (Crewe 1984:211).

An important question, therefore, is whether this turbulence or overall volatility has increased. The implication of the trends in party identification is that it will have done so.

First, however, it is useful background to look at patterns of net volatility. Table 2.5 shows two measures of net volatility. The first column shows the net inter-election volatility, that is the changes in the parties' shares of the vote. Following standard practice we have calculated the index of dissimilarity for the distributions of the vote at each pair of successive General Elections (calculated from table 1.1).[7] The index of dissimilarity is a rather more useful measure than the older one of swing since it takes account of changes in the Liberal (and Other) shares of the vote as well as changes in Conservative and Labour shares. It is the appropriate measure to use in a multi-party system. Moreover, as can be seen from table 1.1, it is the Liberal share of the vote which has shown some of the biggest absolute changes.

As we can see, net volatility tended to be low in the 1950s (the index averaging around 3.5), was slightly higher in the 1960s (averaging 5.1) and peaked in the 1970s (averaging 7.6 but heavily affected by the high figure for February 1974). The 1980s have seen one volatile election and one rather stable one.

TABLE 2.5 Trends in Net Volatility

	Change in the parties' shares of the vote	Mean fall in support for the Government in by-elections
	percentage points	
1945–50	3.8	4.5
1950–51	7.3	2.0
1951–55	2.1	1.9
1955–59	3.2	8.8
1959–64	5.9	13.5
1964–66	4.3	1.8
1966–70	6.0	16.8
1970–February 74	13.3	13.1
February 74–October 74	3.1	0.5
October 74–79	8.2	9.5
1979–83	11.9	11.4
1983–87	3.2	14.0

Source: Table 1.1, Crewe (1985)

In interpreting these figures we have to bear in mind that there have been major changes in the number of Liberal candidates. The number fluctuated quite considerably between 1945 and 1974 (see Butler and Butler 1986:226–8). Thus the Liberals fielded 475 candidates in 1950 but only 109 in 1951, and this might account in part for the rather high net volatility between those two elections. Again, the Liberals fielded 332 candidates in 1970 but 517 in February 1974 and this too might in part account for the record level of 13.3 reached by the index. Some of the volatility, therefore, must be regarded as forced volatility. It tells us about the options facing the electorate as well as about the nature of the electorate itself.

Again, following Crewe's pioneering work, the second column of table 2.5 presents a second measure, namely the mean fall in by-election support for the incumbent government during each inter-election period.[8] We must ignore short periods such as February to October 1974, when only one by-election was held, but in most periods there were enough by-elections to give a reasonable measure.[9]

The second column gives a rather different picture from the first. By-election volatility clearly dates back to the early 1960s and has remained fairly high since then (particularly if we ignore the two short Labour administrations of 1964–6 and February to October 1974). In addition, on this criterion the 1983–87 period turns out not to be a stable one after all but the second most volatile on record.

These by-election results certainly support the argument that the underlying turbulence can be quite high despite a stable General Election outcome. But equally these results suggest that mid-term protests against the government have been with us for over twenty-five years and have shown no tendency over that period to increase in magnitude.

Trends in overall volatility

We turn now to overall volatility between elections. Whereas net volatility can be calculated from the official election results, the pattern of vote-switching between parties—the flow-of-the-vote from one party to another—must be estimated from survey data. The preferred method used by previous investigators has been to draw on panel studies as the basic source of information for the interior of the flow-of-the-vote table and then to adjust the data, using the technique of proportional marginal adjustment, so that the exterior of the table corresponds to the official election outcomes.

The flow-of-the-vote tables constructed by the earlier investigators are shown at the end of this chapter, while table 2.6 gives our estimates for 1983–1987.[10]

TABLE 2.6 Flow of the Vote 1983–87

		Con	Alliance	Lab	Other	Didn't Vote	Leaving electorate	
	Conservative	20.0	2.3	0.5	0.4	3.2	2.1	28.5
	Alliance	2.1	9.2	2.4	0.1	2.4	0.9	17.1
1983	Labour	0.4	1.0	12.7	0.2	3.1	1.2	18.5
	Other	0.2	0.2	0.1	0.5	0.4	0.1	1.4
	Didn't vote	5.9	2.5	4.4	0.3	11.0	1.7	25.7
	Entering electorate	1.9	1.1	2.0	0.1	3.7		8.8
		30.5	16.3	22.1	1.6	23.8	6.0	100.0

Sources: 1983–87 panel study: 1983 and 1987 cross-section surveys

The general pattern shown in table 2.6 is very similar to that found by previous investigators for the earlier elections. Thus the largest percentages fall on the main (top-left to bottom-right) diagonal, representing people who cast their votes in the same way at successive elections (or in the case of non-voting who abstained at both elections). Thus we estimate that, out of all the people who were eligible to vote in 1983 or 1987, 20% voted Conservative on both occasions, 9% voted Alliance on both occasions, 13% voted Labour on both occasions, and 11% abstained both times.

If we sum these percentages on the diagonal, we find that 53% voted the same way at both elections. The table, however, includes many people who were not eligible to vote in one or other election—those entering the electorate as they came of age and those leaving through death or migration. If we recalculate our figures on the basis of those eligible to vote at both elections, our figure of overall stability rises to 63%.

This leaves 37% of people in the off-diagonal cells, that is people who behaved differently at the two elections. As we can see, there was very little direct switching from Labour to Conservative or vice versa (less than 1% in total). This again is a general phenomenon which can be observed in all the flow-of-the-vote tables. There is rather more interchange between Conservative and Alliance and between Alliance and Labour (nearly 8% in total). But the largest off-diagonal cells (containing over 20%) are those involving non-voting.

Non-voting raises serious problems in the measurement of electoral stability. Firstly, there are technical problems of measurement (see Swaddle and Heath 1989). For rather different reasons, neither the survey data nor the official election results give very good estimates of the total level of non-voting. Owing to the ageing of the register before it comes into use, and to the errors it contains even when new, the official results will tend to overestimate non-voting. (Moreover, since the age of the register has varied at different elections, and since errors seem to be increasing over time, this tendency of the official results to overestimate non-voting is not constant.) On the other hand, owing to misreporting and to response bias, surveys tend to underestimate non-voting. Table 2.6 uses the official estimates to calculate the overall levels of non-voting in 1983 and 1987, and as nonvoters tend to be rather volatile, the table will in consequence tend to overestimate the volatility of those voters who really were eligible to vote in both elections.

Secondly, the interpretation of non-voting is not wholly straightforward. As Crewe and his colleagues have suggested (Crewe, Fox and Alt 1977), and as has been confirmed by Swaddle and Heath (1989), very few non-voters are deliberate abstainers. Most non-voting can be ascribed to circumstantial factors such as ill-health, absence on polling day because of work or holidays, and the like. Some of the volatility, then, between voting and non-voting has the character of forced volatility and is caused in part by circumstances outside the voters' control.

This suggests that another useful measure might be the level of stability among those who actually did manage to vote in two successive elections. On this basis we find that overall stability between 1983 and 1987 was 81% leaving only 19% who voted for different parties at the two elections.

We do not wish to suggest that any of these is the correct measure of overall volatility. There certainly seem to have been particular elections when deliberate abstention occurred on a significant scale. Thus between 1966 and 1970 there was an unusually large flow from Labour to non-voting, and this may well have cost Labour the election. So it would probably be wrong to say that non-voting is always forced to the same degree. Restricting ourselves to people who voted in both elections, therefore, will sometimes be a misleading measure of overall volatility. It is probably fairer to say that this measure gives a *minimum* estimate of overall volatility.

We could also get much higher estimates of volatility if we took into account people's behaviour at elections other than General Elections. Given the much lower turnout at local or European elections than in General Elections, overall volatility would certainly increase greatly if we included them in the analysis.[11]

We doubt, then, if it is very sensible to rely on a single measure of overall volatility in the electorate. It is more sensible to look at trends over time, using a variety of measures, to see whether or not volatility (measured in standard ways and, we trust, with constant levels of measurement error) has increased.

TABLE 2.7 Trends in Overall Volatility

	% of combined electorates who changed	% of eligibles who changed	% of voters who changed
1959–64	45	35	18
1966–70	49	34	16
1970–February 1974	51	42	24
October 1974–1979	49	37	22
1979–1983	49	40	23
1983–1987	47	37	19

Notes: the 'combined electorates' include both those entering and those leaving the electorate;
'eligibles' are defined as people who were eligible to vote in both elections;
'voters' are those who were eligible to and voted in both elections.
Source: calculated from tables 2.6, 2.10–2.14

Our next step, then, is to look at the trends over time in our three measures of overall stability. Table 2.7 gives rather little comfort to anyone who believes that there has been a transformation in the electorate. All three measures show much the same changes over time, the differences being rather modest and following no clear trend towards increasing volatility. Volatility was at is highest on all three measures between 1970 and 1974, but since then it has fluctuated. Between 1983 and 1987 it was almost exactly at the average of the thirty year period. Trendless fluctuation might seem to be a sensible way to characterize the pattern or rather the lack of pattern.

It is possible that alternative measures of overall volatility might display more of an upward trend, but we are rather doubtful. Rose and McAllister (1986) suggested for example that there had been "a noteworthy trend up in the proportion of voters floating between parties". They found that it rose from 10% between 1959–64 to 12% between 1970-February 1974, and to 16% between 1979–83. However, we can calculate from table 2.6 that it fell back between 1983–87 to 10%.

There would seem to be no good empirical grounds, therefore, for supposing that overall volatility displays any consistent upward trend (at least over the period covered by our surveys). It has certainly varied, and it seems to have been rather higher in the 1980s than it was in the 1960s. But it was higher still in the early 1970s.

This still leaves us with a paradox. Strength of party identification is related to volatility; the strength of party identification has declined substantially; but volatility has increased very little.

It is easy to exaggerate the extent of the paradox, however. Consider the following simulation. Suppose that strength of party identification was related to volatility in the 1983–87 period in just the same way as it was in the 1966–70 period. Suppose further that strength of party identification declined between 1966 and 1983 in the way that it actually did. We can then calculate by how much volatility would have changed if both these assumptions held true.

This simulation suggests that overall volatility would have been 6% higher in the 1983–87 period than it was in the 1966–70 period. But the second and third columns of table 2.7 suggest that it was in fact around 3% higher.[12] There is still a discrepancy to be sure, but what these calculations bring out is that an apparently dramatic decline in the proportion of very strong identifiers by 25 points (table 2.2) translates into a much less dramatic 6 point increase in volatility.

Our interpretation of the discrepancy is that party identification might in part be measuring people's *satisfaction* with their parties. Now, a decline in satisfaction need not necessarily lead to an increase in volatility (either net or overall) if the opposing parties have also become less attractive. After all, voting behaviour on a rational choice model depends on the perceived difference between the parties not on the absolute level of satisfaction with one's preferred party (Downs 1957).

Fluidity

Comparing tables 2.5 and 2.7 it is fairly clear that overall volatility (the total amount of switching) has followed a rather similar pattern to net volatility (the changes in the distribution of the vote). Thus on both measures volatility was at its highest between 1970 and 1974, and was next highest between 1979 and 1983. The similarity is not surprising since, statistically, the measure of overall volatility is not independent of net volatility. Most obviously, if there is some net volatility there must logically be some overall volatility as well.

A useful additional analysis, therefore, is to control for the level of net volatility. For example, there was much less net volatility between 1983 and 1987 than there had been between 1979 and 1983. So although overall volatility declined, it is interesting to ask whether it declined less than we would have expected given the big reduction in net volatility. In effect, was the underlying turbulence increasing? More technically, did the statistical association (net of the marginal changes) between current and previous vote become weaker? This might shed some light on the question whether the voters' underlying social psychology has changed.

To investigate this question we use log odds ratios. These have the important property that they are statistically independent of the marginal distributions. The symmetrical log odds ratios, which are the ones we deal with here, can be thought of as measuring the degree of fluidity or stickiness between particular parties. A ratio of 0 indicates that the two events are statistically independent, and the larger the value of the log odds ratio, the greater is the stickiness. Fienberg (1980) notes that the odds ratio has several desirable properties but "Surprisingly, this measure appears only rarely in social science research literature, although it is widely used in chemical, genetic and medical contexts" (Fienberg 1980:17).

It should also be noted that log odds ratios are mathematically analogous to the technique of proportional marginal adjustment which has been used uncontroversially by Butler and Stokes (1968), Sarlvik and Crewe (1983), and Rose and McAllister (1986) in constructing flow-of-the-vote matrices. Readers may be reassured to know that the conclusions which follow are formally identical to those that would be obtained if we used the technique of proportional marginal adjustment to set all the flow-of-the-vote matrices to the same marginal distributions.[13]

TABLE 2.8 The Fluidity of the Vote: Symmetrical Log Odds Ratios

	Con: Lab	Con: Lib	Lib: Lab	Con: DNV	Lib: DNV	Lab: DNV
Panel Data						
1966–70	5.0	4.0	4.1	2.5	3.4	2.1
1970–74 (Feb)	4.5	3.8	3.9	2.2	2.5	1.9
1974 (Oct)–79	5.6	3.1	4.0	3.8	3.8	3.8
1983–87	7.2	3.7	3.9	2.4	2.8	2.3
Recall Data						
1959–64	5.3	3.5	4.4	2.5	3.9	2.2
1966–70	5.9	4.4	5.9	2.6	3.1	1.9
1970–74 (Feb)	5.0	3.6	3.9	2.4	2.7	1.8
1974 (Oct)–79	5.4	3.6	3.8	2.7	3.0	2.6
1979–83	5.4	3.6	4.3	2.3	2.8	2.6
1983–87	6.0	3.7	3.5	2.6	3.2	2.8

Sources: British Election Study panel and cross-section surveys

Table 2.8 shows the trends over time in the degree of fluidity between the three main parties, and between each of the main parties and non-voting. We show both the results when panel data are used and those when recall data are employed.[14] In general, these two different data sources give similar results. Some differences are naturally to be expected given the small number of people moving, for example, between Conservative and Labour, and the discrepancies are not particularly worrying. Thus the 95% confidence interval for the Conservative-Labour log odds ratio between 1966 and 1970 is 4.4 to 5.6 in the case of the panel data, and 5.3 to 6.5 in the case of the recall data.[15]

As we can see, there have been some consistent patterns throughout the series of election studies. Thus there is least fluidity between Conservative and Labour; there is rather more fluidity between Conservative or Labour and the Liberals; and there is most fluidity between voting and non-voting. This pattern is repeated (with the exception of the 1974–79 panel) in every single election study and with panel and recall data alike. It is tempting to say that we have here a law of British electoral behaviour.

This general pattern is hardly surprising. Given the greater ideological distance between Conservative and Labour, we would certainly expect to find least fluidity between them. And given the circumstantial factors which affect non-voting, we would also expect to find greater fluidity here.

Let us turn now to the trends over time. Again, no straightforward trend appears towards greater fluidity. Once again, the 1970–74 period appears to be unusual; fluidity appears to have been somewhat greater then than it was either earlier or later. The differences are rather small, but the result is repeated both in the panel and the recall data, giving us some confidence that the result is a real one. But there has been no longstanding trend towards increasing fluidity.

We can construct a simple measure of the overall level of stickiness by averaging the log odds ratios of table 2.8. We find that the average was indeed lowest in the 1970—February 1974 period, but has since recovered to its earlier levels.[16]

A rise in the overall average could of course conceal contradictory trends for some log odds ratios and no trends at all in others. Casual inspection of table 2.8 suggests that this is indeed the case. We can test this more rigorously using log-linear modelling.[17]

This analysis indicates that there has been no trend, in either direction, in the case of the Conservative:Liberal, Conservative:Nonvoting and Liberal:Nonvoting log odds ratios. Both the panel data and the recall data give the same results in this respect and so we can be very confident of these conclusions.

Next, we find hints of a trend towards increasing stickiness in the case of the Conservative:Labour log odds ratio, although the trend reaches statistical significance only in the case of the panel data. The natural interpretation of this trend is that the ideological distance between Conservative and Labour voters has gradually increased (particularly since 1974), thus making it psychologically more difficult for people to switch between them.

Conversely, there are hints of a trend towards increasing fluidity in the case of the Labour:Liberal log odds ratio. According to the recall data this trend is clearly significant, but the panel data in contrast is equally emphatic that there has been no change in the ratio. Given this contradictory evidence, we cannot draw any firm conclusions. However, there

TABLE 2.9 Modelling the Symmetrical Log Odds Ratios

		chi^2	df	p	trend parameter	standard error
		Panel data				
Con:Lab	(1)	22.7	3	0.000		
	(2)	10.9	2	0.004	0.14	0.04
Con:Lib	(1)	2.9	3	0.40		
	(2)	2.5	2	0.29	−0.02	0.04
Lib:Lab	(1)	0.2	3	0.98		
	(2)	0.0	2	0.98	−0.02	0.04
Con:DNV	(1)	8.5	3	0.04		
	(2)	8.1	2	0.02	0.02	0.03
Lib:DNV	(1)	3.6	3	0.31		
	(2)	3.4	2	0.18	−0.02	0.05
Lab:DNV	(1)	16.5	3	0.001		
	(2)	13.2	2	0.001	0.07	0.04
		Recall data				
Con:Lab	(1)	12.4	3	0.03		
	(2)	10.1	2	0.04	0.02	0.01
Con:Lib	(1)	4.0	3	0.55		
	(2)	3.8	2	0.44	−0.01	0.02
Lib:Lab	(1)	21.0	3	0.001		
	(2)	9.4	2	0.05	−0.06	0.02
Con:DNV	(1)	4.7	3	0.45		
	(2)	4.7	2	0.32	0.00	0.01
Lib:DNV	(1)	4.5	3	0.48		
	(2)	4.2	2	0.38	−0.01	0.02
Lab:DNV	(1)	24.5	3	0.00		
	(2)	8.7	2	0.07	0.04	0.01

Source: British Election Study panel and cross-section surveys

are rather good external reasons for supposing that Labour:Liberal fluidity may have increased. In the earlier elections the Liberals did not field candidates in every constituency, and Liberal candidates were particularly lacking in Labour-held working-class seats. The opportunities for switching between Labour and Liberal have therefore increased in the more recent elections.

Finally, both the panel and recall data show a trend towards increasing stickiness for the Labour:Nonvoting ratio. Thus in the early studies there seems to have been rather more fluidity between Labour and nonvoting than there was between Conservative or Liberal and nonvoting, but by the later studies the difference has disappeared. Again, the most plausible explanation is that reluctant Labour identifiers used to abstain as a form of protest whereas latterly they have been more able to use the option of defecting to the Liberals or the Alliance parties in recent elections.

Changing social psychology or changing political circumstances?

Different measures tell different stories. At the one extreme there has been an unequivocal decline since 1964 in the strength of party identification. At the other extreme there has been an equally unequivocal increase in the stickiness between Labour voting and nonvoting. In between there have been no clear trends in wavering, in by-election swings against the government, or in overall volatility.

We would not wish to claim that any single measure is the right measure. Thus party identification, net volatility, overall volatility, and fluidity are different concepts with different uses, not rivals. And while we might expect to find some statistical association between the trends in net and overall volatility, there is nothing intrinsically implausible about their following rather different trends from fluidity. Crewe was right to emphasize that a stable election outcome might be consistent with increasing turbulence in the electorate. Where commentators seem to have been in error is in supposing that turbulence (however defined) was tending to increase. The most that can be said is that overall volatility was slightly higher between 1983 and 1987 than it had been between, say, 1959 and 1964. But the difference is only modest; thus in the earlier of these two periods we found that 35% of eligibles changed their votes whereas in the later period this had increased to 37%.

Moreover, we have enough examples of trends which were promptly reversed at the next election to make us very cautious about extrapolating any of the trends apparent in our data. Thus, while our analysis of the log odds ratios gave hints of a trend towards greater stickiness between Labour and Conservative voting, we would certainly not wish to extrapolate this into the future. If the ideological distance between the Labour and Conservative parties declines, as well it might given the Labour party's policy review, we might expect this trend to be reversed at the next election.

In other words, even the trends which are apparent (and they are few in number and modest in scale), may well be the product of *political* changes rather than of any independent change in the social psychology of the voter. Voters' behaviour will be affected both by their social-psychological predispositions and by political circumstances. If the political parties' behaviour becomes more erratic, for instance, changing their major policies from one election to another, this might well be sufficient on its own to cause increased volatility in voting.

Another important change in political circumstances that may have affected overall volatility is the presence of Liberal or Alliance candidates. We have already noted that a change in the number of parties contesting a seat may lead to some forced volatility. But it is also important to recognize that overall volatility is likely to be higher in a stable three-party system than it is in a stable two-party system. As we have seen, direct switching between the Conservative and Labour parties is very rare. The opportunity of switching to a centre party is one that rather more people will take, and indeed we find that, during the 1966–70 period, overall volatility was four points higher in seats which the Liberals contested at both elections than it was in seats which it contested at neither election.

We do not need, therefore, to introduce theories about the changing social psychology of the voter in order to explain changes in volatility. The changing political circumstances facing the electors may be quite sufficient on their own to account for the fluctuations that have occurred.

TABLE 2.10 Flow of the Vote 1959–64

		1964					
		Con	Lab	Lib	Didn't Vote	Leaving	
1959	Conservative	22.3	2.1	2.9	4.4	3.5	35.2
	Labour	1.8	21.4	1.4	5.2	2.4	32.2
	Liberal	1.0	0.7	1.8	0.6	0.2	4.3
	Didn't vote	3.3	4.9	1.6	9.3	0.6	19.7
	Entering	2.5	3.1	0.5	2.5		8.6
		30.9	32.2	8.2	22.0	6.7	100.0

Source: Butler & Stokes (1974)

TABLE 2.11 Flow of the Vote 1966–70

		1970					
		Con	Lab	Lib	Didn't Vote	Leaving	
1966	Conservative	19.1	0.8	0.4	3.7	2.8	26.8
	Labour	3.2	18.0	0.8	6.5	2.9	31.4
	Liberal	1.5	0.7	2.0	1.1	0.3	5.6
	Didn't vote	3.5	3.5	1.1	12.1	1.0	21.2
	Entering	3.5	5.9	0.8	4.8		15.0
		30.8	28.9	5.1	28.2	7.0	100.0

Source: Butler & Stokes (1974)

TABLE 2.12 Flow of the Vote 1970–February 1974

		1974						
		Con	Lib	Lab	Other	Didn't Vote	Leaving	
1970	Conservative	19.6	2.6	1.9	0.3	3.6	2.4	30.4
	Liberal	0.5	2.9	0.3	0.2	0.6	0.5	5.0
	Labour	1.9	3.3	16.7	0.6	4.1	2.2	28.8
	Other	0.2	0.4	0.1	0.7	0.0	0.1	1.5
	Didn't vote	5.1	3.8	5.3	0.5	9.1	2.1	25.9
	Entering	1.3	1.5	3.4	0.2	1.9		8.3
		28.6	14.5	27.7	2.5	19.3	7.3	100.0

Source: Sarlvik and Crewe (1983)

TABLE 2.13 Flow of the Vote October 1974–79

		1979						
		Con	Lib	Lab	Other	Didn't Vote	Leaving	
1974	Conservative	17.3	1.0	0.7	0.1	2.4	3.0	24.5
	Liberal	3.4	4.7	1.4	0.1	1.9	0.9	12.5
	Labour	2.4	1.5	17.3	0.1	2.9	2.6	26.8
	Other	0.3	0.2	0.4	1.3	0.5	0.1	2.9
	Didn't vote	5.7	1.3	3.2	0.6	10.5	1.4	22.8
	Entering	2.6	1.3	3.6	0.1	3.0		10.5
		31.8	10.0	26.7	2.4	21.2	8.0	100.0

Source: Sarlvik and Crewe (1983)

TABLE 2.14 Flow of the Vote 1979–83

		Con	All	Lab	Other	Didn't Vote	Leaving	
				1983				
1979	Conservative	19.9	2.9	0.9	0.1	5.3	2.2	31.2
	Liberal	1.1	6.0	0.3	0.1	1.6	0.7	9.8
	Labour	1.5	4.5	13.6	0.2	4.5	2.0	26.2
	Other	0.1	0.4	0.2	0.9	0.6	0.1	2.3
	Didn't vote	4.4	2.6	2.6	0.2	11.0	1.0	21.8
	Entering	2.3	1.3	1.6	0.1	3.5		8.7
		29.3	17.6	19.1	1.5	26.5	6.0	100.0

Source: British Election Study 1983 and 1979 cross-section surveys

Notes

[1]Some of the conclusions have now been called into question on methodological grounds. In particular it has been suggested that the apparent lack of attitude consistency found by the earlier studies was due to poor measurement techniques. See Bishop, Tuchfarber and Oldendick 1978; Sullivan, Piereson and Marcus 1978.

[2]In 1983 and 1987 respondents who said they identified with the Alliance were asked whether they identified with the Liberals or the SDP. Only 10 respondents in 1983 and 24 in 1987 insisted on an Alliance identification.

[3]In the 1974 and 1979 surveys, refuseds were coded in the same category as the don't knows and are therefore included with the respondents without a party identification, whereas in the other surveys refuseds are treated as missing data.

[4]Don't knows have been included with not very strong. In the two 1974 surveys, identifiers with minor parties were not asked for their strength of identification, and they have accordingly been omitted from the calculations for 1974. In the 1979 and 1987 surveys strength of identification was asked of respondents who said they were closer to a particular party. To maintain comparability with the earlier surveys, these respondents have been placed in the category not very strong/ don't know irrespective of their reported strength of identification.

[5]Note that Miller, Tagg and Britto (1986) report a rather steadier but less dramatic decline using data from a panel commissioned by the Conservative party and covering the years 1965 to October 1974. They found that "In 1966 42 per cent of identifiers had a very strong identification but this figure had already fallen to 37 per cent in 1970 before dropping to 33 per cent in February 1974 and 32 per cent in October 1974" (Miller, Tagg and Britto 1986:42).

[6] The figure for October 1974 is of doubtful validity. In every other year there is a small number of people who did not answer the question; for example, there were 15 respondents who did not answer this question in 1987. But in October 1974 there were an unprecedented 160 not answereds. Something seems to have gone seriously wrong, either with the administration of the interview or the coding of the data. The most likely explanation is that some interviewers were confused by the preceding question which was to be asked only of respondents in Scotland. In Scotland the question does seem to have been asked correctly, and there is only one missing respondent.

[7] Strictly speaking the index of dissimilarity measures the proportion of voters who would need to change their votes to make the two distributions in question identical. The index is obtained by summing the differences between the two distributions and dividing by 2. Thus the 1983–87 index is $(0.3 + 3.2 + 2.9 + 0.0)/2 = 3.2$. This is sometimes called Pedersen's index. See Pedersen 1979, 1983.

[8] For a detailed analysis of by-elections see Taylor and Payne 1973.

[9] The figures for 1945–1983 are taken from Crewe 1985, table 5.2. Crewe notes that "Calculations for by-elections between 1970 and February 1974 exclude the Speaker's seat, Southampton Itchen, and those cases $(N = 12)$ where there was a non-trivial redistribution of constituency boundaries since the previous general election such that meaningful swing figures could not be calculated" (Crewe 1985:105).

[10] The flow-of-the-vote tables were constructed as follows. First, we obtained the official distribution of voting and non-voting in Great Britain in 1983 and 1987. This gives the marginal distributions. Second, we estimated from the demographic data in Social Trends 19, table 1.3 that 8.8% of the electorate in 1987 would have been new entrants who became eligible to vote for the first time after the 1983 General Election. Their voting behaviour was estimated from the 1987 cross-section survey. This gives us the figures for the bottom row of the table. Third, we estimated from the demographic data in Social Trends that 6.0% of the electorate in 1983 would have died before the 1987 election. (We ignore migration in these estimates since the numbers involved are relatively small and no data on emigrants' previous voting behaviour is available.) We also estimated their age distribution and from the 1983 cross-section survey calculated the voting behaviour of people with this age distribution. This gives us the figures in the final column of the table. Fourth we used the 1983–87 panel study to estimate the voting behaviour of people who were eligible to vote in both elections. These figures were then adjusted, using the technique of proportional marginal adjustment (Mosteller 1968), in order to ensure that the entries in the table sum to the marginal totals. This procedure closely follows that of Butler and Stokes (1974) and of Sarlvik and Crewe (1983).

[11] Including people's party preferences between General Elections would also affect our estimates. In the 1983–87 panel study, we also interviewed people in the autumn of 1986, and thus we have some measures of their party preferences at three points of time. 71% of the respondents (making no adjustments to the marginal distributions) voted or abstained in the same way in 1983 and 1987, whereas 61% gave the same response on all three occasions.

However, this means that some of the people who were volatile between 1983 and 1986 must have returned to their original party (i.e. their 1983 party) in 1987. This homing tendency as it has been called is almost certainly a general phenomenon that occurs, to a greater or lesser extent, in all inter-election periods. (See for example Miller, Tagg and Britto 1986). So while we could increase our maximum estimate of volatility by adding more inter-election time points, the homing tendency makes the meaning of this extra volatility rather hard to interpret.

We should also note that as we increase the number of time-points, so we increase the scope for measurement error and this will artificially increase the measure of volatility (assuming errors are uncorrelated). This is a point which does not seem to be generally recognized. All our measures involve some error, due to transcription errors by interviewers, coding errors and so on as well as to mistakes made by the respondents. These errors will tend to weaken the associations between our variables. In this case they will suggest that there was greater volatility than really occurred. This may become a very serious and misleading problem if we greatly increase the number of time points; what seems to be a lot of volatility may just be a lot of measurement error by the investigators! But measurement error must also be something of a problem even with our own measures taken just at two points of time. In general, if we correct for random measurement error, then our estimates of stability will tend to increase.

[12] The measure of the combined electorates who changed in 1966–70 is of course affected by the extension of the franchise to younger voters and hence by the unusually large number of voters entering the electorate. This is why it gives different results from the other two columns.

[13] The technique of proportional marginal adjustment has the property that the log odds ratios remain unchanged while the marginal totals (and of course the cell percentages) are adjusted. This is why it is such an attractive method for constructing flow-of-the-vote tables: the relationships between the variables (as defined by the log odds ratios and estimated through survey research) remain unchanged while the marginal totals are adjusted to correspond to the official election results.

[14] The log odds ratios have been calculated from the original data rather than from the flow-of-the-vote tables. In theory they ought to give the same results, and in some cases they actually do. However, there are some discrepancies for the 1959–64 period.

[15] It has been usual to question the use of recall data, on the grounds that it is substantially biased (see Himmelweit et al 1978; van der Eijk and Niemoller 1979). And it is certainly true that respondents are particularly prone to misreport votes for the Liberals or Alliance at previous elections. Thus the *marginal* distribution of past vote obtained from recall data is likely to be inaccurate. However, what is not generally appreciated is that the *relationship* between past and present vote is not so greatly affected (a point made in a different context by Weir 1975). Table 2.8 shows that panel and recall data in fact give very similar estimates of the relationships, and indeed the most suspect figures would seem to be those involving nonvoting in the 1974–79 panel. Given the processes of attrition and conditioning that occur in a panel,

it is not perhaps surprising that results for nonvoting are suspect (see
Waterton and Lievesley 1987). It is also worth noting that, with the exception
of the 1974–79 period, the panel data are derived from quite independent
samples from the recall data (see Appendix I).

[16] Thus in the case of the panel data the overall average moves from 3.5 to
3.1, 4.0 and finally 3.7. In the case of the recall data the average moves from
3.6 to 4.0, 3.2, 3.5, 3.5, and finally 3.6 again. We should of course note that
this overall average is an unweighted one and therefore does not take account
of the fact that some of the more fluid categories may be increasing in size.

[17] Our procedure here is to analyse separately each of the 2-by-2-by-n tables
corresponding to the six symmetrical log odds ratios. To each of these tables
we first fit the constant fluidity model; that is we test the hypothesis that the
log odds ratio in question remains constant. (This model fits the three
two-way interactions, namely previous vote by current vote, previous vote by
election, and current vote by election.) We then compute election as a linear
covariate and add to the model the three-way interaction between previous
vote, current vote and the covariate. By computing a linear covariate we use
up only one extra degree of freedom. The results of these models are shown
in table 2.9. The first row for each study shows the results of the constant
fluidity model, while the second row shows the results of adding the linear
covariate.

Chapter 3

The Rational Electorate?

The phrase "secularization of party choice" is an evocative one with its implication of a shift from traditional, habitual action to deliberate, rational action. Theories of this sort have been widespread in sociology and political science, and are by no means new. Scholars throughout the twentieth century (and earlier) have contrasted the rationality of their age with the tradition of previous epochs.

Among contemporary political scientists, Franklin provides much the most thorough treatment of this theme. He concluded that:

> "... the British electorate has moved to a more sophisticated basis for voting choice. No longer constrained to the same extent by characteristics largely established during childhood, British voters are now more open to rational argument than they were in the past. A party which ignores these developments and relies on past loyalties to bring supporters to the polls is unlikely to be as successful as a party which bases its appeal on careful assessment of the needs and wishes of the voting population, and skilfully presents its policies in terms of issues that are meaningful and salient to them" (Franklin 1985:152).

Franklin's theory of issue voting underlies a great deal of contemporary practical politics as well as academic political science. For example, the theory of issue voting would seem to be one element in the policy reviews which the Labour Party initiated in the wake of the 1987 defeat. One of the ideas behind the reviews seems to have been that an alternative policy package might make the party more attractive to the voter. Certainly, this was the view of three writers in a Fabian pamphlet:

> "As the Party sets out its stall for the next general election, it must ensure that it addresses its real weaknesses and does not adopt policies which are

not more popular than their predecessors". (Lipsey, Shaw and Willman 1989).

It must be said at the outset that there is some prima facie evidence in support of the proposition that issues and policies have become more important to the electorate in deciding how to vote. In 1983 and 1987 voters' attitudes towards the issues were more closely associated with the way they voted than had been the case in previous election studies. Attitudes have become better predictors of how people will vote. With technical variations in their statistical analysis, this is the basic evidence on which writers such as Franklin (1985) and Rose and McAllister (1986) rest their case for a rise in issue voting.[1]

As with volatility, however, we need to check whether the changes are due to the changing social psychology of the voter or to changing political circumstances. If the voters have indeed become "less constrained by characteristics established during childhood" and are now more "open to rational argument", then we might well expect their attitudes towards political issues to become more important influences on their vote. But equally, if the Conservative and Labour parties have moved apart in their stands on the issues, we would also expect there to be a stronger statistical association than before between attitudes and vote. Thus, on conventional rational choice lines, if the Labour and Conservative parties move away from the centre, voters with centrist attitudes will switch to the centre parties, while those who vote Labour or Conservative will now be more extreme subsets of the electorate. In effect, Labour and Conservative voters will now be more polarized in their attitudes, and this means that the usual statistical measures will show a stronger relationship between attitudes and voting for these two parties. Changes in the association between attitudes and vote may thus derive from changes in the ideological distance between the parties.[2]

What we need to do, then, is to take account of the distance between the parties. The crucial question becomes whether attitudes and vote have become more closely associated than would be expected given the perceived distance between the parties.

Perceived differences between the parties

Questions on the perceived positions of the parties on specific issues have not been asked in standard form throughout the election study series. There is however a standard measure of the overall difference between the parties which covers the full time-span of the election studies. Respondents were asked:

"Considering everything the parties stand for, would you say that there is a good deal of difference between the parties, some difference, or not much difference?" (BES 1964)[3]

TABLE 3.1 Perceived Differences between the Parties

	Good deal of difference	Some difference	Not much difference	Don't know		N
1964	46	24	26	4	100%	1733
1966	42	26	28	3	99%	1834
1970	32	27	37	3	99%	1828
February 1974	33	30	35	2	100%	2443
October 1974	39	30	30	1	100%	2361
1979	46	29	22	2	99%	1871
1983	82	10	6	2	100%	3952
1987	84	11	5	1	101%	3822

Source: British Election Study cross-section surveys

Table 3.1 shows the trends for this question. As we can see, just under half the electorate thought there was a good deal of difference between the parties in 1964, but this proportion gradually shrank to a third in the early 1970s. Thereafter it began to increase again. By 1979 it was back to the 1964 level and in 1983 it increased dramatically further. With the exception of 1974, these trends also parallel those in the level of Liberal voting. Rational choice theory predicts that, if the two main parties move apart, voting for the centre parties will increase, and broadly speaking this prediction is confirmed.

These findings on perceived differences between the parties are broadly confirmed by a similar series of questions asked by Gallup. The Gallup series goes back to 1951, and shows that the parties were seen as much further apart at that time. They then moved closer together during the late 1950s and 1960s, the period which commentators have often referred to as the era of consensus politics (Kavanagh 1987), before moving apart again in the 1980s.

Strictly speaking, our interest is in the perceptions of our respondents rather than in the objective reality of the differences between the parties. It is what the elector believes to be true that will influence behaviour, not the unread small print in the party manifestos. Nevertheless, the various analyses which have been made of party manifestos suggest that the perceptions of the electors do bear some relation with the content of the manifestos. Charlot (1975) has suggested that there was a substantial narrowing of the difference between the Conservative and Labour policies on the major economic issues (nationalization, planning and the distribution of wealth) between 1945 and 1966, although she suggests that the gap widened again in 1970 when the Conservatives under Mr Heath adopted a much more radical free-market policy.[4] The electorate did not seem to notice this at the time, and nor it must be said have most political commentators, who have failed to notice how much the free market element of Mrs Thatcher's policies owes to Mr Heath.

It also seems to be the case that the Labour party's policies moved further to the left in 1974, with more extensive promises of nationalization than had been seen in their manifestos since the early 1950s. However, Mr Heath's famous U-turn away from free market policies and back to interventionism and government controls effectively moved the Conservatives back towards the centre. The electorate could not unreasonably conclude therefore that the gap had stayed the same. Certainly, on the evidence both of the election surveys and the Gallup surveys, the electorate thought that the gap had not changed much in 1974.

Finally, there can be little doubt that the gap subsequently widened once more between Labour and Conservative under Mr Foot and Mrs Thatcher in 1983. And the absence of major policy changes in 1987 (apart from the largely un-noticed conversion of the Labour party to membership of the EEC) is in line with our respondents' perceptions.[5]

The crucial comparison, therefore, must be between 1964 and 1979. Perceived differences between the parties (and the level of Liberal voting) were rather similar in those two years. If party choice has indeed become secularized, the association between attitudes and vote should therefore have increased in 1979. But if voters' social psychology has stayed constant, the association should have stayed the same. Both theories, on the other hand, predict a stronger association between attitudes and vote in 1983 and in 1987, and so these two most recent elections do not enable us to discriminate between the rival theories.

The relationship between attitudes and vote in 1964

There is one important problem to resolve before we can get down to analysing the relation between attitudes and vote. The different election study teams asked rather different questions about political issues in the different studies. To some extent this reflects the fact that different issues were on the political agenda at different times. For example, in 1966 Butler and Stokes quite reasonably asked questions about Rhodesia which, under Ian Smith, had just declared illegal independence. But equally reasonably these questions were not repeated in later studies. Instead, questions were introduced in 1974 on new items on the political agenda such as North Sea oil.

This would not be a problem if we felt that each election study team had given proper coverage to the issues of the day. We could simply use whichever policy questions each team had thought appropriate to the election they studied. Unfortunately, this is not the case. Partly because they espoused a party identification theory of voting behaviour, Butler and Stokes asked many fewer policy questions than did their successors. We would thus stack the cards unfairly in favour of issue-voting if we compared the ten issue questions of, say, the 1964 survey with the fifty or so questions of the 1987 survey. We begin therefore by looking at the *common* issues which have been covered throughout the election study series. We will then expand our analysis to take account of the further issues covered in individual studies.

The common issues covered in all the election studies, although unfortunately not always asked with identical question wording, are nationalization (and privatization), trade union power, big business power, government spending on social services, defence, immigration and the Common Market. The questions asked on these themes in 1964 were as follows:

"There's also a lot of talk about nationalising industry. Which of these statements comes closest to what you yourself feel should be done? If you don't have an opinion about this, just say so.
A lot more industries should be nationalised.
Only a few more industries, such as steel, should be nationalised.
No more industries should be nationalised, but the industries that are nationalised now should stay nationalised.
Some of the industries that are nationalised now should be denationalised".

"There's a lot of talk these days about nuclear weapons. Which of these statements comes closest to what you yourself feel should be done? If you don't have an opinion, just say so.
Britain should keep her own nuclear weapons, independent of other countries.
Britain should have nuclear weapons only as a part of a western defence system.
Britain should have nothing to do with nuclear weapons under any circumstances."

"Do you think that the Trade Unions have too much power or not?"
"Do you feel that the government should spend more on pensions and social services, or do you feel that spending for social services should stay about as it is now?"
"Do you think that big business has too much power in this country or not?"
"If the question of going into the Common Market comes up again, do you think that Britain should go in or stay out, or don't you have an opinion on that?"
"Do you think that too many immigrants have been let into this country or not?"

To analyse the relation between voting behaviour and attitudes to these issues, we use logit modelling, which is the appropriate technique when we have a dichotomous dependent variable and categorical independent variables (see Fienberg 1980).[6] And since the question about the perceived difference between the parties can be taken to refer to the Labour and Conservative parties, we accordingly focus on whether people voted Labour or Conservative.

Table 3.2 reports the results of this analysis of the 1964 survey.[7] The parameters tell us how strongly each attitude goes with vote, controlling for the other attitudes contained in the analysis.[8] They thus tell us about the *net* relationships. We follow the usual rule of thumb that a parameter must be twice its standard error to be statistically significant. The index of concentration then gives us an overall measure of the relation between attitudes and vote. It is analogous to the variance explained in multiple regression (Haberman 1982).[9]

TABLE 3.2 Logit Model of Attitudes and Vote in 1964
(Conservative vs. Labour)

	Parameter	Standard error
Constant	− 0.23	(0.08)
Nationalization	− 1.19	(0.11)
Privatization	0.59	(0.10)
Trade Union power	0.67	(0.08)
Big business power	− 0.46	(0.08)
Social services spending	− 0.36	(0.09)
Independent deterrent	0.31	(0.07)
Unilateral disarmament	− 0.57	(0.14)
Common Market	0.01	(0.08)
Immigration	− 0.09	(0.11)
Index of concentration	0.40	
N	1333	

Source: 1964 cross-section survey

From table 3.2 we see that in 1964 attitudes to public ownership had the strongest net association with vote, followed by trade union power, big business power, spending on social services, and nuclear weapons. As expected, people who favoured further nationalization, who felt that big business had too much power, who felt there should be more spending on social services, and who favoured unilateral disarmament were relatively inclined towards the Labour party (as shown by the negative signs for these parameters). Attitudes to immigration and to the Common Market had no significant relationship with vote net of the other variables in the model. (In comparing the dichotomous and trichotomous variables, we cannot simply compare the size of the parameters. It is more sensible to look at the ratios of the parameters to their standard errors. Thus in 1964, the parameter for nationalization is over ten times its standard error, while trade union power comes next at eight times its standard error.)

These results suggest that, contrary to the received wisdom, issues were rather important in 1964. If in 1964 people had voted solely out of habitual party loyalty, then we would have expected them to agree with their party on *all* the major issues alike (or, where they disagreed, we would have expected their attitudes to be unrelated to their vote). For example, Labour party supporters would have been expected to adopt their party's line *both* on nationalization *and* on nuclear disarmament.[10] Thus if party identification were the sole source of voters' attitudes towards the issues, then these attitudes would have been strongly associated with each other, deriving in theory from the same common source. And once we had included one attitude in the analysis, the addition of further ones would have had little net effect.[11]

But the fact that attitudes to nuclear weapons had a strong relationship with vote *net* of the other attitudes included in the analysis casts this interpretation into doubt. In other words, the results of table 3.2 suggest that some people were influenced in their voting decision by the parties' stands on nationalization and privatization while others were influenced by their stands on nuclear disarmament. It appears therefore that voters in 1964 might well have been rather more rational and sophisticated than has usually been recognized.

The conventional model of voting behaviour in 1964 stresses the role of childhood socialization in the formation of political attitudes and behaviour (Butler and Stokes 1974, Franklin 1985, Rose and McAllister 1986). Party allegiance was believed to be largely learned through the family (a key element of the party identification theory which Butler and Stokes espoused).

Now there was certainly some truth in this view, but it was always an oversimplification. This can be seen from table 3.3. Here we present the results of two logit models. The first model predicts 1964 vote from the respondents' reports of their mother's and father's party preferences when they (the respondents) were young. The second model includes both parents' party preferences and the respondents' attitudes.[12]

TABLE 3.3 Childhood Socialization, Attitudes and Vote in 1964
(Conservative vs. Labour)

Independent variables	Index of concentration	N
Mother's and father's party preferences	0.24	1311
Mother's and father's party preferences plus respondents' attitudes	0.49	1291

Source: 1964 cross-section survey

As we can see, there is a substantial amount of truth in the notion that party allegiance was learned through the family. The first model shows that parents' preferences help to account for the way respondents voted in 1964. However, the second model shows that attitudes had a great deal of additional explanatory power. The index of concentration rises from 0.24 to 0.49 when we include attitudes as well as our measures of childhood socialization. In short, it is a considerable exaggeration to say that voters were "constrained" by characteristics largely established during childhood. They were surely influenced by them, but even in 1964 childhood socialization was very far from being the whole story.

The changing relationship between attitudes and vote

Identical questions were asked on all these issues in the 1966 cross-section survey and in the 1970 panel survey.[13] The questions on nationalization, trade union and business power have been asked in identical or similar form throughout the rest of the election studies as well (with the exception of the February 1974 survey in which very few issue questions were asked), and there have been questions on defence, government spending, race and the Common Market too, although sometimes with substantial wording changes.[14]

The most serious problem concerns defence. In the 1974 and 1979 surveys the respondents were asked about defence cuts, not about the nuclear deterrent. This change of focus probably reflects the changed nature of the political debate, with argument over the Labour party's policy of cuts in defence spending taking over from nuclear disarmament. There were changes in the wording of the Common Market and race questions too reflecting the changing political situation. For example, once Mr Heath had taken Britain into the Common Market and signed the Treaty of Rome, survey researchers could hardly go on asking whether "Britain should go into the Common Market or stay out" as they had done in the 1960s. Instead, an alternative question was introduced:

> "It is sometimes said that Britain should try to change the terms of entry into the Common Market and if this is not successful, get out ... [what do] you yourself feel should be done?" (BES, October 1974).

Table 3.4 charts the parameters for these questions over the whole series of election studies.

A number of points stand out. First, the rank ordering of the different issues remains rather stable, with public ownership consistently having one of the strongest net associations with vote. (It is interesting to note, however, that privatization has become the major discriminator in the later studies, while nationalization was the major discriminator in the earlier ones.) Trade union power also ranks consistently high, while in six of the seven election studies race comes at the bottom. Only in 1983 and 1987 does race have a significant net association with vote.[15]

The most marked changes are those involving defence. Attitudes towards Britain's nuclear deterrent declined sharply in importance after 1964 and became one of the least important of the seven issues in 1970. Defence cuts were also relatively unimportant in 1974 and 1979 but by 1987 nuclear disarmament had returned as a major issue, and indeed rivalled public ownership and trade union power as an influence on vote.

TABLE 3.4 Attitudes and Vote 1964–87 (Conservative vs. Labour)

	logit parameters						
	1964	1966	1970 (panel)	1974 (Oct)	1979	1983	1987
Constant	− 0.2	− 0.3	− 0.1	− 0.6	− 0.4	− 0.1	− 0.1
Nationalization	− 1.2	− 0.9	− 0.7	− 1.1	− 0.4	− 0.2	− 0.7
Privatization	0.6	0.6	0.7	0.8	0.8	1.0	1.2
Trade union power	0.7	0.7	0.6	1.2	1.1	1.0	1.1
Big Business power	− 0.5	− 0.6	− 0.6	− 0.5	− 0.5	− 0.5	− 0.4
Social Services spending/ welfare benefits	− 0.4	− 0.3	− 0.1	− 0.5	− 0.4	− 0.4	− 0.4
Independent deterrent/ more defence spending	0.3	0.1	0.2	0.4	0.1	0.5	0.0
Unilateral disarmament/ less defence spending	− 0.6	− 0.3	− 0.3	− 0.2	− 0.1	− 0.5	− 1.2
Common Market	0.0	0.1	0.2	0.7	0.2	0.9	0.5
Immigration/race equality	− 0.1	− 0.1	− 0.1	− 0.1	− 0.1	− 0.1	− 0.3
Index of Concentration	0.40	0.34	0.30	0.52	0.39	0.53	0.59
N	1333	1369	793	1462	1275	2307	2114

Sources: BES cross-section surveys and 1970 panel survey

These changes are by no means surprising given the recent history of the Labour and Conservative parties. Nor is the other major change, the emergence of the Common Market as an important issue in 1974 and 1983, particularly surprising. The Common Market was of course one of the key issues which led to the split between the SDP and the Labour party in 1981, and Labour's strongly anti-EEC stance is reflected in the pattern of the parameters.

Overall, the data of table 3.4 cast considerable doubt on the theory that the electorate has become more rational and more influenced by issues. The pattern of the parameters in 1964, 1966 and 1970 rather closely follows that predicted by our hypothesis of constant social psychology: as the Labour and Conservative parties were perceived to come closer together, so the co-efficients generally declined in size over the course of these three surveys. The overall relationship clearly weakened, as can be seen from the decline of the index of concentration from 0.40 to 0.30.

By 1979 the perceived gap between the parties had widened once more, and in keeping with our hypothesis of constant social psychology, the overall relationship between attitudes and vote had recovered almost to its 1964 level. In 1964 the index of concentration had been 0.40; in 1979 it was back at 0.39. There is no indication therefore that issues had become more important bases of party choice in 1979 than they had been in 1964. Our provisional decision, then, must be to reject the theory of the secularization of party choice.

There is, however, one major exception to our hypothesis. October 1974 shows a marked discrepancy from the pattern we had predicted. While table 3.1 suggests that perceived differences between the Labour and Conservative parties in October 1974 were not all that great, table 3.4 shows that the overall relationship between attitudes and vote was even stronger than it had been in 1964. Indeed, on every issue except for defence the parameters were larger in October 1974 than they had been before, and the index of concentration was markedly up on its 1964 level.[16]

It may well be the case, then, that issue voting increased in October 1974. Certainly, the relationship between attitudes and Labour and Conservative voting was a lot stronger than could be explained by party identification theory. It is notable that this is a similar story to that told in chapter 2, when the period between 1970 and February 1974 also proved to be rather unusual, with record levels of volatility.

Expanding the analysis

An important possibility we must now consider is that there were additional issues that were important in the later studies but were not included in the original list of seven issues covered in the 1964 survey. After all, it would be rather surprising if the common issues that were covered throughout the series were always the ones that figured most prominently in the voters' decisions.

In 1964 Butler and Stokes themselves asked about three additional issues concerning the monarchy, the links between the Labour Party and the Unions, and about strikes. In the 1966 and 1970 surveys there were further new questions on tax cuts, the death penalty, links with America, whether Britain gave up its Empire too fast, and on Rhodesia. Rhodesia's unilateral declaration of independence was certainly a new political issue that first came onto the political agenda at the 1966 election, and it is worthwhile seeing if these new items substantially change our results.

TABLE 3.5 Expanded Analysis of Attitudes and Vote
(Conservative vs. Labour)

	Index of concentration						
	1964	1966	1970 (panel)	1974 (Oct)	1979	1983	1987
Common attitudes	0.40	0.34	0.30	0.52	0.39	0.53	0.59
Common attitudes plus topical ones	0.43	0.42	0.37	0.53	0.43	0.55	0.62

Source: BES cross-section surveys and 1970 panel survey

As we can see from table 3.5, they do. The index of concentration increases in 1964, 1966 and 1970 when we include the extra issues, much of the work being done by the question on links between the Labour party and the unions in 1964, and by the question on Rhodesia in 1966 and in 1970. The new question on Rhodesia tends to compensate for the fact that nuclear disarmament seems to have been declining in electoral importance, and thus in the expanded analysis the downward trend in the relationship between attitudes and vote is somewhat reduced.

A very large number of issues were covered in the later studies from October 1974 on, and it would be a rather unfair comparison with the earlier studies to include them all. What we prefer to do is to expand our analysis to include those issues which the investigators of each survey seemed to have regarded as most important. For example, there were a small number of questions which the October 1974 investigators judged to be so important that both the respondents' attitudes and their perceptions of the parties' positions were asked. The same was true in 1979, 1983 and 1987. We therefore add the limited number of questions which each set of investigators seemed to regard as most important for the year they studied, and we make the assumption that each set of investigators was equally competent in judging the political agenda of their day.

In October 1974 there was only one additional issue which received this favoured treatment, namely North Sea oil. Its inclusion does not change our results very much. It had little effect on vote, net of the other issues already included, and so the overall relationship scarcely changes.

In 1979 the new, privileged questions were on the political system, tax cuts, incomes policy and unemployment, which had of course begun to rise under Labour giving Saatchi and Saatchi the opportunity for their famous election poster "Labour isn't working". These new questions boost the index of concentration for 1979, much as the extra questions did in 1964 and 1966. They do not therefore modify our initial conclusion that issue voting was at much the same level in the three elections.

Finally, in 1983 and 1987 the new, privileged questions covered tax cuts and government spending, unemployment and inflation, and law and order. Attitudes to law and order do not make a significant net contribution, but attitudes to tax cuts and government spending and to inflation and unemployment do have significant net relationships with vote. However, their inclusion in the model weakens some of the other relationships and so the overall relationship is little .changed.

The explanation for this is fairly straightforward. Attitudes towards, for example, unemployment and inflation correlate quite highly with those towards nationalization and privatization, which were already included in our original model. Their net impact is therefore going to be low since their effects have already in large part been picked up.

There appears to be no need therefore to change our provisional conclusions. Indeed, the main way in which the expanded analysis modifies our initial conclusions is to suggest that there were higher levels of issue voting towards the beginning of our period, in 1966 and 1970, than we had previously thought. It is the years in which the original model gave relatively low indices of concentration that have been most affected, whereas those years when the index was already high benefit little from the extra questions.

This analysis reinforces, therefore, our conclusion that voters were rational and sophisticated in the 1960s just as they are today, and that the changes since then are largely to be explained by the changes in the ideological positions of the parties. This conclusion is even more convincingly reinforced if we include Liberal voting in the analysis. One of the advantages of logit modelling and of the index of concentration is that they can be applied to a multi-category dependent variable. We do not have to restrict ourselves to the Conservative: Labour dichotomy but can look simultaneously at Conservative, Labour and Liberal voting. This also solves, to a considerable extent, the problem of the changes in ideological distance between the two main parties.

What we find is that, when we include Liberals, the explanatory power of issues is substantially reduced. This is not unexpected. Liberal voters are not as distinctive as voters for the other two main parties in their attitudes. But we also find that the explanatory power of attitudes remains effectively constant over time. Thus the index of concentration moves from 0.28 in 1964 to 0.29 in 1987. The fact, then, that a rise in issue voting is apparent only when we restrict ourselves to Labour and Conservative voters reinforces our view that it was the ideological polarization between the Labour and Conservative parties, rather than changes in the voters' social psychology, that accounts for our earlier findings.

These results are markedly at odds with those reached by Franklin in his analysis of the same period. In particular, Franklin found a steady increase in the total effects of attitudes on voting choice between 1964 and 1979 (Franklin 1985: tables 6.4 and 6.5).

There are a number of methodological reasons which could account for the differences between our results and Franklin's.[17] For example, Franklin controls for various aspects of childhood socialization in his analysis. As we have shown in table 3.3, attitudes had a strong relationship with vote in 1964, even after controlling for parental preferences. But it is also quite possible that the balance between childhood socialization and the voters' current attitudes has changed, the importance of socialization, relative to issues, declining since 1964.

Table 3.6 tests this hypothesis by including in our analyses measures of childhood socialization, namely mother's and father's party preferences when the respondent was growing up. (Unfortunately, the question about mother's party preference was not asked in 1974, and this year therefore has to be excluded from the analysis.)

As we can see, the explanatory power of childhood socialization was indeed rather lower in the three later surveys. In particular, the index of concentration for the relation between childhood socialization and vote falls from 0.24 in 1964 to 0.19 in 1979. The differences are not great, but they are in line with Franklin's hypothesis that political attitudes and party allegiance are not learned in childhood to quite the extent that they used to be.

However, we should also note that there has been a substantial increase in social mobility over the last quarter century. In 1964 47% of the respondents

TABLE 3.6 Childhood Socialization, Attitudes and Vote 1964–87
(Conservative vs. Labour)

Independent variables	Index of concentration					
	1964	1966	1970 (panel)	1979	1983	1987
Mother's and father's party preferences	0.24	0.26	0.29	0.19	0.21	0.19
Mother's and father's party preferences, plus respondents' attitudes	0.49	0.46	0.47	0.48	0.59	0.62

Source: BES cross-section surveys and 1970 panel survey

were in the same social class as their father had been, while 53% had experienced intergenerational social mobility. In 1987, however, intergenerational mobility had increased to 60%. Once again, then, it may not be people's social psychology but their situations which have changed. In the 1980s people may still learn their political attitudes through the family in much the same way as previous generations did. And in the 1960s people who were socially mobile might have changed from their parents' party allegiance much as the mobile do today. The point is that there are now more mobile people in the electorate, and hence the intergenerational transmission of political allegiance has declined.

The evidence does indeed support this hypothesis. Among the immobile, the effects of parents' party on one's current vote was just as strong in 1987 as it had been in 1964 (the index of concentration being 0.30 and 0.29 in 1964 and 1987 respectively).

Rationality and volatility

Our major conclusion, then, is that voters have displayed a fair amount of rationality and sophistication throughout the past quarter century. Even in the early 1960s they were merely influenced, rather than constrained, by childhood socialization and, while we do not doubt that many voters had strong party identities, their attitudes towards the major political issues do not seem to have followed the party line any more closely than they do today.

These results are of course closely in line with those of chapter 2, when we showed that overall volatility had changed little over the same period. At another level, however, it might be thought that there is something of a paradox in the conclusions of these two chapters. Earlier writers had tended to emphasize the role that habitual party loyalties played in maintaining electoral stability. Our results, however, seem to suggest that a sophisticated and rational electorate can also be fairly stable in its voting behaviour.

The solution to the paradox is almost certainly that attitudes themselves are rather stable. The early writers such as Butler and Stokes (and the Americans such as Converse from whom their work derived) believed that individual attitudes were rather unstable and that it was traditional loyalty which provided the cement binding voters to the parties. More recent research, however, has shown that the instability of attitudes which they found was most probably an artefact of poor questionnaire construction. Modern techniques of attitude measurement suggest that basic attitudes are rather stable after all (Heath and McDonald 1988).

Of course, attitude stability will produce voting stability only if the parties' positions are stable too. The more parties change their positions, the greater volatility we may find among the electorate. The polarization in the parties' positions in 1983 may thus help to explain why overall volatility was somewhat higher between 1979 and 1983 than it was between 1983 and 1987, when the parties' ideological positions remained more or less stationary. It also suggests that overall volatility may increase again at the next election if the parties are perceived to have come closer together.

Appendix: The Questions Used for Tables 3.4 and 3.5

In order to maximize comparability with the earlier studies, questions have been dichotomized throughout (with the exception of the questions on nationalization/privatization and on nuclear weapons/defence, which have been treated as trichotomies throughout). Don't knows have been included throughout. Alternative procedures for dichotomizing the questions and for allocating don't knows lead to some differences in the parameters, but do not affect the overall conclusions which we reach in the chapter.

Nationalization

The questions used on nationalization are: 1964—23a; 1966—20a; 1970—22; October 1974—21a; 1979—24a; 1983—37; 1987—36a.

In 1987, the question was changed to "Just to make sure about your views, are you generally in favour of more nationalization of companies by government, more privatization of companies by government, or—should things be left as they are now?"

Trade Union Power

The questions used on trade union power were: 1964—24; 1966—21; 1970—24; October 1974—59; 1979—56a; 1983—38a; 1987—110. In 1987 the question was asked in the self-completion supplement.

Big Business Power

The questions used on big business power were: 1964—26; 1966—25; 1970—29; October 1974—60; 1979—56b; 1983—38b; 1987—111. In 1987 the question was asked in the self-completion supplement.

Welfare State

The questions used on government spending on social services are: 1964—25a; 1966—22a; 1970—25; October 1974—22a; 1979—22a; 1983—45a; 1987—43a.

In 1970 a separate code was used for spending more on pensions, but we have combined this with the code for spending more on social services.

In 1974 and 1979 the question used was worded as follows:

"Now we would like to ask what you think about social services and benefits. Which of these statements do you feel comes closest to your own views?
Social Services and benefits have gone much too far and should be cut back a lot.
Social Services and benefits have gone somewhat too far and should be cut back a bit.
Social Services and benefits should stay much as they are.
More social services and benefits are needed."

In 1983 and 1987 the question used was worded: "Thinking first about the welfare benefits that are available to people today. Would you say they have gone too far, are they about right or have they not gone far enough?"

Defence

The questions used on defence are: 1964—22a; 1966—19a; 1970—20; October 1974—26j; 1979—26h; 1983—24a; 1987—27.

In October 1974 and 1979 respondents were asked "How do you feel about the reduction of Britain's military strength?" In 1983 a 21 point scale was introduced to measure attitudes to nuclear weapons. Respondents were asked:

"One of the election issues was whether the government should keep or get rid of nuclear weapons in Britain.
Please look at this card. People who are convinced that we should get rid of all nuclear weapons in Britain without delay will put a tick in the last box on the left while those who are convinced that we should increase nuclear weapons in Britain without delay will put a tick in the last box on the right. So, as you can see, people who hold views that come somewhere between those two positions will tick a box somewhere along here—POINT TO BOXES FROM LEFT TO CENTRE—or somewhere along here—POINT TO BOXES FROM RIGHT TO CENTRE.

First, would you tick the box anywhere along the scale that comes closest to your own views about nuclear weapons in Britain."

In 1987 the original 1964 question was reintroduced.

Common Market

The questions used on the Common Market are: 1964—27a; 1966—26a; 1970—30; October 1974—20a; 1979—27a; 1983—43b; 1987—24a.
    In October 1974 the following question was asked:

"It is sometimes said that Britain should try to change the terms of entry into the Common Market and if this is not successful, get out. Which of the following statements on this card comes closest to what you yourself feel should be done? If you haven't a view on this, just say so.
It is alright for Britain to stay in the Common Market on the present terms.
Britain must stay in the Common Market but should try hard to change the terms.
Britain must change the terms and should leave the Common Market unless they improve.
Britain should get out of the Common Market no matter what."

In 1979 the following question was asked:

"Some people think that Britain should be more willing to go along with the economic policies of other countries in the Common Market. Others think that we should be readier to oppose Common Market economic policies. Which of the statements comes closest to your views?"

In 1983 the question asked was "Which of the three statements on this card comes closest to your own views on the Common Market?
Britain should leave the Common Market without further ado.
Britain should stay in the Common Market provided we can get better terms.
Britain should stay in the Common Market anyway."
    In 1987 respondents were asked: "Do you think that Britain should continue to be a member of the EEC—the Common Market—or should it withdraw?"

Race

The questions used on race are: 1964—33a; 1966—35a; 1970—42a; October 1974—26e; 1979—26e; 1983—45g; 1987—43f.
    In October 1974 and 1979 the following question was used "And how do you feel about recent attempts to ensure equality for coloured people in Britain?". Respondents were offered five options "gone much too far", "gone a little too far", "is about right", "not gone quite far enough", "not gone nearly far enough".

In 1983 and 1987 respondents were asked "[how about] Attempts to give equal opportunities to black people and Asians in Britain?". They were offered three options in 1983—"gone too far", "about right" and "not gone far enough"—and five options in 1983.

Questions used in the expanded analysis

In the expanded analyses nonsignificant items from the previous analyses were deleted as were any extra items which proved not to have significant net relationships with vote.

1964: Questions on Trade Union links with the Labour party (question 28), the importance of the Royal Family (question 29) and on strikers (question 31) were added.

1966: Questions on Britain's ties with America (question 31), the death penalty (question 27), Rhodesia (question 30a), taxes (question 23) and the decline of Empire (question 24) were added to those asked in 1964.

In the question on Rhodesia policy respondents were asked: "Which of these statements comes closest to what you yourself feel should be done about Rhodesia?

Grant independence on the terms Ian Smith wants.

Negotiate a peace settlement with Smith's Government.

Go on using economic sanctions until Smith gives in.

Use force against Smith's Government"

1970: the same questions were used (from the panel study) as for 1966.

October 1974: The only additional issue (on which party position was ascertained) concerned North Sea oil (question 19a).

1979: Four extra questions were examined. Question 13a asked about attitudes towards the political system, question 25a asked about job creation schemes, question 23a about reducing taxes and spending on Government services, and question 66a on incomes policy. It should also be noted that there were additional questions (on which party position was ascertained) covering trade union legislation and race. These to a large extent duplicate the common questions on trade union power and race, and have not therefore been included in the analysis.

1983: Questions on unemployment and inflation (question 28a), taxes and social services (question 31a) and law and order (question 41a) were included in the expanded analysis. These questions used the same 21 point scale format used to measure attitudes to nuclear weapons (question 24a).

1987: As in 1983, attitudes towards unemployment and inflation (question 28a), taxes and social services (question 29a) and law and order (question 39a) were included in the expanded analysis. These questions were answered on an 11 point scale rather than the 21 point scale used in 1983. Questions were also asked on redistribution and on welfare using the same format to obtain the respondents' positions and their perceptions of the parties' positions, but these were not intended to measure issues but underlying ideological dimensions, and have therefore been excluded from the present analysis.

Notes

[1]Franklin's method is to "construct an index measuring the extent of issue-based support for any political party by establishing for each of a number of issues, the extent to which each respondent considers it a salient issue, the position he takes on that issue, and the identity of the party (if any) which he views as taking the same position" (1985:132–3). Rose and McAllister (1986) use the more straightforward method of calculating the increment in the variance in vote which is explained by attitudes. This is analogous to the method we use in this chapter.

[2]This problem is particularly important for Rose and McAllister's analysis. In principle, Franklin's method avoids the difficulty, since changes in party position should in theory affect the voter's views about the identity of the party which takes the same position as he does himself. Unfortunately, however, questions about the parties' positions on the issues have generally used very broad categories and are therefore likely to have masked a great deal of change in the perceived distance between the respondent and the parties on the issues. For example, in 1964, 1966 and 1970 respondents were asked "which party would be more likely to nationalise some more industry—the Conservatives or Labour, or wouldn't there be any difference between them on this?" (BES 1964). It would be quite reasonable for respondents to give identical answers on the three occasions, even if they believed that the distance between the parties (and between themselves and the parties) had changed considerably. In practice, therefore, Franklin is unable to control satisfactorily for the changes in the perceived positions of the parties. In 1983 and 1987 we tried to devise questions that would deal with this problem, but of course we cannot implement our questions retrospectively.

[3]The questions used for table 3.1 were: 1964—13; 1966—11; 1970—11a; February 1974—8; October 1974—8; 1979—5; 1983—6d; 1987—14d.

The words "good deal" were replaced by "great deal" from February 1974 onwards. From 1979 onwards the wording was changed and the Labour and Conservative parties specified. Thus in 1979 respondents were asked: "Considering everything the Conservative and Labour parties stand for, would you say that there is a great deal of difference between them, some difference, or not much difference?" In 1983 and 1987 the words "deal of" were deleted. We should also note that in 1983 and 1987 the question was immediately preceded by some items on differences between, for example, the Liberal and Social Democratic parties. This may have affected responses.

[4]Robertson's analysis of party manifestos also indicates that the party difference was greater in 1970, although in other respects he reaches very different conclusions from those of Charlot. See Robertson 1987, Laver 1984.

[5]Strictly speaking our questions do not tell us about the perceived distance between the parties but about the proportions who perceived a great deal of difference. We assume however that the two are closely related.

[6]Our strategy in this book is to use logit models when we have a dichotomous dependent variable and categorical independent variables, to use logistic

regression when we have a dichotomous dependent variable and ordered independent variables, and to use linear regression when we have ordered dependent and independent variables.

[7] One problem is the treatment of don't knows. In general, we might expect the don't knows to be the people least interested in political issues and therefore the least likely to engage in issue voting. If there has been an increase in issue voting, this might largely operate through a reduction in the number of don't knows, and therefore their exclusion might bias our results against the secularization of party choice hypothesis.

We have therefore decided to include the don't knows in the analysis. Since in many cases they are few in number, we have not assigned them to a separate category of their own but have assigned them to one of the existing categories. In the case of the trichotomous variables—nationalization and nuclear disarmament—we have included them in the middle category and in the case of the dichotomous variables we have included them in the larger of the two categories. The alternative procedure of assigning them to a separate category does not affect the index of concentration, but does produce some rather unstable parameter estimates.

[8] In the case of the two trichotomous variables we have set the middle category to zero and the parameters thus contrast the effects of the two other categories with the middle one. In the case of the dichotomous variables, we contrast the first category with the second.

[9] We have repeated these analyses using multiple regression and the variance explained follows exactly the same pattern as the index of concentration.

[10] Less informed voters would not have adopted their party's issue positions, since they would not have known what they were. But in any case we would not expect there to be a significant relation between these ill-informed voters' attitudes and their political behaviour.

[11] We must be a little bit cautious in interpreting the net relationships in table 3.2. We should not infer that each statistically significant relationship indicates that the specific issue in question influenced voting. Dichotomous, or even trichotomous, measures are not nowadays regarded as particularly good ways to measure attitudes (see Pierce and Rose 1974; Heath and McDonald 1988). It is quite likely that the measures are in part tapping, in an imperfect way, various underlying values. This is very likely to be the case with attitudes towards nationalization and trade union power, which tend to go together and which are probably both tapping a more fundamental left-right dimension; but it is less likely to be the case with attitudes towards nuclear disarmament, which were only weakly associated with the other attitudes making up the left-right dimension in 1964. (For further analysis of these problems see chapters 11 and 12.)

[12] In these two logit models the dependent variable is the log odds of voting Conservative or Labour. In the first model the independent variables are mother's party preference and father's party preference (four categories—Conservative, Labour, Liberal, Other plus none/don't know). In the second model the additional independent variables are attitudes towards nationalization and privatization, trade union power, big business power, social services spending, the independent deterrent and unilateral disarmament (coded as for

table 3.2). Attitudes towards immigration and towards the Common Market were excluded as they did not have significant relationships with vote in table 3.2.

[13] Unfortunately, some of the key questions such as those on public ownership and nuclear weapons were not asked in the 1970 cross-section survey. We have therefore used the 1970 panel survey. However, we should note that the panel necessarily excludes young voters who entered the electorate in 1970 and that the panel will have been affected by the processes of selective attrition described in Appendix III. It is likely therefore that the 1970 panel wave would show a stronger relationship between attitudes and vote than would have been the case in a cross-section survey.

For a number of themes there are alternative questions that could be used. We have checked that, when alternatives are used, the pattern of the coefficients does not change markedly from that reported in table 3.4.

[14] The wording changes mean that we must be cautious about interpreting changes in the parameters, although in general our experience is that wording changes have a smaller impact on the relationships between variables than they do on the marginal distributions.

[15] The absence of a significant net association between race and vote in 1970 is surprising given the literature on the effect of race in the 1970 election (see for example Miller 1980, Studlar 1978). We should also note that the larger sample sizes in 1983 and 1987 make it easier to find statistically significant relationships.

[16] The increase in the index of concentration to 0.59 in 1987 must be taken with a pinch of salt. For the 1987 analysis we have had to use two questions from the self-completion supplement. People who were less interested in politics were disproportionately likely not to return the self-completion supplement, and such people also exhibit a weaker relation between attitudes and vote.

[17] Some of the main methodological differences are that Franklin uses linear regression rather than logit analysis; he constructs an index of attitude preference; he estimates the reciprocal relations between the attitude index and party identification; and he controls for prior variables such as parent's party and social class and party identification.

We have unfortunately been unable to replicate Franklin's analysis, as he does not give sufficient details about the questions used in his analysis. However, it is likely that the main source of the discrepancy is Franklin's estimation of the reciprocal relations between attitudes and party identification. We do not ourselves believe that the attempts to estimate reciprocal relations are entirely satisfactory as they are highly vulnerable to the particular assumptions which have to be made in order to obtain mathematical solutions. This is especially likely to be a problem in the present case, since party identification, attitudes and vote are highly intercorrelated and problems of multicollinearity are therefore rather serious even before attempts to estimate reciprocal relationships are attempted. We therefore prefer methods such as those of Rose and McAllister which keep closer to the data.

Chapter 4

Tactical Voting

In most studies of electoral behaviour the fundamental assumption is usually made that people vote for the party they like best. But in Britain the first-past-the-post electoral system sometimes leaves the voter facing the choice between voting for his or her favourite party or trying to defeat the one liked least. If a voter reckons that his favourite party is bound to lose in his constituency, but that his second preference party and the party he likes least both have a chance of winning, he may decide that it makes more sense to vote tactically for his second preference party. Thus a Labour voter living in a constituency where his party's candidate is likely to come third may decide to support the local Alliance candidate in the hope of securing the defeat of the local Conservative. Such behaviour seems indeed to be more rational than sticking doggedly to one's partisan inclinations.

The way that people vote, then, may be influenced not only by their preferences for the parties, but also by the tactical situation which they face. The political parties have always been aware of this. The cry, "A Liberal Vote is a Wasted Vote" has long been used by Conservative and Labour candidates to try and dissuade people from voting Liberal. But in the 1980s the tactical situations facing voters have become more varied. Whereas in 1964, 89% of constituencies saw Conservative and Labour candidates share first and second place, in 1987 only just over half (52%) did.

It can be argued, too, that the tactical situation has been crucial to the electoral outcome. The Conservatives' parliamentary dominance has perhaps been founded upon a fragmentation of the opposition vote. If that vote had coalesced around the locally more popular opposition candidate, the Conservatives might have been defeated. Tactical switching between Labour and Alliance might therefore be an antidote to continued Conservative rule.

Accordingly, the 1987 election saw for the first time in Britain organized attempts by two pressure groups to make people aware of the possibility of voting tactically. The philosophy of the two groups was slightly different. One, the Centre for Electoral Choice founded by Lord Young of Dartington, simply aimed to promote awareness among the electorate of the possibility of tactical voting. But the campaign which received the greater publicity was TV '87. This had been founded following a number of articles in the left-wing weekly, the *New Statesman*, (Fishman & Shaw 1989) and had the explicit aim of trying to defeat the incumbent Conservative government by persuading Alliance supporters to vote Labour in Conservative-held seats where the Alliance had no chance of winning, and encouraging Labour voters to switch to the Alliance in seats where their party's cause was hopeless. Their principal method was to publish lists indicating which of Labour and the Alliance appeared on the evidence of local and national opinion polling and past election results to have the better chance of defeating the incumbent MP in Conservative-held constituencies.

Whether or not people do or might be prepared to vote tactically thus moved into the centre stage of British electoral politics. And if indeed there had been a secularization of party choice, we should surely find that voters were now more prepared to consider what, in the light of the tactical situation, was the most effective and rational way of casting their vote. As Galbraith and Rae have suggested: "In a de-aligned electorate with a more 'consumerist' as opposed to 'solidary' approach to voting, the major barriers to tactical voting arising from class or party identification are removed" (Galbraith and Rae 1989:128).

In this chapter, therefore, we examine how widespread was the incidence of tactical voting in 1987. Is there any evidence that, in response to the tactical voting campaigns and the decline in partisanship, it was more common in 1987 than in 1983 or at earlier elections? Is there any indication that tactical voting might become more widespread in future?

The incidence of tactical voting

In both our 1983 and 1987 surveys we attempted to identify who had voted tactically by asking respondents the following question[1]:

"Which one of the reasons on this card comes closest to the main reason you voted for the Party you chose?
I always vote that way.
I thought it was the best party.
I really preferred another Party, but it had no chance of winning in this constituency.
Other (Please specify)" (BES 1983)

The message of our surveys is unequivocal. The efforts of the pressure groups failed to increase the amount of tactical voting. In the 1987 survey, just 6.0% of those who voted said that they really preferred another party.[2] In 1983 the figure was almost identical—5.9%![3]

We also have other evidence from our 1987 survey that supports this conclusion. We asked all those respondents who voted for one of the three major parties to tell us in their own words why they voted as they did. Here perhaps we might have tapped more fully into the reservoir of tactical voting, since respondents could say that the tactical situation was only one of the reasons for their choice rather than the main reason. But just 6.5% of major party voters indicated in their replies a tactical motivation for their vote.

The proportion of tactical voters differed, however, among the parties. It proved to be a higher proportion of the total vote secured both by Labour and (more especially) by the Alliance than by the Conservatives. Whereas 4% of those who voted Conservative said that their support was tactical, this was true of 6% of Labour voters and as many as 11% of those who turned out for the Alliance.

These results are very similar to those obtained by Galbraith and Rae in their analysis, using aggregate data, of tactical voting in 1987. They suggested that around 10% of Alliance votes in 1987 were tactical ones in constituencies where they ran second to the Conservatives in 1983, with a rather smaller proportion of Labour votes being tactical. (Galbraith and Rae did not consider tactical voting for the Conservative party.)

The pressure groups failed, then, to awaken a greater willingness to vote tactically. But, just as importantly, not all of the tactical voting which did occur was directed against the Conservative party.

TABLE 4.1 Preferred and Actual Votes of Tactical Voters 1987

Preferred Party	Actual vote				
	Conservative	Labour	Alliance	Other	All
Conservative	—	5	9	1	15
Labour	7	—	25	1	33
Alliance	23	18	—	0	41
Other	1	9	1	—	11
All	31	32	35	2	100% (N = 200)

Source: 1987 cross-section survey

Table 4.1 shows that although the Alliance won the support of more tactical voters than any other party, it also lost the support of more potential supporters. Thus, of the tactical voters in our sample, the Alliance gained 35% from other parties, but it also lost 41%. And this loss was not just to Labour. Indeed, far from providing some of the fuel for an anti-Conservative majority, the Alliance actually lost slightly more votes to the Conservatives than they did to Labour through tactical voting. Further, as Conservative tactical votes for the Alliance were relatively few (which is not surprising given that there were few seats where the Conservatives started in third place behind the Alliance), it was the Conservatives, and neither Labour nor the Alliance, who were the principal net beneficaries from tactical voting.

TABLE 4.2 Preferred and Actual Votes of Tactical Voters 1983

Preferred Party	Actual vote				
	Conservative	Labour	Alliance	Other	All
Conservative	—	5	5	1	11
Labour	9	—	24	1	34
Alliance	25	22	—	0	47
Other	2	3	2	—	7
All	36	30	31	2	99%
					(N = 177)

Source: 1983 cross-section survey

Equally, there is no evidence from table 4.2 that the level of tactical switching between Labour and the Alliance was any higher in 1987 than it was in 1983. In 1983 as in 1987 approximately one-quarter of all tactical switches were from Labour to the Alliance while another fifth (22% in 1983 compared with 18% in 1987) were from Alliance to Labour. Far from persuading the opposition parties' electoral forces to unite against the Conservatives, TV '87 seems to have had no impact at all upon the willingness of Labour and Alliance voters to make an anti-Conservative tactical switch.

Why is tactical voting so rare?

The failure of the tactical voting campaign to induce more switching between Labour and the Alliance raises a number of important questions. Why is the electorate apparently so reluctant to vote tactically? Surely an electorate which has become more sophisticated and less committed would show a greater willingness to vote tactically than is evident from our survey.

One crucial requirement for any tactical voting campaign to be successful is that voters should accurately perceive the tactical situation in their own constituency. They need to be aware of the likely rank order and distance between the parties locally. Indeed, much of the effort of the tactical voting campaigns was taken up with trying to advise the electorate of precisely this information. For whereas in a parliamentary by-election there are often a number of well publicized local opinion polls from which the potential tactical voter can gain the information she or he needs, in a general election the state of the national campaign dominates political discussion.

In practice we have little firm evidence on voters' knowledge of the tactical situation. But it is interesting to note that tactical voting generally occurred where one would have expected it to. Thus fully 84% of people who switched from Labour to the Alliance did so in constituencies where the Alliance shared first and second places with the Conservatives.

However, accurate information is only a necessary not a sufficient condition for tactical voting. In his discussion of tactical voting in Britain, Cain (1978) notes that "...strategic [tactical] voting occurs when individuals perceive that their second preference has a better chance of winning than their first, and when the utility difference between their first and second preferences are small" (Cain 1978:642). Tactical voting, then, requires not only that voters have adequate knowledge of the local tactical situation, but also that they have the required pattern of preferences to make a tactical switch.

Cain's formulation of the required pattern of preferences is not quite complete. He correctly notes that voters need to be relatively indifferent between their first choice party winning and their second choice party winning. But, in addition, the incentive to vote tactically is greater if voters also have a strong preference for their second party over their least preferred party. There is less incentive for a voter to make a tactical switch to his second choice party if he does not much care whether that party wins or his least preferred does. The most likely tactical voters are therefore people who are indifferent between two parties but are clearly antagonistic towards a third.[4]

That this pattern of preferences is typical of tactical voters can be seen in table 4.3. (The limited number of tactical voters in our survey means that of necessity the table confines its attention to the three most common kinds of tactical switching.) In our 1987 survey we asked respondents how strongly they were in favour of or opposed to each of the political parties. We asked "Please choose a phrase from this card to say how you feel about (each party)—strongly in favour, in favour, neither in favour nor against, against, strongly against" (BES 1987).

TABLE 4.3 Attitudes towards the Parties

	Mean attitude towards				
	Con	Lab	Lib	SDP	N
Preferred Alliance: voted Conservative	2.2	4.1	2.4	2.5	(47)
Preferred Alliance: voted Labour	4.4	2.3	2.3	2.2	(36)
Preferred Alliance: voted Alliance	3.4	3.6	2.1	2.3	(748)
Preferred Labour: voted Alliance	4.2	2.0	2.7	2.6	(50)
Preferred Labour: voted Labour	4.1	1.7	3.1	3.3	(993)

Source: 1987 cross-section survey

In table 4.3 we calculate the voters' average strength of feeling towards the different parties. The higher the score, the more strongly they feel against the party in question. For example, the third row of the table shows that (non-tactical) Alliance voters tended to feel more or less equally in favour of the Liberal and Social Democratic parties (scoring 2.1 and 2.3 respectively) and more or less equally opposed to the Conservative and Labour parties (scoring them 3.4 and 3.6 respectively).

If we then compare these figures with those for the tactical voters who preferred the Alliance but actually voted Labour, we see a marked difference. They are effectively indifferent between the Labour party (scoring 2.3) and the two centre parties, but much more strongly opposed to the Conservatives (rating 4.4).

The difficulty for any tactical voting campaign is that the combination of an appropriate set of preferences with an appropriate constituency situation is not all that common. These two conditions need to be present in combination for a tactical vote to be cast, but the combination is relatively rare.

TABLE 4.4 Preferences, Tactical Situations and Tactical Voting

	% Voting tactically	
	Voters who were indifferent between their 1st and 2nd parties	Other voters
Preferred party 1st or 2nd in 1983	13.7	1.8
	(373)	(2078)
Preferred party 3rd or lower in 1983	35.0	10.5
	(160)	(457)

Note: figures in brackets give base frequencies.
Source: 1987 cross-section survey

This can be seen from table 4.4. First of all, around 17% of voters were indifferent between their two preferred parties. Furthermore, around 20% were registered in constituencies where their preferred party had been in third place (or lower) at the last election. However, only 5% of voters had the required combination of preferences and opportunities. This group did indeed show much the highest level of tactical voting, although at 35% it might be felt to leave some room for tactical voting campaigns to have an effect.

Nevertheless, the data of table 4.4 demonstrate that the problem for any tactical voting campaign is not only knowledge but also motivation and

opportunity. Attempts to end the threat of a Conservative one-party dominance by encouraging an exchange of votes between Labour and the Alliance
are bound to be limited by the fact that the potential pool of voters with the
required motivation and registered in appropriate constituencies is rather
small.

We must add that another problem for the campaign was that, faced with
a choice between Conservative and Labour, many Alliance voters in fact
preferred to see a Conservative victory. Indeed, far from clearly forming part
of an opposition block of votes, people who preferred the Alliance were more
likely to say that the Conservatives were their second choice party (51%) than
Labour (33%).

Tactical voting since 1964

We have thus seen that tactical considerations influenced only a small
proportion of the electorate in 1987, and that little has changed in this respect
compared with 1983. But even the 6% of tactical voting in the 1980s may be
an increase over the proportion voting tactically in the 1960s. In order to test
this possibility we now take a longer time perspective and compare the
incidence of tactical voting in the 1980s with the level in the 1960s.

We face a number of difficulties in undertaking this task. First of all, the
election surveys of the 1960s did not ask respondents whether they voted
tactically or what their second choice party was. We thus have to find some
indirect measure of tactical voting. Secondly, as we noted earlier, in the 1960s
there was far less variation in the tactical situation than in the 1980s. With
just 64 constituencies in which the Liberals came either first or second in
1964, for example, there are relatively few respondents to the election surveys
of the 1960s who were registered in constituencies where the Liberals could
be expected to have benefited from tactical voting. Tactical switching from
Labour to the Liberals, which was one of the major forms of tactical voting
in the 1980s, is thus likely to be largely absent in the 1960s.

In other words, it is quite possible that tactical voting has increased, not
because voters have become more rational, but because the opportunities to
cast a tactical vote have increased.

In order to deal with the measurement problem we adopt the following
strategy. We define as tactical voters those who identified with one party but
actually voted for another. Of course, some Liberal identifiers would not have
had the option of casting a Liberal vote, since no Liberal candidate stood in
their constituency, and accordingly we exclude such constituencies from the
analysis.

Using this measure we then compare the incidence of tactical voting in
different types of constituency, thus controlling for the structure of opportunities. The types of constituency are defined according to the election results
at the prior election. Because of the small numbers involved, we have
amalgamated the 1966 and 1970 surveys, and compare them with the 1987
results (using the same measurement procedures). For the same reason we
have ignored Conservative identifiers altogether, since even by amalgamating

surveys we cannot scrape up enough respondents in seats where the Conservatives came third in the 1960s.

TABLE 4.5 Tactical Voting in 1966/70 and 1987

Liberal/SDP identifiers

Vote	1966/70		1987	
	Con/Lab seats	Other seats	Con/Lab seats	Other seats
Liberal	78	76	76	85
Other	22	24	24	15
	100%	100%	100%	100%
	(129)	(34)	(235)	(365)

Labour identifiers

Vote	1966/70		1987	
	Con/Lib seats	Other seats	Con/Alliance seats	Other seats
Labour	72	93	76	88
Other	28	7	24	12
	100%	100%	100%	100%
	(32)	(511)	(283)	(765)

Sources: 1966, 1970 and 1987 cross-section surveys

Table 4.5 shows that voters were indeed more likely to depart from their party identification when their party was in third place. For example, in 1987 24% of Labour identifiers defected in constituencies where Labour was in third place (or lower), but only 12% did so in other constituencies (in most of which Labour was in first or second place). The difference is statistically significant and gives us some confidence in this measure of tactical voting.

In the earlier period the results are rather mixed. There was a statistically significant tendency for Labour identifiers to defect in Conservative/Liberal seats. Indeed, the relationship was somewhat stronger in the earlier period than it was in 1987. Liberal identifiers on the other hand do not appear to have voted tactically in the earlier elections.[5]

The numbers involved are, of course, very small and we must be cautious about drawing conclusions from them. If we pool the results for Labour and Liberal identifiers (giving us somewhat larger numbers), we find that there has been no statistically significant increase in voters' willingness to vote tactically.[6]

To be sure, the *total* amount of tactical voting has almost certainly increased. Of the Labour and Liberal identifiers covered by table 4.5, 22%

in the earlier period were registered in constituencies where their party lay third, compared with 31% in the later period. Tactical voting has therefore probably grown, perhaps from around 3% to its current 6%; but we should ascribe this to the changed opportunities for tactical voting rather than to changes in the sophistication of the voters.

Finally, these results suggest that some part of Labour's decline at the polls may be due to tactical voting. As we can see from table 4.5, in the earlier period only 6% of Labour identifiers were registered in constituencies where the Conservatives and Liberals shared first and second places. By 1987 27% were so registered, and a fair proportion of this 27% voted tactically for one of the Alliance parties. To put the matter another way, in the 1960s Labour was almost certainly a net beneficiary of tactical voting, gaining more votes from the Liberals than it lost to them. By the 1980s, as table 4.1 shows, this position had reversed and Labour lost more tactical votes to the Alliance than it gained.

Notes

[1] One of the dangers in asking people the reason why they voted in a particular way is that the way in which the question is put may suggest that a particular answer is expected. Thus if we were simply to have asked our respondents whether or not they had voted tactically, respondents might have been lead into responding that indeed they had done so. So in this question we made tactical voting (i.e. preferring another party which had no chance of winning) one of a number of possible reasons for voting, even though our only interest was in identifying those who had voted tactically.

[2] This figure excludes 13 respondents who said that they really preferred another party which had no chance of winning, but who when asked a follow-up question as to which that party was named the same party as they had actually voted for. In addition, some respondents who gave an 'other' answer said that they had voted against a party or that their vote was a tactical one. If these respondents are also regarded as tactical voters (again excluding those who named as their preferred party the party they actually voted for), the proportion of 1987 voters who voted tactically rises to 6.3%. In all subsequent analyses in this chapter it is this 6.3% of voting respondents who are counted as tactical voters. This procedure cannot however be followed in the case of the 1983 survey as none of the respondents who gave an 'other' answer were asked if there was a party they would have voted for.

[3] Eight respondents who said that they really preferred another party and who named as their preferred party one of the Alliance parties, but reported voting for the other Alliance party, are excluded from this figure.

[4] In practice, however, whatever the strict logic of rational choice may be, Cain is right in thinking that the main factor is the utility difference between the voter's two preferred parties. This is shown clearly in table 4.6N. This table shows the probability of casting a tactical vote according to the gaps between the voter's first and second preference and between his second and third preference parties. (The first preference party is defined as the party voted

for [question 8a] except in the case of tactical voters, for whom it is the party nominated as preferred [questions 9b, 9c].

TABLE 4.6N Strength of Preference and Tactical Voting

		% who voted tactically				
Difference	4	—				
in feeling	3	18	3			
towards	2	14	4	1		
2nd and 3rd	1	15	3	2	0	
choice	0	11	2	1	2	2
parties						
		0	1	2	3	4

difference in feeling
towards 1st and 2nd choice
parties

Source: 1987 cross-section survey

As we can see, tactical voting is much the highest among people who were indifferent between their first and second choice parties, and it then falls sharply as we move to people who had a definite preference between their first and second choice parties. (Compare the first two columns of the table.) This column effect is clearly stronger than the row effect.

[5] If we include abstentions as well as actual votes, we find a slight tendency for Liberal identifiers to vote tactically in the earlier period.

[6] The loglinear model which includes relationships between type of seat and period, between type of vote (for own party vs. for other party) and period, and between type of vote and seat yields an acceptable fit to the data; $chi^2 = 2.57$ with 1 df, $p = 0.109$. This model in effect tests whether people's willingness to vote tactically has remained constant over time.

Chapter 5

The Withering Away of Class?

One of the most controversial topics in the discussion of contemporary British politics has been the role of social class. The orthodoxy established by Butler and Stokes in the 1960s was a combination of party identification theory and class theory. Party identification, they held, derived from class identification. Thus they wrote: "the individual, identifying with a particular class, forms a positive bond to the party which looks after the interest of the class ... " (Butler and Stokes 1974:88) and they gave examples of people who voted Labour because "To me Labour is for the working class. It is only right to vote for people who will try to help you" (1974:88).

Just as the theory of party identification has waned in intellectual popularity, so class theory has gone out of fashion. Indeed, the two are sometimes explicitly linked. As Crewe has argued: "the period of partisan dealignment is also one of class dealignment: it is easier to vote against one's class once party loyalties weaken, easier to abandon one's party once class loyalties wither" (1984:193). Crewe (1984), Dunleavy and Husbands (1985), Franklin (1985), Robertson (1984), and Rose and McAllister (1986) all seem to accept that the social classes, and particularly the working class, have weakened and lost their social cohesion and ideological distinctiveness. There has been talk of a "loosening" of the social structure (Butler and Kavanagh 1984:8), an "opening up" of the electorate (Rose and McAllister 1986:82), a process of "class secularization" (Robertson 1984:86) and a decline in the "ideological consciousness and solidarity of the working class" (Crewe 1986:633).

Perhaps the clearest statement comes from Robertson who argues that "The old classes have ceased to be cultural communities, witness the decline in class consciousness and class loyalty" (1984:222) and "We are forced to the conclusion that class in anything resembling the overall communitarian and ideological sense is vanishing from British politics" (1984:102).

The precise sociological mechanisms involved in this process of class dealignment or class secularization have not always been clearly spelled out. But the dominant theme has been the fragmentation of the classes. For example it has been argued that there is now a new working class of affluent skilled manual workers, many of whom are homeowners living in the South, who do not share the economic interests of the old, less affluent working class in Northern industrial communities (Crewe 1981:293–6; Crewe 1984:196; Crewe 1986; cf Butler and Kavanagh 1988). Associated with this is a growth in the proportion of people in mixed situations. Owing to increased social mobility and the increased participation of women in the labour market where they are concentrated in white-collar jobs, there is now a larger proportion of the working class than there used to be with some kind of middle-class ties such as a white-collar spouse or white-collar in-laws. "The significance of the preceding data is that voters in mixed-class situations are subject to partisan cross-pressures. . . Here, therefore, is one important source of the crumbling of the working-class Labour vote: the rapid erosion of the 'pure' working class" (Crewe 1984:199).

These arguments apply not only to the working class. It is also argued that there is now a new middle class of public sector employees (McAdams 1987; Kriesi 1989), or of young highly educated postmaterialists who have different values and political priorities from the old middle class (Inglehart 1971, 1977, 1981; Lipset 1981).

This thesis of class secularization is particularly important as it is offered as a causal explanation of the electoral decline of the Labour party, and the rise of the Alliance. For example Franklin argued that the decline of class "opened the door to explosions in minor party voting such as were seen in 1974 and 1983" (Franklin 1985:105). Similarly, in their analysis of the 1983 General Election, Butler and Kavanagh suggested that "Social class, another factor which had stabilized the two-party system, continued to weaken. As social structure became 'looser', so Britain became less two-party and two-class" (Butler and Kavanagh 1984:8).

There has, however, been dissent from this new orthodoxy (Heath, Jowell and Curtice 1985; Goldthorpe 1987; Marshall et al 1988; Weakliem 1989.) For example, in the most thorough recent study of class in modern Britain, Marshall, Newby, Rose and Vogler concluded:

"Our findings do not support the popular belief that we are witnessing a long-term decline in class loyalties and attitudes. Just as the structural processes associated with class have persisted into the late twentieth century, in the face of sustained attempts at egalitarian reform by successive governments in post-war Britain, so too have the ideological differences associated with a class-based culture" (Marshall et al 1988:182).

Similarly, in *How Britain Votes* our central argument was that, while the classes had indeed changed in size, there was little evidence that they had changed in sociological character—in their social cohesion or ideological distinctiveness. We argued that they still had the potential for collective class action, and that the rise of the Alliance owed more to political factors—the failure of the other parties when in office or their changed policy stances—than to sociological ones.

This is not the same as saying that the classes are today highly unified with a developed sense of class consciousness. The image of a unified, cohesive and solidary working class was an inaccurate representation even in the 1960s (just as an image of traditional voters voting purely out of party loyalty was inaccurate). As contemporary research from the 1960s showed there was already a new affluent working class in the 1960s with instrumental orientations towards politics (Goldthorpe, Lockwood, Bechhofer and Platt 1968) and a new middle class of unionized, public sector workers with radical values (Parkin 1968). Butler and Stokes too emphasized instrumental or materialistic reasons for class voting in the 1960s (1969:83). So the new emphasis on instrumental voting in the 1980s is the rediscovery of an old phenomenon.

Absolute and relative class voting

The major evidence in favour of the class secularization thesis comes from data on the relation between class and vote. We shall begin by reviewing these data and then turn to more detailed examination of direct evidence on class awareness, class fragmentation and so on.

At the outset we need to repeat the distinction which we introduced in *How Britain Votes* between absolute and relative class voting. The level of absolute class voting is simply the overall proportion of voters who support the party of their class.[1] Relative class voting on the other hand refers to the relative strength of a particular party in the different social classes; it measures the relationship between class and party after controlling for any across-the-board movements between the parties. (The distinction is analogous to that between overall volatility and fluidity which we drew in chapter 2.)

These two measures need not move in parallel. Thus if the Labour party lost votes to the Alliance in all classes alike, then absolute class voting would decline but relative class voting would stay unchanged. Conversely, if Labour maintained its share of the working-class vote unchanged while gaining middle-class votes from the Alliance, relative class voting would decline but absolute class voting would stay unchanged.

Now absolute class voting has indeed declined. As table 5.1 shows, in 1964 64% of voters cast their ballots for the party of their class and this fell to 52% in 1983, a level at which it remained in 1987.[2] There is no dispute about this. There has thus been a real change in British politics—fewer people vote for the party of their class. However, it is also apparent that this decline coincides with the rise of the Liberal party (later the Alliance). As we can see, there were particularly large drops in absolute class voting in the years of Liberal strength. Other things being equal, a rise in the voting strength of the Liberals (defined by most writers as a non-class party) must *logically* lead to a decline in absolute class voting. So of course we cannot use the decline in absolute class voting to explain the rise of the Liberals since the two are

TABLE 5.1 Absolute Class Voting 1964–87

	Middle-class Conservative plus working-class Labour as % of all voters	Middle-class Conservative or Liberal plus working-class Labour as % of all voters
1964	64.0	70.7
1966	64.4	69.9
1970	60.2	64.4
February 1974	55.5	66.5
October 1974	57.4	68.6
1979	56.7	64.3
1983	51.7	66.9
1987	51.6	66.3

Note: For definitions of 'middle class' and 'working class' see footnote 2.
Source: calculated from table 5.2

logically related. We cannot decide from this evidence whether it was the decline of class which opened the way to the rise of the Liberals or the electoral popularity of the Liberals which reduced class voting (Heath, Jowell and Curtice 1986).[3]

We should note, however, that the decline in absolute class voting is much less dramatic if we define the Liberal and Social Democratic parties as middle-class ones, along with the Conservatives. One of the more puzzling features of contemporary British political science is the belief that the Liberal party (latterly the Alliance) draws its support evenly from across the class structure. As we shall see, it does not. Moreover, if we add middle-class Liberals to middle-class Conservatives, as we do in the second column of table 5.1, the decline in absolute class voting becomes much less marked. It drops just over four points in 23 years instead of the original twelve. And Liberal surges now seem to be associated with increases, not decreases, in absolute class voting.

However, we believe that a measure of *relative* class voting is more relevant for assessing theses of class secularization and of a loosening or an opening up of the classes. If the classes have indeed become looser and lost their social cohesion and ideological distinctiveness, then we would expect the relationship between class and vote to have become weaker. For example, we would expect Labour's relative strength in the working class to have declined and for its vote to have become more evenly spread across the different social classes.

Of course, there might be political explanations for a changed relationship, too: if the Labour party changed its electoral strategy and put forward policies which appealed to the new middle class rather than to the old working class, this might also weaken the relationship between class and vote. The

Labour party's recent emphasis on nuclear disarmament, which is not an issue which appeals particularly to the working class voter, might in principle have had this effect (cf Przeworski and Sprague 1986).

A loosening of the classes, however, might be expected to take a gradual and more continuous form whereas changes in political strategy might be more episodic. (Hence in our earlier work we talked about "trendless fluctuation" in the relationship between class and vote.) Certainly, many of the processes of loosening described above—the spread of owner-occupation in the working class or the growth of women's employment in white-collar jobs—can be shown to be long-run and gradual trends whereas Labour's emphasis on unilateralism, for example, is clearly associated with two particular elections, those of 1983 and 1987.

The class schema

Unfortunately, most of the writers who subscribe to the class secularization thesis have used an oversimple dichotomous measure of social class. Following John Goldthorpe's work (Goldthorpe 1980, 1982, 1987) our preference, which we have explained in full in earlier publications, is to adopt a five-class model and log-linear statistical techniques. (For a critique of dichotomous measures of class see Korpi 1972. On the merits of Goldthorpe's class schema see Heath, Jowell and Curtice 1985; Marshall, Newby, Rose and Vogler 1988. On the statistical side see Heath, Jowell and Curtice 1987; Evans, Heath and Payne 1989.)

The five-class schema which we use is as follows:[4]

—the Salariat (managers, professionals and administrators)
—Routine Nonmanual Workers (clerks and secretaries)
—the Petty Bourgeoisie (employers and the self-employed)
—Foremen and Technicians
—the Working Class (rank and file manual employees in industry and agriculture)

These five classes are distinguished according to their degree of economic security, their authority within the workplace, their prospects of economic advancement and their sources as well as levels of income. The schema is accordingly based on employment status as well as on occupation. Thus for example, the self-employed plumber is in a different class from the foreman plumber or from the rank-and-file employee plumber. These distinctions of employment status are, as we showed in *How Britain Votes*, rather important in understanding voting behaviour.

The petty bourgeoisie is perhaps the most interesting innovation of Goldthorpe's schema. It contains small employers and own-account workers. What distinguishes members of this class is not their occupations as such but their conditions of employment—they are all independents directly exposed to market forces rather than cushioned by bureaucracy or trade union membership (cf Elliott, McCrone and Bechhofer 1988). Their income is by no means the highest of the five social classes, but they are the most inclined to the Conservatives.

This schema, then, distinguishes classes according to their economic interests rather than according to their standard of living or lifestyle (as the market research schemas do), or according to their prestige and standing in the community (as the official schema of the Registrar-General does).[5]

Changes in relative class voting

Table 5.2 shows how these five classes distributed their votes over the 1964–1987 period covered by the election studies. (Because of the very small numbers involved, voters for other parties have been excluded.)

Inspection of table 5.2 shows some consistent patterns in the parties' relative strength. The Labour party is strongest in the working class (and next strongest in the adjacent class of foremen and technicians); the Conservatives are strongest in the petty bourgeoisie (and next strongest in the salariat); and the Liberal and Social Democratic parties are strongest in the salariat. With a couple of exceptions (the Liberals in 1970 and in February 1974), these propositions hold true in every election survey.

There are also some clear across-the-board changes between 1964 and 1987. Thus the Liberals (joined by the SDP) did better in every single class in 1983 and 1987 than they had done in any of the previous six elections (with the exception of the routine nonmanual class in the two 1974 elections). Similarly, the Labour party fared worse in 1983 and 1987 in every single class (except the petty bourgeoisie) than it had done in any of the previous elections. These across-the-board changes reflect the marked overall decline in support for Labour and the rise in support for Liberals in these elections. The Conservatives in contrast have not seen such marked overall changes in support, except in 1974, and in their case there are few across-the-board changes to be observed.

However, there also appear to be some changes in the parties' relative strengths and weaknesses. In particular, Labour gained votes in the salariat, but lost them in the working class, between 1964 and 1970. It is this kind of change we need to analyse in order to test the thesis of class secularization.

To analyse table 5.2 more rigorously and to check whether these apparent changes could have arisen through sampling error, we use log-linear modelling.[6] One major advantage of log-linear modelling is that it distinguishes the strength of the association between class and vote from the other changes that are taking place, namely the changing sizes of the classes and the changing overall shares of the vote going to the three main party groupings, either of which would otherwise confound the calculations. On the one hand, the past twenty-five years have seen a marked contraction of the working class and an expansion of the salariat; in 1964 the working class (as defined above and including the non-voters) amounted to 51% of the electorate but by 1987 this had fallen to 36%. On the other hand, there have been marked changes in the parties' electoral fortunes with the Labour vote fluctuating between

TABLE 5.2 Class and Vote 1964–87

	Salariat	Routine nonmanual	Petty bourgeoisie	Foremen & technicians	Working class
1964:					
Conservative	62	58	75	38	25
Labour	19	26	14	46	68
Liberal	18	16	12	15	7
	99% (268)	100% (197)	101% (102)	99% (117)	100% (691)
1966:					
Conservative	61	49	67	34	24
Labour	25	41	19	61	71
Liberal	15	10	15	5	5
	101% (280)	100% (216)	101% (102)	100% (111)	100% (707)
1970:					
Conservative	62	51	70	39	33
Labour	29	41	19	56	61
Liberal	9	9	11	5	6
	100% (288)	101% (187)	100% (110)	100% (111)	100% (603)
February 1974:					
Conservative	54	45	68	39	24
Labour	22	29	19	40	60
Liberal	24	26	13	22	16
	100% (410)	100% (329)	100% (164)	101% (106)	100% (848)
October 1974:					
Conservative	52	44	71	35	21
Labour	23	32	13	52	64
Liberal	25	24	16	13	15
	100% (399)	100% (307)	100% (137)	100% (114)	100% (785)
1979:					
Conservative	61	52	77	45	32
Labour	22	32	13	43	55
Liberal	17	17	10	11	13
	100% (378)	101% (209)	100% (130)	99% (150)	100% (604)

[*Continued next page*

TABLE 5.2—*Continued*

	Salariat	Routine nonmanual	Petty bourgeoisie	Foremen & technicians	Working class
1983:					
Conservative	55	53	71	44	30
Labour	13	20	12	28	49
Liberal & SDP	31	27	17	28	21
	99% (793)	100% (547)	100% (227)	100% (183)	100% (1127)
1987:					
Conservative	56	52	65	39	31
Labour	15	26	16	36	48
Liberal & SDP	29	23	20	24	21
	100% (839)	101% (576)	101% (245)	99% (176)	100% (1024)

Source: British Election Study cross-section surveys

49% in 1966 and 28% in 1983. In asking whether the association between class and vote has weakened, we must therefore control for these changes.

A further advantage of using log-linear modelling is that it enables us to include all three major parties in the analysis and not just two. Most previous studies of the class-party relationship have concentrated on Labour and Conservative voting, relying on the convenient assumption that the Liberals (or Alliance) drew their support from a cross-section of the electorate. As can be seen from table 5.2 this assumption is incorrect, and it is clearly preferable to recognize in our statistical analysis that Britain has had a multi-party system for much of the period.

It is useful to begin with the independence model (that is, the model which hypothesizes that there was no statistically significant relationship between any of our three variables, namely class, party and election). As might be expected this model gives a very poor fit to the data of table 5.2. The deviance (the difference between the actual frequencies of table 5.2 and the frequencies predicted by the model) is very substantial and it is extremely unlikely that such differences would have occurred by chance.

We then successively introduce the relationships between class and election, between class and vote, and between election and vote. Table 5.3 shows the results of these three models.

First of all, we introduce the relationship between class and election in order to test the hypothesis that the sizes of the classes varied significantly over the eight elections. We know this to be the case from other sources (see chapter 13) and, true enough, this model makes a significant improvement to

TABLE 5.3 Loglinear Models of the Relationship between Class, Vote and Election

Model	Deviance	df	p
1. Class, election, vote	3063	106	0.000
2. Class by election, vote	2813	78	0.000
3. Class by election, class by vote	629	70	0.000
4. Class by election, vote by election, class by vote	85	56	0.008

14897 unweighted cases

Source: calculated from table 5.2

the fit. Deviance falls by 250 with the loss of 28 degrees of freedom, and we have no hesitation in accepting the hypothesis.

The second step is to add the relationship between class and vote. The deviance now falls by a further 2184 (with the loss of only 8 degrees of freedom). Again, this is a highly significant improvement.

The third step is to add the relationship between vote and election (in addition to the other two relationships) in order to test the hypothesis that there were across-the-board changes in the parties' electoral fortunes. We see a further improvement in fit. Deviance falls by a further 544 with the loss of 14 degrees of freedom, another highly significant improvement.

It is important to be clear what this third model means. Its essential feature is to postulate that *relative class voting was equally strong at all elections*. It takes account of the facts that class is related to vote, that the classes changed in size, and that the parties' shares of the vote also changed. But it assumes that these changes in share of the vote took place across-the-board—thus affecting all classes in the same manner and leaving the strength of association between class and vote unchanged. In other words, the model postulates that there has been a constant relationship between class and vote, controlling for class size and vote shares. For this reason, we can term it the constant relative voting model.

This model correctly classifies 97.4% of respondents, but the discrepancies between the predictions of the model and the observed data of table 5.2 are still statistically significant. We must therefore reject the hypothesis that the relationship between class and vote was identical in all elections. We therefore move on to consider the form that these changes took.

As we observed earlier, if the thesis of class secularization holds true, we should expect a gradual and continuous decline in the strength of association between class and vote to have taken place. If, on the other hand, specific political factors have been at work, we would expect the changes to have been more episodic.

To analyse the pattern that these changes have taken, it is helpful to inspect the class/vote log odds ratios. In a table containing five classes and three categories of vote, there are altogether 30 log odds ratios that we might want to inspect. To illustrate the patterns, however, we shall simply focus on three; we look at the three relationships between Conservative and Labour voting, between Conservative and Liberal voting, and between Liberal and Labour voting in the salariat and working classes. Diagram 5.4 plots these three log odds ratios over time.

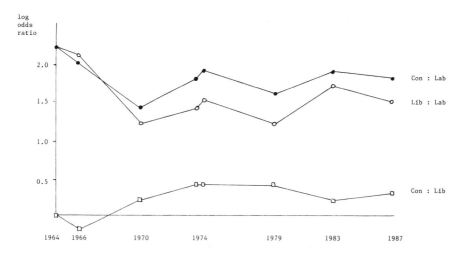

DIAGRAM 5.4 Salariat: working class log odds ratios

Source: calculated from table 5.2

Looking first at the Conservative: Labour log odds ratio, we see that this declined rapidly between 1964 and 1970. There is however no further decline after 1970. The ratio fluctuated thereafter in an apparently trendless way, rising in 1974, falling in 1979 (but not to as low a level as in 1970), rising once more in 1983 but falling in 1987. The constant relative voting model predicts that this particular log odds ratio will be 1.8 throughout and we may note that this is the value of the 1987 ratio.

Turning next to the Liberal: Labour log odds ratios, three points are worth mentioning. First, they are in general only slightly lower than the Labour: Conservative ones. The Liberal party is thus much closer to the Conservatives than to Labour in its relative support in the salariat and working class. Secondly, they follow much the same pattern over time as with the Conservative: Labour ratio, declining until 1970 and then fluctuating. Thirdly, however, we should note that the Liberal: Labour log odds ratio declines rather more over the period as a whole than does the Conservative:Labour one. So if there has been relative class dealignment, it is here that one has most hope of finding it. However, we shall see later in this chapter that there is a rather more promising political explanation for this change.

Finally, we come to the Conservative:Liberal log odds ratio. Throughout, this is very much lower than the other ones, reflecting the fact that the two parties are more similar in their patterns of class support. Indeed, in 1964 the log odds ratio was zero, indicating that their relative strength in the salariat and working class was identical. A modest gap then emerges in the 1970s and persists thereafter, suggesting that the Liberals have moved slightly away from the Conservatives and towards the Labour party in their pattern of class support.

None of these cases, however, appears to conform to the pattern of a gradual, continuous trend.[7] We can test rigorously for trends using log-linear modelling as we did in chapter 2, and the results are shown in table 5.5. This table compares constant relative voting models with linear trend models. As we can see, the trend which comes closest to statistical significance is that for Liberal and Labour voting.

TABLE 5.5 Modelling the Salariat: Working Class Log Odds Ratios

		chi²	df	p	Trend parameter	Standard error
Con:Lab	(1)	15.9	7	0.03		
	(2)	14.7	6	0.02	−0.006	0.006
Lib:Lab	(1)	19.8	7	0.01		
	(2)	16.5	6	0.01	−0.013	0.007
Con:Lib	(1)	6.9	7	0.44		
	(2)	6.2	6	0.40	0.006	0.007

Source: calculated from table 5.2

The thesis of gradual class secularization looks distinctly unpromising, therefore, leaving political explanations as the prime contenders. We consider some of these in the final section of this chapter, but first we examine some more direct evidence on class secularization.

Class conflict and class awareness

Previous writers have attempted to infer processes of class secularization from trends in class support for the parties, and the models we have used so far in this chapter also infer secularization, or rather lack of secularization, from the pattern of relative class voting. Ideally, however, we should look for more direct evidence of class loyalties and class solidarity.

Unfortunately, we do not have the necessary data to measure class loyalty, but there is a substantial amount of material on perceptions of class. First of all, Butler and Stokes asked their respondents in 1964 "On the whole, do you think that there is bound to be some conflict between different social classes or do you think they can get along together without any conflict?". This question was repeated in February 1974 (at the time of the miners' strike) and in 1987.

TABLE 5.6 Conflict between the Classes 1964–87

	% who think ...				
	Bound to be conflict	Can get along	Don't know		N
1964	42	52	6	100%	(1741)
1966	41	54	5	100%	(1868)
1970 (panel)	32	64	4	100%	(1098)
February 1974	51	44	5	100%	(2454)
1987	51	45	4	100%	(3811)

Sources: British Election Study cross-section surveys and 1966–70 panel study

As we can see, in 1964 42% of respondents thought that there was bound to be some conflict between the classes. This rose to 51% in 1974 at the time of the miners' strike, an increase which is scarcely surprising in view of the open conflict at this time between the government and the miners. Yet, when we repeated this question thirteen years later in 1987, we found that the proportion was still 51% despite the apparently more peaceful social conditions.

Abercrombie and Warde report an even more marked increase in class awareness since 1964. Gallup have regularly asked the question "There used to be a lot of talk in politics about the 'class struggle'. Do you think there is a class struggle in this country or not?". As we can see from table 5.7, the proportion who agree that there is a class struggle rises steadily from 48% in 1964 to 74% in 1984, again with a marked surge in February 1974 at the time of the miners' strike. (Abercrombie and Warde 1988).

It is always rather reassuring for the social researcher to find that two quite independent sources of evidence tell the same story. These two sources leave us in little doubt that people's perceptions of society have changed, but in the opposite direction to that predicted by the decline of class thesis.

The British Election Surveys have also asked people whether they think of themselves as belonging to a particular class. In 1964 Butler and Stokes asked "Do you ever think of yourself as belonging to a particular social class? [If

TABLE 5.7 Perceptions of the Class Struggle 1964–84

	\% thinking there is a class struggle in Britain		
	Is	Is not	Don't know	
July 1964	48	39	13	100\%
June 1972	58	29	13	100\%
January 1973	53	33	14	100\%
February 1974	62	27	11	100\%
April 1975	60	29	11	100\%
April 1981	66	25	9	100\%
March 1984	74	20	6	100\%

Source: Abercrombie and Warde 1988

yes] Which class is that?''. Half the respondents answered the first question in the affirmative and then placed themselves either in the middle or the working class. Respondents who did not initially think of themselves as belonging to a social class, or who mentioned classes other than middle or working, were then asked: "Most people say they belong either to the middle class or to the working class. If you had to make a choice, would you call yourself middle class or working class?" This set of questions has been used almost unchanged in every single election study since (except 1966 when a rather different procedure was used).[8]

We must emphasize that these questions do not necessarily tap class consciousness or class solidarity. When people answer, they may simply be thinking of the type of job they do or their level of income. We would be over-interpreting the answers if we inferred from them class loyalty, since they are essentially cognitive not normative questions. If tables 5.6 and 5.7 tell us about people's perceptions of society, these questions probably tell us about people's perceptions of themselves. On the other hand, respondents' self-perceptions, as measured by these questions, are quite strongly associated with their voting behaviour (cf Heath and Evans 1988; Robertson 1984).

One striking feature of table 5.8 is the stability of the answers over time. They fluctuate much less than the proportions voting Labour and Conservative. It is also notable that the proportion who are unwilling to assign themselves to a class remains low throughout the period.[9] Unlike the trends in party identification, for example, there is no sign here that the unattached are growing in number. The parallels which some scholars have drawn between party identification and class identification are not evident in the time trends. (In particular, compare table 5.8 with table 2.1.)

While there are modest increases in the proportions of people assigning themselves to the middle class and a corresponding decline in working-class identification over the period, they are scarcely surprising in view of the gradual contraction of the working class, objectively defined, over the same

TABLE 5.8 Subjective Class 1964–87

% who described themselves as . . .

	Middle class	Working class	don't know		N
1964	29	66	5	100%	(887)
1966	30	66	4	100%	(1860)
1970	33	63	4	100%	(732)
February 1974	33	63	4	100%	(2443)
October 1974	33	62	4	99%	(2341)
1979	33	62	5	100%	(1849)
1983	34	59	6	99%	(3897)
1987	34	62	4	100%	(3795)

Note: Figures are based on the combined responses to the prompted and unprompted questions.
Source: British Election Study cross-section surveys

period and the gradual expansion of higher level jobs in the salariat. These changes also have much more of the glacial character that one might expect with long-run social change. They provide a marked contrast with the large and episodic fluctuations in support for the political parties.

It is, however, of interest to check whether the relationship between objective and subjective class has been changing, and whether the changes parallel those found between objective class and vote. Table 5.9 gives us our answers.

TABLE 5.9 Objective and Subjective Class 1964–87

Class self-image	Salariat	Routine nonmanual	Petty bourgeoisie	Foremen & technicians	Working class
1964:					
Middle	57	41	44	20	15
Working	33	58	41	74	82
None	10	1	15	6	4
	100% (150)	100% (103)	100% (54)	100% (69)	101% (417)
1966:					
Middle	60	38	49	21	15
Working	34	57	44	75	83
None	6	6	7	4	3
	100% (334)	101% (264)	100% (124)	100% (133)	101% (872)

[Continued next page

TABLE 5.9—*Continued*

Class self-image	Salariat	Routine nonmanual	Petty bourgeoisie	Foremen & technicians	Working class
1970:					
Middle	62	43	43	27	15
Working	33	54	49	70	82
None	6	3	8	3	3
	101% (135)	100% (96)	100% (49)	100% (59)	100% (318)
Feb 1974:					
Middle	58	44	46	32	17
Working	36	53	47	64	80
None	5	3	6	4	3
	99% (465)	100% (383)	99% (190)	100% (123)	100% (1063)
Oct 1974:					
Middle	57	42	41	26	17
Working	37	53	53	70	80
None	6	5	7	4	3
	100% (492)	100% (369)	101% (173)	100% (138)	100% (996)
1979:					
Middle	60	34	47	26	15
Working	35	62	47	69	81
None	5	4	6	5	5
	100% (444)	100% (248)	100% (152)	100% (189)	101% (751)
1983:					
Middle	54	38	40	30	19
Working	37	56	50	65	76
None	9	7	10	5	4
	100% (917)	101% (662)	100% (276)	100% (225)	99% (1457)
1987:					
Middle	58	35	32	18	17
Working	36	61	60	79	80
None	6	4	8	3	3
	100% (983)	100% (684)	100% (303)	100% (213)	100% (1241)

What we find is a small decline in the strength of the association between 1964 and 1987. For example, the salariat:working class log odds ratio falls from 2.2 to 2.0 over this period. However, while there does seem to be a slight weakening of the association between objective and subjective class, the timing of the fall is rather different from that with vote. In the case of vote, the most dramatic change occurred in 1970 when relative class voting reached its nadir. But relative class awareness showed no sign of decline in 1970. Indeed, the salariat:working class log odds ratio was slightly up at 2.3!

TABLE 5.10 Loglinear Models of the Relationship between Class, Class Image and Election

Model	Deviance	df	p
1. Class, election, class image	2698	106	0.000
2. Class by election, class image	2421	78	0.000
3. Class by election, class by class image	114	70	0.001
4. Class by election, class by class image, election by class image	73	56	0.06
16 314 unweighted cases			

Source: calculated from table 5.9

As with class voting we can use log-linear analysis to model the relationship between objective and subjective class and to hunt for linear trends. In table 5.10 we proceed exactly as we did in table 5.3, successively adding relationships to the model. The results confirm our impression that episodic fluctuations are rather smaller than they were with class voting, and the final model of table 5.10 gives a rather better fit than did the equivalent model in table 5.3. Indeed, in the present case the discrepancies between the observed data and the predictions of the model are not significant at the .05 level.

We could stop at this point and say that our final model was a satisfactory one and that there has been no change over time in the relationship between objective and subjective class. However, it is interesting to take the final step of introducing linear time trends, and these do in fact make a further significant improvement in fit.[10] There is, then, some evidence after all for a process of class secularization over this period. But the scale of the process is very small and its pace is very gradual.

This evidence highlights the distinctiveness and autonomy of the changes in class voting. For example, it must make it very unlikely that the fall in class voting in 1970 could have had anything to do with class secularization. Class awareness within the working class clearly did not crumble in 1970, yet the Labour vote did. This suggests rather strongly that the loss of Labour votes in the working class in 1970 had much more to do with political processes than with class processes. It gives no support to Franklin's idea that the decline of class "opened the door to explosions in minor party voting" (Franklin 1985:105).

Equally, if the Labour party had been able to maintain its vote in the working class in the way that class awareness has been maintained, its share of the working-class vote would have fallen only by a couple of points, not the twenty points it actually suffered. On this evidence, then, there may have been a very modest amount of class secularization (perhaps due to processes like social mobility) but it has only minimal relevance to explaining political change.

The story of *How Britain Votes* does need to be modified, therefore. We have now found that a modest process of class secularization probably did occur. This process takes exactly the form one might expect from gradual processes of social change. It is "glacial" in character (an expression that Crewe rightly uses to describe social change). And it looks very different from the episodic fluctuations in class voting.

As we have emphasized, our questions on people's class self-images do not directly measure class consciousness, class loyalty or solidarity. On the other hand, other research on class processes is closely in line with our results on class self-images. For example, in their study of trends in social mobility Goldthorpe and Payne (1986) found no tendency towards increased openness in the class structure. Similarly, in their study of long-run trends in class inequalities in education Heath and Clifford (1990) found only very modest changes since the beginning of the century.[11]

These results should therefore put paid to "dualistic historical thinking" which contrasts loyal and cohesive social classes in the 1960s with open and calculating classes today. There is no direct sociological evidence that such a transformation has occurred. Certainly, classes today are much like the classes of yesterday in their self-images.

While there has been no transformation, we certainly do not wish to claim that contemporary classes are loyal and solidaristic. We agree with Robertson's scepticism about the existence of class in a "communitarian" sense in Britain today. Rather, our interpretation is that there were already substantial elements of a calculating and instrumental approach in the class politics of the 1960s (and probably of much earlier periods too). In other words, we believe that there has been a *contingent* relation between class and voting throughout our period.

In explaining the decline in absolute class voting, or the episodic changes in relativities, we therefore think it is better to focus on contingent political factors such as the failures of the Labour party to deliver the goods to their voters when in office. It is time to put the political back into political science.

Political explanations

There is a wide variety of political factors that could in principle explain the episodic changes in relative class voting. For example, there might be one-off political explanations for particular outcomes in particular years. Thus Labour's working-class supporters may have been particularly disillusioned by its failures to pursue working-class interests when in office in the late 1960s and mid 1970s (cf Alt 1979, 1984). It is rather notable that the two elections which exhibited the lowest levels of relative class voting (and indeed of absolute class voting on the more inclusive definition of table 5.1) were those of 1970 and 1979, which followed periods of Labour government.

Another relevant consideration is that class voting tends to be somewhat weaker among young people than it is among those who are more established in their occupational careers. Many young people start their careers in relatively low-level jobs but expect to be promoted before too long. They may well regard their initial class positions as merely temporary and therefore define their class interests somewhat differently from their older workmates. Since the franchise was of course lowered to 18 in 1969, it is not therefore implausible that relative class voting might have been generally somewhat higher in the 1960s than it was thereafter. A once-for-all change of this kind would seem to be quite likely.

Perhaps most interesting however is the impact of Liberal candidates on class voting. Remember that the Liberals contested just over half the constituencies in 1964, 1966 and 1970, and the ones which they chose to contest tended to be rather more middle class. This cannot account for the 1970 results, but it could perhaps explain why class voting has generally been lower in the later elections.

Table 5.11 compares class voting in the seats contested by the Liberals in 1964 with that in the other constituencies where there were no Liberal candidates. The results are of considerable interest. We find that class voting, whether defined in absolute or relative terms, was higher in the seats without Liberal candidates.

Consider absolute class voting. Using the same procedures as for table 5.1 (column 1) we can calculate that 75% of voters in seats without Liberal candidates voted for their class parties, but only 57% did so where Liberals stood. Thus there is a difference of 19 points in the level of absolute class voting in the two types of constituency. We can compare this with the 12 point decline in absolute class voting between 1964 and 1987 shown in table 5.1.

The differences in relative class voting are also of interest. Compare, for example, the log odds of voting Conservative or Labour in the salariat and working class respectively. Where there were no Liberal candidates in 1964, this log odds ratio reached 2.5, but where Liberals stood it was only 1.9.

It is quite possible, therefore, that it has been the intervention of Liberal candidates, not class secularization, that has reduced both absolute and relative class voting. And it is particularly likely that Liberal interventions can explain why the class pattern of Liberal support has moved slightly away from

TABLE 5.11 Liberal Candidates and Class Voting 1964

	Con	Lab	Lib		N
	Constituencies where Liberal candidate stood				
Salariat	57	18	25	100%	(196)
Routine nonmanual	52	23	25	100%	(124)
Petty bourgeoisie	71	12	17	100%	(69)
Foremen and technicians	35	39	26	100%	(69)
Working class	28	60	12	100%	(379)
	Con	Lab	Lib		N
	Constituencies where no Liberal candidate stood				
Salariat	77	23	0	100%	(75)
Routine nonmanual	68	32	0	100%	(75)
Petty bourgeoisie	82	18	0	100%	(33)
Foremen and technicians	44	56	0	100%	(48)
Working class	22	78	0	100%	(315)

Source: 1964 cross-section survey

the Conservatives' and towards that of the Labour party (as we reported in table 5.5). In 1964, the Liberal party was more likely to field candidates in Conservative-held, middle-class seats and so their support had more of a middle-class character. In 1974 they increased their number of candidates; the extra candidates were necessarily fielded in Labour-held, working-class seats; and so their class support moved a bit closer to that of Labour.

Now we cannot prove causality from the evidence of table 5.11. We cannot be sure that it was the Liberal interventions that reduced class voting. It is perfectly possible that the seats in which Liberals chose to field candidates were ones where class voting was already rather lower. What we can do, however, is to examine what subsequently happened to class voting in the seats which the Liberals did not contest in the 1960s. If the causal hypothesis is correct, we would expect to see the high levels of absolute and relative class voting in these seats decline to the levels of the seats which the Liberals had contested in the 1960s.

Table 5.12 shows that this has indeed happened.[12] Following the same procedure as before, we find that absolute class voting in 1987 was virtually identical in the two types of seat: it was 51% in the seats which the Liberals had contested back in 1964, and 52% in the seats which they had not contested then. Again, in 1987 the Conservative:Labour log odds ratio for the salariat and working class was identical at 1.5 in both types of seat.

TABLE 5.12 Liberal Candidates and Class Voting 1987

	Con	Lab	Alliance		N
	Constituencies where a Liberal candidate stood in 1964				
Salariat	58	12	31	101%	(462)
Routine nonmanual	58	19	23	100%	(300)
Petty bourgeoisie	64	14	22	100%	(143)
Foremen and technicians	42	30	29	101%	(84)
Working class	39	38	23	100%	(449)
	Constituencies where no Liberal candidate stood in 1964				
Salariat	46	25	28	99%	(197)
Routine nonmanual	39	39	22	100%	(152)
Petty bourgeoisie	59	25	16	100%	(61)
Foremen and technicians	35	46	19	100%	(63)
Working class	24	60	16	100%	(353)

Source: 1987 cross-section survey

Even this evidence does not prove the causal connection, although it is certainly consistent with it. We cannot therefore be sure that any or all of our explanations are correct either singly or in combination. Our point is that political explanations of the kind we have put forward—the number of seats contested by the Liberals, the extension of the franchise, the failure of Labour governments to satisfy their supporters—are in many ways more plausible than those which focus on changes in the character of the social classes.

Notes

[1] The conventional approach is to divide the class structure into two—a middle class of nonmanual workers and a working class of manual workers. Absolute class voting then becomes the sum of middle-class Conservative voters and working-class Labour voters (see Sarlvik and Crewe 1983). This assumes that the Liberal and Social Democratic parties are not class parties.
[2] Table 5.1 is derived from a collapsed version of table 5.2. The salariat, routine nonmanual class and petty bourgeoisie have been combined to form the middle classes and foremen and technicians have been combined with the working class.

[3] We must emphasize that Franklin, the writer who has most cogently argued that the decline of class voting opened the way for the rise of the Liberals, does not use absolute class voting as his measure. Instead, he uses the linear regression coefficient of class on vote, which is effectively a measure of relative class voting in our sense.

[4] The class schema is based on occupational group and employment status, as defined by OPCS. Over the years OPCS have changed their classifications of occupational groups. The data in the present book have been coded according to the 1980 classification (OPCS 1980) whereas *How Britain Votes* used the 1970 classification (OPCS 1970). In order to maintain comparability over time, the codes used in the earlier election studies have been reassigned (using a look-up table published by OPCS which crosstabulates the 1970 and 1980 occupation groups) to classes so as to conform as closely as possible to the 1980 class schema. Note that OPCS's 1970 classification also differed from their 1960 classification in some respects, although the differences are not as great as those between the 1970 and 1980 classifications. Again we have tried to allocate codes to classes so as to obtain maximum comparability with the 1980 class schema. The computer programs which we used for this purpose are available on request.

We have also taken the opportunity to rectify a few anomalies in the earlier class schema used in *How Britain Votes*. The result is to enlarge the working class slightly compared with our earlier procedure. For a detailed comparison of the two class schemas based on the 1970 and 1980 classifications respectively see Goldthorpe and Payne (1986).

[5] We should note that respondents are assigned to these five classes on the basis of their present or last main occupation (if unemployed or retired). More specifically, respondents who are economically active or retired are allocated according to their present or last main occupation. Respondents who are not economically active or retired, but who have an economically active or retired spouse, are allocated to a class on the basis of their spouse's present or last main occupation. (Following conventional OPCS procedure, unemployed respondents who are seeking work are defined as economically active.) This procedure could not be followed exactly in the 1964, 1966, 1970 and October 1974 election surveys since wife's occupation was not ascertained. In these four surveys it is only women who were not economically active or retired who could be allocated to their spouse's class.

Widows and the divorced/separated were not asked for their former husband's occupation and accordingly have been omitted throughout if they were not themselves economically active or retired.

[6] Most writers have used the Alford index or related measures such as regression coefficients, metric or standardized, in OLS regression to measure relative class voting. See Alford 1962; Crewe 1984; Franklin 1985; Rose and McAllister 1986. For critiques of this approach see Heath, Jowell and Curtice 1987; Evans, Heath and Payne 1989.

OLS regression assumes that the dependent variable is a continuously measured variable with a normal distribution and homoscedastic error variance. When the dependent variable is a dichotomous one, these assumptions are not met. OLS regression gives a reasonable approximation in many cases but the more skewed the dependent variable, the more serious becomes the violation of the assumptions. Techniques of loglinear modelling and logistic regression are now available to deal with dichotomous dependent variables and are to be preferred (Cox 1970; Aldrich and Nelson 1984).

It should be noted that, in the case of the two-class two-party model the Alford index is formally equivalent to the unstandardized regression co-efficient, and thus must suffer from the same drawbacks. Thus, the more skewed the distribution, the more problematic becomes the index. In effect, floor and ceiling effects come into operation thus limiting the value which the index can reach. This is analogous to the point made by Cox that, with a skewed dependent variable, OLS regression may predict probabilities that are greater than 1 or less than 0.

Dunleavy has suggested that the index of dissimilarity be used to measure relative class voting (Dunleavy 1987). However, as we showed in our reply (Heath, Jowell and Curtice 1988), the index of dissimilarity tells an almost identical story to that told by our preferred technique of loglinear modelling and quite clearly contradicts Dunleavy's own assertion that there was an "accelerated phase of class de-alignment . . . in the late 1970s, when the way in which voting patterns converged across different occupational classes was significantly different from what had gone before" (Dunleavy 1984).

[7] We can also undertake a global test for the full set of thirty log odds ratios. Again we find that the hypothesis of a linear trend should be rejected. As table 5.3 showed, the constant class voting model yields chi^2 of 85 with 56 degrees of freedom (p = 0.008). The addition of linear trends in the relations between class and vote reduces chi^2 by 14 for the loss of 8 degrees of freedom, a change that is not significant at the .05 level.

[8] In 1966 a split half design was used with half the respondents being administered the standard closed question and the other half being asked an open-ended question. The documentation is unclear, but it appears that the corresponding variables in the data file (VAR0819 and VAR0820) are composite measures, which should therefore be treated with caution.

[9] The proportion who assigned themselves unprompted to a class is a lot lower and is also more volatile. It does not however show any clear downward trend. The figures are:

    1964—59%
    1966—na
    1970—44%
    February 1974—39%
    October 1974—44%
    1979—49%
    1983—57%
    1987—50%

[10] The introduction of linear trends in the class by class self-image relationships yields chi^2 of 49 with 48 degrees of freedom, a reduction of 24 in deviance for the less of 8 degrees of freedom. This change is significant at the 0.01 level.

We should note that this final model fits eight new parameters. These parameters are not constrained to be the same size or even of the same sign, and indeed the fitted parameters do differ in both respects. In other words, the model simply tests the hypothesis that there are linear trends, not that there are linear trends towards secularization. However, we do find that the negative parameters are not significantly different from zero whereas there are some positive parameters which are significant. More specifically, if we focus specifically on middle and working class self-images in the salariat and working class respectively and model this particular log odds ratio, we find a statistically significant linear trend towards secularization.

[11] One dissenting study is that of McPherson and Willms (1987). They found that class relativities in education had narrowed in Scotland since the mid-1970s, although they note that this was not true at the higher levels of attainment. They attribute the change in part to comprehensive reorganization, which had begun earlier and proceeded further than in England.

[12] Because of boundary changes it is not possible to identify with any precision current seats which the Liberals did or did not contest in 1964. We have included in the analysis of table 5.12 only those seats where we are reasonably confident that the seats broadly correspond, and have excluded all seats where we had major doubts. It should be noted that the task of identifying seats is made slightly easier by the fact that there was a considerable degree of geographical clustering in the seats which Liberals contested in 1964, so in many cases boundary revisions affected adjacent seats all of which had been contested by the Liberals.

Chapter 6

The New Middle Class

While we have found little evidence for processes of class secularization, we certainly do not wish to claim that the classes are internally homogeneous, exhibiting high degrees of class loyalty and solidarity. The petty bourgeosie is perhaps the most homogeneous, but the other classes are all divided both by opposing interests and by ideology. Our claim is simply that many of these internal divisions are long-standing ones, going back at least as far as the first election studies in the 1960s, and probably long before that too. Differences in social origin and religion are perhaps the most notable of these old cleavages.

A number of writers have also suggested that there are now new cleavages within the classes, and in particular that there is now a new middle class, based on professional employees in the public sector, with substantially different ideology and interests from those of the old middle class of managers and businessmen. Some writers have emphasized the distinctive interests of the new middle class, their position in the public sector giving its members an interest in government spending on the welfare state. Other writers have emphasized their distinctive ideology and value priorities, and believe them to constitute a New Left that values quality of life rather than the economic goals valued by the Old Left of the working class.

As we shall see in this chapter, there is good evidence that these new cleavages have indeed grown in importance and that the salariat has in the 1980s become a more divided class than it used to be. We begin, however, with the old cleavages of religion and social origin.

Religion

The importance of religion has recently been rather neglected in the study of British voting behaviour, as indeed it was in *How Britain Votes*.[1] In

85

general, most writers have contrasted the unimportance of religion in Britain with its much greater importance in many European countries. Now it may well be true that religion is a more important source of political loyalties elsewhere (as it most certainly is in Northern Ireland); and it is also true that religion is less important in Britain than is social class; but as we shall see religion is as important a division within the salariat as some of the new cleavages such as public sector employment to which most contemporary research energy has been devoted.[2]

TABLE 6.1 Religion and Vote in the Salariat 1987

	Conservative	Alliance	Labour	Other		
Church of England	65	27	8	0	100%	(391)
Presbyterian	54	26	13	7	100%	(46)
Nonconformist	42	42	15	2	101%	(60)
Catholic	50	24	25	2	101%	(68)
Other	52	26	19	4	101%	(54)
None	44	29	25	2	100%	(231)

Source: 1987 cross-section survey

Table 6.1 shows that, within the salariat, Anglicans are the most inclined to vote Conservative, while Nonconformists, Catholics, people of no religion, and people of other religions (e.g. Muslims, Sikhs) are much less inclined towards the Conservatives.[3] The Conservative vote of 65% among Anglicans is one of the highest levels of support for the Conservatives that we shall find. The Alliance vote of 42% among Nonconformists is the highest level of Alliance support we shall find in any class. And the Labour votes of 25% among Catholics and among the non-religious are again some of the highest levels of Labour voting that we shall see in the salariat.

There are probably somewhat different reasons for the voting patterns of each religious group. In the case of Catholicism, the link probably has less to do with religion per se than with the Irish question. A large number of British Catholics are of Irish origin and, as Hornsby-Smith has shown, "For historical reasons, largely grounded in differences between the political parties with respect to the Irish question, Catholics have disproportionately given their allegiance to the Labour Party" (Hornsby-Smith 1987 164–5, cf Hornsby-Smith and Lee 1979:37–9,174–5).

The position with the other religions probably has little do with religion per se either. The other religions are rather heterogeneous, but they include some Sikhs and Muslims who, for reasons probably more to do with ethnicity and related political issues disproportionately support the Labour party.

In the case of Nonconformists and the non-religious, the links probably have less of an ethnic explanation. Historically, Nonconformity is of course associated with Liberal voting. Wald (1983) explains this link in terms of the dissenting and free-thinking nature of the various Nonconformist churches and of the similarly free-thinking, anti-establishment stance of the Liberal party in the nineteenth century and of its earlier Whig predecessors. Today, however, it could be argued that the Labour party is an even clearer home for anti-establishment free-thinking, and it is perhaps this that makes it relatively attractive to agnostic or atheist dissenters.

A distinction can be drawn, then, between the members of the Established Church, who tend to be traditionalist in their social attitudes, and the various dissenting traditions. We must emphasize that we are dealing here with the rank and file of the Established Church not the elite, many of whom will be a great deal more free-thinking than their parishioners. There may well be a growing divergence between the attitudes of the Church of England's elite and that of ordinary Church members. Incidentally, there is evidence of a marked change in the social basis of recruitment to the ministry over the past one hundred years, with bishops and clergy coming from much less socially elite backgrounds than they used to (see Thompson 1974). The social basis of rank-and-file membership has probably changed much less, and this may well have some connection with the growing divergence between elite and mass opinions in the Church.

The continued importance of religion comes as something of a surprise, given the earlier research documenting its decline. For example Wald (1983), using aggregate data, documents the gradual decline of the religious cleavage in Britain during the first half of the twentieth century and its gradual replacement by class. And Butler and Stokes' (1969) cohort analysis of the first election studies in the 1960s showed that the association between religion and voting was much weaker in the younger age groups than it had been in the old. As the older age groups have since died, we might have expected to find that religion too had died as a source of political allegiance.

Unfortunately, when we turn to the 1964 study for comparisons with 1987, we find some major procedural changes. Butler and Stokes asked their respondents "What is your religion?" But subsequent investigators (including ourselves) have followed Sarlvik and Crewe's practice, introduced in 1974, asking "Do you belong to any religious denomination?"

Butler and Stokes' formulation takes it for granted that respondents *do* have a religion, whereas the later formulation leaves it an open question. In answer to Butler and Stokes' question hardly anyone had the nerve to deny that they had a religion, and the change in survey practice in 1974 coincided with a large increase in the number of respondents saying they had no religion. But the change in the question wording means that we are not really comparing like with like.

However, Butler and Stokes did ask a supplementary question about the frequency of church attendance, and our best plan is to use this in conjunction with the question on religious affiliation. We therefore combine together people admitting to no religion with the people claiming to have a religion but never attending church. Table 6.2 shows the trends with this revised formulation.

The two panels of table 6.2 show some across-the-board changes of the kind that became familiar in chapter 5. Thus Conservative voting in the

TABLE 6.2 Religion and Vote in the Salariat 1964 and 1987

	1964					
	Conservative	Liberal	Labour	Other		N
Church of England	72	11	16	1	100%	(123)
Presbyterian	74	22	4	0	100%	(23)
Nonconformist	51	29	20	0	100%	(45)
Catholic	—	—	—	—	—	(12)
Other	—	—	—	—	—	(3)
None and non-attenders	47	20	30	3	100%	(64)

	1987					
	Conservative	Alliance	Labour	Other		N
Church of England	67	25	8	0	100%	(266)
Presbyterian	63	19	13	6	101%	(32)
Nonconformist	40	46	13	2	101%	(48)
Catholic	46	24	29	2	101%	(59)
Other	52	25	18	5	100%	(44)
None and non-attenders	50	30	19	2	101%	(401)

Sources: 1964 and 1987 cross-section surveys

salariat was generally down in 1987, while Alliance voting was substantially up.

After taking account of these across-the-board changes, we find that there has been no clear tendency for the relation between religion and voting behaviour to weaken. There are occasional hints of change, but none of them is anywhere near statistical significance.[4] They are certainly nothing like the size of the changes that Wald and Butler and Stokes had noted earlier in the century.

However, while the relationship between religion and voting in the salariat has scarcely changed, it would be wrong to say that nothing has changed. There has in fact been a marked growth in the number of nonreligious people in the salariat. In 1964, 23% of the salariat said that they had no religion or never attended church. By 1987 this had risen to 47%. This is one of the biggest social changes that we shall find.

Social background

Our second old cleavage within the salariat derives from social origins. Abramson (1972) for example suggested that middle-class Labour voting was largely to be explained by upward mobility from the working class. He showed that Butler and Stokes' measures underemphasized the importance of upward mobility and that it in fact represented a major contributor to class-deviant voting. His explanation for the phenomenon was largely in terms of family traditions of Labour voting (although he also mentioned the possibility that the upwardly mobile may move into less well-paid jobs within the middle class and that this may in part account for their Labour votes).[5]

Social origins have also been linked to the new cleavages within the middle class. Whereas Abramson argued that working-class origins explain middle-class Labour voting, Inglehart has argued that "formative affluence" (of which middle class origins would be a good indicator) accounts for the rise of a New Left within the middle class. He argues that people who grew up in conditions of formative affluence, where they were freed from the usual worries about economic security, will develop new value priorities, placing a higher value on the quality of life than on the Old Left issues of economic growth (Inglehart 1971, 1977, 1981).

While Inglehart's theory was not formulated specifically for the British case, Alt and Turner (1982) found some evidence consistent with his proposition from the British Election Surveys. They found a group of "silk stocking socialists" who came from middle-class backgrounds and had taken jobs in the public sector.

Of course, the two theories are not necessarily incompatible. Abramson's theory may help to explain the distribution of Old Left orientations in the salariat while Inglehart's may help to explain New Left orientations. As Rallings (1975) has cogently argued, there may in fact be two quite distinct types of middle-class Labour voter.

TABLE 6.3 Social Origins and Vote in the Salariat 1987

Social origins	Conservative	Alliance	Labour	Other		N
Salariat	56	32	11	1	100%	(276)
Routine nonmanual	63	24	13	1	101%	(72)
Petty bourgeoisie	68	21	11	0	100%	(110)
Foremen, technicians	52	31	14	2	99%	(86)
Working class	45	29	24	2	100%	(249)

Source: 1987 cross-section survey

Table 6.3 offers some hope to both theories. First, Labour voting is significantly higher among upwardly mobile people from working-class origins, and we may also note that Conservative voting is at its highest among people from petty bourgeois origins.

Second, there are also hints of a curvilinear relationship between social origins and voting behaviour. While Conservative voting rises as we move from working-class origins, through foremen, to petty bourgeois origins, it then declines again as we move on up to routine nonmanual backgrounds and finally to the second generation members of the salariat. And this suggests that Inglehart's theory of formative affluence may also have some truth in it.

On the other hand, it is clear that Abramson's theory is the more powerful. People from working-class origins are clearly more likely to be Labour voters than are those from affluent salariat backgrounds. Indeed, in 1987 49% of all Labour voters in the salariat came from working class origins.

TABLE 6.4 Social Origins and Vote in the Salariat 1964

Social origins	Conservative	Liberal	Labour	Other		N
Salariat	68	15	15	1	99%	(72)
Routine nonmanual	58	11	21	11	101%	(19)
Petty bourgeoisie	67	27	6	0	100%	(48)
Foremen and technicians	54	15	31	0	100%	(13)
Working class	56	16	28	0	100%	(98)

Source: 1964 cross-section survey

Turning next to a comparison with the 1964 data, the curvilinear relationship that we noted in 1987 was not evident in 1964. And we should note that this too is in line with Inglehart's theory, since in 1964 most second-generation members of the salariat would have grown up in an environment of insecurity during wartime or the pre-war depression.

However, with this exception, the association between origins and vote was very similar in 1964 and 1987. Indeed, the model which postulates that the relationship stayed the same has an excellent fit to the data.[6] Like the religious cleavage, then, the old cleavage of social origins shows little sign of decline.

Unlike the case of religion, however, there has been a decline, not a growth, in the size of the more Labour-inclined group. Thus people from working-class origins made up 39% of voters in the salariat in 1964, but by 1987 this had fallen to 31%. This therefore tends to cancel out to some extent the potential gains to Labour from the decline of religion.

Education

A number of writers have found a connection between higher education and liberal political attitudes or Liberal voting (Inglehart 1977; Heath, Jowell and Curtice 1985; Heath and Topf 1985). Indeed, higher education has often been noted as a key source of New Left values.

As we can see from table 6.5, support for the Alliance is markedly higher among graduates than it is at lower educational levels. To be sure, even among graduates the Alliance does not manage to take the lead, but this is one of the highest levels of support for the Alliance that we shall find in any group, exceeded only by the support from Nonconformists that we saw

TABLE 6.5 Qualifications and Vote in the Salariat 1987

Highest qualification	Conservative	Alliance	Labour	Other	N	
Degree	39	39	22	1	101%	(207)
Technical and professional	57	26	15	2	100%	(326)
O- or A-level	67	21	9	2	99%	(141)
Below O-level	64	31	3	3	101%	(39)
None	58	25	17	1	101%	(139)

Source: 1987 cross-section survey

earlier. Furthermore, graduates are now a much larger proportion of the salariat than are Nonconformists, and so in this sense education is a rather more important basis of Alliance voting.

Table 6.5 also exhibits a rather interesting curvilinear relationship between education and voting, with support for Labour in the salariat being highest among graduates at one extreme and among the unqualified at the other. This parallels our findings on social origins, and is of course in part due to the fact that the two sets of people largely overlap: graduates are much more likely to have come from salaried origins while the unqualified are most likely to have come from working-class origins.

TABLE 6.6 University Education and Vote in the Salariat

	1964					
	Conservative	Liberal	Labour	Other	N	
University education	46	32	21	0	99%	(28)
Other	63	17	19	1	100%	(243)

	1987					
	Conservative	Alliance	Labour	Other	N	
University education	39	39	22	1	101%	(207)
Other	60	25	13	2	100%	(645)

Sources: 1964 and 1987 cross-section surveys

The 1964 study did not collect information on people's other qualifications, and so we must restrict ourselves to higher education. As we can see, the Liberals were relatively strong among graduates in 1964, just as they were in 1987. And once again we find that the strength of the association has not changed significantly over time.[7] Higher education cannot, therefore, qualify as a new cleavage, although the numbers of the higher educated within the salariat have certainly been expanding. From being 10% of the salariat in 1964 they had risen to a quarter of the salariat in 1987.

Occupational divisions within the salariat

The old cleavages based on religion, origins and education, then, have shown little or no tendency to wither away. They remain major sources of differentiation within the salariat. Let us now turn to specific measures of the new cleavages based on sector and occupation.

There have been many different theories of the new middle class. A number of writers have emphasized the different interests of the old and new classes. Some of these concentrate on occupational divisions (Brint 1984; Kriesi 1989), while others focus on sectoral divisions (McAdams 1987; Dunleavy 1980a, 1980b; Dunleavy and Husbands 1985). Thus McAdams advanced the hypothesis that those who work for government rather than in the private sector will have an interest in expanding government intervention in the economy and will accordingly be more left wing. Similarly, Dunleavy and Husbands argued that "a potential conflict of interest is established between public sector employees advancing their wage levels (and interested in expanding services) and private sector employees anxious to minimize their tax burdens" (Dunleavy and Husbands 1985:22).

Despite its apparently platitudinous character, this proposition was not in fact supported by McAdams' American data although there was some support for it in Dunleavy's British data.[8]

Writers such as Kriesi (1989) on the other hand have suggested that the crucial division may not be between public and private sectors but between the "technocrats" who run large-scale organizations and the rank-and-file professional "specialists" who are more concerned with maintaining the integrity of their disciplines in the face of bureaucratic control.[9] Kriesi describes

"... an opposition of interests between, on the one hand, the technocrats in private enterprises *and* public bureaucracies who try to manage their organizations most efficiently and, on the other hand, the specialists who try to defend their own and their clients' relative autonomy against the intervention of the "technostructure". Ideal-typically, it is the specialists in the private *and* in the public spheres who constitute the new class and who mobilize in [new social movements]" (Kriesi 1989:1085).

Kriesi's Dutch data did not support this proposition either, but favoured the more limited one that it was the "social and cultural" specialists (teachers and social workers for example) rather than professional specialists in general who were radical. In this respect, Kriesi's results support Parkin's much earlier study of CND supporters in Britain, when he found that the "welfare and creative" professions were disproportionately represented in the anti-nuclear movement (Parkin 1968; see also Cotgrove and Duff, 1980).

We must note however that Parkin emphasized the process of selective recruitment to these occupations rather than any distinct interests which they engendered. Thus Parkin argued that middle-class radicals were highly selective in their choice of occupations, choosing ones which were amenable to their prior political and moral values. The new middle class was thus more of a sanctuary for radicals rather than a cause of their radicalism (Parkin 1968:185).

Table 6.7 looks at the voting behaviour of Dunleavy's public sector employees in the salariat, of Kriesi's specialists, and of Parkin's welfare and creative occupations. Respondents are classified according to their own occupations, and are distinguished from people who were economically inactive at the time of the survey.

TABLE 6.7 Occupational Divisions within the Salariat 1987

	Conservative	Alliance	Labour	Other		N
Public sector	40	32	26	2	100%	(212)
Private sector	57	29	13	2	101%	(281)
Specialists	44	31	24	2	101%	(266)
Technocrats	56	29	14	2	101%	(287)
Welfare and creative	32	33	34	1	100%	(162)
Business and administrative	58	28	12	2	100%	(391)
Economically inactive	63	26	9	1	99%	(299)

Source: 1987 cross-section survey

As we can see there is a difference in the voting behaviour of public and private sector employees (the former including nationalized industries, national and local government). In both sectors, the Conservatives are the largest single bloc, followed by the Alliance. But it is clear that Labour is *relatively* stronger in the public sector, although Labour voting is still a lot lower among these members of the salariat than it is among, for example, manual workers in the private sector (see chapter 7). We must, therefore, keep these results in perspective. As befits their privileged positions in the salariat, both the public and private sector employees incline more to the Conservatives than to any other party. If we equate the New Left with Labour voters in the public sector, then they are merely a minority of a minority.

Very similar results are obtained when we compare technocrats (including both managers in industry and officials with managerial responsibility in government) and rank-and-file specialist employees such as teachers, technicians and social workers.[10]

We may note that these differences are of roughly similar order of magnitude to the old cleavages which we have already seen. However, when we turn to Parkin's concept of the welfare and creative professions we obtain rather larger differences.[11] In 1987, this group divided its votes almost equally between the three main party groupings. The 34% of its votes which it gave Labour is in fact the highest level of Labour voting which we shall find in any group within the salariat.

These distinctions between public and private sector, technocrats and specialists, and welfare and creative occupations to a large extent overlap. Thus the welfare and creative professions include many specialists who are employed in the public sector, in particular teachers, doctors and social workers, although it also includes some such as clergy, journalists, artists, actors and musicians who work in the private sector. To a considerable extent, therefore, we are simply redescribing the same set of people in different ways.

What we need, therefore, is a multivariate analysis in which we analyse sector and occupation simultaneously. When we do this, we find that it is the welfare and creative distinction that is doing most of the work. Sector has no statistically significant effect once we control for the welfare and creative occupations.

TABLE 6.8 Logit Models of Sector, Occupation and Vote in the Salariat 1987

Independent variables	Public/Private sector parameter	Welfare and Creative/ Business and Admin. parameter
1. Sector	−0.53 (0.13)	—
2. Occupation	—	−0.81 (0.13)
3. Sector and occupation	−0.20 (0.15)	−0.78 (0.15)
4. Plus controls for social origins, religion and higher education	−0.19 (0.16)	−0.68 (0.18)
5. Plus further control for income	−0.17 (0.17)	−0.65 (0.19)

Note: Figures in brackets give the standard errors.
Source: 1987 cross-section survey

This can be seen rather clearly from table 6.8, in which we report a series of logit models. In the first model we begin with the simple relationship between sector and vote (Labour versus Conservative) without controlling for any other variables. The logit parameter here is analogous to the log odds ratio that can be calculated from table 6.7. (In the parameterization which we use it is simply half the log odds ratio.) As we can see, the parameter is more than twice its standard error, and thus tells us that there is a statistically significant difference in the voting behaviour of public and private sector workers in the salariat.

The second model carries out the equivalent analysis for the welfare and creative occupations, and we can see that the relationship with vote is even stronger than in the case of sector.

The third model looks simultaneously at sector, occupation and vote. We now see, when we control for welfare and creative occupations, that the sectoral effect is no longer significant. And in the fourth model we check our results by controlling for the other variables described earlier in this chapter—social origins, education, and religion. These additional controls do not lead us to modify our conclusions. It remains true that the welfare and creative professions are distinctive in their voting behaviour.

The belief that the public sector is a home to middle-class radicals is not however wholly without foundation. Certainly, the great majority of the welfare and creative professionals are employed in the public sector, and they constitute around half of all public sector employees in the salariat. But public sector employees who are not members of the welfare and creative professions (civil servants and managers of nationalized industries for example) do not differ significantly from private sector employees in their voting patterns. And private sector welfare and creative professionals (who are admittedly very few in number) are also relatively radical in their voting behaviour. Of course, even the welfare and creative professionals are not all that radical: they divide their votes evenly between the three parties.

This finding must cast serious doubt on the theories of public sector or specialist interests. After all, if there were distinctive public-sector interests, we would expect these to affect the behaviour of public-sector administrators and managers as well as public-sector welfare workers.[12] The fact that they do not casts serious doubt on the theory of interests, or at the very least suggests that these interests are not recognized by many of the participants.

Of course, it could be that there are distinct interests associated with the welfare and creative occupations. Most obviously, these may be the least well-paid members of the salariat (cf Rallings 1975). But this does not appear to be the case either. While they are not the best-paid jobs in the salariat, they are not the worst-paid. If we control for income, we still find very marked differences between the voting patterns of the welfare and creative occupations and those of the business and administrative occupations. This can be seen from the final model of table 6.8, which shows that controls for income do not substantially modify our earlier conclusions. Parkin's rival theory of selective recruitment to the welfare and creative occupations looks, therefore, to be a more promising one.

On the other hand, the political distinctiveness of the welfare and creative professionals appears to be a rather new phenomenon, and it may be therefore that a political rather than a social explanation is needed for their voting behaviour in 1987. As we can see by comparing tables 6.7 and 6.9 their voting behaviour was much less distinctive in 1964, and was on a par with that of the specialists.[13] (The 1964 survey did not ask questions about the public/private sector division.) Moreover, much the same pattern is repeated in most of the other election surveys. While there are fluctuations (as one would expect given the small numbers involved) in the earlier surveys, 1987 stands out as the one in which the welfare and creative professionals differed most

TABLE 6.9 Occupational Divisions within the Salariat 1964

	Conservative	Liberal	Labour	Other		N
Specialists	52	24	23	1	100%	(75)
Technocrats	63	17	20	1	101%	(97)
Welfare and creative	50	26	22	2	100%	(50)
Business and administrative	62	17	20	2	101%	(127)
Economically inactive	67	16	17	0	100%	(93)

Source: 1964 cross-section survey

from the rest of the salariat (see table 6.10 below). The suddenness of the change in 1987, therefore, makes it look much more like a reaction to political events than the product of autonomous social forces.

Even if we accept the idea that the welfare and creative occupations constitute a new middle class, a crude distinction between the old and the new middle classes does not do justice to the complexities of the social sources of voting behaviour. In addition to the welfare and creative occupations, we are still left with three other major characteristics which have significant relationships with voting within the salariat—social origins, religion, and education (and there are also further associations with housing tenure, trade union membership and region).

Lying behind these complexities, however, we believe there are two more general social processes at work. On the one hand, as we have suggested, a number of our measures, particularly higher education, Nonconformity, agnosticism and atheism, and perhaps membership of the welfare and creative occupations may be associated with dissenting, free-thinking orientations. On the other hand, some measures such as father's class will be associated with family traditions of voting.

In essence then, we have two main sources of Labour voting in the salariat—family traditions and intellectual dissent.[14] There is in contrast one main source of Alliance voting, namely dissenting and free-thinking orientations. Finally the Conservative party appeals most to the socially and materially privileged members of the salariat. To put the matter slightly more colloquially, the Conservative party appeals to the orthodox members of the establishment; the Alliance parties have tended to appeal to the dissenting elements of the establishment; the Labour party both to the upwardly mobile members of the salariat and to the dissenters.

The divided salariat

There are two senses in which a cleavage might be new or might become more important. On the one hand, as we have just seen, existing groups like the welfare and creative professions might change their voting behaviour. On the other hand, a group such as university graduates who were previously small, albeit distinct in their voting behaviour, might grow in size thus becoming a quantitatively more important force.

We can put these two components of newness together using the index of dissimilarity. Table 6.10 compares the profiles of Labour and Conservative voters in the salariat over the years 1964 to 1987. In addition to the characteristics covered earlier in this chapter, we add trade union membership, housing tenure and region.[15]

TABLE 6.10 The Changing Profile of Conservative and Labour Voters in the Salariat 1964–87

| | Index of dissimilarity | | | | | |
| | --- | --- | --- | --- | --- | --- |
	1964	1970	1974 (Oct)	1979	1983	1987
Religion	17	24	—	25	25	23
Social origins	24	31	26	30	21	23
Higher education	4	3	2	7	8	17
Welfare and creative occupations	7	11	21	13	15	31
TU membership	10	12	23	26	37	29
Housing tenure	21	17	17	30	13	19
Region	14	7	4	8	13	21

Source: 1964–1987 cross-section surveys

Table 6.10 brings out both the continuities and the changes over time. On the one hand, we can see that there has been no real change with respect to social origins and housing (working-class origins and local authority housing tending moreover to go together). In 1987, Labour and Conservative voters in the salariat differed in their profiles to almost exactly the same extent as they did in 1964.

On the other hand, we can see major increases in political polarization with respect to higher education, membership of the welfare and creative occupations, and trade union membership. (In the cases of higher education and trade union membership the index of dissimilarity has increased because the proportion of the salariat who are graduates or union members has increased; in the case of the welfare and creative professionals, the proportion has stayed the same and it is, as we have just seen, their voting behaviour that has changed relative to other groups.)

Table 6.11 repeats the analysis of dissimilarity for the Liberal voters in the salariat. Given the very small numbers of Liberals in the earlier surveys, the figures must have a rather large sampling error and we have to be cautious about their interpretation. One point is clear, however. Throughout, the Liberals have been closer to Conservative than to Labour voters in their social origins and housing tenure (and, less clearly, region). This of course

TABLE 6.11 The Changing Profiles of Liberal Voters in the Salariat 1964–87

		Indices of dissimilarity					
		1964	1970	1974 (Oct)	1979	1983	1987
Religion	Con:Lib	24	27	—	14	11	13
	Lib:Lab	21	13	—	26	19	16
Social origins	Con:Lib	9	24	15	12	6	10
	Lib:Lab	26	26	15	18	22	17
Higher education	Con:Lib	11	14	9	11	10	16
	Lib:Lab	−7	−11	−7	−4	−3	2
Welfare occupations etc.	Con:Lib	11	18	13	11	10	11
	Lib:Lab	−5	−15	−13	5	5	20
TU membership	Con:Lib	12	19	9	14	13	9
	Lib:Lab	−1	22	20	13	24	20
Housing tenure	Con:Lib	2	5	5	4	2	2
	Lib:Lab	20	14	14	27	12	17
Region	Con:Lib	19	9	10	8	8	10
	Lib:Lab	20	20	9	7	14	19

Source: 1964–1987 cross-section surveys

mirrors our earlier finding in chapter 5 that Liberal voters are closer to the Conservatives in their current class positions.

Secondly, there are hints of a realignment between Labour and the Liberals. Thus in the earliest surveys, the Liberals were actually stronger than Labour among graduates and among members of the welfare and creative occupations (indicated by the minus signs). By the later surveys, the position had reversed. This, if we are correct, should probably be seen as the end of a longer-term process whereby the Labour party has taken over from the Liberals the role of principal spokesman for dissent on civil rights, equal opportunities and the like.

However, our most striking finding is the way in which the social profiles of Conservative and Labour voters have diverged between 1964 and 1987. On three of the seven social characteristics covered by table 6.10, Conservative and Labour have moved substantially apart; on none have they moved substantially closer. In this sense, we can conclude that the salariat is now more divided than it used to be.

We can check this result more rigorously using multivariate analysis. If we conduct a logit analysis of Labour and Conservative voting within the salariat (using social origins, housing tenure, religion, university education, trade union membership and welfare and creative occupations as our independent variables), we find a marked increase in the extent to which these social characteristics statistically predict Labour:Conservative voting. The measure of concentration increases from 0.17 in 1964 to 0.29 in 1987.

However, we should note that, if we include Liberal/Alliance voting in the analysis, the index of concentration remains unchanged at 0.12 both in 1964 and 1987. This parallels our results on issue voting reported in chapter 3. There we found that Labour and Conservative voters had become more polarized in their attitudes towards issues, but, once we included Liberal and Alliance voters in the analysis, overall polarization had not increased. The parallel results on issues and on social structure in turn suggest that the same basic explanation may underly both phenomena. In other words, it may be the ideological changes in the positions of the Labour and Conservative parties, rather than autonomous social changes among the voters, that account for the differences between 1964 and 1987.

Notes

[1] Exceptions to this neglect of religion include Bochel and Denver 1970, Miller and Raab 1977, Moyser 1978 and Wald 1983.

[2] Franklin (1985) rightly points out that there are two senses of important. For example, a variable may be important in the sense that it has a large coefficient in a logit or regression analysis, but it may be a variable that distinguishes only a small number of people. Ethnicity is a good example of this: black and Asian respondents are much more likely to vote Labour than are white respondents, but only a small proportion of the electorate is black. Religion, however, is important in both senses (at least within the salariat).

[3] One problem in the coding of religion is the treatment of Presbyterians. In England the Presbyterians have combined with the Congregationalists to form the United Reformed Church, and it is therefore appropriate to include them in the Nonconformist category. This is not the case in Scotland, where the Presbyterian Church of Scotland is the established Church, and thus has an analogous relation to the State to that held by the Church of England. Since the voting behaviour of Presbyterians tends to be closer to that of members of the Church of England, we have decided to combine them with the Anglicans. Alternative treatments do not materially affect our results.

[4] If we carry out a global test of the relation between religion and vote over time, we find that the constant relative voting model (that is, the loglinear model containing the three two-way relationships between religion, vote and election) gives an excellent fit: $chi^2 = 7.05$ with 8 degrees of freedom, $p = 0.53$. (For this analysis voters for other parties are excluded and, because of the small numbers, Catholics are combined with people from other religions.)

[5] We should note that there has also been a very large literature on the general effects of mobility on voting. In particular there has been considerable debate about the relative effects of upward and downward mobility: do the upwardly mobile defect from Labour to a greater extent than the downwardly mobile defect from the Conservatives? Following Sobel (1981, 1985) it is now generally recognized that diagonal reference models are the most appropriate for analysing the effects of mobility. For an application of these to voting behaviour see de Graaf and Ultee (1987).

[6] In the case of social origins, vote and election, the constant relative voting model yields a chi^2 of 9.4 with 8 degrees of freedom; p = 0.308 (Again, voters for other parties are excluded).

[7] In the case of university education, vote and election the constant relative voting model yields a chi^2 of 1.10 with 2 df; p = 0.577.

[8] Thus Dunleavy (1980b: table 4) found a statistically significant effect of sector on alignment, after controlling for class. He found no significant effect of sector on alignment after controlling for unionization as well as sector, but since it is reasonable to suppose that sectoral location is causally prior to union membership, this is not a worrying finding for his thesis.

[9] This approach has some similarities with the earlier discussions of a new working class of technicians. See Mallet 1963; Touraine 1966; Gorz 1976; Gallie 1978.

[10] The public/private sector distinction is based on a recode of V50F: categories 2,3,4 and 5 are included in the public sector. The technocrat/specialist distinction is based on a recode of V50A2: categories 1,2,5,6,8 are included as technocrats and categories 3 and 9 as specialists.

[11] The welfare and creative professions are defined in terms of the OPCS Classification of Occupations 1980. Following Parkin we include school teachers, clergymen, medical occupations, scientists, architects, lecturers, social workers, journalists, artists, actors and musicians. More precisely, we include occupation groups 10.1, 10.2, 11.0, 13.3, 14.0, 15.1, 15.2, 16.0, 17.1, 17.2, 17.3, 17.4, 17.5, 17.6, 19.0, 20.1, 21.1, 21.2, 24.1, 24.2, 24.3, 31.1. With a larger data set it might be possible to check the inclusion of these groups.

[12] Dunleavy could, consistently with his earlier publications, argue that public sector interests are mediated by union membership, and that it is the low level of unionization among public-sector administrators which accounts for their relatively high Conservative voting. There is in fact a high correlation between union membership and the welfare and creative occupations. However, we find that there is still a significant effect of welfare and creative occupations on vote even after controlling for both sector and unionization.

[13] In the case of the welfare and creative professionals, vote and election, the constant relative voting model does not give a good fit to the data. It yields a chi^2 of 7.65 with 2 degrees of freedom; p = .022. We therefore accept the hypothesis that there has been a changed relationship.

[14] This analysis has a lot in common with Rallings' account of two types of middle-class Labour voter. Rallings' first type consists of people who are subjectively middle class and who are more likely to be highly educated and to hold professional jobs; his second type consists of people who are subjectively working class and who are more likely to be council tenants and working in office/shop employment. They constitute a kind of disguised working class. In practice, many of Rallings' second type would probably be found in our routine non-manual class rather than in the salariat proper.

[15] We have not included the 1966 survey in this analysis since neither housing tenure nor TU membership was ascertained in that survey. The 1974 data come from the October survey.

Church attendance was not measured in either of the 1974 surveys, and so we have not been able to construct our measure of religion for that year.

In calculating the indices of dissimilarity we have tried to construct measures that are as closely comparable over time as possible. In the cases of religion, social origins, higher education, and the welfare and creative occupations they correspond to the distinctions used in the tables for 1964, i.e. six categories for religion, five for social origin, two for higher education, and three for welfare and creative occupations (the economicallcy inactive being the third category). We use three categories for TU membership (members, non-members and people not in work); three categories for housing tenure (owners, private renters and local authority tenants) and five categories for region (Scotland, Wales, North, Midlands and South).

Chapter 7

The New Working Class

We now turn to the fragmentation of the working class. Two of the most interesting and influential treatments are those by Crewe (1987) and by Dunleavy and Husbands (1985). Crewe was particularly concerned with the decline of the old, Labour-inclined working class and the growth of a new, more Conservative working class. He contrasts the traditional working-class communities of the North, living on council estates and belonging to trade unions with the new working class composed of affluent, private sector owner-occupiers in the South of England. Writing after the 1987 election he suggested:

> "My post-mortem survey of the 1983 election concluded that Labour's claim to be the party of the working class was sociologically, if not ideologically, threadbare. The Labour vote remained largely working class; but the working class was no longer largely Labour. The party had come to represent a declining segment of the working class—the traditional working class of the council estates, the public sector, industrial Scotland and the North, and the old industrial unions—while failing to attract the affluent and expanding working class of the new estates and new service economy of the South. It was a party neither of one class nor one nation; it was a regional class party.
>
> The 1987 [Gallup] survey reinforces each of these conclusions. . . . In one important sense the picture is even gloomier for Labour this time. Government policies are producing a steady expansion of the new working class, and diminution of the old. Council house sales, privatisation, the decline of manufacturing industry (on which the old unions are based) and the steady population drift to the South have re-structured the working class. The new working class is not only the dominant segment but increasingly dominant. Demography and time are not on Labour's side" (Crewe 1987).

Similar arguments have been advanced by Rose and McAllister (1986), Butler and Kavanagh (1988), Harrop and Miller (1987) and others. They have become the orthodox interpretation of the relationship between Labour and the working class.

The essence of Crewe's argument is that there has been a change in the social composition of the working class—that there has been a spread of owner-occupation, a decline of employment in manufacturing industry and in the membership of the associated trade unions, and a drift of the population to the South. Dunleavy and Husbands, on the other hand, argue that new cross-cutting cleavages have emerged. They focus on new interests deriving from the changing role of the state, and in particular from state employment, state provision of housing and transport, and dependency on state benefits (such as social security). State employment they see as cross-cutting both the middle and working classes, while the other two cleavages centering on consumption and state benefits they see as particularly relevant to the working class.

We have already met their theory of production sector cleavages in chapter 6 and need not rehearse their argument now. On the consumption side their argument is that the Labour party is seen as the party of collective or state provision, and attracts the votes of people dependent on state provision, while the Conservatives attract the votes of people who have access to private provision. Dunleavy and Husbands see the growth of consumption cleavages as a major factor in explaining class dealignment particularly within the working class (1985:21–25). Most middle-class voters have for a long time had access to private provision of housing and transport and so these consumption cleavages do not, they argue, divide the middle class to any great extent. In contrast the working class is divided in its access to private consumption of housing and transport and, they appear to suggest, has become politically more polarized in recent years. They write:

"The second structural change underlying class dealignment has been the polarization of consumption patterns between a commercial, commodity mode and a public service mode. In some areas, such as education and health care until very recently, publicly organized consumption has been the dominant form of provision. In other areas, commercial firms have operated virtually without competing public agency involvement. In neither situation should we expect to see strong consumption influences on political alignment. If 95 per cent of people consume a good or service in one way, then there is little incentive for any political party to appeal to the minority 5 per cent, since the potential votes to be gained are small. However, where the electorate is much more evenly divided between those involved in private and public sector consumption, as in housing and transport, then the situation is transformed" (1985:22).

The crucial point, for Dunleavy and Husbands, is that in housing and transport the Conservative and Labour parties have come to take up opposite sides on the question of public or private provision and these thus become interests with political relevance. They conclude "With this background we might expect housing and transport locations to become more important influences on political alignments" (Dunleavy and Husbands, 1985:22–24).

Dunleavy and Husband's is not a theory of autonomous demographic change but of deliberate political policy. Their crucial point, with which we are in complete agreement, is that the extent to which an interest is politicized can vary as the political parties adopt different stances towards it. They rightly argue that interests on which the parties take similar stands will not lead to differences in political behaviour. We cannot therefore simply read off how an individual will vote from his or her objective interests. We also need to know whether, and in what form, the interests are politicized.

Simplifying somewhat, then, Dunleavy and Husbands are concerned with the politicization of issues like housing whereas Crewe is more concerned with the spread of owner-occupation.

Sector and union membership

In the salariat we found that public sector workers were indeed less inclined to support the Conservatives, although the picture was complicated by the welfare and creative occupations. Once we controlled for welfare and creative occupations, the differences between the sectors disappeared and we were led to doubt the existence of distinct public sector interests, or at least of interests that were perceived by the voters to be politically relevant. In the working class of course there are by definition no members of the welfare and creative occupations, but table 7.1 shows that the political differences between working-class public and private sector employees are rather modest. They do not in fact reach statistical significance. In effect, then, this confirms our rejection of the theory of distinct interests based on production sectors.[1]

TABLE 7.1 Sector and Vote in the Working Class 1987

	Conservative	Alliance	Labour	Other		(N)
Private sector	32	20	47	1	100%	(484)
Public sector	26	19	54	1	100%	(173)
Economically inactive	32	22	46	1	101%	(368)

Source: 1987 cross-section survey

Trade union membership is a second, employment-related, feature that is prominent in accounts of the old working class. Dunleavy in particular argues that public-sector interests are largely mediated by trade union membership, and he is certainly correct in arguing that public-sector workers are more likely to be unionized.[2]

TABLE 7.2 Trade Union Membership and Vote in the Working Class 1987

	Conservative	Alliance	Labour	Other		(N)
TU member	26	23	50	1	100%	(295)
Not a member	40	19	40	0	99%	(277)
Economically inactive	28	20	51	1	100%	(461)

Source: 1987 cross-section survey

As we can see, there is indeed a tendency for working-class Trade Union members to favour the Labour party. The political difference between members and non-members is, however, rather less than it was in the salariat. This may well be because in the salariat trade union membership has something of a voluntary character, whereas in the working class it more often goes with the job. Thus in the salariat it is likely that union membership to a larger extent reflects people's prior political values, while in the working class the association between union membership and vote may have more of a causal character.

At all events, whatever the causal interpretation, the relationship is a modest but statistically significant one. However, it is one that has, if anything, declined in importance. As we can see from table 7.3 the association of Trade Union membership with Labour voting in the working class was rather stronger in 1964 than it was in 1987. Thus, in 1964 there was a twenty-four point gap between members and nonmembers in their support for Labour. By 1987 the gap had fallen to ten points.[3]

TABLE 7.3 Trade Union Membership and Vote in the Working Class 1964

	Conservative	Liberal	Labour	Other		(N)
TU member	20	4	76	0	100%	(245)
Not a member	36	11	52	1	100%	(193)
Economically inactive	22	5	73	0	100%	(245)

Source: 1964 cross-section survey

On the other hand, Crewe is right to point to the decline of union membership within the working class. Whereas in 1964 35% of the working-class respondents were union members, by 1987 this figure had fallen to 27%. It is not entirely clear, however, what the economic causes or the political consequences of this decline have been. Firstly, in part, the decline reflects the growth of unemployment in the working class. The unemployed are likely to leave their trade unions, but as we shall see in chapter 10, there is no evidence that the unemployed also desert Labour. To this extent, therefore, the decline of union membership will not lead to a decline in Labour voting.

There is however a second reason for the decline in union membership which is likely to have had more implications for Labour voting. Thus some people may have moved from employment in unionized factories (perhaps in traditional heavy industries) to non-unionized employment. Insofar as the level of unionization affects people's voting patterns, this component of the decline will have had some impact on Labour voting in the working class. (For further studies of these issues see Gallie 1989; Elias 1990).

Housing

There are much bigger political differences, and larger social changes, when we turn to housing. As is well known, housing tenure does have a significant relationship with voting in the working class (just as it does in the salariat). Indeed, it is one of the stronger relationships which we shall find.

TABLE 7.4 Housing Tenure and Vote in the Working Class 1987

	Conservative	Alliance	Labour	Other		(N)
Owner	37	23	39	1	100%	(574)
Other	41	15	45	0	101%	(74)
L.A. tenant	20	18	61	2	101%	(377)

Source: 1987 cross-section survey

In table 7.4 we have divided respondents into owner-occupiers, local authority tenants, and a miscellaneous category (which is largely composed of people renting privately, but also includes tied cottages and the like). As we can see, 61% of the working-class local authority tenants voted Labour in 1987, the highest proportion that we have as yet encountered (although we shall find higher ones in due course).

TABLE 7.5 Housing Tenure and Vote in the Working Class 1964

	Conservative	Liberal	Labour	Other		(N)
Owner	35	10	56	0	101%	(220)
Other	26	4	70	0	100%	(191)
L.A. tenant	17	6	76	1	100%	(280)

Source: 1964 cross-section survey

However, housing is in no way a new cleavage. As we can see from table 7.5 there was just as strong a relationship between housing tenure and vote in 1964 as there was in 1987.[4] To be sure, there have been some changes. Most notably the Labour share of the vote has plummeted, but it has done so among working-class owner-occupiers and local authority tenants alike, while the Alliance vote has correspondingly increased. Perhaps most interestingly of all, the Conservative share of the vote has remained more or less the same. In 1964 they obtained 35% of the votes of working-class owner-occupiers; in 1987 they obtained 37%.

So although there have been some changes in the overall support for Labour and the Alliance, the relative levels of support have stayed much the same. Thus, we find that Labour voting was 22 points higher in 1987 among local authority tenants than it was among owner-occupiers in the working class. The corresponding gap in 1964 was 20 points.[5] The expectation that housing locations will have become more important influences on political alignments is not therefore substantiated.

While housing is not a new cleavage, Crewe's thesis that owner-occupation has become more widespread within the working class is clearly correct. Thus in 1964 owner-occupiers made up only 32% of the working class whereas by 1987 they made up 56%. To a large extent, this expansion has come at the expense of private renting, and the proportion of local authority tenants has fallen only from 41% to 37% over period. (Although as with union membership this was not a steady decline. Rather, it rose until 1979 and then declined under Mrs Thatcher 's two administrations.)

Since private renters were not as left-wing as local authority tenants, the impact of the spread of home ownership on voting patterns is probably not quite as large as might initially be thought. Furthermore, there must be some doubt about the causal relationship between housing and voting behaviour. We look into this further in chapter 8 when we examine the impact of council house purchase on voting behaviour. It is clear from the analysis of chapter 8 that purchasers were already somewhat more inclined to favour the Conservatives than were the people who decided not to purchase their council houses. Once again, then, the statistical association (in this case between housing tenure and voting behaviour) may in part reflect patterns of selective mobility. To paraphrase Parkin, home-ownership may not be a cause of individualism but a sanctuary for those who place a greater value on individual effort.

We do not wish to suggest that selective mobility wholly accounts for the association. The social networks established in homogeneous council estates, or the material interests deriving from property ownership, surely both play a part as well. But whatever the causal mechanisms involved, it is clear that the spread of owner-occupation within the working class cannot explain to any great extent why the Labour vote within the working class has crumbled. Remember that tables 7.4 and 7.5 showed that Labour lost votes across the board among working-class owner-occupiers and local authority tenants alike. It is simply not the case that the old working class of tenants remained faithful to Labour while the new working class of home owners defected. The major factors which lost Labour votes in the working class, whatever they were, affected local authority tenants as well as home owners.

Region

While there are substantial differences between owners and tenants in their voting behaviour, these are more than matched by the regional differences in voting.

TABLE 7.6 Region and Vote in the Working Class 1987

	Conservative	Alliance	Labour	Other		(N)
Wales	14	13	69	4	100%	(71)
Scotland	10	21	62	8	101%	(92)
North	24	16	59	0	99%	(345)
Midlands	38	23	40	0	101%	(245)
South	44	26	30	0	100%	(281)

Source: 1987 cross-section survey

As we know from the aggregate statistics, Conservative voting in 1987 was particularly low in Scotland and Wales, and was highest in the South of England. A similar pattern occurs with Alliance voting (although the Alliance was somewhat stronger in the South West). However, what is not immediately apparent from the aggregate statistics is that these regional differences are greater among working-class voters than among those in the salariat. For example, if we compare the North and the South we find a gap of twenty-nine points in Labour voting in the working class compared with a gap of twelve points in the salariat.

TABLE 7.7 Region and Vote in the Working Class 1964

	Conservative	Liberal	Labour	Other		(N)
Wales	15	3	79	3	100%	(76)
Scotland	17	0	82	1	100%	(34)
North	24	9	66	0	99%	(213)
Midlands	27	2	71	0	100%	(154)
South	29	11	60	0	100%	(217)

Source: 1964 cross-section survey

It has also been evident from the aggregate statistics that the regional differences have grown markedly over the past thirty years. This can again be seen clearly from table 7.7. In 1964 there were some differences of the same kind as in 1987 but of very different magnitude. For example, Labour voting was only six points higher in the North than it was in the South in 1964 compared with the twenty-nine points of 1987.[6]

Here then we have our clearest example of a new cleavage within the working class. From having no significant relationship with vote in 1964, region has become almost the largest division in 1987.

The explanation for this growth in the regional division is not entirely clear. It is fairly straightforward to rule out various possibilities, but it is not so easy to put something persuasive in their place. (See Johnston, Pattie and Allsopp 1988 for a detailed examination of the growth of regional differences over the 1979–87 period).

First, it is clear that the changing social composition of the regions is not the answer. While the North and Scotland are indeed more working class than the South, they have seen much the same expansion of the salariat and contraction of the working class that the South has seen. Similarly with housing, trade union membership and the like. We therefore find substantial regional differences in voting even after controlling for these other social characteristics.

TABLE 7.8 Logit Models of Region and Vote in the Working Class

	Regional parameters		
	Without controls	With controls for social origins, TU membership and housing tenure	With further controls for social context
Scotland	0	0	0
Wales	0.12 (0.24)	0.16 (0.28)	0.24 (0.29)
North	0.46 (0.19)	0.55 (0.22)	0.64 (0.23)
Midlands	0.87 (0.19)	0.91 (0.22)	0.99 (0.23)
South	1.09 (0.19)	1.10 (0.22)	1.13 (0.23)

Note: Figures in brackets give the standard errors
Source: 1987 cross-section survey

This is shown in table 7.8, which gives the results of a succession of logit models. In the first model we simply look at the relation between region and vote in the working class, without any controls for other aspects of social structure. We take Scotland as our baseline, and the parameters then show how large the differences are in the other regions. As we can see, there is no significant difference between Scotland and Wales in their propensity to vote Conservative or Labour in 1987, while there are highly significant differences in the Midlands and, even more so, in the South.

In our second model we then include controls for social origins, trade union membership and housing tenure. As we can see, these fail to reduce the regional parameters.

The third model takes account of the local social context as well. There has been considerable debate about the impact of local social context on voting behaviour (see for example Miller 1978, Dunleavy 1979, Johnston 1983, Kelley and McAllister 1987), and it has sometimes been suggested that the more heterogeneous social environments of the South can explain the lower level of Labour voting there. However, the third model refutes this hypothesis. What we have done here is to add a variable which measures the class composition of the respondent's neighbourhood. This variable does indeed have a significant relationship with vote (even although housing, social origins and union membership are already included in the analysis) but it fails to reduce the regional parameters.

The different social environments of Britain fail, then, to explain, the regional differences in voting behaviour. An alternative strategy is to look at the economic differences between the regions. The South, for example, undoubtedly has higher incomes and lower unemployment than the North, Scotland and Wales. To some extent, however, the social variables which we have already included in our models (variables such as housing tenure and neighbourhood) will themselves be correlated with the economic variables of income and unemployment, so we should not have very high expectations of economic explanations.

One way to proceed in testing the economic explanations is to add them as further control variables such as income to the models of table 7.8. It should come as no surprise that this strategy fails to work: the regional parameters remain unchanged.

An alternative strategy is to look at the aggregate data on regional income and unemployment. After all, it may not be the individual's own income or experience of unemployment that is crucial so much as the regional level. People may be influenced not only by their own personal experiences but also by the collective experiences of the group to which they belong. Thus individuals might perceive that their own individual interests are largely influenced by those of their group or locality: even if they themselves are not unemployed at the moment, they may believe that their likelihood of becoming unemployed will depend on the local unemployment rate. An explanation along these lines could also account for the fact that regional differences are greater among the working class than among the salariat. The working class tends to be less mobile geographically and thus more dependent on local labour markets.

Table 7.9 shows the regional trends in personal disposable income from official sources.[7] (These of course cover the population as a whole and not simply the working class). They show very clearly the regional inequalities: the North, Scotland and Wales have consistently had lower average income than the Midlands and South. But these differences seem to be long-standing ones, going back to 1974 when the official series begins.[8] They are not new cleavages to the extent that the political cleavages are new.

Table 7.9 Regional Trends in Personal Disposable
Income

	1974	1979	1983	1987
Scotland	94.1	95.4	96.9	96.1
Wales	88.1	90.7	90.1	86.2
North	95.1	95.2	93.5	93.0
Midlands	97.7	96.9	93.3	92.8
South	108.9	108.0	111.8	112.1
UK	100.0	100.0	100.0	100.0

Source: Regional Trends

Nor are all the changes in the predicted direction. Scotland, for example, has got somewhat closer to the national average in income over this period, whereas Scottish support for the Conservatives has fallen. Conversely, the Midlands have become relatively worse off, but their support for the Conservatives has risen.

Regional differences in income, therefore, do not appear to hold the key, but trends in unemployment may perhaps be more relevant to understanding working-class voting, since it is the working class who are of course particularly vulnerable to unemployment.

Table 7.10 Regional Trends in Unemployment (%)

	1966	1970	1974	1979	1983	1987
Scotland	2.9	4.2	4.1	8.0	14.9	15.3
Wales	2.9	3.9	3.8	8.0	16.0	14.8
North	1.6	3.2	3.0	6.4	15.1	14.7
Midlands	1.3	2.3	1.8	4.4	13.1	11.2
South	1.1	1.8	1.4	3.4	9.3	8.5
UK	1.6	2.6	2.7	5.8	12.9	11.7

Source: Regional Trends

As table 7.10 shows, the regional inequalities are again long-standing.[9] Indeed, relative unemployment rates are even more stable than the levels of personal disposable income. The South, for example, has the lowest unemployment rate in every year covered by table 7.10. Next come the Midlands, which do not show the relative decline that we saw with personal disposable income.

However, while regional inequalities in unemployment are long-standing, the absolute differences have grown markedly. There was, for example, only a half-point difference between North and South in 1966. This had increased to three points in 1979 and six points in 1987. It may well be that it is people's perceptions of these absolute differences that have been most important in explaining the growing regional differences in electoral behaviour.

We do not have the data to pursue this question further, but this would appear to be the most promising line of explanation. Certainly, it is clear that *individual* differences in income, unemployment and so on cannot explain the regional differences in voting behaviour. Perceptions of the *community's* economic situation might therefore provide the answer.[10]

Ethnicity

There is, finally, one further new cleavage which we ought to mention, namely ethnicity. As the numbers involved are rather small, we have simply distinguished respondents of South Asian or Afro-Caribbean origin from all others. This might be regarded as a measure of colour, but we resist this interpretation. We do so partly because it is offensive; and partly because we believe that the notion of ethnicity better captures the social processes at work.

TABLE 7.11 Ethnicity and Vote in the Working Class 1987

	Conservative	Alliance	Labour	Other		(N)
White	31	21	46	1	99%	(985)
Other	17	7	76	0	100%	(46)

Source: 1987 cross-section survey

Nevertheless, our crude measure replicates the results obtained by other researchers showing a marked inclination of black respondents to the Labour party (see Anwar 1986, Charlot 1985). As we can see, the effect of ethnicity is a large one, although it is a large effect that affects only a small number of people. Only 4% of our working-class respondents (51 in all) were classified as black. (And there is accordingly a large confidence interval in our estimate). Nevertheless, the 76% support for Labour is the very highest that we encounter. This is also of course a new cleavage in the sense that there were virtually no black members of the electorate in 1964 when our surveys began.

The explanation for the Labour orientation of black voters is not entirely clear. The reasons black respondents themselves usually give is that "Labour is for the working class" rather than for specifically ethnic reasons (Anwar 1986, Charlot 1985). However, as we can see, the behaviour of black respondents is markedly more Labour-inclined than that of other working-class respondents. Furthermore the difference cannot be accounted for by other individual characteristics of black respondents such as their social origins, housing tenure and so on.

TABLE 7.12 Logit Models of Ethnicity and Vote in the
Working Class

Independent variables	Ethnic parameter
1. Ethnicity (without controls)	− 0.52 (0.19)
2. With controls for social origins, tenure, region and TU membership	− 0.89 (0.23)
3. With further controls for unemployment and income	− 0.95 (0.25)

Note: Figures in brackets give standard errors.
Source: 1987 cross-section survey

To demonstrate this we carry out the same kind of multivariate analysis that we did with region. Table 7.12 first looks at the relationship between ethnicity and vote without any controls. This relationship is highly significant statistically. In the second model we add controls for social origins, tenure, region and trade union membership. As we can see, the ethnic parameter actually increases in size. It is unusual for parameters to increase in size and significance after controls, but in this particular case it should not be all that surprising. Thus Labour voting tends to be rather higher in the North than in the South, but the ethnic minorities are generally more likely to live in the South; the first model compares the voting behaviour of Asians and blacks with those of the working class as a whole, while the second model in effect contrasts them with working-class people in the South.

It is frequently argued that the ethnic minorities form a kind of underclass, being more likely to have the less skilled, less well-paid and more insecure jobs in the working class. There is some truth in this, but further controls for income and unemployment fail to explain the ethnic pattern of voting. Nor do controls for the social character of the respondent's neighbourhood explain the ethnic difference.

In other words, the political behaviour of blacks is not to be explained by their class situation, however broadly defined. They are much more inclined to the Labour party than white voters in similar class situations, housing, local milieux, and so on. As in the case of region, therefore, individual economic and social factors do not seem to be the answer. Perceptions of group interests or processes of group identification are more plausible explanations.

Fragmentation and volatility in the working class

The working class, then, is certainly fragmented, most notably by region, ethnicity, housing and, to a lesser extent, by union membership. We should also note that, as with the salariat, there are significant differences associated with religion and social origin although not with education.

It is also quite clear that the working class has been fragmented throughout our period. As with the salariat, fragmentation is not a new phenomenon. Housing and union membership have long been associated with voting patterns, and while Crewe and others have been right to note the spread of owner-occupation and the decline of union membership within the working class, these changes can go only a little way towards explaining the crumbling of the Labour vote. (See chapter 13 for a further exploration of this.) The one really major change is the rise of a regional division.

The index of dissimilarity is a useful way to summarize the magnitude of these various cleavages. As we noted in chapter 6, this index takes account both of the proportion of people affected and of the size of the effects. Essentially, it tells us how different the parties are in the social profiles of their voters. Table 7.13 shows the trends over time in the Labour : Conservative differences.

TABLE 7.13 The Changing Profile of Conservative and Labour Voters in the Working Class

	Conservative : Labour Index of dissimilarity					
	1964	1970	1974 (Oct)	1979	1983	1987
Social origins	27	21	25	20	17	17
Religion	17	18	—	10	15	7
Housing tenure	18	8	28	16	29	24
TU membership	18	16	23	13	14	12
Region	9	13	17	19	31	31
Skill level	1	0	2	4	5	1

Source: BES cross-section surveys

The table shows rather dramatically the rise of region; from being almost the smallest of our divisions in 1964 it has become the largest in 1987. Housing comes next in size, followed by social origins, trade union membership and religion. We have also included differences between skilled and less skilled workers in the table, since it is frequently claimed that one of the major changes in recent elections has been the tendency for skilled workers to abandon Labour. As we can see, however, differences between skilled and less skilled workers have been comparatively small throughout.

These are, then, rather different lines of fragmentation from the ones we saw in the salariat. Education and irreligion, which we interpreted as sources of ideological dissent in the salariat, prove to be more minor sources of differentiation in the working class. Instead, the major differences in the working class are those associated with region, social origin, housing tenure, and ethnicity.

Nor do we find that there are distinctive variables such as education associated with Alliance voting in the working class as they were in the salariat. In the working class, the Liberals are consistently closer to the Conservatives than to Labour in their patterns of housing tenure and in their regional distribution (just as they were in the salariat). And they are straightforwardly midway between Conservative and Labour in their social origins and religion. (The trade union pattern is more surprising but may have something to do with the changing pattern of Liberal candidates in working-class seats that we described in chapter 5.)

TABLE 7.14 The Changing Profile of Liberal Voters in the Working Class

		Indices of dissimilarity					
		1964	1970	1974 (Oct)	1979	1983	1987
Social origins	Con:Lib	16	9	15	8	7	9
	Lib:Lab	14	15	11	12	13	10
Religion	Con:Lib	14	13	—	12	7	4
	Lib:Lab	15	20	—	14	16	6
Housing tenure	Con:Lib	11	7	9	5	11	8
	Lib:Lab	22	5	20	14	20	17
TU membership	Con:Lib	9	6	3	13	6	10
	Lib:Lab	27	18	24	3	9	4
Region	Con:Lib	24	9	6	11	9	7
	Lib:Lab	34	13	16	12	22	24
Education	Con:Lib	—	—	—	10	4	3
	Lib:Lab	—	—	—	10	10	6

Source: BES cross-section surveys

Overall, these factors do not seem to divide the working class to quite the same extent that they divide the salariat. With the exception of region, the indices of dissimilarity between Labour and Conservative voters in the working class tend to be rather lower than those we saw in chapter 6, and if we construct a multivariate logit model of Conservative and Labour voting in the working class, using the main explanatory variables described in this chapter (namely social origins, housing tenure, region, religion, trade union membership, and ethnicity), we obtain a measure of concentration of 0.17. In the salariat, the same variables (but including education and the welfare and creative occupations in place of ethnicity) yielded a measure of concentration that is 70% higher at 0.29. In other words, these particular structural measures are more strongly associated with Labour and Conservative voting in the salariat than they are in the working class.

Labour and Conservative voters in the working class, therefore, are more similar in their social profiles than they are in the salariat. In this particular sense, then, we can say that the working class is more homogeneous than the salariat. Or, to put it somewhat differently, the old and new working classes are not as far apart politically as are the old and new middle classes.

Again, unlike the salariat, there has been little overall change between 1964 and 1987 in the social profiles of Labour and Conservative voters in the working class. While the regional divide has become more important, other divisions such as trade union membership have become somewhat less important, and the net change is rather small. Thus the index of concentration in 1964 was 0.14, little lower than in 1987.[11]

TABLE 7.15 The Voters' Ideological Positions

	Mean score of . . .		
	Conservative voters	Alliance voters	Labour voters
Voters in the salariat			
Left-right scale	0.88	−0.05	−0.81
Liberal-authoritarian scale	0.08	−0.29	−1.22
Nuclear scale	0.66	−0.30	−1.05
Countryside scale	−0.19	−0.42	−0.29
Voters in the working class			
Left-right scale	0.23	−0.27	−0.78
Liberal-authoritarian scale	0.40	0.19	0.09
Nuclear scale	0.49	0.04	−0.44
Countryside scale	0.03	−0.03	0.26

Source: 1987 cross-section survey

Various interpretations of these findings are possible. Part of the explanation may be that ideological factors associated with education and religion are more important in the salariat, and the ideological changes in the parties' positions may thus have had more impact in the salariat. In the working class, in contrast, pragmatic considerations may be more important than ideological ones.

We can test this interpretation by comparing the ideological differences between the voters in the salariat and in the working class. Accordingly in table 7.15 we report the scores of Conservative, Alliance and Labour voters on four ideological dimensions. (For details of the construction of these four dimensions see chapters 11 and 12.)[12] A positive score represents a right-wing position while a negative score represents a left-wing position.

As we can see, on three of the four dimensions the ideological differences between Labour and Conservative voters are very much larger in the salariat than in the working class. Take, for example, the left-right dimension which is concerned with such issues as nationalization and privatization and which represents perhaps the most fundamental division between the Conservative and Labour parties. In the salariat the gap between Labour and Conservative voters on this dimension was 1.69. In the working class it was only 1.01. Similarly on the nuclear dimension the gap was 1.71 in the salariat but only 0.93 in the working class.

The one exception is the countryside dimension, which is in many ways a rather anomalous one in 1987 and played a relatively small role in voting behaviour. The notions of left and right do not apply particularly well to countryside issues, and it was in fact Liberals in the salariat who were the most favourable towards the protection of the countryside while Labour voters in the working class were the least favourable.

Following on from the arguments of chapters 2 and 3, we might expect the greater ideological polarization of Labour and Conservative voters in the salariat to lead to a lower degree of volatility between them. And this indeed proves to be the case.

TABLE 7.16 Fluidity in the classes 1983–87

	log odds ratios		
	Con:Lab	Con:Lib	Lib:Lab
Salariat	6.94	3.91	3.32
Routine nonmanual	6.46	3.43	3.38
Petty bourgeoisie	6.77	3.78	3.50
Foremen, technicians	5.29	5.58	3.33
Working class	5.19	3.09	3.15

Source: 1983–87 panel study

Table 7.16 calculates measures of fluidity for each of our five classes. The lower the measure (described in detail in chapter 2), the higher the fluidity. As we can see, Conservative:Labour fluidity is highest in the working class and declines as we move up to the salariat. Similar patterns, although less marked, are also apparent with the Liberals.

Our various pieces of evidence, therefore, fit together rather well. Labour and Conservative voters in the working class are closer together both in their social profiles and in their ideological positions than are their peers in the salariat. They are also more likely to switch from one party to the other, perhaps because they feel the psychological jump required to be a rather smaller one. And while, as we explained in chapter 2, fluidity is a different concept from net or overall volatility, it may be that bigger swings can be expected in the working class.

Notes

[1]To be sure, other studies have also found small differences between the sectors of a similar order of magnitude to those of table 7.1, and we would

not therefore wish to place too much weight on the level of statistical significance. Nonetheless, it is clear that sectoral location is not a major source of cleavage within the working class.

[2] See also Webb (1987) for an analysis of the changing relationship between trade union membership and vote.

[3] As in chapter 6 we can test whether the constant relative voting model fits the data on TU membership and vote in 1964 and 1987 (tables 7.2 and 7.3). Fitting this model we obtain a chi^2 of 9.5 with 2 degrees of freedom; $p = 0.009$. (As in chapter 6 we exclude the voters for minor parties because of their small numbers.) We can therefore reject the hypothesis that the relationship between union membership and vote was the same in these two elections.

We should note, however, that the weakening of the relationship has not been a steady one, the political polarization between members and non-members reaching a peak in 1974 (the log odds ratio reaching 1.3) and only declining thereafter.

[4] Again we can fit the constant relative voting model to the data of tables 7.4 and 7.5. We obtain a chi^2 of 2.7 with 4 degrees of freedom; $p = 0.602$. We therefore have no hesitation in accepting the hypothesis that the relationship between tenure and vote was the same in 1964 and 1987.

[5] It would be wrong, however, to suggest that the relationship between tenure and vote in the working class has stayed constant over time. It has in fact fluctuated quite markedly, the Conservative:Labour owner:L.A. tenant log odds ratio starting at 1.0 in 1964, falling to 0.4 in 1970, rising to 0.8 in 1974, falling again to 0.6 in 1979, rising to 1.3 in 1983 and then back to 1.1 in 1987. This pattern of rise and fall is in fact very similar to the pattern which we saw in chapter 5 when we examined the trends in relative class voting.

This similarity in the trends in the housing log odds ratio and the original class trends suggests that common causes lie behind them. Housing does not follow a distinct pattern of its own, as might have been expected if housing were a distinct interest, autonomous from social class.

[6] Fitting the constant relative voting model to the data of tables 7.6 and 7.7 we obtain a chi^2 of 41.3 with 8 degrees of freedom; $p = 0.000$. It is quite clear therefore that the relationship between region and vote in the working class was not the same in 1987 and 1964.

[7] Personal disposable income is defined as total personal income minus taxes on income, National Insurance contributions, transfers abroad, and taxes paid abroad.

[8] Earlier official data are available on income before taxes, and these also show regional differentials.

[9] In calculating the unemployment rate we have taken total employees plus registered unemployed as the denominator. This is the practice that has generally been followed by the official statistics, and in fact is the only basis which we can use for constructing a long time series. However, in the last few years the official sources have enlarged the denominator, adding the self-employed and members of the armed forces. This of course reduces the official unemployment rate, and explains why our figures are rather higher than the official ones.

[10] In their aggregate analysis of electoral geography Johnston, Pattie and Allsopp (1988) found that constituency levels of unemployment were significantly associated with change in constituency voting patterns over the 1979–1987 period. What is needed to pursue the matter further is the integration of individual-level and constituency-level variables, using the techniques of multi-level modelling. We shall be attempting this in subsequent publications.

[11] Once again we should note that this finding applies only to Labour and Conservative voting. If we include Liberal/Alliance voters as well, the index of concentration becomes 0.11 in 1964 and 0.10 in 1987.

[12] Note that these are standardized scales, with scores for the sample as whole (i.e. for all classes combined) standardized with mean zero and standard deviation 1.

Chapter 8

The Extension of Popular Capitalism

Anthony Heath with Geoff Garrett

While class and religion are probably little affected by government action, other aspects of social structure—education and housing in particular—are much more susceptible to political intervention. On the whole, Labour governments have been more ambitious in the educational field, whereas the two Thatcher administrations have concentrated more on housing and share ownership. They have vigorously pursued the sale of council houses to their tenants and sold off major nationalized industries to private shareholders.

The sale of council houses was promoted from the beginning of the first Thatcher term. Over one million council houses, approximately 5% of the total housing stock, were sold to their tenants in the period 1980–1987.[1] The terms of the sales were highly advantageous to buyers. The enabling 1980 and 1984 Housing Acts not only guaranteed to purchasers a government-sponsored mortgage, but also dictated that the sale price of houses be discounted from 33% to 60% below their market valuations.

Participation in the government's privatization of publicly-owned corporations has been even more extensive than was the case with council house sales. It has been estimated that the programme of sales almost doubled share ownership to around a quarter of the population. (The exact figures will depend on whether one takes individuals or households as the units.)[2] There were only a few small privatizations in the first Thatcher administration, but the programme expanded rapidly after the government's re-election in 1983 with the sales of British Aerospace, British Airways, British Gas, British Telecom, Britoil, Jaguar, Rolls Royce and the TSB.

As was the case for purchasers of council houses, the benefits of purchasing shares in privatized companies were very large. Vickers and Yarrow (1988)

120

have shown that consistent and extensive undervaluation by the government of corporations in public flotations (column b of table 8.1) and great demand for the shares (column c) allowed investors in the privatizations to reap substantial windfall profits (column d).

TABLE 8.1 Major Privatizations in Britain 1979–87

Company	Gross proceeds (mill. £) (a)	Under valuation (mill. £) (b)	Oversubscription (multiple) (c)	First day profits (%) (d)
1979–1983				
Amersham International	63	20	25.6	32
Assoc. Brit. Ports	22	5	35	23
British Aerospace (1981)	149	21	3.5	14
B.P.	290	3	1.5	1
Cable & Wireless (1981)	224	39	5.6	17
1984–1987				
British Aerospace (1985)	550	66	5.4	12
British Airways	900	315	32	68
British Gas	5603	519	4	25
British Telecom	3916	1295	5	86
Britoil	450	54	10	12
Cable & Wireless (1985)	602	3	2	0.5
Jaguar	294	25	8.3	8
Rolls-Royce	1360	496	9.4	73
T.S.B.	1360	483	8	71

Source: Vickers and Yarrow (1988: 174–7)

In both cases, then, there were important windfall profits to the purchasers, profits which might be expected to lead to short-term electoral benefits to the Conservative party. On the usual theories of retrospective voting, we might expect the voters affected to reward the Conservative government which had provided these windfalls and to punish the Labour party which had opposed them, and which might conceivably take away these benefits in future. (Although whether the rational voter will reward a political party for a *one-off* benefit is a moot point.)

More substantial electoral claims have also been made for the Conservative government's policy. Home and share ownership have often been shown to be close correlates of voting behaviour. French political scientists have advanced the notion of patrimoine—one's stake in the country's wealth—as a major, perhaps *the* major, determinant of how one votes (Capdeville and Dupoirier 1981). Monica Charlot has recently demonstrated that the concept applies equally well to Britain (Charlot 1989), and table 8.2 confirms her results with our 1987 survey.

TABLE 8.2 Le Patrimoine

	Vote in 1987					
	Conservative	Labour	Other	Did not		(N)
Home- and share-owners	55	12	22	11	100%	(1005)
Home-owners w/o shares	38	25	22	16	101%	(1589)
Share-owners in rented property	33	30	20	17	100%	(132)
Non-owners	20	45	16	19	100%	(963)

Source: 1987 cross-section survey

As we can see, people with more assets were more likely to vote Conservative (or Alliance) while those who neither owned shares nor homes were more likely to report a Labour vote. If we had data on the size of these assets, we would doubtless find that the association was even stronger.

Because of this association, it has been widely argued that the sale of council houses and shares has been of long-term electoral benefit to the Conservatives. Both sorts of purchasers have a new-found stake in property and in the price of that property, and hence have a longer-term interest in political arrangements that protect and enhance these investments. The government, it is therefore claimed, has succeeded in expanding its social base and in undermining Labour's. For example, according to Andrew Gamble, "There can be no doubt that this policy has been a masterstroke for the government. It has made a significant inroad into the traditional Labour vote" (Gamble 1987:15). Similar views were expressed in many of the post-mortems published in the immediate wake of the 1987 result.

But the data reported in table 8.2 do not provide us with a firm basis for drawing conclusions about the electoral consequences of *extending* home and share ownership. For that we need some kind of longitudinal data. Table 8.2 provides a snapshot of the electorate. It simply shows us that at the last election home owners and shareholders were more likely to vote Conservative than were tenants and people without shares. It does not necessarily follow from this that, when individuals become owner-occupiers or shareholders, they then also change their voting behaviour. For the people who decided to purchase shares or to buy their council homes may already have been more likely to vote Conservative before they made their purchase. We therefore need to see if their behaviour has changed since making the purchase.

In order to investigate these questions about change, we conducted a small panel study, separate from the main 1987 cross-section survey. That is to say, we reinterviewed respondents to the 1983 survey and we can thus relate changes in their voting behaviour to changes in their social and demographic characteristics. We should note however that panel studies suffer from the problems of attrition and conditioning, and the surviving members of the panel will thus not be representative of the population as a whole (see Appendix III).

Share purchase

Table 8.3 explores the relation between changes in share ownership and changes in voting between 1983 and 1987. Since the bulk of the privatizations took place between these two elections this is a reasonable period to focus on, although it is also conceivable that, on a rational expectations model, voters had already anticipated their windfall gains in deciding how to vote in 1983.[3]

TABLE 8.3 Share Purchase and Vote

	Vote	
	1983	1987
Non-Purchasers		
Conservative	45	42
Labour	26	31
Other	29	27
	100%	100%
(N)	(438)	(471)
'New' Recruits		
Conservative	55	53
Labour	14	16
Other	31	32
	100%	101%
(N)	(127)	(135)
Enthusiasts		
Conservative	64	70
Labour	14	10
Other	22	20
	100%	100%
(N)	(95)	(102)
Other Share-owners		
Conservative	56	62
Labour	16	14
Other	29	24
	101%	100%
(N)	(69)	(70)

Source: 1983–87 panel study

We asked our respondents in the 1987 wave of the panel "do you (or your partner) own, or have you ever bought shares in any of these recently privatized companies?" and we gave them a checklist of the major share issues since 1983. We also asked them whether they owned any other shares quoted on the stock exchange, including unit trusts.

On the basis of this information we have divided our respondents into four categories; first, in the top panel, are respondents who reported that they neither purchased any of the privatized share issues nor owned any other shares. These respondents make up 61% of the panel respondents but, because of selective attrition, this is certainly an underestimate of their numbers in the electorate as a whole. (Our cross-sectional data give an estimate of 71% of households without shares which is almost identical to the GHS estimate.)

Second, we have respondents who purchased the privatized issues but owned no other shares. They make up 17% of the panel respondents. They can be thought of as the new recruits to Mrs Thatcher's popular capitalism. Third, we have respondents who both purchased the privatized issues and owned other shares. They make up 13% of the sample and can be thought of as the enthusiasts for popular capitalism. (Unfortunately, we do not know the timing of this group's purchase of their other shares. Some will have been long-standing share-owners while others will have been introduced to share purchase by the privatizations.) And fourthly we have respondents who owned other shares but failed to take advantage of the windfall gains of the privatizations.

As we had expected from table 8.2, there are quite marked differences between the four sets of respondents in their voting behaviour. The non-purchasers in the top panel have the lowest propensity to vote Conservative while the enthusiasts have the highest propensity. The new recruits fall about midway in between (at least as far as Conservative voting is concerned).

However, the striking feature of the table is how little change in the voting patterns of these four groups took place between 1983 and 1987. We might have expected that the new recruits would have moved away from the non-purchasers and would have become more similar to the other members of the property-owning democracy in their pattern of voting. As we can see however from the top two panels, there was little change in their relative propensities to vote Conservative, Labour or Alliance. The new recruits were already more inclined to the Conservatives in 1983, and they remained that way. The 10 point differential barely changed. And the new recruits, just like the non-purchasers (and of course the electorate overall), showed a modest net increase in Labour voting between 1983 and 1987.

There are however signs of change when we look at the bottom two panels of table 8.3. In both these panels we see an increase in Conservative voting and a decline in Labour voting. Insofar as there is any pattern of change, then, it is that the new recruits are akin to the non-purchasers while the enthusiasts are akin to the other share-owners. In other words, table 8.3 divides up, as far as change is concerned, not into purchasers versus non-purchasers of the privatized shares but into owners versus non-owners of other shares.[4]

So while the privatizations have certainly extended popular capitalism perhaps to a quarter of the electorate, it is not clear that this has had any direct effect on the purchasers' voting behaviour. The purchasers were already more inclined to vote Conservative before they bought the privatized share issues, and the new recruits show no sign of rewarding the Conservatives for their windfall gains.

On the other hand, the privatizations may have had an *indirect* effect. They may have stimulated some people to go on and buy other shares on the stock market, and this in turn may have increased their propensity to favour the Conservatives. We cannot, unfortunately, pursue this question any further since we do not know the timing of these other share purchases.[5] We are, however, a little sceptical of this idea. Given the pattern of change shown in table 8.3, a more natural hypothesis is that the enthusiasts and the other share-owners had features in common which explain their increased support for the Conservatives.

Nor is there any sign that their increased stake in capitalism has made the new recruits any more supportive of the existing order. In both waves of the panel we asked our respondents "whether you agree or disagree that income and wealth should be redistributed towards ordinary working people". Table 8.4 shows how their attitudes changed between 1983 and 1987.

TABLE 8.4 Share Purchase and Attitudes

	% Opposing redistribution	
	1983	1987
Non-purchasers	39 (531)	34 (533)
New recruits	46 (147)	38 (146)
Enthusiasts	61 (109)	60 (111)
Other share-owners	52 (77)	50 (76)

Note: Figures in brackets give the base frequency.
Source: 1983–87 panel study

The pattern of change is not unlike that of table 8.3, and clearly refutes the hypothesis that the new recruits would become more attached to the existing economic order. To the contrary they show a clear swing to the left (as do the non-purchasers). Once again, moreover, the enthusiasts and the other share-owners show a common pattern, their attitudes towards redistribution remaining more or less unchanged. (And since actual inequality has increased over this period, constant responses to the survey questions are tantamount to a real shift to the right. See chapter 11 for a further discussion of this point.)

Our analysis fails, then, to show that privatization per se had any electoral impact on the purchasers. In particular, the new recruits have neither rewarded the Conservatives for their windfall gains nor become more attached to the economic order. Claims about the effects of popular capitalism simply failed to recognize that the share purchasers were not a random selection of the electorate in the first place. (See Norris 1990 for further analyses on the same lines.)

TABLE 8.5 The Characteristics of Share Purchasers

	Non-purchasers	New recruits	Enthusiasts	Other share-owners
% working class	44	23	12	23
% in paid employment	53	62	59	66
% income over £8000	50	71	78	78
% home-owners	63	88	93	85
% living in South and Midlands	55	64	67	65
N (minimum)	(2306)	(464)	(345)	(222)

Source: 1987 cross-section survey

The distinctive character of share purchasers becomes very clear from table 8.5. Share purchasers and share-owners were generally more advantaged than the non-purchasers. They were less likely to be working class and more likely to be in paid employment and to have above-average incomes. These are of course characteristics which tend to go with Conservative voting anyhow.

It is not unreasonable to conclude, therefore, that the extension of popular capitalism largely extended share ownership to a group that was already relatively privileged and relatively inclined to the Conservatives. It was a case of the windfall gains going to people who were already well-off, or to put the matter somewhat differently, of the Conservative party rewarding their own supporters.

Council house purchase

Houses, even council houses, are rather larger assets than most of the share-holdings we have been discussing, so they might well have more electoral impact on the purchasers. The buyers of council houses are also a rather different group from the new shareholders, being more likely to have social characteristics typical of Labour rather than of Conservative voters. Here then there is more potential for the Conservatives to reach beyond their own supporters and to inflict electoral damage on Labour.

The council house purchasers are also a much smaller group than the shareholders. Unfortunately, this means that there are too few such respondents in our panel study to undertake a sensible analysis. We have instead to turn to our cross-section data, using respondents' recall of how they voted at previous elections.

TABLE 8.6 Council House Purchase and Vote A

	1979	1983	1987
L.A. tenants			
Conservative	21	22	21
Labour	70	64	61
Other	10	15	18
	101%	101%	100%
(N)	(531)	(531)	(483)
Council house purchasers			
Conservative	36	42	35
Labour	52	42	35
Other	11	16	30
	99%	100%	100%
(N)	(149)	(149)	(139)
Other home-owners			
Conservative	59	58	54
Labour	29	24	21
Other	13	18	25
	101%	100%	100%
(N)	(1587)	(1587)	(1472)

Source: 1987 cross-section survey, respondents who were eligible to vote in all three elections

Table 8.6 uses recall data from the 1987 cross-section survey to look at the voting behaviour of people who changed their housing tenure. Recall data are not ideal for our purposes; in particular there is the well-known tendency for respondents to under-report past voting for the Alliance or Liberal party. However, we have been able to carry out various checks which suggest that this bias is more or less constant across the table and therefore does not affect our main conclusions. Thus, in the 1983 study we asked people whether they were likely to buy their council houses, and if we use these prospective 1983 data rather than the retrospective 1987 data we obtain the same patterns of change in voting behaviour.[6]

Table 8.6 shows how home owners, council-house purchasers, and council-house tenants reported voting in 1979, 1983 and 1987. Only those respondents who were eligible to vote in all three elections are included in the table. We look at this longer time period because many of the council house purchases took place between 1979 and 1983, and thus some of the electoral consequences could already have occurred by 1983. (It is still of course possible that voters had already anticipated their purchases when making their 1979 decisions, but we have no way of pursuing this since we do not have any information on our respondents' 1974 vote.)

The top panel of table 8.6 covers the 21% of respondents who were council tenants in 1987. The middle panel covers the 6% of respondents who bought their council houses between 1979 and 1987. And the bottom panel covers owner-occupiers other than those who had bought council houses. They make up 64% of respondents. There is also a residual category, making up 8% of respondents, who were in other tenures such as private renting, housing cooperatives, tied cottages and the like. (Note that in the case of the top and bottom panels we cannot identify what proportion transferred *into* the category between 1979 and 1987. Thus a few people might have moved from owner-occupation to council tenancy during this period, and some former council tenants might have bought houses on the open market.)

As we had expected from table 8.2, there are quite marked differences in the voting behaviour of the three categories. In particular, we see that the purchasers were about midway between the council tenants and the home owners in 1987 in their support for the Conservative and Labour parties.

More importantly, however, we can see that the purchasers were already more prone to vote Conservative in 1979 than were the other council tenants, and the gap does not widen between 1979 and 1987. Reported Conservative voting was 15 points higher among the future purchasers in 1979; it was 20 points higher in 1983, when some of this group had completed their purchases; but it was only 14 points higher in 1987 when the whole of the group had purchased their council houses. There is little indication, therefore, that the sale of council houses produced *new* recruits for the Conservatives.

However, inspection of table 8.6 does suggest that perhaps council house sales did hurt Labour. Among the continuing tenants reported Labour voting fell by 9 points; among the other home owners it fell by 8 points; but among the purchasers it fell by 17 points. The Labour vote does therefore seem to have declined rather faster among the purchasers than it did among the other two groups. More rigorous analysis confirms the conclusion that the purchasers were more likely than the continuing tenants to defect from Labour.[7]

There is also some evidence of change in the purchasers' attitudes towards the economic order. In table 8.7 we look at the attitudes towards redistribution of those who said, in 1983, that they were likely to purchase their council houses and of those who said, in 1987, that they actually had done so.

TABLE 8.7 Council House Purchase and Attitudes

	% Opposing redistribution	
	1983	1987
L.A. tenants	19 (888)	12 (799)
Likely/actual purchasers	21 (123)	23 (101)
Other home-owners	44 (2564)	33 (2579)

Note: Figures in brackets give the base frequency.
Sources: Column 1—1983 cross-section survey. Column 2—1987 cross-section survey, respondents who were eligible to vote in 1983

As we can see, the continuing tenants and the other home owners both show the shift to the left that we saw earlier in table 8.4. The purchasers, on the other hand, have moved if anything to the right. Compared with the other two groups, then, the purchasers do stand out. They seem to have resisted the more general move to the left, and the hypothesis that council-house purchase has influenced political attitudes cannot be rejected.

Clearly, we must be cautious about these conclusions since we do not have adequate panel data to test them. However, the various pieces of evidence on the attitudes and voting behaviour of the purchasers are quite consistent and make good sociological sense. As we saw in chapter 2, direct switching from the Labour party to the Conservatives is relatively rare. If the general effect of council house purchase is to shift people's attitudes somewhat towards the right, then the natural consequence would be for their political preferences to move somewhat towards the right as well. In other words, a modest shift in attitudes, of the kind we saw in table 8.7, is likely to lead to a modest shift across the political spectrum from Labour towards the centre parties rather than all the way to the Conservatives.

The impact of this on Labour's fortunes will not have been very great, however: 6% of these respondents were purchasers, and among the purchasers the Labour vote appears to have fallen by perhaps 8% more than it fell among the tenants; 8% of 6% comes out as 0.5% of the electorate as a whole. In contrast, the total Labour share of the vote in the electorate fell from 37% in 1979 to 31% in 1987.

The major social process, therefore, is not conversion from one party to another but selective mobility. As with share purchase, the council-house purchasers were not a random selection of local authority tenants. They differed beforehand in ways that made them more inclined to the Conservatives than those who stayed behind. Council-house purchase, for example, is not likely to have the same feasibility for older, retired tenants as it does for those with secure, well-paid employment. Nor are some council flats as desirable properties to buy as some of the semi-detached houses. It is hardly surprising, therefore, to find that purchasers were much more likely than the other local authority tenants to be in paid employment. They were also less likely to be working class, and accordingly their household income was substantially higher than that of people who stayed behind in council housing.

TABLE 8.8 The Characteristics of Council House Purchasers

	L.A. tenants	Purchasers	Other home-owners
% working class	68	50	26
% in paid employment	37	72	61
% income over £8000	23	70	71
% living in South and Midlands	43	60	63
N (minimum)	(737)	(183)	(2136)

Source: 1987 cross-section survey

To be sure, the house purchasers were not as advantaged as the share purchasers, at least with respect to social class. The programme of council house sales thus did reach a rather different group from the privatization programme. Nor was the government rewarding its own supporters through the council houses sales to the same extent that it was with the share issues. Whereas in 1979 the Conservatives got over 50% of the votes of the future recruits to popular capitalism, they received less than 40% of the votes of the future home owners.

In both cases, however, there were marked prior differentials between purchasers and non-purchasers. It is this fact, and the pattern of selective mobility that followed from it, that largely explains the association between vote and property ownership with which we began this chapter.

TABLE 8.9 The 'Residualization' of Council Housing

	1979	1983	1987
% in semi- and unskilled work			
L.A. tenants	44	47	51
All respondents	25	27	26
% in paid work			
L.A. tenants	58	42	37
All respondents	63	56	56

Sources: 1979, 1983 and 1987 cross-section surveys

This pattern of selective mobility has also led to a process of "residualization" of council housing (Forrest and Murie 1984). This can be seen rather clearly from table 8.9 which looks at the changing social makeup of local authority tenants. The fall in the number of tenants in paid employment is particularly striking. Tenants are, therefore, a group which has rather rapidly been changing in character. While we have seen little evidence that changes in housing tenure influence people's politics, the reverse causal processes should not be underestimated: politics certainly influences housing.

Notes

[1] These figures come from Social Trends 1989, table 8.9 and refer to sales of dwellings owned by local authorities and new towns in the United Kingdom.
[2] The General Household Survey 1989 shows that 21% of adults owned shares and 28% of households did so.
[3] We can explore this idea using our panel respondents' recall of their 1979 vote. This is done in table 8.10N. As we can see, reported Conservative voting

fell by 3 points among new recruits and enthusiasts, but remained steady among the nonpurchasers, between 1979 and 1983. This does not therefore support the idea that future purchasers rewarded the Conservatives in 1983 for the expected windfall gains.

TABLE 8.10N Share Purchase and Vote 1979–87

	1979	1983	1987
Non-Purchasers			
Conservative	43	43	42
Labour	39	26	30
Other	17	31	28
	99%	100%	100%
(N)	(404)	(357)	(371)
New Recruits			
Conservative	57	54	53
Labour	27	15	16
Other	16	32	31
	100%	101%	100%
(N)	(135)	(117)	(124)
Enthusiasts			
Conservative	67	64	69
Labour	16	13	10
Other	17	23	21
	100%	100%	100%
(N)	(93)	(83)	(87)
Other Share-owners			
Conservative	59	55	62
Labour	23	17	15
Other	19	28	23
	101%	100%	100%
(N)	(65)	(60)	(61)

Source: 1983–87 panel study. Respondents eligible to vote in 1979

[4]We can check these results more formally with loglinear models. Table 8.11N shows the results of fitting a series of models to the three-way 1983 vote by 1987 vote by share purchase table (1983 vote and 1987 vote being divided into Conservative, Labour and Other, and share purchase being divided into non-purchasers, new recruits, enthusiasts, and other share-owners as in table 8.3).

TABLE 8.11N Loglinear Models of the Relationship between 1983
Vote, 1987 Vote and Share Purchase

Model	Deviance	df	p
1. 1983 vote, 1987 vote, shares	723	28	0.000
2. 1983 vote by 1987 vote, shares	55	24	0.000
3. 1983 vote by 1987 vote, shares by 1983 vote	34	18	0.01
4. 1983 vote by 1987 vote, shares by 1983 vote, purchase by 1987 vote	31	16	0.01
5. 1983 vote by 1987 vote, shares by 1983 vote, ownership by 1987 vote	24	16	0.09

Source: 1983–87 panel study

As we can see, there is a highly significant relationship between 1983 vote
and 1987 vote (model 2), and also a significant relationship between 1983 vote
and share purchase (model 3). In model 4 we then introduce a binary variable
which distinguishes purchasers from non-purchasers of the privatized shares.
The introduction of the relationship between this variable and 1987 vote does
not make a significant improvement to the fit. In model 5 we introduce an
alternative binary variable which distinguishes owners from non-owners of
other shares. The introduction of the relationship between this variable and
1987 vote does make a significant improvement to fit.
[5]We obtain slightly different results when we conduct the same analysis on
the cross-section data. As we can see from table 8.12N, the cross-section data
confirm our main conclusion: there is no tendency for the new recruits to
reward the Conservative party. Conservative voting fell by 5 points between
1983 and 1987 among new recruits compared with 4 point falls among
non-purchasers and among enthusiasts. Among the other share-owners the
fall was only 1 point.

TABLE 8.12N Share Purchase and Vote:
Recall Data

	1983	1987
Non-Purchasers		
Conservative	41	37
Labour	41	38
Other	18	25
	100%	100%
(N)	(1952)	(2160)

[Continued next page

TABLE 8.12N—*Continued*

	1983	1987
'New' Recruits		
Conservative	57	52
Labour	27	22
Other	16	27
	100%	101%
(N)	(445)	(470)
Enthusiasts		
Conservative	74	70
Labour	8	5
Other	18	25
	100%	100%
(N)	(340)	(331)
Other Share-owners		
Conservative	60	59
Labour	21	19
Other	19	22
	100%	100%
(N)	(207)	(217)

Source: 1987 cross-section survey

However, while the Conservatives do not appear to have benefited from share purchase, according to the data of table 8.12N, there are signs that Labour lost. As we can see, the Labour share of the vote fell by 5 points among the new recruits compared with a fall of 3 points among non-purchasers. This pattern is very similar to the one we find with respect to council house purchase, which we discuss in the next section.

[6]Table 8.13N gives the results of this prospective analysis. The first column gives results from the 1983 cross-section survey and the second column from the 1987 cross-section. In the case of the 1983 data, we divide respondents into those who at that time were owner-occupiers, those who said they were likely to buy their council houses (or were already negotiating to do so), and those who said they were not likely to do so (or did not know). In the case of the 1987 data we classify respondents into those who were L.A. tenants in 1987, those who had purchased their council houses between 1983 and 1987, and other owner-occupiers. The 1987 data include only those respondents who were eligible to vote in 1983.

TABLE 8.13N Council House Purchase and Vote B

	1983	1987	1987
L.A. Tenants			
Conservative	21	23	22
Labour	57	62	58
Other	22	15	20
	100%	100%	100%
(N)	(706)	(625)	(561)
Likely/Actual Purchasers			
Conservative	33	45	33
Labour	52	39	36
Other	16	16	31
	101%	100%	100%
(N)	(95)	(82)	(75)
Other Home-owners			
Conservative	53	57	53
Labour	19	25	22
Other	28	19	26
	100%	101%	101%
(N)	(2123)	(2020)	(1846)

Source: Column 1—1983 cross-section survey. Columns 2 and 3—1987 cross-section survey, respondents who were eligible to vote in 1983

As we can see, the proportion of likely purchasers in the 1983 survey tallies well with the proportion of actual purchasers in the 1987 survey. And we can also see that, in the case of the L.A. tenants and the other owner-occupiers, Labour voting increased between 1983 and 1987, nonvoting declined, and Conservative voting showed little change, corresponding closely to the actual election outcomes. The likely purchasers, however, showed a higher Labour vote, and a lower Alliance vote, in 1983 than the actual purchasers showed in 1987. This prospective analysis therefore confirms the conclusions of the retrospective analysis that purchase was associated with a switch from Labour to the Alliance.

[7]To check these conclusions more rigorously we carried out two sets of logit analyses on the council-house tenants and purchasers (in other words excluding the other home-owners). In the first set of analyses we treat 1987 vote as a Conservative:non-Conservative dichotomy and in the second as a Labour:non-Labour dichotomy. In both sets we first look at the relationship between vote and purchase without any controls and second at the relationship with a control for 1979 vote. It is of course also possible that the effect of purchase on vote is due to other changes which have affected the voters.

Table 8.8 suggested that employment situation and income are the two factors most strongly associated with council house purchase, and we therefore control for these.

TABLE 8.14N Logit Models of Vote and Council House Purchase

	logit parameters	
	Con vs. Non-Con	Lab vs. Non-Lab
Without controls	0.37 (0.09)	−0.47 (0.09)
After controls for 1979 vote	0.17 (0.14)	−0.39 (0.13)
After further controls for employment situation and income	0.05 (0.16)	−0.32 (0.15)

Source: 1987 cross-section survey

We can see that, in the set of analyses where our dependent variable is Conservative versus non-Conservative voting (column 1), purchase does not have a significant relationship with 1987 vote, net of 1979 recalled vote. In the second set, however, when the dependent variable is Labour versus non-Labour voting (column 2), there is a significant relationship, which remains even after controlling for employment situation and income.

Chapter 9

Pocket-book Voting

While the extension of popular capitalism was perhaps one of the most notable achievements of Mrs Thatcher's second administration (even if it did not have the expected electoral consequences), political commentators placed even more weight on her government's economic successes in accounting for her victory in 1987. Ivor Crewe argued that "Here, quite simply and obviously, lies the key to the Conservative victory" (Crewe 1987). Similarly, Butler and Kavanagh argued:

> "A majority of voters thought that the economy in general and their own family finances were improving. Perceptions of whether the economy was getting better were clearly correlated with changes in voting behaviour since 1983. Those who thought their family fortunes had improved were highly likely to defect to the Conservatives. A reverse pattern was found among switchers to and from the Labour party. Pocket-book politics—the voters' perceptions of the economy and their family finances—were potent electoral forces, and the Conservatives were seen by enough voters to have delivered the goods" (Butler and Kavanagh 1988:273).

This notion of pocket-book voting has been one of the most popular among the lay public and indeed among politicians. Harold Wilson for example once claimed "All political history shows that the standing of a Government and its ability to hold the confidence of the electorate at a General Election depend on the success of its economic policy". Butler and Stokes even managed to find a quotation from 1814: "A Government is not supported a hundredth part so much by the constant, uniform, quiet prosperity of the country as by those damned spurts which Pitt used to have just in the nick of time" (Brougham to Thomas Creevy; quoted in Butler and Stokes 1969:389).

There are two main sources of evidence on pocket-book voting—survey data and aggregate data. The survey data also allow us to explore whether it is the voter's own personal pocket-book or perceptions of national economic fortunes that play the larger role in the voter's decision. These are sometimes termed the egocentric and the sociotropic approaches respectively (see for example Kinder and Kiewiet 1981). We begin with the egocentric approach.

Personal experiences

In the panel study we asked respondents "Since the last general election, in June 1983, would you say that your *own* standard of living has increased a lot, increased a little, stayed the same, fallen a little or fallen a lot?"

Respondents' assessments of change in their standard of living are bound to be rather subjective, and we should be more cautious about them than about their reports of share or house purchase. There is almost inevitably the danger that, in an interview devoted to electoral matters, respondents will unconsciously tend to rationalize their voting decisions. Labour voters for example may give the interviewer rather jaundiced accounts of their economic fortunes since they may feel called upon to justify the way they voted. We should, therefore, probably regard our survey results as tending to overestimate the extent of pocket-book voting.

Table 9.1 follows the same basic procedure as the one which we used in analysing share and house purchase. We divide the sample into those who thought their own standard of living had increased, those who thought it had stayed the same, and those who thought it had deteriorated. And we then compare the voting behaviour of these three groups in 1983 and 1987.

As with our previous analyses of this kind, there are marked differences in how our three groups voted beforehand in 1983. There was a large Conservative lead in 1983 in the top panel of table 9.1 (that is, among people who subsequently reported that their standard of living had increased) and an even larger opposition lead in the bottom panel (among people who subsequently reported that their standard of living had fallen). If we accept people's reports at their face value, we must conclude that the Conservative government was effectively rewarding its own supporters through its economic policies and penalizing supporters of the opposition parties. (For a discussion of the widening economic inequalities in Britain under Mrs Thatcher see chapter 10).

We also see the pattern predicted by Butler and Kavanagh with Conservative voting rising slightly among people who felt their standard of living had increased, while Labour voting rose among those who felt their standard of living had fallen. However, the increase in Conservative voting in the top panel is much smaller than the Labour increase in the bottom panel. Rather than people rewarding the Conservatives for improvements in their family fortunes, it looks as though the major process is one of punishing the Conservatives for falling living standards. More rigorous analysis confirms the visual inspection of the table.[1]

We can make an estimate of how potent an effect this was by carrying out a simple simulation. Let us suppose that, instead of winners outnumbering losers by nearly two-to-one as they do in table 9.1, the numbers were evenly

TABLE 9.1 Own Standard of Living and Vote

Own standard had ...	1983	1987
Improved		
Conservative	57	58
Labour	19	18
Other	24	24
	100%	100%
	(270)	(286)
Stayed the same		
Conservative	53	52
Labour	17	20
Other	30	28
	100%	100%
	(310)	(325)
Fallen		
Conservative	32	26
Labour	38	43
Other	31	31
	101%	100%
	(144)	(162)

Source: 1983–87 panel study

balanced.[2] This is not quite the same thing as supposing that there was zero economic growth (since growth is consistent with a small number of winners gaining substantially while a larger number of losers lose modestly). Nevertheless, a comparison between the electoral results of our simulation and the actual electoral outcome will indicate the kind of electoral difference that a modest improvement in economic performance might achieve.

The results of this simulation suggest that the Conservatives would have lost around two and a half points, the Labour party would have gained around two points, and the other parties would have gained half a point if losers had equalled gainers. These are of course substantially larger gains and losses than those we saw in chapter 8, but they would not have made the difference between victory and defeat. The Conservatives' share of the vote would still have topped 40% and their Parliamentary majority, although reduced, would have survived.

Assessments of national economic conditions

One reason why people's pocket-books do not have larger effects on their voting may be that voters believe that changes in their own real incomes have little to do with government actions and may owe more to their own efforts (a promotion for example or extra overtime worked) or to chance factors. Insofar as voters attribute the changes in their standard of living to nongovernmental action, then the relationship between their own experiences and their voting behaviour will surely be weakened.

An alternative suggestion, therefore, is that voters may be more influenced by the overall economic indicators, such as the level of unemployment or inflation. Kiewiet for example has argued:

"In contrast, according to proponents of the national assessments hypothesis, most people readily perceive trends in the nation's economy to be a product of the policies pursued by those in power. An individual may attribute a personal loss of income to unwise investments or to a cutback in overtime hours, but believe a drop in GNP results from the ineptitude of the current administration. A worker who has been laid off will blame it on his or her company losing a contract to a competing firm, but see a rise in the unemployment rate as the consequence of Republican macroeconomic policies. In short, trends in the nation's economy, in most people's minds, reflect directly upon the performance and policies of the government party. Their own personal economic fortunes, in contrast, generally do not." (Kiewiet 1983:24)

In practice, however, we find that people's perceptions of their own personal situation and of the national one go rather closely together—perhaps because both are subject to a more general tendency to rationalize one's voting decision, or perhaps because people's perceptions of the national situation are coloured by their own experiences, or vice versa. For example, we find that around 70% of people who reported that their own standard of living had improved also reported that the general standard of living had improved. Similarly, people who thought that their own standard of living had fallen tended to take the same view of the national situation.

Because of this similarity, people's assessments of the national situation go with vote in much the same way that assessments of their own situation did. This becomes clear from table 9.2. We again see a one-point Conservative increase in the top panel (among people who thought the general standard of living had improved) while there is again a five-point Labour increase in the bottom panel (among people who thought that it had fallen).

The one major difference between the two tables is that assessments of the national situation are even more strongly associated with prior vote than are assessments of one's own standard of living. Thus in table 9.1 Conservative voting in 1983 was 25 points higher in the top panel than it was in the bottom panel; in table 9.2 it was 41 points higher. This suggests that there is even more of a subjective element in these national perceptions than in the personal ones.

Perhaps for this reason, if we carry out a multivariate analysis in which both personal and national assessments are included, the national ones prove to be the more important predictors of vote-switching. Indeed, once we control for

TABLE 9.2 General Standard of Living and
Vote

General standard had . . .	1983	1987
Improved		
Conservative	67	68
Labour	11	10
Other	23	21
	101%	99%
	(295)	(309)
Stayed the same		
Conservative	50	49
Labour	19	22
Other	31	29
	100%	100%
	(209)	(223)
Fallen		
Conservative	26	23
Labour	40	45
Other	34	32
	100%	100%
	(206)	(226)

Source: 1983–87 panel study

national assessments, personal assessments no longer have a significant impact.

Table 9.3 shows the results of a series of multivariate logit models in which we include our respondents' reports both of their own and of the general standard of living. The dependent variable is Conservative versus Labour voting.

The first model looks at the relationship between changes in one's *own* standard of living and vote in 1987 without any statistical controls. (This is equivalent to an analysis of Conservative and Labour voting in the second column of table 9.1.) As we can see, people who thought their own standard of living had fallen were significantly less likely to vote Conservative.

The second model looks at reports of changes in the *general* standard of living. The parameters are even larger; in other words, there was an even bigger difference in the votes of people who thought the national standard of living had risen and those who thought it had fallen.

The third and fourth models control for prior vote in 1983 (and are thus equivalent to the three-way tables underlying tables 9.1 and 9.2). They confirm what we had already inferred from tables 9.1 and 9.2: people who thought that their own standard of living had fallen (the third model) or who thought that

TABLE 9.3 Logit Models of the Standard of Living and 1987 Vote (Conservative vs. Labour)

| | logit parameters | | | | | |
| | Own standard | | | General standard | | |
Independent variables	improved	stayed the same	fell	improved	stayed the same	fell
1. Own standard of living	0	-0.10 (0.11)	-0.84 (0.13)			
2. General standard of living				0	-0.53 (0.13)	-1.27 (0.13)
3. Own standard and 1983 vote	0	-0.10 (0.23)	-0.63 (0.29)			
4. General standard and 1983 vote				0	-0.57 (0.28)	-1.16 (0.29)
5. Own standard, general standard and 1983 vote	0	0.21 (0.27)	-0.09 (0.34)	0	-0.62 (0.31)	-1.13 (0.32)

Note: Figures in brackets give standard errors.
Source: 1983–87 panel study

the general standard of living had fallen (the fourth model) were significantly less likely to stay loyal to the Conservatives in 1987.

Finally, we include reports both of one's own and of the general standard of living in the same model (the fifth model). This time, the parameters for one's own standard of living fail to get anywhere near statistical significance, while the association with the general standard of living survives unscathed. The sociotropic interpretation, therefore, survives while the egocentric one fails. Just as our discussions of region and ethnicity suggested, individual experiences do not seem to carry as much weight as collective ones.

Some further evidence consistent with this comes from our open-ended material. Early in the interview we asked people to say in their own words why they supported their current party. In table 9.4 we have grouped the reasons they gave under six main headings—personal pocket-books, the government's management of the country, specific issues or ideologies, social class, personal or family loyalty, leadership, and a category of general approval for the party without any specific content. (Table 9.4 reports the positive reasons that people gave for their choice. There were also some, although not as many, negative reasons. Respondents could of course give more than one reason, so the totals in table 9.4 can exceed 100 per cent, and other reasons which do not fit neatly into any of our seven categories were also given. Alliance voters in particular gave reasons like "time for a change".)

TABLE 9.4. Reasons for Choice of Party

	% mentioning each type of reason		
	Conservative voters	Labour voters	Alliance voters
Pocket-book	18	18	5
Management of the country	45	6	6
Issues/ideology	42	41	33
Social class	8	38	5
Loyalty	13	33	7
Leadership	29	7	9
Best party	27	14	26
N	(1405)	(1000)	(754)

Source: 1987 cross-section survey

As we can see, quite a lot of voters for all three main parties explained their choice in terms of their personal pocket-books. "Financially I am better off" said one Conservative voter. "I feel that [the Conservatives] were the party who would do most for me and my family. I felt that my standard of living and way of life was better preserved under the Conservatives" said another.

However, in the Conservative case (and it was after all the Conservatives who might be expected to benefit most from pocket-book considerations), references to economic self-interest were far outnumbered by references to the party's general competence in managing the economy and running the country. Some reasons referred specifically to the government's management of the economy, for example "I think over the last 8 years they've started to turn the corner over the economy and their policies seem to be on the right road for recovery". Other people referred to the government's general competence without specifically mentioning the economy: "I think they've done a fairly good job over the last 4 years".

As with the questions on one's own and the general standard of living, we might expect the two types of answer to go together, and indeed they do to some extent. However, when we analyse the structure of the reasons people volunteered, we find that a much more powerful relationship is between pocket-book reasons and social class reasons.[3] In other words, the people who mentioned their own pocket-books were also relatively likely to mention the interests of their social class as a reason for their choice of party. It would appear that people link their own self-interest with that of their social class, and indeed many reasons that we have coded as pocket-book ones explicitly mentioned "people like me". "I think they would give more to people like me" said one Labour voter. "Just generally much better for people like us" said a Conservative voter.

Egocentric and sociotropic reasons, self-interest and group-interest are not perhaps so different after all. On this evidence, then, pocket-book voting and class voting may not be rivals but rather may be different aspects of the same phenomenon.

Official data on the economy

Given the problems of rationalization and subjectivity that beset respondents' reports, whether from open-ended or from closed questions, it is clearly desirable to check our results against more objective data. We turn next, therefore, to the official data on real income. These do not allow us to distinguish egocentric from sociotropic interpretations, but do give us another way of assessing the relationship between changes in standards of living and changes in vote.

Table 9.5 shows the changes in real personal disposable income at 1985 prices over the last twenty-five years. There are of course many other economic indicators that have been used in the analysis of government popularity such as the rate of inflation, the level of unemployment and the balance of payments. But real personal disposable income (after taxes and transfers) is the official category that corresponds most closely to the lay notion of standard of living. It is also the variable that American studies have found to be consistently the best predictor of election outcomes (Kramer 1983) and can be said to represent the bottom line in evaluating government economic performance.

The first column of table 9.5 shows real income at the end of each administration (that is, in the quarter in which the election occurred) over our period.[4] The second column shows the annual rate of increase over each

TABLE 9.5 Economic Growth and Electoral Performance

	Real personal disposable income at 1985 prices	Average annual rate of change since previous election	% Change in previous year	Change in incumbent government's share of vote
October 1959	53.4			
October 1964	64.9	4.0	3.2	− 5.9
March 1966	69.1	4.3	6.4	+ 4.0
June 1970	73.2	1.4	4.6	− 5.0
February 1974	83.7	3.6	1.0	− 8.5
October 1974	84.8	2.6	(1.3)	+ 2.0
May 1979	91.5	1.6	4.5	− 2.2
June 1983	96.1	1.2	2.6	− 1.5
June 1987	105.7	2.4	2.4	− 0.2

Source: *Economic Trends* (1989); Table 1.1

government's period of office. According to these data, Mrs Thatcher's second administration was a rather average one, while her first administration was the poorest on record. Thus real incomes grew at an average of 1.2% per year over the course of the 1979–83 Conservative government—slightly worse than Mr Wilson's and Mr Callaghan's Labour governments managed in the late 1960s and late 1970s. Mrs Thatcher's second administration managed rather better, but the average annual growth rate of 2.4% was still well short of Sir Alec Douglas-Home's or Mr Heath's achievements.

This is not the place to go into the details of Mrs Thatcher's economic record. But these data are so at variance with the usual portrayal of her government's record that they require some comment. First, we must emphasize that these data come from the government's own offical economic statistics (Economic Trends 1989). Secondly, we should point out that government spokesmen, when talking of the economic miracle, tended to emphasize the improvement in manufacturing productivity, and this does indeed seem to have increased quite markedly since 1979.

Finally, to make a fair assessment of the government's record it would be necessary to compare the figures with those of other major industrial economies. Britain's economic growth is certainly affected by world economic conditions as well as by the government's handling of the economy. Recent attempts by economists to compare British performance with those of other industrial economies have reached much the same conclusion as that of table 9.4: the performance of the economy under Mrs Thatcher has been rather average.[5] (See Layard and Nickell 1989, Coutts and Godley 1989.) Whether voters are aware of these international comparisons is another matter.

Still, the fact that Mrs Thatcher's economic record has been rather average should be comforting to advocates of pocket-book voting, since her electoral record, as judged by votes cast for the Conservative party, hardly qualifies as an electoral miracle either.

It should be said in Mrs Thatcher's defence, however, that there appears to be a negative incumbency effect in table 9.5. The only incumbent administrations which have actually increased their share of the vote have been Mr Wilson's two brief ones of 1964–6 and February to October 1974. Every administration over our period which served for four or more years has lost votes. We have to go back to the 1951–55 Conservative administration to find one that served more or less a full term without actually losing votes. This negative incumbency effect is consistent of course with our finding that voters tended to punish the Conservatives for a fall in their standard of living but not to reward them much for an increase.

Inspection of table 9.5 suggests that there has been little relation between the incumbent administration's electoral success and the annual growth rate which it achieved over its period of office. Mr Macmillan and Sir Alec Douglas-Home presided over a period of generally high growth, but the Conservatives went down to defeat in 1964. Similarly the average growth rate under Mr Heath was rather better than that under Mrs Thatcher, but Mr Heath lost more votes at the subsequent General Election than any other Prime Minister in this period (although some of this loss will have been due to the extra Liberal candidates in the 1974 election). Correlating the annual growth rate with the change in the government's share of the vote confirms this conclusion (that is, correlating columns 2 and 4). The correlation proves to be effectively zero (0.03).

An alternative, and quite persuasive view, is that it is not so much the *average* over the government's lifetime that is important but the record over the preceding year or so. The electorate, it is said, have short memories. A number of American studies have found that "change in per capita real disposable income over the course of the election year has been the best predictor of the incumbent party's electoral fortunes" (Kiewiet 1983:7).[6]

The third column of table 9.5 shows the percentage increase in real personal disposable income over the last year of an administration's life.[7] This does yield a higher correlation with the change in the incumbent administration's share of the vote, which now rises to 0.37. Since this is based only on eight elections, it does not actually reach statistical significance, but given the similar findings from American studies we are inclined to accept it.

It would not be sensible with so few observations to undertake sophisticated statistical analysis. There are of course numerous possibilities for alternative analyses. For example, instead of assuming that voters remember only the previous year's economic performance, we might give some additional, but lesser, weight to previous years (cf Fiorina 1981). This might help to explain anomalous results like that of 1970 when a pre-election boom failed to bring electoral success. To undertake more elaborate analysis of this kind we would need to include many more observations (perhaps like Kramer's original path-breaking paper going back to the beginning of the century).[8]

There is however one extra exercise which is perhaps worth carrying out. We can carry out an elementary regression analysis of the national-level data in order to summarize the relationship between the changes in the government's share of the vote and the changes in real personal disposable income over the previous year. For the eight elections covered here we find that a 1% change in real income (in the year preceding the election) was associated with 0.85% change in the government's share of the vote.[9]

While this is not strictly comparable with the simulation which we carried out on the effects of personal experiences on vote-switching, the two exercises are clearly yielding rather similar, and modest, estimates of the effects of economic fortunes on election outcomes. They are also of broadly similar magnitude to those reached by American researchers (e.g. Marcus 1988).

Government responsibilities

The pocket-book theory of voting is based on the not unreasonable premise that one of the prime responsibilities of government is to manage the economy and to improve people's living standards. This is what Butler and Stokes termed a "valence" issue. Valence issues are ones on which the electorate broadly agrees and debate therefore focuses on government performance in securing, say, economic growth rather than on whether growth is a good thing. In contrast Butler and Stokes defined "position" issues as ones on which there is fundamental ideological disagreement. The classic position issues are those like nationalization and privatization, income redistribution, or nuclear disarmament.

Furthermore, since parties' stands on the major position issues tend to be relatively stable over time, it makes good sense to suppose that government performance on the valence issues will tend to be the main explanation of the net movements between the parties at General Elections.

The distinction between valence and position issues is, however, almost certainly overdrawn. Even the value of economic growth, the classic valence issue, is now disputed by the Green party and should perhaps now be regarded as a position issue.

Moreover, there are also other potential valence issues which might challenge management of the economy as an explanation of electoral swings. Some relevant evidence on this comes from the British Social Attitudes Survey of 1985. Respondents were asked:

> "On the whole, do you think it should or should not be the government's responsibility to . . .
> . . . provide a job for everyone who wants one
> . . . keep prices under control
> . . . provide health care for the sick
> . . . provide a decent standard of living for the old
> . . . provide industry with the help it needs to grow
> . . . provide a decent standard of living for the unemployed
> . . . reduce income differences between the rich and poor?"

These questions were also asked, in identical format, in the United States and the comparisons make interesting reading.

TABLE 9.6 Government Responsibilities in the USA and Britain

% saying the government definitely should:	USA	Britain
Provide a decent standard of living for the old	40	78
Provide health care for the sick	35	86
Keep prices under control	29	60
Provide industry with the help it needs to grow	16	53
Reduce income difference between the rich and the poor	16	45
Provide a decent standard of living for the unemployed	15	43
Provide a job for everyone who wants one	13	37

Source: Davis (1986)

As we can see, providing health care for the sick actually comes top of the British list, with the greatest public consensus. Next comes a decent standard of living for the old. In contrast, control of inflation and unemployment (and even economic growth) look more like the position issue of income redistribution.

It is also of considerable interest that the British electorate differs rather markedly from the American electorate in this respect (Davis 1986; see also Evans and Durant 1989). Americans are much less likely to see any of these things as government responsibilities. This perhaps explains why there is a negative incumbency effect in Britain but not in America. The British seem to expect more of their government, and so there is more that can go wrong and undermine government popularity.

The theory of pocket-book voting, therefore, probably ought to be widened to become a more general theory of government performance. As we can see from table 9.7, our evidence suggests that perceptions of government performance in other areas like the health service were associated with vote-switching in much the same way as were the economic assessments.

In table 9.7 we look at assessments of the standards of health and social services. One striking feature of the table is that the majority of people felt that standards had fallen. Whereas people who felt the general standard of living had risen outnumbered those who thought it had fallen by nearly two-to-one, people who thought that the standards of health and social services had risen were outnumbered by one-to-seven.

Once again, to be sure, we see that people's perceptions are strongly associated with their prior party preferences. The same subjectivity is involved with perceptions of standards in the NHS as with the economic ones. Indeed, they may be even greater. Whereas 1983 Conservative voting was 25 points higher in the top panel of table 9.1 than it was in the bottom panel, and 41 points higher in the top panel of table 9.2 than in the bottom panel, the gap in table 9.7 is a remarkable 53 points.

TABLE 9.7 Standard of Health and Social Services and
Vote

Standard of services had ...	1983	1987
Increased		
Conservative	77	78
Labour	7	10
Other	16	12
	100%	100%
	(68)	(72)
Stayed the same		
Conservative	78	75
Labour	6	9
Other	16	16
	100%	100%
	(165)	(171)
Fallen a little		
Conservative	51	53
Labour	20	17
Other	29	30
	100%	100%
	(226)	(245)
Fallen a lot		
Conservative	24	22
Labour	37	43
Other	39	35
	100%	100%
	(259)	(281)

Source: 1983–87 panel study

And once again we see that people who thought that the standards of the
health and social services had fallen a lot were more likely to switch to
Labour. There is a six point rise in the Labour vote between 1983 and 1987
in the bottom panel of table 9.7, much as there was in the bottom panels of
tables 9.1 and 9.2.

In addition to the standard of living and the standard of the health
and social services, we also asked our respondents about their perceptions
of changes in prices, unemployment, taxes, crime, strikes, education, and
safety from the threat of war. We can expand the multivariate analysis of
table 9.3 to include these other changes, and the results are given in table
9.8.[11]

TABLE 9.8 Logistic Regression of Changes in Standards and
Vote (Conservative vs. Labour)

Independent variables	Regression parameters
Prices	0.10 (0.14)
Unemployment	0.08 (0.08)
Taxes	0.05 (0.08)
Own standard of living	− 0.06 (0.09)
General standard of living	− 0.24 (0.09)
Standard of health and social services	− 0.22 (0.10)
Crime	− 0.09 (0.07)
Strikes	0.16 (0.08)
Quality of education	− 0.07 (0.10)
Britain's safety from threat of war	− 0.10 (0.09)
Vote in 1983	2.22 (0.28)

Note: Figures in brackets give standard errors.
Source: 1983–87 panel survey

We now find that the general standard of living is joined by strikes and health and social services. None of the other changes reaches statistical significance, but we must remember that perceptions of some of these different changes will tend to go together. We must not make too much of the finding that, for example, perceptions of changes in the health and social services have a significant effect whereas perceptions of changes in the quality of education do not. People who think one has fallen are rather likely to think that the other has fallen too and we should not try to disentangle them.[12]

There is also some evidence that assessments of the general standard of living represent a kind of summary of the respondents' perceptions of these various changes.[13] It is often argued that the health and education services provided by the welfare state are part of the "social wage", and ought therefore to be included along with one's money wages in calculating the standard of living. The voter may well include these already in assessing his own or the general standard of living.

Some circumstantial evidence in favour of this proposition comes from a comparison between the objective evidence of table 9.5 and survey data on people's perceptions of changes in their real incomes.

In 1974, 1979, 1983 and 1987 (BSA survey) respondents were asked "Looking back over the last year or so, do you think that your income has fallen behind prices, kept up with prices or has gone up by more than prices?" This question is not ideally phrased, since people seem rather unwilling to admit, or unable to calculate, that their incomes have actually risen by more than inflation. If we took the figures at face value we should come to the conclusion that Britain had experienced negative growth in real incomes over the last fifteen years! Nevertheless, they give us a basis for comparing the voters' perceptions of their changing fortunes at the time of recent general elections.

TABLE 9.9 Perceptions of Changes in Real Income

% thinking that their income had . . .

Year	gone up by more than prices	kept up with prices	fallen behind prices	don't know	N	
1974	5	41	51	2	99%	(2346)
1979	6	32	60	2	100%	(1860)
1983	8	40	49	2	99%	(3939)
1987	9	44	45	2	100%	(2847)

Sources: October 1974, 1979 and 1983 BES cross-section surveys; 1987 BSA survey

The perceptions reported in table 9.9 are clearly at variance with the official data of table 9.5 on changes in real personal disposable income. Most notably, 1979 saw one of the largest changes in real income over the year before the election, but it was the year when the largest proportion of people thought their income had fallen behind prices. The official statistics define *real* income in terms of purchasing power after inflation, so the two different measures are getting at roughly similar things, but the discrepancy between them is striking.

Nor can the results be explained by a money illusion. Price inflation was certainly quite high at the time of the 1979 election, running at an annual rate of 11%, but it was substantially lower than inflation in October 1974, when it had been running at 17%. So we cannot explain people's pessimistic views about their real incomes in 1979 in terms of the rate of inflation.

It is in our view more plausible to suppose that it was people's experiences of the winter of discontent in 1979 that led them to take a rather gloomy view of their own real incomes. Power cuts and uncollected rubbish sacks have a rather obvious and immediate impact on voters' lives. It is by no means unreasonable for people to include these in their assessments of their own standard of living, or indeed to include other factors like the quality of public health and education services.

Our conclusions must necessarily remain rather tentative. The individual-level analyses show that the British voter holds governments responsible for a wide range of outcomes, not just for management of the economy, and that perceptions of changes in the strike rate and the quality of the health and social services go with changes in voting. The aggregate-level analysis suggests that the performance of the economy in the year before the election is related to changes in the government's share of the vote, but that it is far from the whole story in explaining short-run electoral swings.

Now just as net volatility is a different concept from overall volatility, so analyses of individual perceptions do not necessarily give us a sound basis for drawing conclusions about the effects of aggregate changes in strikes, health,

TABLE 9.10 Perceptions of Change in Prices etc.

	increased	stayed the same	fallen	don't know	N
		% thinking that prices, etc. had increased, stayed the same or fallen since the 1983 General Election			
Prices	94	4	1	1	100% (869)
Unemployment	67	12	19	2	100% (865)
Taxes	27	17	49	7	100% (869)
Own standard of living	37	42	21	1	101% (868)
General standard of living	39	29	29	3	100% (869)
Standard of health and social services	9	22	67	2	100% (869)
Crime	87	6	7	1	101% (869)
Strikes	12	15	72	1	100% (869)
Quality of education	5	21	68	6	100% (869)
Britain's safety from threat of war	28	57	12	3	100% (869)

Source: 1983–87 panel study

education or defence (see Kramer 1983 for a detailed discussion of this point). Nonetheless, it is clear that we need to introduce explanations over and above pocket-book ones, narrowly defined, in order to account for the Conservatives' electoral fortunes.

As table 9.10 shows, people were more inclined to think that standards of living had risen than fallen, that strikes and taxes had fallen, and that safety from the threat of war had improved between 1983 and 1987. But these Conservative successes were balanced by perceptions that prices, unemployment and crime had increased, and that the quality of health and social services and of education had fallen. It may well be that the Conservatives' failure to increase their share of the vote in 1987, despite their economic record, was because in the electorate's eyes their perceived successes were balanced by their perceived failures.

Notes

[1]Table 9.1 of course simply shows the net outcomes of the patterns of switching. Table 9.11N shows the actual pattern of switching. As we can see, switching to the Conservatives in the top panel was actually rather low, although not as low as in the bottom panel. But by no stretch of the imagination could we say that people who thought their fortunes had improved were highly likely to defect to the Conservatives.

TABLE 9.11N Standard of Living and the Flow of the Vote

			1987 vote			
		Conservative	Labour	Alliance		N
	Improved					
	Conservative	92	1	7	100%	(145)
	Labour	7	76	18	101%	(45)
	Alliance	16	16	68	100%	(62)
	Stayed the same					
1983	Conservative	88	2	10	100%	(155)
Vote	Labour	2	91	7	100%	(45)
	Alliance	17	13	71	101%	(85)
	Fell					
	Conservative	65	5	30	100%	(43)
	Labour	0	96	4	100%	(50)
	Alliance	10	17	73	100%	(41)

Source: 1983–87 panel study

Following a similar procedure to chapter 8, we can fit logit models to the three-way table 9.11N in order to test for significance. This is done in table 9.3 above.

[2] Our procedure for this simulation was to reweight the percentages in the second column of table 9.1 (that is the 1987 votes). We assumed that there were 224 respondents whose standard of living increased (instead of the actual 286) and we assumed that there were 224 respondents whose standard of living fell (instead of the actual 162). We also assumed that the number who reported their standard of living stayed the same was unchanged at 325. These hypothetical frequencies were then used to weight the actual percentages. We should of course note that the panel study shows a surplus of Conservative voters and a deficit of Labour voters (see Appendix III), and so these figures should strictly be adjusted further.

[3] Table 9.12N shows the results (after rotation) of a factor analysis of the positive reasons given by Conservative voters. (Very similar patterns are found among Labour voters, although not to the same extent among Alliance voters.)

TABLE 9.12N Factor Analysis of Positive Reasons Given by Conservative Voters

	Factor 1	Factor 2	Factor 3
Pocket-book	0.75	0.08	−0.08
Management of the country	−0.33	0.48	0.33
Issues/ideology	0.25	0.59	0.09
Social class	0.73	0.02	0.06
Loyalty	0.02	−0.79	0.14
Leadership	−0.26	0.04	0.67
Best party	−0.30	0.02	−0.70
Eigen value	1.44	1.27	1.02
Percentage of variance explained	20.6	18.1	14.6

Source: 1987 cross-section study; open-ended questions

As we can see, pocket-book reasons and class reasons tend to go together and are the major elements of the first factor. The second factor suggests that people who mentioned family or personal loyalty were unlikely to mention issues and ideology. Similarly, the third factor suggests that people who mentioned Mrs Thatcher's leadership were unlikely to say that the Conservatives were simply the best party.

[4] There is inevitably some error here, since elections occur at different points within a quarter. In particular, the 1966 election occurred at the very end of a quarter.

[5] Bruno Paulson has made some comparisons for us between annual rates of growth in GDP under British administrations since 1964 and those in Germany and Italy for comparable periods. His calculations indicate that the annual growth rate in Britain under Mrs Thatcher's first administration was 1.1 points lower than the German/Italian average while it was 0.7 points higher under her second administration. However, we should also note that the annual growth rate of GDP was 2.8 points lower than the German/Italian

average under Mr Wilson's second administration and 0.9 points lower under the Wilson/Callaghan administration.

[6] Much of the American work has been on congressional elections, for example Kramer 1971, Tufte 1975. On Presidential elections see for example Stigler 1973 and Fair 1978.

[7] In the case of the February-October 1974 administration we have simply taken the percentage increase over the first quarter of the year.

[8] Another strategy is of course to use the monthly opinion polls to measure government popularity. This greatly increases the number of observations, but one difficulty with this approach is that the determinants of government popularity mid-term may be rather different from the determinants of election outcomes. Models which predict mid-term popularity may not do so well at general election time. There is a huge and controversial literature on these models of government popularity. See for example Goodhart and Bhansali (1970) and Frey and Garbers (1971) for a debate over an early and ill-fated attempt to predict government popularity. Most recently debate has focused on the impact of the Falklands War on government popularity. See for example Sanders, Ward and Marsh (1987), Norpoth (1987), Franklin (1987).

[9] The constant term in this regression is -4.9, indicating that a government which presides over zero growth in the year before the election loses nearly 5% of its share of the vote.

We must emphasize that this analysis merely summarizes the relationships described in table 9.5. We do not regard it as a causal or predictive analysis, since there are many other variables which would need to be included in a proper causal analysis, for example changes in the parties' ideological positions, government performance with respect to the welfare state and war, the number of Liberal candidates, and so on.

[10] To simplify the presentation of table 9.8 we have carried out a logistic regression, treating each of the independent variables (the perceptions of changes in prices etc.) as continuous five-point scales, with the exception of 1983 vote, which is treated as a binary (Conservative versus non-Conservative) variable. The dependent variable is the log odds of voting Conservative or Labour.

[11] The results of a factor analysis of the various perceptions is shown in table 9.13N. The loadings shown are those after rotation.

We should note that similar results are obtained if we carry out factor analyses for Conservative, Labour and Alliance voters separately.

[12] Perceptions of changes in the general standard of living had the highest loading on the first factor extracted before rotation.

TABLE 9.13N Factor Analysis of Perceptions of Change

	Factor 1	Factor 2	Factor 3	Factor 4
Prices	0.61	-0.25	-0.15	0.15
Unemployment	0.42	-0.68	0.15	0.05
Taxes	0.78	-0.01	-0.10	-0.04
Own standard of living	-0.09	0.03	0.87	0.01
General standard of living	-0.19	0.32	0.76	0.03
Standard of health and social services	-0.01	0.68	0.40	0.08
Crime	0.09	-0.02	-0.14	0.78
Strikes	0.67	0.05	-0.05	-0.09
Quality of education	0.07	0.75	0.16	0.04
Britain's safety from threat of war	-0.11	0.08	0.19	0.68
Eigen value	2.63	1.33	1.10	1.03
Percentage of variance explained	26.3	13.3	11.0	10.3

Source: 1983–87 panel study

Chapter 10

Economic Inequality

Most political commentators have concentrated on the economic advances made under Mrs Thatcher—Britain's rising prosperity, the spread of home-ownership and share-ownership (see for example Butler and Kavanagh 1988). It is however also quite clear and uncontroversial that the economic benefits have not been equally spread. One of the most notable features of the 1980s under Mrs Thatcher's first two administrations has been the increased economic inequality between rich and poor. As the economists Layard and Nickell report "On inequality, the record is clear: it has increased hugely" (Layard and Nickell 1989:21).

The long-run trends in the distribution of income have been towards greater equality. For example, Soltow (1968) looked at data from 1436, 1688, 1801 and more recent years up to 1962–63, and found a convincing trend towards greater equality. The Royal Commission on the Distribution of Income and Wealth (the Diamond Commission), which was appointed by the Wilson government in 1974, looked in detail at the postwar period. They also found a clear trend toward equality, with a marked decline in the share received by the top 1%, and a rather smaller decline in the share of the top 10%. Thus in 1949 the top 1% received 6.4% of all income but this had fallen to 3.5% in 1976–77. (See also Rubinstein 1986.)

The period from 1979, however, has seen a movement back towards greater inequality. The official publication *Economic Trends* (1988) helpfully gives the evidence. The authors divide households up into quintiles, that is into income bands each of which contains 20% of households, the quintiles being arranged in order from richest to poorest. They then look at the proportion of total national income going to each quintile. If there were complete income inequality, each quintile would of course receive 20% of total income. In practice, of course, the distribution of income is far from equal (although not as unequal as the distribution of wealth).

156

The authors of the *Economic Trends* article pursue various ways of calculating income, but the results are essentially the same: the share of the top quintile has risen by several points (the exact figure depending on which definition one uses), while the shares of the remaining four quintiles have each fallen by around 1 point. Of course, a 1-point fall for the bottom quintile is a rather more serious matter than a 1-point fall for the middle quintile since it is a much larger proportion of their already small share.[1]

TABLE 10.1 The Changing Income Distribution

	1975	1979	1983	1986
Disposable Income				
Top quintile	38	39	40	42
2nd quintile	24	25	24	24
3rd quintile	18	18	18	17
4th quintile	13	12	12	11
Bottom quintile	6.6	6.5	6.8	6.2
	100%	100%	100%	100%
Income after cash benefits and all taxes				
Top quintile	39	40	42	45
2nd quintile	24	25	24	24
3rd quintile	18	18	17	16
4th quintile	12	11	11	10
Bottom quintile	6.2	6.1	6.0	5.1
	100%	100%	100%	100%

Source: *Economic Trends* (1988: 114)

Other evidence suggests that, within the top quintile, it was those with the highest income who have benefited most in the 1980s. Layard and Nickell, for example, show that it is the top percentile that has shown the biggest increase in real gross earnings. Thus, between 1979 and 1988 they show that real take-home pay for a man in the top percentile rose by 73% compared with an increase of 13% for a man in the bottom decile. We should not therefore equate growing income equality in any simple way with inequality between the classes. The top 1% is of course only a tiny minority of the salariat. Nor should we equate the bottom quintile with the working class. A majority of the currently-employed working class are in fact in the middle income bands. As we shall see later, the bottom quintile is largely composed of pensioners, the unemployed, and people on social security.

The increase in inequality has probably had a variety of causes. In part it may be due to increased demand for highly-skilled professional and managerial labour—the same phenomenon that gave rise to the expansion of the salariat. This will have had little to do with government policies. However, it may also be due to specific government policies, such as the taxation system which has become much less progressive, with a reduction in the higher rates of tax (Hansard 17 May 1988:423), and a shift in the balance of taxation from direct to indirect taxes, which are less progressive than income tax.

The increase in unemployment has also increased the numbers of people living on or near the poverty line. It is of course arguable how far the increase in unemployment was due to government action as opposed to world trade conditions. It is also arguable whether people on unemployment benefit or other forms of social security are actually in poverty. What is not arguable is that, on the government's own (continually revised figures) unemployment was around 10% in 1987 compared with 5% when the Conservatives took office in 1979.

Previous research on unemployment closely parallels that on shares and housing. It has shown, for example, that the unemployed are markedly more inclined to the Labour party than are people in work (Cautres 1989). But nor are the unemployed a random cross-section of the electorate. They are disproportionately likely to be drawn from the less skilled jobs within the working class, and from declining areas and industries, particularly in the North and Scotland (Nickell 1980). We would therefore expect them to have been more inclined to the Labour party even before they became unemployed. The undoubted correlation between unemployment and Labour vote, as shown by cross-sectional data, is therefore no guarantee that an increase in the overall level of unemployment will lead to a concomitant increase in Labour voting.

This is the conclusion reached by Marshall and his colleagues in their analysis of the electoral effects of unemployment. From their 1984 national survey they concluded:

"Nor are the unemployed exceptional in their political make-up. A majority vote Labour—but this is to be expected given the social characteristics of those who are selectively recruited into the ranks of the jobless. ... Political allegiance is determined prior to the event of unemployment, and largely unaffected by it ... unemployment itself would seem to have no direct impact on voting choice, since the overall patterns of vote switching among those in and out of work are very similar" (Marshall et al 1988b:218).

There have even been suggestions that the Labour party might lose votes through unemployment. There is a considerable literature suggesting that the unemployed may become passive and withdrawn and less inclined to participate in the political process. (The classic statement of this theme is Jahoda, Lazarsfeld and Zeisel 1933. Cf Bakke 1933, Schlozman and Verba 1979). Thus Marshall and his colleagues found that the unemployed were less likely to participate in union activities or other pressure group activities. More of them said that they would not turn out to vote. "The implication is clear: unemployment induces political quiescence rather than political mobilization" (Marshall et al 1988b:222). (However, for a rather more positive view of the unemployed see Liem and Liem 1988.)

The political implications of growing income inequality are not entirely obvious either. Broadly speaking, two main theories can be identified, namely the absolute income hypothesis and the relative income hypothesis. Political scientists have tended to adopt an absolute income hypothesis (and so it must be said do Conservative politicians). They concentrate on the fact that real standards of living have been increasing, even for the poor, and hence expect to see a shift to the right as real incomes increase.[2] This kind of idea has a long pedigree. At the beginning of the century Werner Sombart argued that "all socialist utopias come to grief on roast beef and apple pie". After the Eastern European revolutions of 1989, however, one is now tempted to stand this proposition on its head and argue that it is the *lack* of roast beef and apple pie on which socialist utopias come to grief.

Sociologists, on the other hand, have tended to adopt a relative rather than an absolute approach to income. This is clearest in the again notorious debates about the concept of poverty, although it is also applicable (quite independently of the outcome of the poverty debate) to voting behaviour. The sociological approach emphasizes that it is people's *comparisons* with others that are important (see the classic studies of Stouffer et al 1949 and Runciman 1966). Thus, even if people are absolutely better off than before but nonetheless believe they are falling behind their peers, they may tend to become dissatisfied with their lack of relative progress and hence punish the government (insofar as they believe that the government is responsible for their plight).

Both theories predict a widening of differentials under Mrs Thatcher. The absolute income hypothesis, however, predicts that Conservative voting will increase particularly among the top quintile, which has seen the largest absolute increase in real income. The relative income hypothesis on the other hand predicts that Conservative voting will decline in the lowest quintile, which has not shared to the same extent as the others in the general rise in living standards.

Income inequality and voting behaviour

Questions on income were asked both in the 1979 and 1987 surveys. There are some differences in the question; for example in 1979 respondents were asked about their own (or joint if married) income *after* tax. In 1987 they were asked about household income *before* tax. The distinction between income after tax and income before tax will of course have a large effect on the absolute figures respondents report. But (with one important exception) it is unlikely to have much effect on people's ranking in the income distribution. On the whole, people who come in the top quintile before tax will be the same people who come in the top quintile after tax.

A more serious problem is that in both studies, as in most surveys, respondents were asked to place themselves in income bands rather than to specify a particular figure, and these bands do not correspond neatly to percentile or quintile groups. What we have done, therefore, is to amalgamate the bands in order to produce groups of similar size in the two studies. More elaborate methods of interpolation could be used, but the results look pretty clear-cut without resorting to elaborations. Other sources of error are likely to be more serious.

TABLE 10.2 Family Income and Vote 1979 and 1987

| Income band | 1979 | | | | | |
	Conservative	Labour	Liberal	Other		N
1 (top)	82	13	5	0	100%	(56)
2	56	25	15	4	100%	(112)
3	45	36	17	3	101%	(342)
4	37	46	15	2	100%	(213)
5	42	43	14	1	100%	(235)
6	36	45	18	1	100%	(187)
7 (bottom)	46	43	10	1	100%	(134)

| | 1987 | | | | | |
	Conservative	Labour	Alliance	Other		N
1 (top)	70	8	21	1	100%	(112)
2	57	17	24	2	100%	(288)
3	52	19	26	2	99%	(689)
4	42	32	25	1	100%	(577)
5	37	42	20	1	100%	(471)
6	30	46	23	1	100%	(441)
7 (bottom)	32	45	23	1	101%	(267)

Sources: 1979 and 1987 cross-section surveys

Table 10.2 shows the relationship between income and vote in 1979 and 1987. We have divided respondents into seven income bands which are reasonably comparable between the two studies. The top band covers the 4% of respondents with the highest family income. The next band covers a further 8–10% of respondents, and so on until we come to the poorest 10–11% of respondents in the last of our seven income bands.

The 1979 picture is quite an interesting one in its own right. The top band was markedly more Conservative than the next band, and Conservative voting declined steadily as we move down to the 50th percentile (band 4). Within the bottom 50%, however, income does not seem to differentiate the voters in any straightforward manner. The poorest band (the bottom 11%) were in fact more Conservative than people around the 50th percentile. We must of course be a little bit careful because these figures are based (particularly at the two extremes) on quite small numbers and will be subject to sampling error. Still, the story for 1979 seems fairly clear (and is confirmed by data from the October 1974 survey).

The data from 1987 yields a very different picture. All four of the top income bands have tended to abandon Labour for the Alliance while the bottom three bands, in contrast, have tended to maintain their support for Labour and to desert the Conservatives (again for the Alliance), particularly so in the case of the poorest band. The net result is of course a widening of the differentials (as measured by odds ratios). This conclusion is confirmed by loglinear analysis.[3]

There has, then, been quite a marked change between 1979 and 1987. The increased income inequality under the last two Conservative administrations goes with a clear change in the statistical association between income and vote. The lower bands are less inclined to the Conservatives than they used to be; the higher bands are less inclined to Labour. (One rather anomalous result is the fall in the level of Conservative support in the top income band. However, given the very small numbers in this band in the 1979 survey, it is probably wise to treat the 1979 figure as a sampling error.[4]

As with some of the other changes we have seen, however, we must ask whether this is simply due to selective mobility from one income band to another. The data of table 10.2 do not on their own prove that the increased inequality has *caused* the changed pattern of voting. Instead, we may have something analogous to the residualization of council housing. Most obviously, some left-wing manual workers (perhaps previously employed in traditional heavy industries) may have become unemployed and thus have moved from the middle or higher income bands to the lowest income bands. We may simply be witnessing a redistribution of Labour voters into different income bands analogous to the redistribution of Conservative voters into different housing categories.

The composition of the different bands may thus have changed, and table 10.3 shows that it has indeed, and in a quite dramatic way.

In table 10.3 we classify people according to their family's economic situation. Thus if either partner is in paid employment, we have allocated them to the employed category. If either partner is retired, and neither is in paid employment, we have allocated them to the retired category, and so on. Of course, in many cases, there will not be a partner, and the respondent is then straightforwardly allocated on the basis of his or her own economic situation.[5]

As we can see, there have been some quite major changes between 1979 and 1987 in the overall distribution of respondents. Thus in 1987 there were fewer families in the employed category than there had been in 1979, and there have been corresponding increases in the numbers of retired and unemployed.

These processes have particularly affected the lowest income bands, where the changes have been rather dramatic. Thus families with paid employment have almost completely disappeared from the lowest income band, which is now largely composed of the retired (mostly state pensioners) and the unemployed. Our figures probably overstate this change somewhat, since we are comparing after tax incomes in 1979 with before tax incomes in 1987.[7] Nevertheless, the direction of change is certainly correct. There can be little doubt that people on social security, state pensioners, and the unemployed are among those with the lowest incomes. The growth in their numbers must inevitably squeeze out some of the employed from the bottom 10%.

TABLE 10.3 Family Income and Economic Situation

Income band	Paid work	Retired	Unemployed	Student	Other		N
			1979				
1 (top)	91	8	0	2	0	101%	(63)
2	99	1	0	0	0	100%	(129)
3	98	1	1	0	0	100%	(393)
4	93	7	0	0	0	100%	(248)
5	82	15	1	0	2	100%	(293)
6	49	41	4	4	3	101%	(231)
7 (bottom)	54	30	3	7	6	100%	(168)
			1987				
1 (top)	92	4	1	3	0	100%	(136)
2	94	2	2	2	0	100%	(333)
3	93	5	1	1	1	101%	(793)
4	85	12	2	1	1	101%	(656)
5	67	24	5	1	3	100%	(559)
6	22	54	16	1	6	99%	(519)
7 (bottom)	7	62	21	3	7	100%	(322)

Sources: 1979 and 1987 cross-section surveys

Government statistics also show that it is the real incomes of people on state pensions which have most signally failed to keep up with the overall rise in national prosperity (Social Trends 1989).

TABLE 10.4 The Votes of People in the Two Lowest Income Bands

Families with members	Conservative	Labour	Alliance	Other		N
In paid work	34	50	16	0	100%	(113)
Retired	38	35	26	1	100%	(334)
Unemployed	12	69	17	2	100%	(115)
Other	26	46	26	1	99%	(106)

Source: 1987 cross-section survey, respondents in the lowest two income bands

As we can see from table 10.4, the unemployed are by far the most left-wing of the different groups on low income, followed by the people in paid employment, people looking after the home, and finally the retired. Both in 1979 and in 1987 the retired, despite their poverty, were fairly close to the national average in their support for the main political parties. We should also note in passing that the transition from paid employment to retirement, even though for most people it means a sharp reduction in income, does not seem to be associated with any major change in support for the political parties.

The question therefore arises whether we are simply observing selective recruitment to the ranks of the unemployed or political radicalization on the part of the unemployed.

Unemployment and party preference

The right way to proceed must be to carry out the same kind of analysis that we conducted with share and council house purchase. That is, we should ideally compare the voting patterns of people before and after they became unemployed with the corresponding patterns for people who were in work throughout. Unfortunately, as with council house purchase, the number of unemployed people in our panel study is too small for useful analysis, and we must therefore use recall data from the 1987 cross-section survey.

TABLE 10.5 Unemployment and Vote

Families with members:	1979	1983	1987
In paid work			
	49	50	47
	37	31	28
	14	19	25
	100%	100%	100%
	(1662)	(1555)	(1524)
Retired			
	49	51	47
	40	36	29
	11	13	24
	100%	100%	100%
	(736)	(703)	(658)
Unemployed			
	20	19	17
	70	67	68
	10	14	15
	100%	100%	100%
	(115)	(107)	(106)

Source: 1987 cross-section survey, people eligible to vote in 1979

Table 10.5 gives the voting histories of people from families in paid work, retired families, and unemployed families respectively. Some of the unemployed will have been out of work for more than the eight years covered by table 10.5, but for most their current period of unemployment will have begun under the two Conservative administrations.[7]

The results of table 10.5 also broadly parallel those of share and council house purchase. First, we see that it was not a random cross-section of the electorate that experienced unemployment. As we had expected, the unemployed were much more likely to have been Labour voters, and much less likely to have been Conservative voters, in 1979 than were people in work.

Marshall's suggestion of "selective recruitment to the ranks of the jobless" is certainly confirmed by our data. It does not however appear to be the whole story. Rather, there seems to be some degree of polarization in the voting behaviour of those in work and those out of work. Thus among people in work, Conservative voting holds up at nearly 50% in all three elections while Labour voting falls by nine points; similarly, among the retired, Conservative voting holds up while Labour voting falls by eleven points. Only among the unemployed does Labour voting hold up.

More rigorous analysis confirms the conclusion that the unemployed differed significantly from the other groups in their loyalty to Labour. Thus in table 10.6 we report the results of logit models analogous to those used in chapter 8. As we can see, the unemployment parameter is highly significant in the second model (four times its standard error) while the retired parameter is nowhere near significant.[8] In other words, people from retired families were indistinguishable from those in paid work in the way they changed their vote between 1979 and 1987, whereas the unemployed were clearly distinct.

TABLE 10.6 Logit Models of Vote and Unemployment

	Dependent Variable	
	Conservative vs. Non-Conservative	Labour vs. Non-Labour
Constant	0.71 (0.10)	0.51 (0.07)
1979 Vote:		
Conservative	0	0
Labour	1.87 (0.07)	−2.04 (0.09)
Liberal	1.35 (0.08)	−0.61 (0.13)
Other	2.04 (0.30)	−1.15 (0.19)
1987 Family Situation:		
Paid work	0	0
Retired	0.00 (0.07)	−0.01 (0.07)
Unemployed	0.42 (0.17)	−0.64 (0.15)
N	(2288)	(2288)

Note: Figures in brackets give standard errors.
Source: 1987 cross-section survey, respondents eligible to vote in 1979

Table 10.6 also suggests that the effects of unemployment on vote are rather larger than those we saw with house purchase on vote. Of course, we must be careful about drawing causal conclusions from these data, since we are relying on recall material. The same problem of course affected our analysis of council house purchase which we looked at in chapter 8, and it is striking that the measured effect of unemployment is more significant (in the statistical sense) than that of house purchase. While we cannot be certain in either case that there was a causal effect, the case for saying that unemployment has an effect on one's voting behaviour is clearly the stronger one.[9]

Unemployment and participation

Previous research has suggested that unemployment leads to political quiescence. If that is true, the political effects which the recall data indicate will be rather reduced by the lower turnout of the unemployed.

Respondents' reports to interviewers about their turnout at General Elections are notoriously unreliable. Respondents to the British Election Surveys have consistently reported much higher levels of turnout than the official results, usually in the order of ten points higher. As part of our research programme, we checked these reports against the official results. The party which someone votes for is of course secret, but official records are kept (and are available for public inspection) showing who actually turned up to vote. The results, which have been reported by Swaddle and Heath (1989), are rather encouraging. They indicate that much of the gap between the official results and the survey estimates of turnout can be explained by the limitations of the Electoral Register and by failure of the politically apathetic to respond to surveys. The actual amount of exaggeration by respondents to the British Election Survey proved to be rather small.

TABLE 10.7 Political Participation

	Not in the labour market	In paid work	Unemployed
Official turnout	84 (1418)	83 (2111)	73 (200)
Reported turnout	86 (1449)	87 (2169)	76 (208)
Contacted MP	26 (1119)	23 (1753)	18 (155)
Signed petition	65 (1180)	79 (1879)	70 (169)
Been on a demonstration	7 (1057)	16 (1713)	24 (152)
Joined protest group	6 (1039)	10 (1684)	9 (150)

Note: Figures in brackets give base frequencies.
Sources: official records; 1987 cross-section survey

In table 10.7 we give both the official data and our respondents' recall of their turnout.[10] As we can see, they give substantially the same results:

turnout was around ten points lower among the unemployed than it was among the rest of the electorate. (Note that in this analysis and the ones that follow in this section we look at individuals who were unemployed rather than at respondents from unemployed families.)

However, we should not too rapidly jump to the conclusion that the unemployed are politically quiescent. We also asked our respondents about various other forms of political participation. We asked: "Suppose a law was being considered by Parliament which you thought was really unjust and harmful. Which, if any, of the following things do you think you ought to do? And which of these things have you ever done? Contacted your MP, signed a petition, gone on a demonstration, joined a protest group."

As we can see, the unemployed were rather less likely to have signed a petition or contacted an MP, but they were more likely to have gone on a demonstration.

These results should not surprise us, since the unemployed will tend to have understandable reasons for choosing one kind of protest activity in preference to another. Most of them come from the industrial working class, and demonstrations and marches may be rather more in line with the political culture of the working class than are letters to MPs.

Similarly, we must ask whether the lower turnout of the unemployed is a consequence of unemployment or of the other characteristics which go with, but precede, unemployment.

As with our analyses of the effects of house purchase and so on, there are two strategies we can pursue; we can either conduct a longitudinal analysis of the same people over time, or we can employ multivariate modelling to control statistically for other relevant variables. Both techniques lead to the conclusion that unemployment per se has rather little effect on turnout.

Our first method uses recall data for the earlier years, and so in order to maintain comparability we have used respondents' reports of their turnout in 1987 as well. Table 10.8 shows that the people who were unemployed in 1987 reported low turnout in 1979 and 1983 as well. There is little sign here that the experience of unemployment has reduced levels of turnout. Rather, the data suggest that the kinds of people who become unemployed were less likely to turn out and vote in the first place. This is confirmed by our second method of analysis.

Our second method is to control statistically for the other variables which are known to be related to turnout. Crewe, Fox and Alt (1977) and Swaddle and Heath (1989) have looked at this question and come to very similar conclusions. Age, marital status, length of residence, and social class have all been found to have significant relationships with turnout: the young are less likely to turn out and vote, as are the single, new residents, and the working class. As it happens, the young, the single, and the working class are also more at risk of unemployment.

Our method, therefore, is to look at the relationship between turnout and unemployment, controlling for these other variables. For this analysis we can use the official records of turnout, and we restrict the analysis to the unemployed and those in paid work.

TABLE 10.8 Reported Turnout and Unemployment

	1979	1983	1987
People not in the labour market			
Voted	90	90	87
Did not vote	10	10	13
	100%	100%	100%
N	(1243)	(1229)	(1237)
People in paid work			
Voted	85	87	89
Did not vote	15	13	11
	100%	100%	100%
N	(1631)	(1620)	(1621)
Unemployed			
Voted	75	84	82
Did not vote	25	16	18
	100%	100%	100%
N	(138)	(137)	(137)

Source: 1987 cross-section survey, respondents eligible to vote in 1979

TABLE 10.9 Logit Model of Turnout

Constant	0.55 (0.05)
18–29	0
30–44	0.16 (0.07)
45–59	0.42 (0.08)
Old resident	0
New resident	−0.37 (0.08)
Married	0
Single	−0.17 (0.07)
Salariat	0
Intermediate classes	−0.15 (0.07)
Working class	−0.16 (0.07)
In paid work	0
Unemployed	−0.16 (0.10)
Not in labour market	−0.10 (0.08)
Chi^2	101.9
df	73
N	2441

Note: Figures in brackets give standard errors.
Source: 1987 cross-section survey, respondents aged 18–59

As we can see, there are the expected significant relationships between turnout and age, marital status, and length of residence. Social class does not quite reach statistical significance, but nor does unemployment.

We should note that the sign of the unemployment parameter is in the predicted direction, hinting that unemployment may reduce turnout. On the other hand, there is always the worry with this kind of statistical analysis that we have omitted other relevant variables (and that their inclusion would have further reduced the size and significance of the unemployment parameter). We must therefore, until a larger panel study becomes available, remain rather sceptical about the alleged tendency of unemployment to lead either to political quiescence in general or to low turnout in General Elections.

Embourgeoisement?

The unemployed, then, were already quite markedly inclined towards the Labour party before they became unemployed. And the balance of evidence favours the conclusion that the experience of unemployment has influenced their political behaviour too. They do not show the same tendency as the rest of the working class over the 1979–87 period to defect from Labour to the Alliance. Rather, they have generally remained loyal to Labour, and the rather small number who originally voted Conservative has declined yet further.

This interpretation, however, does not really conform to simple versions either of the political scientists' absolute income hypothesis or of the sociologists' relative income hypothesis. To be sure, there is some evidence in favour of both camps. The unemployed have almost certainly experienced large falls in their absolute standard of living. So, however, have new pensioners, and state pensioners in general have experienced a fall in their real incomes relative to the population as a whole over the last decade with few if any consequences for their voting behaviour.

To pursue this matter further we would need to have detailed evidence about the kinds of people with which the unemployed and the retired compare themselves. Our hypothesis is that the unemployed continue to compare themselves with people in work, while the pensioners compare themselves with other retired people.

Apart from the unemployed, there is little sign that any of the other groups have deviated significantly from the across-the-board swings in support for the parties. We might have expected to find that low-paid workers (who will presumably have benefited rather little from economic prosperity under the Conservatives) would have been more likely to defect from the Conservatives, while the better paid will have been more likely to swing to their support. But table 10.10 suggests that this has not happened.

As we can see, the unemployed stand out as the one group which maintained its Labour vote over the 1979–1987 period. Apart from this, there are hints that the retired were a little more likely to defect from the Conservatives to the Alliance. And among those in paid work, there are hints that it was the lowest paid, not the affluent, who were most likely to switch

TABLE 10.10 Voting Change 1979–87

Families with members:	Conservative	Labour	Other	N
Top two income bands				
in paid work	−2	−7	+10	(261)
3rd income band				
in paid work	−5	−11	+16	(459)
4th income band				
in paid work	−2	−8	+10	(354)
retired	−1	−11	+12	(65)
5th income band				
in paid work	0	−6	+7	(219)
retired	−4	−12	+16	(112)
Bottom two income bands				
in paid work	+1	−10	+9	(81)
retired	−4	−11	+15	(368)
unemployed	−6	0	+7	(78)

Source: 1987 cross-section survey, people eligible to vote in 1979

to the Conservatives (although none of these differences is near statistical significance). There is little sign of embourgeoisement here.

Notes

[1]Disposable income is defined as gross income minus income tax and employees' National Insurance contributions. Income after cash benefits and all taxes is defined as disposable income minus rates and indirect taxes (such as VAT, stamp duties, motor vehicle duties etc.). The data source for these calculations is the Family Expenditure Survey, and the unit of analysis is the household.

TABLE 10.11N Loglinear Models of the Relationship between Income, Vote and Election

Model	Deviance	df	p
1. Income, election, vote	345	32	0.000
2. Income by election, vote	331	26	0.000
3. Income by election, Income by vote	81	14	0.000
4. Income by election, Income by vote, Vote by election	37	12	0.000

Sources: 1979 and 1987 cross-section surveys

170   UNDERSTANDING POLITICAL CHANGE

[2]To be sure, political scientists have focused most of their attention on the rising living standards of the affluent workers in the middle income groups rather than of the lower income groups, witness the notorious embourgeoisement debate (Abrams, Rose and Hinden 1960; Goldthorpe et al 1968; Crewe 1973; Hope 1975; Kavanagh 1990; Heath 1990).

[3]Table 10.11N shows the results of a series of models analogous to those we fitted in the case of class and vote. As we can see, we must reject the hypothesis that the relationship between income and vote was the same in 1979 and 1987.

[4]Recall data from 1987 shows no sign that the top income band was particularly likely to defect from the Conservatives to the Alliance. Thus among those eligible to vote both in 1979 and 1987 in the top income band, the proportion voting Conservative remained constant at 70%, the proportion voting Labour fell six points to 6% and the proportion voting for other parties increased six points to 24%.

[5]The 1979 study uses fewer categories for measuring people's economic situation than does the 1987 study. We should note that in 1979 the disabled were included with the retired, whereas in 1987 the two categories were distinguished and we have felt it preferable to place the disabled in the "other" category if they were aged under 60. In both studies we have reallocated people aged 60 or over from the "other" category to the retired category. These are mainly women who had never had a job.

[6]The main problem is the poverty trap caused by high marginal rates of taxation as people move from unemployment to employment. For people caught in the poverty trap their ranking in the income distributions before and after tax will thus be somewhat different. Dilnot and Stark (1986) however show that the numbers involved are rather small.

[7]Some 71% of the unemployed had last held a paid job within five years, 15% within 5–10 years, 4% over 10 years ago, and 9% had never held a paid job.

[8]If we control for additional variables, namely class, father's class, tenure, region, qualifications, religion and ethnicity, the size of the unemployment parameter is somewhat reduced but remains over twice its standard error.

[9]It is not entirely clear why our results differ from those of Marshall and his colleagues. Marshall has pointed out to us that their measure of previous vote was far from ideal: their respondents were asked "Have you ever voted for another party at a general election?" but the way they voted at particular elections was not ascertained. It may be that this accounts for the discrepancy.

[10]The official records show whether a postal vote was issued to an elector and whether a (nonpostal) vote was recorded with respect to the register entry in question. We cannot ascertain whether the postal votes were actually returned, but we have assumed that they were. We should also note that, because of double entries in the electoral register, some respondents may have voted with respect to addresses other than the one issued to our interviewers.

Chapter 11

The Great Moving Right Show

One of the most influential conclusions about the 1979 election result was that there had been a sea-change in popular attitudes. In their treatments of the 1979 election, Sarlvik and Crewe (1983) and Robertson (1984) showed that public opinion had moved markedly to the right on issues such as nationalization and welfare spending in the years between 1974 and 1979, and it is likely that this played a significant part in Mrs Thatcher's first election victory. Sarlvik and Crewe estimated that the Conservatives gained 4.4 percentage points as a result of these shifts to the right (Sarlvik and Crewe 1983:195).

Various explanations can be put forward for this sea-change. It was too sudden and too large to be explained by social changes such as the contraction of the working class or the spread of owner-occupation, and so it almost certainly had some kind of political explanation. On the one hand it might have been a negative reaction to the experience of the Wilson and Callaghan administrations, which had presided over a series of strikes in nationalized industries and had delivered low economic growth. On the other hand, it might have been due to the positive attractions of Mrs Thatcher's political philosophy, which marked in some respects a break from previous Conservative thinking.

In a classic paper Stuart Hall described the Great Moving Right Show that took place after Mrs Thatcher became leader of the Conservative party in 1975 (Hall 1979; see also Jessop et al 1984, 1985 and Hall 1985) while Crewe and Searing (1988) have talked about Mrs Thatcher's crusade to change social values. As she herself remarked "I came to office with one deliberate intent. To change Britain from a dependent to a self-reliant society—from a give-it-to-me to a do-it-yourself nation; to a get-up-and-go instead of a sit-back-and-wait-for-it Britain" (quoted in Rentoul 1989).

Despite her subsequent victories at the polls, Mrs Thatcher does not seem to have had quite the same success with popular attitudes after 1979 as she perhaps had before. True, Ralf Dahrendorf has claimed that "Mrs Thatcher has, in her nine years as prime minister, probably effected a deeper change in social values than any other democratic politician in the post-war period" (Dahrendorf 1988). But in their analyses of British Social Attitudes and Gallup data respectively Curtice (1986) and Crewe and Searing (1989) have found that the electorate has in fact tended to shift back towards the left in recent years. Crewe has even gone so far as to talk of Mrs Thatcher's "crusade that failed".

Whether or not Mrs Thatcher's crusade to change values succeeded, there is another important possibility to consider. The Great Moving Right Show may have been important not so much in changing attitudes but in influencing votes. On conventional rational choice lines, if a party shifts position while the voters stay in the same place, patterns of voting can be expected to change. Downs' original rational choice theory assumed a one-dimensional political world (Downs 1957). However, it is now recognized that political attitudes have more of a two-dimensional (or indeed multi-dimensional) character. On the one hand there is the conventional left-right dimension which is concerned with economic issues such as equality, nationalization and the welfare state. And on the other there is a liberal-authoritarian dimension which largely cross-cuts the left-right one and which is concerned more with social issues such as law and order.

It was this liberal-authoritarian dimension which Hall seems to have had particularly in mind when he wrote about the Great Moving Right Show. Hall used the phrase "authoritarian populism" to describe the different ideological themes associated with the Great Moving Right Show, and he laid particular stress on notions like authority and standards:

> "[Thatcherism] is a particularly rich mix because of the resonant traditional themes—nation, family, duty, authority, standards, self-reliance—which have been effectively condensed into it. Here elements from many traditional ideologies . . . have been inserted into and woven together to make a set of discourses which are then harnessed to the practices of the radical right and the class forces they now aspire to represent" (Hall 1979:17).

This authoritarian populism is particularly interesting to the political scientist. Firstly, it is the ideological element which most clearly distinguishes Mrs Thatcher's beliefs from those of her predecessors as Conservative leader such as Edward Heath. An emphasis on the free market and on privatization is not distinctively Thatcherite. Edward Heath for example abolished retail price maintenance (a euphemism for price fixing) when he was President of the Board of Trade and on economic issues his 1970 manifesto looked quite like Mrs Thatcher's 1979 manifesto. Mr Heath may have changed his views subsequently, but it is not at all obvious that their economic philosophies— with their emphases on competition, reduced taxation and less government intervention—were initially all that different either from each other's or from traditional Conservative beliefs. Mrs Thatcher's moral philosophy, however, is very different from Mr Heath's.

Secondly, whereas Mrs Thatcher was probably moving away from the average voter by moving to the right on economic issues, she was moving closer to them on moral issues. For example, her preference for the ultimate deterrent of the death penalty is much more in tune with popular, grassroots opinion than with that of the educated liberal establishment. Her public views on race, too, are more in tune with popular opinion than those of her predecessors. Whereas Mr Heath sacked Enoch Powell for his River of Blood speech in 1968, Mrs Thatcher publicly went on record before the 1979 election on the dangers of being swamped by immigrants.

Now Mrs Thatcher's populism may not have changed people's attitudes, but it may have changed their votes. It may have enabled her to win votes from groups outside the liberal establishment, in particular perhaps from traditional working-class voters. The Great Moving Right Show may thus have contributed to a realignment of British politics, foregoing support from the educated but making up for these losses by capturing so-called working-class authoritarians.

Attitudes in the electorate

In assessing these theories, it is important to recognize the multi-dimensional character of social and political values. Issues like privatization and the free market can be thought of as belonging to the conventional left-right dimension around which British politics has largely been organized in the postwar period. Other left-right issues include unemployment and inflation, economic inequality, trade unions, and government spending. Attitudes towards these different issues tend to go together. A major social basis of this left-right dimension is social class, and hence it is the salariat and the petty bourgeosie that tends to be furthest to the right on these issues. Indeed, it may be sensible to regard attitudes towards these issues as reflections, in part, of class interests.

Issues like the death penalty, on the other hand, belong to a different dimension. Attitudes towards the death penalty have more in common with attitudes towards race and immigration than they do with nationalization, and their social basis is education, not class. In particular, it is the least educated members of the electorate (who are of course also concentrated in the working class) who are most likely to adopt authoritarian attitudes towards crime, race or the family.

These two dimensions become clear from table 11.1, which show the results of a factor analysis of selected items from the 1987 survey.[1] We have excluded issues to do with defence and the environment from this analysis, and will turn to them in the next chapter.

As we can see, issues like unemployment, redistribution and nationalization are central to the first, left-right dimension whereas the death penalty and race are central to the second. A number of issues like welfare benefits and trade unions link to both dimensions, while other issues like abortion and pornography are weakly linked to either. If we carried out a more elaborate

TABLE 11.1 Factor Analysis of Social and Political Attitudes

	Factor 1	Factor 2
Create jobs	0.73	0.01
Redistribute income	0.70	−0.01
Get rid of poverty	0.65	0.06
Put money into NHS	0.65	0.00
Nationalize/privatize companies	0.60	0.11
Welfare benefits gone too far	0.54	0.32
Introduce stricter TU legislation	0.41	0.39
Give workers more say	0.40	0.03
Death penalty	0.00	0.77
Stiffer sentences	−0.07	0.74
Equal opportunities for blacks and Asians	0.20	0.61
Give more aid to poor countries	0.20	0.57
Equal opportunities for women	0.21	0.29
Sex in films	0.03	0.22
Abortion on NHS	−0.04	0.17
Eigen value	3.41	1.84
Variance explained	22.70	12.30

Source: 1987 cross-section survey

analysis, we would find that these issues divide into a number of sub-dimensions. For example, attitudes towards abortion and pornography might be better treated as a separate subdimension, although one that is somewhat more closely related to the liberal-authoritarian one than to the left-right dimension.

Overall, these two dimensions largely cross-cut each other and have rather different social bases.[2] Their relationships with different aspects of social structure are shown in table 11.2.[3]

As we can see, social class (and class-related variables) dominates the analysis of the left-right dimension. Left-wing attitudes are predictably more common among people from the working class or from working-class origins, renting council houses, belonging to trade unions, and living in the North of England. However, we should also note that the young are significantly more left-wing than the old, and that women are more left-wing than men.

Education is unrelated to left-right attitudes, but it dominates the analysis of the liberal-authoritarian dimension. The only other significant association is with religion, members of the other religions being more liberal than members of the established churches or people with no religion.[4] Perhaps surprisingly, age and class do not have significant relationships with authoritarianism once we have controlled for education. Of course, older people tend to have less education than younger people and the working class tend to have less education than the salariat. So it remains true that older people and working-class people are in general more authoritarian. What the regression

TABLE 11.2 Regression Analysis of Attitudes towards Left–Right and Liberal–Authoritarian Issues

	Dependent variable	
Independent variables	Left–Right scale	Liberal–Authoritarian scale
Class	0.20**	−0.04
Father's class	0.13**	−0.03
Housing tenure	0.13**	−0.02
TU membership	0.07**	0.02
Region	0.10**	0.00
Education	0.01	−0.28**
Churches of England and Scotland	0.04*	−0.01
Other Churches	−0.05*	−0.08**
Age	0.14**	0.03
Sex	0.06**	0.04
R²	0.17	0.11
N	2921	2647

*Significant at the 0.05 level.
**Significant at the 0.01 level.
Source: 1987 cross-section survey

analysis does, however, is to suggest that it is not age or class in itself that leads to authoritarianism, but the lack of education that these people have received.[5]

Changing attitudes

Table 11.3 brings together in summary form the changes in attitudes towards the main issues on the left-right dimension for the 1974–1987 period.[6]

As Sarlvik and Crewe have demonstrated, there were marked shifts between 1974 and 1979 in attitudes towards nationalization and welfare benefits.[7] None of the other changes between 1974 and 1979 is statistically significant, however. Rather than a general sea-change of attitudes, there seem to have been rather specific shifts in public opinion. Perhaps we should think of them as currents running in the direction of privatization and self reliance.

The years since 1979 also present a complex pattern. As Crewe and Searing's evidence suggested, the move back to the left has been quite striking on the issue of welfare benefits.[8] Here it would seem that Mrs Thatcher is increasingly out of touch with public opinion, and her crusade has surely failed. There are similar moves to the left on industrial democracy and trade union legislation, and rather lesser ones (at least in absolute terms) on poverty and the NHS. On the other hand, there have been no major changes in attitudes towards nationalization or the redistribution of income and wealth.

TABLE 11.3 Changing Left–Right Attitudes

% agreeing that the government should:	October 1974	1979	1983	1987
Redistribute income and wealth to ordinary working people	54	52	48	50
Spend more money to get rid of poverty	84	80	81	86
Nationalize more companies	30	16	16	16
Privatize some companies	20	38	38	31
Not introduce stricter laws to regulate TU's	—	16	32	33
Give workers more say in running places where they work	58	55	68	76
Put more money into the NHS	84	87	85	90
% Agreeing that:				
Welfare benefits have not gone too far	22	17	28	34

Source: BES cross-section surveys

The difficulty with interpreting these changes is of course that the world has been changing around the electorate. Thus on the public ownership of industry, 41% of the electorate in 1979 favoured the status quo, while in 1987 48% did so. But the status quo of 1987 was a very different one with many fewer nationalized industries. As we reported in chapter 8, British Gas, British Telecom, British Airways and so on had moved into the private sector. It would surely be fair to conclude from these data that Mrs Thatcher had secured public acceptance for her programme of privatization. In this sense her crusade had succeeded.

This problem of the world changing around the electorate applies to many of the other issues too. Thus the two Conservative administrations put through quite an extensive programme of trade union legislation; the eligibility rules for welfare benefits were changed; income inequality increased.

On some of these issues, therefore, like trade union legislation, poverty, and the NHS it is possible that the electorate, rather than moving to the left, has simply stayed in the same place. Their changed responses to our questions may simply reflect the changing situation they face. Either way we would agree that Mrs Thatcher failed in her attempts to radicalize the electorate on these issues, but we ought to be more cautious about claims that the electorate has actually moved to the left.

It could be argued, moreover, that there has been public acceptance of the increase in inequality just as there has been for the programme of privatization. As we saw in chapter 10, inequality has increased under Mrs Thatcher, with the top 1% making substantial gains. But the data in table 11.3 give little indication that the electorate has reacted against this.[9] On the two rather fundamental issues of public ownership and inequality, then, Mrs Thatcher seems to have been rather more successful.

Turning next to the liberal-authoritarian dimension, there are a number of relevant questions which were asked regularly from 1974 to 1987, and these are collected together in table 11.4. There are no major shifts to the right like that on nationalization, although on most of the items there were movements of a couple of points to the right between 1974 and 1979.

TABLE 11.4 Changing Liberal-Authoritarian Attitudes

% agreeing that:	October 1974	1979	1983	1987
The right to show nudity and sex in films and magazines has gone too far	63	65	62	65
The availability of abortion on the NHS has gone too far	40	41	27	28
The attempts to give equal opportunities to blacks have gone too far	26	28	18	28
The government should not give more aid to poor countries	46	47	—	42
Britain should bring back the death penalty	—	69	56	74
People who break the law should be given stiffer sentences	95	90	77	80

Source: BES cross-section surveys

The period since 1979 is again a rather confused one, with no very clear pattern emerging. Certainly, there is no evidence that the electorate has generally followed Mrs Thatcher in the direction of authoritarian populism. On abortion and foreign aid the electorate seems to have moved away from the right, and on most of the other items it is probably safest to conclude that there has been little real change.[10]

The effects on voting

We turn now to consider whether Mrs Thatcher's distinctive philosophy brought distinctive patterns of support for the Conservative party. For these purposes let us distinguish between the Free Market Right and the Author-itarian Right. We define the former as people who were in favour of "more privatization of companies by government" and the latter as people who thought that "attempts to give equal opportunities to black people and Asians in Britain" had gone too far. (We have chosen these two questions because they are ones on which there is a high degree of methodological consistency over time, and because they have been the most politicized items from the two dimensions).[11] The Free Market Right and the Authoritarian Right overlap to some extent, and this gives us a third group which we can term the Consistent Right.

TABLE 11.5 Social Class and the Right

	Consistent Right	Free Market Right	Authoritarian Right	Centre and Left		
Salariat	12	29	13	47	101%	(990)
Routine nonmanual	9	22	16	53	100%	(689)
Petty bourgeoisie	16	28	16	39	99%	(306)
Foremen, Technicians	10	19	17	54	100%	(213)
Working class	8	14	26	53	101%	(1247)

Source: 1987 cross-section survey

Table 11.5 shows that the Free Market Right (and the Consistent Right) was, as expected, much more numerous in the petty bourgeoisie and the salariat than it was, for example, in the working class. Conversely, the Authoritarian Right was much more numerous in the working class than in the salariat (probably for reasons to do with lack of education rather than with class per se, as we explained earlier). Just as the sale of council houses gave the Conservatives the chance to win votes from groups normally associated with the Labour party, so appeals to the Authoritarian Right would seem likely to threaten Labour's strongholds.

In table 11.6 we then chart the voting behaviour of these groups from 1974 to 1987. A clear pattern emerges. Firstly, we see that the Conservatives were much stronger throughout among the Free Market Right and the Consistent Right; Labour was stronger among the Left and Centre; and the votes of the Authoritarian Right were more evenly distributed between the three parties (although as their working-class character befits, they tended more towards Labour than to the Conservatives).

As we would also expect, there were a number of across-the-board changes over time. In all four categories, for example, the Liberal vote fell in 1979 but then recovered in 1983.

It is, however, the deviations from these across-the-board changes which are particularly interesting. And the most striking deviation is the success of the Conservatives among the Free Market Right and the Consistent Right. Here they increased their share of the vote quite markedly between 1974 and 1987. And it would appear that they did so largely at the expense of the Liberals, who did not make the gains here that would have been expected given their overall performance.

Conversely, the Conservatives merely held their own among the Authoritarian Right and lost slightly among the Left and Centre, while the Liberals gained substantially at Labour's expense. Rather surprisingly, Labour's

TABLE 11.6 The Changing Vote of the Right

	October 1974	1979	1983	1987
Consistent Right				
Conservative	63	80	74	83
Labour	9	10	8	4
Other	28	10	18	13
	100%	99%	99%	100%
	(126)	(184)	(238)	(317)
Free Market Right				
Conservative	65	70	71	77
Labour	10	15	7	6
Other	25	15	22	17
	100%	100%	100%	100%
	(253)	(418)	(990)	(687)
Authoritarian Right				
Conservative	35	39	37	36
Labour	47	44	41	38
Other	18	17	22	26
	100%	100%	100%	100%
	(358)	(252)	(350)	(572)
Left, Centre				
Conservative	27	27	26	25
Labour	51	56	43	45
Other	21	17	31	30
	99%	100%	100%	100%
	(1218)	(686)	(1609)	(1623)

Source: BES cross-section surveys

performance was much of a muchness in all four groups, their share of the vote falling by between 4 and 9 points.

We must be careful in interpreting these results. They are of course based not on a panel study but on four successive cross-section surveys. This means that there is plenty of scope for selective mobility between the different categories, and some of the increase in Conservative voting among the Free Market and Consistent Right in 1979 could have been due therefore to Conservative voters becoming more right wing in their attitudes rather than right-wing voters switching to the Conservatives. However, this can hardly explain the changes (and, in the case of the Authoritarian Right, the lack of change) after 1979.

It seems reasonably safe to conclude, therefore, that authoritarian populism per se failed to gain the Conservatives votes.[12] It was among people who favoured privatization that the Conservatives gained. Authoritarians who did not favour privatization showed no sign of moving to the Conservatives.

These results have interesting parallels with those we saw in chapter 8 on share and council house purchase. There, using the 1983–87 panel study, we found that it was among existing share-holders not among the new recruits to popular capitalism that the Conservatives gained votes, while it was the Alliance that gained votes among council house purchasers at Labour's expense. The picture, then, is one of the Conservatives strengthening their position in their existing strongholds, whether defined in economic or ideological terms, rather than making converts in foreign territory.

This should not perhaps be so surprising after all. While it may be Mrs Thatcher's authoritarian populism that particularly annoys the educated establishment, the parties have not openly campaigned for votes on issues such as the death penalty. The differences between the parties have been more covert than overt. Even issues of immigration and racial equality have been treated in a somewhat bipartisan way in the House of Commons (if not in local authorities). Labour, when in office, had a policy not entirely dissimilar from the Conservatives of restricting immigration, while the Conservatives have not actually repealed Labour's race relations legislation. The electorate could be forgiven for seeing little difference between Conservative and Labour in their stands on liberal-authoritarian issues. In contrast, little needs to be said about the perceived differences between the parties on nationalization and privatization.

Diagram 11.7 brings out the differences in the perceived positions of the parties rather clearly. We asked our respondents to mark, on an eleven-point scale, where they perceived the parties to stand on issues such as nationalization and privatization and law and order. As we can see, the parties were perceived to be rather close together on law and order. Indeed, of all the issues we asked about, this is the one on which they were perceived to be closest.

Conversely, the parties were perceived to be much further apart on the issue of nationalization and privatization, and it was in fact the issue on which the perceived gap was greatest between Labour and Conservative.

In general, the greater the perceived difference between the parties on an issue, the stronger is the relationship between the electorate's attitudes to the issue and their vote. Thus, of the issues we covered in these position scales, attitudes towards nationalization were most strongly associated with vote and attitudes towards law and order were least strongly associated with vote. This proposition might seem something of a truism but there is an equally plausible rival hypothesis, namely that the issues which the electorate deems most important will be most strongly associated with they way they cast their votes. The evidence, however, does not favour the latter hypothesis.

Table 11.8 shows the perceived differences between the parties on the issues, their perceived importance, and the strength of the relationship between the respondents' attitudes and vote.[13] There can be little doubt that perceived differences win the day.

DIAGRAM 11.7 Perceived Positions of the Parties

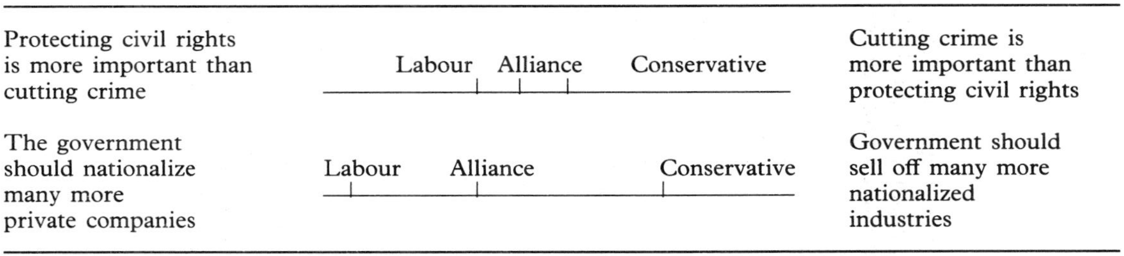

| Protecting civil rights is more important than cutting crime | | Labour Alliance Conservative | Cutting crime is more important than protecting civil rights |
| The government should nationalize many more private companies | Labour Alliance | Conservative | Government should sell off many more nationalized industries |

Source: 1987 cross-section survey

TABLE 11.8 Perceived Differences, Perceived Importance and Voting

	Perceived difference between Conservative and Labour parties	% Saying the issue was extremely important in deciding about voting	Relationship between respondents' attitude and Conservative vs. Labour voting
Nuclear Defence	5.9	39	0.19
Unemployment/inflation	4.0	69	0.17
Health and Social Services	4.1	59	0.17
Nationalization/privatization	6.2	19	0.22
Law and order	1.9	60	0.04

Sources: 1987 cross-section survey (columns 1 and 3), 1983–87 panel study (column 2)

We cannot of course be certain about the causal processes that lie behind these findings, but it does seem plausible to suppose that Mrs Thatcher's authoritarian populism failed to win converts because it simply was not perceived by the electorate as being anything like as distinctive as her radical programmes on privatization of industry.

Notes

[1] For this analysis we have imposed a two-factor solution. The factor loadings shown are those after rotation. The questions used for the analysis are questions 30b, 38b, 33b, 33d, 36a (combined with 36b), 43a, 37a, 37b, 121n, 121l, 43f, 38d, 43b, 43c, 43j. Don't knows have been included with the middle responses.

[2] If we carry out an oblique rotation we find that the two resulting factors have a correlation of 0.23. The two indexes which we use as dependent variables in our regression analyses have a correlation of 0.19. We should note however that the correlation between the indices is higher among more educated respondents, reflecting their tendency towards greater ideological consistency.

[3] The two dependent variables are Likert scales measuring left-right and liberal-authoritarian attitudes respectively. Scores on the two scales have been standardized with mean of 0 and standard deviation of 1. For the left-right scale we used the questions on job creation, redistribution, poverty, NHS spending and nationalization. Cronbach's alpha for this five-item scale was 0.73. For the liberal-authoritarian scale we used the questions on the death penalty, stiffer sentences, racial equality and foreign aid. Cronbach's alpha for this four-item scale was 0.67.

We have treated the independent variables as follows. Class and father's class are treated as five-point scales ordered from working class, foremen, routine nonmanual, salariat and petty bourgeoisie. Tenure is a three-point scale ordered council tenant, other and home owner. TU membership is a dummy variable distinguishing members from all nonmembers. Region is a dummy variable distinguishing Scotland, Wales and the North from the Midlands and South. Qualifications is a seven-point scale ordered none, other, CSE etc., O level, A level, professional, degree. Religion is made up of two dummy variables distinguishing members of the Church of England and Church of Scotland, and members of the other Churches from people with no religion or not attending church. Sex is a dummy variable.

[4] Members of the other religions include Sikhs, Muslims and so on who might be expected to take liberal views on questions of racial equality. We should also note that religion has a significant relationship with attitudes towards abortion. See table 11.9N.

TABLE 11.9N Regression Analysis of Attitudes towards Abortion

Independent variables	Standardized regression coefficients
Class	0.01
Father's class	− 0.03
Housing tenure	− 0.04
TU membership	0.02
Region	− 0.07**
Education	− 0.04
Churches of England and Scotland	0.04
Other Churches	0.17**
Age	0.11**
Sex	0.08**
R^2	0.06
N	2980

*Significant at the 0.05 level
**Significant at the 0.01 level
Source: 1987 cross-section survey

[5] We must emphasize too that these results are merely suggestive not conclusive of causality. The interpretation of associations with age is of course particularly problematic because of the need to disentangle life-cycle, period and cohort effects. Education is also not straightforward since the rapid expansion of education in the past thirty years means that the meaning of the different categories may not be constant over time. In short, we cannot be sure that the liberalism displayed by the rather select group of highly-educated older people in our sample will be shown by the less select group of young highly educated people when they age. As ever, cross-sectional analysis cannot prove causality.

[6] In interpreting these changes we should remember, first, that design effects will tend to increase the confidence intervals and, second, that the particularly low response rate in 1979 will have introduced additional response bias.

[7] Sarlvik and Crewe used the questions 1974, 22a and 1979 22a on social services and benefits to demonstrate the move to the right on the welfare state. The difficulty with this question is that "social services and benefits" include a rather large range of items. Respondents may have had rather different items in mind and may not have changed their attitudes equally on all of them. Comparing the results of the questions on welfare benefits and NHS spending shows clearly that different trends may occur with regard to different elements of the welfare state.

[8] There is however some interesting evidence from Harris and Seldon (1987) which, while confirming the shift back to the left in recent years, suggests that attitudes may not have moved all the way back to where they were in the 1960s (see Harris and Seldon 1987, table 3).

[9] There are hints of differences in the electorate's responses to poverty and to redistribution, with slightly increased support for spending to get rid of poverty but slightly reduced support for redistribution towards ordinary working people. There is nothing logically inconsistent in this: the electorate may be unhappy with the plight of the poor but be unconcerned about the increased inequality between the top 1% and the middle ranks of ordinary working people. On the other hand, given all the problems of measurement error and sampling error, it would be unwise to read very much into these differences.

[10] There are several methodological problems that should be mentioned. First, three-point scales not five-point scales were used in 1983. Three-point scales tend to encourage respondents to use the midpoint, and therefore some of the differences between 1983 and the other years may simply be artifactual. Secondly, the questions on the death penalty and on stiffer sentences were asked in the self-completion supplement in 1987, and as Appendix III shows this introduces additional response bias. Thirdly, there have been some wording changes between the surveys, particularly in the case of the question on the death penalty.

[11] A preferable strategy would be to use scales to measure these two dimensions over time, rather than to use individual questions, but unfortunately there has not been enough methodological consistency in question wording and so on in the case of the main liberal-authoritarian items to make this possible.

[12] In table 3.3 we saw that the parameter for race was rather higher in 1987 than it had been in previous years, and this gives a hint that authoritarian populism may have been more influential in 1987 than it had been before. However, table 3.3 does not suggest that race has generally been more important in the three elections when Mrs Thatcher led the Conservative party.

[13] The perceived differences between the parties are the differences between the mean scores of the Labour and Conservative parties on questions 23B and C, 28B and C, 29B and C, 34B and C and 39B and C in the 1987 cross-section survey. The percentages for perceived importance come from question 12A

of the 1987 panel wave. Note that the percentages for unemployment and inflation have been combined, while the item on health and social services does not mention taxation.

The measures of strength of relationship are the regression parameters in a series of bivariate logistic regressions. The same conclusions are reached if a multivariate analysis is conducted.

Chapter 12

Green and Nuclear Issues

We have not so far had anything to say about green and nuclear issues—nuclear disarmament, nuclear power and the protection of the environment. They do not belong squarely either to the left-right or to the liberal-authoritarian dimension, but nonetheless may be of some political importance. Certainly, it has been generally accepted that Labour lost votes both in 1983 and 1987 because of its anti-nuclear defence policies, and table 11.8 at the end of the last chapter showed that only nationalization and privatization ranked ahead of nuclear defence in strength of relationship with voting.

Green and nuclear issues may also be of more general significance for understanding long-run developments in contemporary politics. They have been regarded by many writers as key elements of the New Politics (Dalton 1988) and they have been closely associated with the rise of new political movements and parties such as the peace movement and the Green party in Germany (and in Britain in 1989 in the Euro-elections). Inglehart and Rabier (1986) for example have talked about the shift from class-based politics to quality of life politics, and protection of the environment figures prominently in many people's assessment of the quality of life. It is widely assumed, therefore, that these quality of life issues are likely to remain important elements of late twentieth-century politics, and indeed might become the basis for some political realignment, either through the emergence of new Green parties or through changes in the policies and patterns of social support for established parties.

A key finding from Germany, which has heavily influenced interpretations of the green phenomenon, is that Greens tend to be younger, highly educated, and middle class (Bürklin, 1981, 1985, 1987). Many writers have also assumed that these quality of life issues do not appeal to the traditional working class in the way that they do to the middle-class intelligentsia. This has led Lipset for example to talk about two different Lefts—one composed of a quality of life-oriented intelligentsia, the other of the traditional, economically-oriented working class. He writes:

"Thus there are now two Lefts, the "materialist" and the "post-materialist", which are rooted in different classes. A conflict of interest has emerged between them with respect to the consequences of policies that affect economic growth. The materialist Left wants an ever-growing pie so that the less privileged can have more, while the postmaterialists are more interested in the quality of life. . . . Both Lefts are often in the same party (Democratic, Social Democratic, even Communist, as in Italy), but they have different views and interests. . . . The New Politics intelligentsia does not like trade unions, which, like business, it considers "materialistic" rather than "public interested". Some workers move right as a result, to more conservative groupings, which espouse growth, favour a competitive mobile society, and retain beliefs in traditional social values. The Left, however, picks up support from the growing ranks of the intelligentsia. Thus, the correlations between class and party voting have been reduced" (Lipset 1981:510–11).

While Lipset advanced this analysis as a general account of political change in advanced post-industrial societies, it clearly has a great deal of relevance to the British situation. It suggests that there may be an important trade-off for the Labour party: the more recruits it tries to win from the New Left, the more votes it will lose from the Old Left.

Quality of life issues per se did not feature very prominently in the 1987 election, and became much more salient politically in the 1989 Euro-elections when the Green party obtained an unprecedented 15% of the vote in Britain. More visible in 1983 and 1987 were the issues of nuclear defence and nuclear power, issues which have of course been closely associated with the Green party in Germany.

In both General Elections the Labour manifesto proposed that a future Labour government would adopt a non-nuclear defence policy, for example phasing out Polaris, cancelling Trident and removing American nuclear missiles from British soil. The 1987 manifesto was rather less strident than the 1983 manifesto and did not commit itself to "carry through in the lifetime of the next parliament our non-nuclear defence policy" as it had done in 1983. But it still said quite clearly that "We say that it is time to end the nuclear pretence and to ensure a rational conventional defence policy for Britain."

The Conservatives were equally clearly in favour of retaining nuclear weapons: "We will retain our independent nuclear deterrent and modernise it with Trident." And the Alliance policy, reached after some compromises between the Liberals and the SDP, lay somewhere in between: "we accept the obligations of NATO, including the presence of Allied bases and nuclear weapons on British soil . . ." but "we would be prepared to include Britain's nuclear weapons in disarmament negotiations".

There was also a big difference between the parties in their policies on nuclear power. But all the parties were in favour of protecting the green belt and the countryside, reducing pollution, and conserving wild-life.

We begin this chapter, as with the preceding one, by looking at the structure of attitudes. First, how do the green issues fit into the two-dimensional structure described in chapter 11 and what tradeoffs do they involve?

The structure of attitudes

We have a number of questions in the 1987 survey which measure nuclear and green issues, covering nuclear disarmament, nuclear power and protection of the countryside. Our first step is to conduct a factor analysis of these items as we did in chapter 11 for the left-right and liberal-authoritarian dimensions.[1]

TABLE 12.1 Factor Analysis of 'Green' Attitudes

	Factor 1	Factor 2
U.S. missiles	0.73	0.00
British missiles	0.76	0.01
Nuclear disarmament	0.70	0.03
Nuclear power stations	0.72	−0.09
Risks of nuclear power	0.68	−0.10
Building in country areas	0.00	0.49
Damage to countryside	−0.04	0.78
Development in countryside	−0.00	0.80
Protection of wildlife	−0.08	0.63
Eigen value	2.64	1.86
Percentage of variance explained	29.30	20.70

Source: 1987 cross-section survey

We immediately obtain an interesting and important result. The green issues we have mentioned do not form a single green dimension but instead fall onto two quite separate dimensions. The basis of the two dimensions is also quite clear—one is nuclear and one non-nuclear.[2] The results, shown in table 12.1, are remarkably clear cut. Attitudes towards nuclear power clearly go with attitudes towards nuclear disarmament, not with attitudes towards the countryside. Conversely, attitudes towards industrial damage to the countryside, development, building houses in country areas, and protection of wildlife all go together and not with nuclear power.

We can construct attitude scales as we did before for the left-right dimension. The five nuclear questions prove to form a good scale with a high level of internal consistency. With only four items the countryside scale is not quite so satisfactory but is still acceptable on the usual criteria.[3] The two scales moreover have a rather low correlation of 0.09.

We thus have two quite distinct and empirically unrelated types of green issue. This suggests that there are also likely to be two rather different sorts of green voter, and such proves to be the case.

TABLE 12.2 Regression Analysis of Attitudes towards Nuclear and Countryside Issues

Independent variables	Dependent variable	
	Nuclear scale	Countryside scale
Class	0.04	−0.06*
Father's class	0.07**	0.01
Housing tenure	0.05*	−0.08**
TU membership	0.06**	0.01
Region	0.04*	−0.14**
Education	−0.06**	−0.12**
Church of England or Scotland	−0.08**	0.02
Other Churches	0.05**	−0.04*
Age	0.09**	0.04*
Sex	0.14**	−0.04*
R^2	0.06	0.07
N	2666	2623

*Significant at the 0.05 level
**Significant at the 0.01 level
Source: 1987 cross-section survey

The similarities and differences in the social bases of nuclear and green attitudes become very clear from table 12.2. Here we report the results of regression analyses, again following the same procedures as for table 11.2. Table 12.2 shows that region, education and housing tenure are most strongly associated with green attitudes towards the countryside. In this case it is the owner-occupiers, the well-educated and Southerners who are most likely to favour protection of the countryside. As Lipset suggested, it is the middle-class intelligentsia who are most "postmaterialist" in the sense of favouring protection of the countryside at the expense of industrial development.

It is a rather different pattern, however, when we turn to nuclear issues. Sex, age and religion prove to have the strongest relationship with attitudes towards the nuclear issues. People who are opposed to nuclear weapons and nuclear power thus tend to be young, female and irreligious. They are not especially middle class, and are in fact more likely to have come from working-class origins and to be council tenants.

We also note that, both with nuclear and countryside attitudes, the relationships with social factors are rather weaker than they were in the case of left-right or liberal-authoritarian attitudes. (This is clear both from the coefficients and from the variance explained.) This suggests that these various green attitudes are less anchored in the social structure, and may perhaps be more volatile and open to change. We return to this point later.

This analysis of the structural sources of nuclear and countryside attitudes also suggests that the conflict of interest, or at least of attitudes, between the anti-nuclear left and the egalitarian left may be rather less than previous commentators had supposed. While, as Lipset had correctly observed, the protection of the countryside appeals to different sorts of people from traditional left-wing economic policies and may involve a fundamental conflict of interest, it is not at all obvious that anti-nuclear policies need be so damaging to traditional left-wing groups and concerns. Indeed, it could be argued (and no doubt has been within the Labour party) that the two are complementary, not antagonistic: it could be argued that reliance on nuclear power and nuclear weapons is damaging to working-class interests in that the former reduces the demand for traditional working-class jobs in the coal industry while the latter relies on the purchase of American-made weapons rather than British ones which give employment to the indigenous working class.

In line with this interpretation we find that the social characteristics of anti-nuclear voters are relatively similar to those of traditional left-wing voters (as measured by the left-right scale in chapter 11).[4] Similarly, attitudes towards the nuclear issues correlate positively and relatively highly with attitudes towards the left-right dimension, while attitudes towards the countryside issues correlate weakly and negatively.[5] In other words, people who are anti-nuclear also tend to be quite left-wing on economic issues, while people who are pro-countryside tend if anything to be slightly right-wing on economic issues. And this is rather good news for a party like the Labour party which attempted to combine anti-nuclear with left-wing economic policies. The dilemmas and trade-offs look as though they may be rather less than had been supposed.

Changes over time

Unfortunately, we have rather few questions on nuclear or countryside issues which were asked in previous election studies, and we cannot attempt to construct scales for the earlier studies as we can with the 1987 survey. We have to make do as best we can with isolated questions.

In 1964, 1966 and 1970 Butler and Stokes did ask a question on nuclear disarmament. This question was dropped by Sarlvik and Crewe, who asked nothing about nuclear disarmament in any of the three studies of February 1974, October 1974 and May 1979 (no doubt because the issue had largely dropped off the political agenda). Some new questions on nuclear weapons were then introduced in 1983, and were repeated in 1987 together with the old Butler and Stokes question on nuclear disarmament, a question which we replicated in 1987.

Butler and Stokes did not, however, look at issues to do with nuclear power or the countryside, which were not on the political agenda at that time. It is not until 1974 that we have a question on protection of the countryside and it was not until 1979 that the investigators added a question on nuclear power.

Table 12.3 shows how attitudes towards these various questions have changed over time.[6]

TABLE 12.3 Changing Attitudes to Green Issues

	All	Conservative	Liberal/ Alliance	Labour	Con:Lab log odds
			% thinking that Britain should have nothing to do with nuclear weapons		
1964	10	4	14	16	1.5
1966	14	7	14	19	1.1
1970 (panel)	15	9	16	22	1.0
1987	15	3	16	36	2.9

% opposing expansion of nuclear power

	All	Conservative	Liberal/ Alliance	Labour	Con:Lab log odds
1979	29	28	40	36	0.4
1983	29	18	36	54	1.7
1987	40	23	48	66	1.9

% favouring greater protection of the countryside

	All	Conservative	Liberal/ Alliance	Labour	Con:Lab log odds
October 1974	86	90	88	85	−0.5
1979	87	91	90	87	−0.4
1987	79	81	85	74	−0.4

Sources: BES cross-section surveys except 1970, where the 1966–70 panel is used

Among the electorate as a whole, attitudes towards nuclear defence do not appear to have changed very much over the last twenty years. The 1987 pattern is indeed very close to that which Butler and Stokes found in 1966. A much clearer long-run change emerges however when we look at the extent to which the voters for the three parties differ in their attitudes towards nuclear weapons. As we can see, the gap between the three sets of voters was far wider in 1987 than it had been in any of the three Butler and Stokes surveys, the Labour:Conservative gap widening from 13 points in 1970 to 33 in 1987.[7]

Somewhat similar results emerge when we turn to nuclear power. Because of changes in question wording we have to be careful about the changes in overall totals between 1979 and 1983. We would be unwise to conclude from these data that public attitudes had become more hostile towards nuclear power. But once again, as with nuclear weapons, we find that the polarization between Conservative, Labour and Alliance voters on nuclear power was considerably higher in 1983 and 1987 than it had been in 1979, the Conservative:Labour gap moving from eight points to a massive forty-three points.

Finally, we come to the countryside issues. This time we find very little change, either overall or in polarization between the voters. A change in question wording means that the fall in the overall percentage favouring protection of the countryside cannot be interpreted. But it is very clear, both from the responses to this and to the other countryside questions, that the voters for the three parties are not polarized on countryside issues as they are on the left-right and nuclear issues.[8]

There can be very little doubt, then, that the nuclear issues, on which the party policies and manifestos became polarized, are also the ones on which the voters for the three parties became polarized, while neither the party manifestos nor the attitudes of Conservative, Labour and Alliance voters differ much on the countryside issues. And while it would be nice to have more extensive evidence from earlier surveys, it is also reasonably clear that voters were much more polarized on nuclear issues in 1983 and 1987 than they had been in earlier election surveys.

Effects on voting or effects on attitudes?

It is not an entirely straightforward matter to test what effects these changes in party policy had on voting. One way to proceed is to chart the voting behaviour of the Old Left and the New Left in recent elections as we did in the case of the Free Market Right and the Authoritarian Right in chapter 11. This give us a first, provisional view of the problem.

Given the paucity of nuclear questions in the earlier election studies, we have little option but to use the question on nuclear power to identify the New Left. This covers the years 1979 to 1987, which of course span Labour's change of policy. To identify the Old Left we have rather more choice of questions in this period, and have chosen to use the question on redistribution of income and wealth.[9]

TABLE 12.4 Social Class, the Old Left and the New Left

	Consistent Left	Old Left	New Left	Non-Left		N
Salariat	19	17	17	47	100%	(985)
Routine nonmanual	25	23	17	35	100%	(688)
Petty bourgeoisie	20	20	16	44	101%	(302)
Foremen and technicians	24	28	14	33	99%	(213)
Working class	30	33	12	25	100%	(1238)

Source: 1987 cross-section survey

These two questions are of course correlated, and there are some people who were left-wing both on redistribution and on nuclear power. This gives us a third category which we can term the Consistent Left. Table 12.4 then shows the class distribution of the different Lefts in 1987.

As expected, the Old Left is much more numerous in the working class, while the New Left is slightly more numerous in the salariat, and the Non-Left is correspondingly much more numerous in the petty bourgeoisie and salariat.

Turning next to the voting behaviour of the Left, table 12.5 also shows some familiar patterns. As expected, the Old Left and the Consistent Left were likely to support Labour in 1979, while the New Left and the Non-Left were more inclined to the Conservatives.

TABLE 12.5 The Changing Vote of the Old and New Lefts

	1979	1983	1987
Consistent Left			
Conservative	26	12	15
Labour	56	62	59
Other	18	26	26
	100%	100%	100%
	(247)	(582)	(831)
Old Left			
Conservative	34	32	39
Labour	53	37	34
Other	13	31	27
	100%	100%	100%
	(537)	(929)	(782)
New Left			
Conservative	57	41	39
Labour	22	25	28
Other	21	34	33
	100%	100%	100%
	(205)	(353)	(466)
Right, Centre			
Conservative	65	69	71
Labour	20	11	10
Other	15	20	19
	100%	100%	100%
	(557)	(1317)	(1120)

Source: BES cross-section surveys

The changes over time, however, are very different from those we saw in chapter 11. Whereas the Conservatives strengthened their position among the Free Market Right, and made little headway among the Authoritarian Right, the Labour party lost a great deal of ground between 1979 and 1983 among the Old Left, but strengthened its position both among the New Left and among the Consistent Left.

At first sight, then, Lipset's interpretation does seem to be correct and there do seem to have been quite substantial trade-offs between the anti-nuclear policies of the New Left and the redistributive policies of the Old Left. The change in policy in 1983 coincides with a major change in voting patterns.

The interpretation of these results is not, however, at all straightforward. Table 12.5 is based on three cross-section surveys, not on a panel study, and selective mobility between categories is therefore a major potential difficulty.[10] Thus Labour supporters may have brought their attitudes on nuclear issues into line with the party's. The sixteen-point fall in Labour support among the Old Left may therefore reflect the emigration of the Labour faithful to the Consistent Left, leaving a much less Labour-inclined Old Left behind. Conversely, the six-point rise in Labour support among the Consistent Left may simply reflect the arrival of these migrating Labour faithful.

Table 12.6 offers some support for this idea. Here we look at the changing correlations over time between various measures of the left-right, nuclear and countryside dimensions. Nationalization is one of the key elements of the left-right dimension, and as noted earlier a standard question has been asked throughout the series of election studies. We use this question as a proxy for the left-right dimension (which we are unable to measure in the earlier surveys).[11]

TABLE 12.6 Correlations between Attitudes to Nationalization and Attitudes towards Green Issues

	Nuclear disarmament	American missiles	Nuclear power	Protection of countryside
1964	0.11	—	—	—
1966	0.07	—	—	—
1970 (panel)	0.06	—	—	—
1974 October	—	—	—	− 0.01
1979	—	—	0.07	− 0.02
1983	—	0.23	0.21	—
1987	0.22	0.31	0.28	− 0.05

Source: BES cross-section surveys except 1970, where the 1966–70 panel is used.

As we can see, the correlation between attitudes to nationalization and those towards nuclear issues were higher in 1983 and 1987 than they had been previously, while those with the countryside remained small. (We should note that these correlations between individual items are much lower than those between the attitude scales, largely because a question with three possible responses is a much blunter measuring instrument, involving much more noise and measurement error, than a twenty-point attitude scale.)

Thus 1983 appears to mark a change in the *structure* of voters' attitudes. In 1987, as we saw, attitudes towards nuclear power and nuclear weapons tended to go together and to be correlated with the attitudes that make up the left-right dimension. The same phenomenon was true in 1983, but it does not appear to have held true to the same extent in earlier years. It appears very plausible, then, that the changes in party policy led some voters to change their attitudes and to bring them into line with their party's.

We cannot be sure that this wholly explains the changes shown in table 12.5, but it is likely that it goes some way towards explaining them and that the actual effects on voting, as opposed to the effects on attitudes, were substantially less than first appeared from table 12.5.

We should also note that a comparable change in the structure of attitudes does not appear to have occurred to anything like the same extent with the liberal-authoritarian issues.

TABLE 12.7 Correlations between attitudes to nationalization and attitudes towards Liberal-Authoritarian Issues

	Death penalty	Stiffer sentences	Equal opportunities for blacks	Aid to poor countries	Abortion on NHS
1974 October	—	—	0.10	0.13	0.09
1979	−0.13	−0.12	0.09	0.11	−0.01
1983	−0.08	−0.08	0.07	—	0.03
1987	−0.11	−0.06	0.06	0.11	0.02

Source: BES cross-section surveys

Table 12.7 looks at the correlations over time between various measures of liberal-authoritarian attitudes and attitudes towards nationalization. There is no sign here of any change in the structure of attitudes. The correlations remain low throughout, displaying no particular time trend. In particular it is interesting to observe that Mrs Thatcher's authoritarian populism did not seem to have any effects on the structure of attitudes in 1979 (or thereafter) comparable to the 1983 changes on nuclear issues.[12]

We should remember, however, that Hall's concept of "authoritarian populism" also included the resonant traditional theme of nation as well as that of authority. We should not assume that the changes in the structure of attitudes in 1983 were solely due to the Labour party's adoption of anti-nuclear policies under Mr Foot. The change may also owe something to the Falklands War and the opportunity which the victory gave Mrs Thatcher to weave themes of nation and patriotism into her free market ideology.

Room for manoeuvre?

All the same it is clear that very different processes have occurred in the cases of the Authoritarian Right and the New Left. Whether we look at the problem from the perspective of the relationship with vote (as in tables 11.6 and 12.5) or from the perspective of the structure of attitudes (as in tables 12.6 and 12.7), it is clear that the liberal-authoritarian issues have seen nothing like the changes of the nuclear ones.

The two perspectives do however have very different political implications. If we adopt the voting perspective of table 12.5 we come to the conclusion that Labour lost votes heavily among the Old Left because of its espousal of nuclear policies. If we adopt the alternative approach of table 12.6 we reach more limited conclusions about the electoral consequences of anti-nuclear policies and rather more optimistic ones about a political party's ability to shape public attitudes.

These two perspectives correspond to what we have elsewhere termed the "bottom up" and the "top down" approaches to explaining political change (Heath, Jowell, Curtice and Evans 1990). The prevailing assumption among British political commentators is that the structure of attitudes is determined independently of the political parties and thus represents a constraint upon them to which they must adapt. We call this the bottom-up interpretation of the relationship between voters' attitudes and party policy. An alternative view, following party identification theory, is that voters may adopt the attitudes associated with their party. We term this the top-down interpretation. On this latter interpretation, the correlation between left-right and anti-nuclear attitudes in the mass electorate increased in the 1980s because the Labour and Conservative parties packaged them together. Conversely, the fact that countryside attitudes did not go together with them may be because the parties had not at that time taken distinct stands on them.

We do not wish to advocate a one-sided top-down theory in place of the one-sided bottom-up theory that is currently dominant. Political parties have some freedom for manoeuvre, but not complete freedom. The left-right and nuclear scales are highly, not perfectly, correlated. As we pointed out in chapter 3, if party identification theory were the whole story, we might expect the correlations to be even higher. While the parties may be able to shape some of their supporters' attitudes, and surely have more freedom of manoeuvre than is commonly supposed, they do not have complete freedom of manoeuvre on all issues and attitudes.

Some attitudes, moreover, may be rooted more firmly in alternative social institutions and structures, and we doubt if the political parties will have much freedom of manoeuvre in relation to, say, attitudes towards the family, divorce, or abortion as they do towards nuclear or countryside issues. Institutions such as the churches may be important social anchors for attitudes towards the family, and these may well therefore be attitudes which, from the political parties' point of view, it would be realistic to treat as given and to which they should therefore adapt.

Attitudes towards green issues, however, whether the nuclear or the countryside ones, do not appear to be so firmly rooted in social structure and institutions and on these issues, then, the parties may have more room for manoeuvre.

Notes

[1] The questions used in the factor analysis are as follows: 1987, questions 25a, 25b, 27, 43d, 115b, 43k, 116a, 116b, 117c. Don't knows have been included with the middle response for each item.

[2] Similar results have been obtained, using British Social Attitudes data, by Heath (1986) and Aish (1989).

[3] Cronbach's alpha for the nuclear scale is 0.76 and for the countryside scale is 0.62. To some extent the high internal reliability of the nuclear scale reflects technical as well as normative consistency (see Heath 1986 for a discussion of these concepts). For example, if one believes that nuclear weapons make Britain less safe, it must be technically correct to try and get rid of them (although multilateral as well as unilateral disarmament could be a technically consistent response). Normative consistency is demonstrated more by answers to the nuclear power and nuclear disarmament questions, and is at a roughly similar level to the normative consistency on the left-right scale.

[4] If we compare our four regression analyses of left-right, liberal-authoritarian, countryside and nuclear attitudes, we find that the signs for the various structural coefficients are identical in the case of left-right and nuclear attitudes.

[5] Thus the correlation between the nuclear and left-right scales is 0.45, between the nuclear and liberal-authoritarian scales is 0.31, between the countryside and left-right scales is −0.09, and between the countryside and liberal-authoritarian scales is 0.11. All the correlations are significant at the 0.01 level.

[6] The questions used in table 12.4 are as follows:
1964: 22a.
1966: 19a.
1970 (panel): 20.
October 1974: 27m.
1979: 38k, 38n.
1983: 45e.
1987: 27, 43d, 116a.
The questions on nuclear weapons have the same wording throughout. However, there are quite substantial wording changes in the case of nuclear power and protection of the countryside. We are carrying out methodological work to investigate the effects of these wording changes.

[7] Evidence of a large gap between Labour and Conservative supporters on nuclear issues in the 1980s is also present in the British Social Attitudes surveys.

[8] Attitudes to the countryside do however have a significant association with voting behaviour, even after controlling for the other attitude scales. This is

shown in table 12.8N, where we report the results of three logistic regressions. (These results have been obtained using the PROBIT procedure of SPSSX. In this procedure, the regression coefficients are divided by 2 and 5 added to the intercept.)

TABLE 12.8N Logistic Regression of Attitudes and Vote

Independent variables	Dependent Variable		
	Labour vs. Conservative	Alliance vs. Conservative	Labour vs. Alliance
Left–right scale	1.11 (0.06)	0.54 (0.04)	0.61 (0.05)
Liberal–authoritarian scale	0.16 (0.04)	0.21 (0.03)	−0.05 (0.03)
Nuclear scale	0.46 (0.04)	0.31 (0.04)	0.20 (0.03)
Countryside scale	−0.13 (0.03)	0.03 (0.03)	−0.18 (0.03)
Constant	5.38 (0.04)	5.12 (0.03)	4.73 (0.04)
N	1990	1837	1463

Source: 1987 cross-section survey

As we can see, the left-right scale has the strongest association with vote in all three cases, followed by the nuclear scale. The countryside scale does however have a significant association with Labour:Conservative and Labour:Alliance voting.

[9]We have checked our results using the question on nationalization. The size of the Old Left and Consistent Left is much reduced if we use the question on nationalization, but the changes in the pattern of voting remain much as before.

[10]Note that the use of recall data, as with the analysis of council house purchase, would not solve our problems here. In the case of council houses people's reports of whether or not they purchased are likely to be fairly reliable. People's reports of their attitude change, however, are much less likely to be reliable (see Lievesley and Waterton 1985), and for that reason were not asked in the survey. Without information on attitude change, however, it is impossible to sort out the relative extents of vote-switching and selective mobility.

[11]The same pattern of results is obtained for 1974 to 1987 using the question on redistribution of income and wealth, but the correlations are generally rather lower. To maintain comparability responses have been collapsed to three categories throughout. Don't knows have been included with the midpoint.

[12] Our conclusions here are very similar to those reached by Studlar (1974) in his analysis of the 1959–72 period. He concluded that "on colour issues the British public is an autonomous element, not easily subject to persuasion by political leaders." (Studlar 1974:381)

Chapter 13

Components of Change

In this final chapter our aim is to bring together the different themes described earlier and to see how far they can, either singly or in combination, explain the political changes of the last twenty-five years.

Many writers have suggested that the parties now have to contend with a less committed electorate, less anchored by traditional ties of loyalty to class or party. Our evidence has cast some doubt on this proposition. We doubt if the social psychology of the electorate has changed much if at all over the last twenty-five years. Overall volatility, for example, has increased by a few points; but this can be explained by the shift from a two-party to a three-party system as the Liberals became a national force fielding candidates in all constituencies. There is thus no need to postulate that the voters' social psychology has changed in order to account for the small change in volatility.

Similarly, it has been argued that voters have become more sophisticated, and it is indeed true that (on some criteria) voters' attitudes have become more strongly associated with Labour and Conservative voting. But this can be explained by the increased ideological distance between the Labour and Conservative parties without any need to postulate that voters have become more rational.

On the other hand, it is quite clear that there have been important changes. The social composition of the electorate has changed: it is now more middle-class, less religious, more educated, and more unequal. There have also been important political changes. The franchise has been extended. Voters have the option of voting for at least three parties, not just two. The ideological positions of Labour and Conservative have changed.

So while the social psychology of the voter may not have changed much, the social and political conditions under which the parties competed for votes in the 1980s have certainly been rather different from those of the 1960s. And they are likely to be different again in the 1990s, particularly if we move to a four-party competition with Green candidates in most seats, or if Labour moves back towards the centre of the ideological spectrum.

In this final chapter we assess the extent to which these various social and political changes can explain the varying fortunes of the parties over the 1964–1987 period. Over this period, the Conservative party more or less held its share of the vote; the Labour party saw its share fall by around 13 points, while the Liberal/SDP Alliance share rose by 12 points. In explaining these changes we turn first to social changes such as the contraction of the working class, the expansion of owner-occupation, and the decline of religion. Many although by no means all of these changes are autonomous of the political process, while others are more reversible. A Labour government might, perhaps, be able to reverse the decline in trade union membership, or slow down the expansion of owner-occupation, but it is very doubtful whether it (or any other government) could reverse the contraction of the working class or the decline of religion. These social changes thus represent basic conditions which the parties have to accept.

The political changes have also been of more or less reversible kinds. On the one hand, it is doubtful whether any party could remove the franchise from the 18–20 year-olds who were granted it in 1968. But on the other hand changes such as the formation of the SDP or the policy shifts of the Labour and Conservative parties away from the centre in the late 1970s and 1980s would seem to be eminently reversible. In between come such political changes as the intervention of Liberal candidates or of Green candidates in the future. These largely represent constraints on the other parties, although of course they could be reversed by the Liberal Democrat or Green parties themselves.

In assessing the impact of these changes, this concluding chapter will necessarily be rather more speculative than any which has preceded it. The core of the preceding chapters has been descriptive. We have tried to document the changes in, for example, overall volatility or relative class voting. To be sure, we have also presented causal interpretations of our findings, and in social science these must necessarily have a tentative and provisional character. In the absence of real life experiments, survey data can never be conclusive of causality. At most we can say that the balance of the evidence favours one interpretation rather than another.

To assess the impact of social or political change, moreover, we clearly have to make some causal assumptions. As our data and methods improve, we shall no doubt be able to make better causal assumptions. We hope that other scholars will be able in due course to improve upon the procedures used in this chapter. In the meantime, just as we have noted the provisional character of our causal interpretations in previous chapters, so we must emphasize the provisional character of the following attempts to account for political change.

Social change

Over the last twenty-five years the electorate has changed quite markedly with respect to its social class composition, housing tenure, education, religion, and so on. As we have seen, the *associations* between these characteristics and voting behaviour have (with a few notable exceptions like region) remained fairly stable throughout the period, but the *proportions* with the different characteristics have changed quite substantially. If we assume that the associations indicate causal links, then it follows that these social changes may explain some of the long-run changes in voting behaviour that have occurred.

For example, while there is little evidence for the thesis of class secularization, there is a great deal of evidence that the size of the different classes has changed over the past twenty-five years, the working class contracting and the professional, managerial and technical occupations in the salariat expanding. There is general agreement that the size of Labour's electoral base has therefore been declining, while that of the centre parties and of the Conservatives has been expanding. While it is highly unlikely that social changes of this type can explain the election-to-election fluctuations in party popularity, they do suggest that the natural level of the Labour vote will have been falling.

Previous studies have estimated that social change can explain nearly half of the thirteen-point fall in the Labour vote between 1964 and 1987 (Heath, Jowell and Curtice 1985, Franklin 1985, Heath and Mcdonald 1987). These estimates have been reached by means of a simple simulation. In *How Britain Votes*, for example, we assumed that the parties retained the same *level* of support in each class that they did in 1964, but we adjusted the *size* of each class according to its expansion or contraction between 1964 and 1983. This exercise told us how the parties would hypothetically have fared if the only sources of change had been the changing size of the classes (and, crucially, if other things had remained equal).

Social Class

A changing class structure seems to be a common feature of all industrialized societies, whatever the colour of their politics. This is not to suggest that even the class structure is altogether autonomous of politics (see for example Garnsey 1975 on the occupational structure of the Soviet Union.) But we doubt if British government action, even Conservative attempts to reduce the public sector, have had much effect other than reclassifying some people from one sector to another.

The Census provides us with the most authoritative data on the changing occupational structure. The Census categories are not quite identical to those we have used in the construction of our social classes, but we have arranged them so that they approximate as closely as possible to our categories.[1] Table 13.1 shows the changing distribution of the economically active population of Great Britain.

As we can see, there was rather little change in the occupational structure between 1951 and 1961, but thereafter change proceeded much more rapidly. Between 1961 and 1981, for example, the proportion of managers and professionals (roughly equivalent to our salariat) increased from 14% to 25% of the labour force while skilled manual workers declined from 24% to 16%. By 1981 less than half the labour force was in the three main manual

TABLE 13.1   Distribution of the Economically Active Population by Occupational Category in Great Britain 1951–81

	1951	1961	1971	1981
Employers and own account	6.7	6.4	6.5	6.4
Managers and administrators	5.4	5.3	8.0	10.1
Professionals and technicians	6.6	9.0	11.1	14.7
Clerical and sales	16.3	18.6	19.5	19.3
Supervisors and foremen	2.6	2.9	3.9	4.2
Skilled manual	23.8	24.1	20.2	16.0
Semi-skilled manual	26.6	25.1	19.3	19.0
Unskilled manual	11.9	8.5	11.6	10.4
Total	99.9%	99.9%	100.1%	100.1%
GB labour force (000s)	22,514	23,639	25,021	25,406

Source: Heath and McDonald (1987)

categories. Recent survey evidence suggests that these trends have been continuing throughout the 1980s (see for example the reports of the General Household Survey and the Labour Force Survey).

The labour force is not of course the same concept as the class structure. Measures of the labour force take the individual as the unit of analysis, while our measure of social class also includes economically inactive spouses (and of course the retired) as well. We should note that some of these changes in the labour force coincide with greater participation of women, particularly married women, in paid employment. Different procedures for allocating married women to social classes will therefore produce slightly different pictures of the extent of change (see Heath 1990).[2]

Using the British Election Survey data, we can now construct a model to estimate the effect of these changes in the class structure on the parties' shares of the vote. We estimate that, other things being equal, the changing shape of the class structure would have led to an increase of 3.8 points in the Conservative share of the vote, a 4.5 point decline in Labour's share, and a 0.7 point increase in the Liberal/Alliance share.[3]

Religion

A second major social division in most industrial societies is that based on religion, and we have seen that even in Britain it has rather more importance than is usually recognized. There is also little doubt that there have been important changes in Church membership. Authoritative data are provided by Brierley (1988) and are summarized in table 13.2.[4]

For the major Protestant denominations, the trends show some parallels with the changes in the labour force and class structure. Change was rather slow between 1950 and 1960, but then there was a more rapid, and

TABLE 13.2 Church Membership (%)

	1950	1960	1970	1980	1985
Church of England	8.6	7.9	6.8	4.6	4.1
Church of Scotland	3.4	3.3	2.8	2.2	2.0
Nonconformist	4.9	4.5	3.6	2.8	2.5
Catholic	NA	NA	4.7	4.6	4.2
Other Christian	NA	NA	0.7	0.7	0.8
Hindus	NA	NA	0.1	0.3	0.3
Sikhs	NA	NA	0.2	0.3	0.4
Muslims	NA	NA	0.6	1.4	1.9
Jews	NA	NA	0.3	0.3	0.2
Others	NA	NA	0.1	0.4	0.4
All	NA	NA	19.9	17.6	16.8
G.B. population aged 15 and over (000's)	37,828	39,360	40,993	42,973	44,014

Source: Brierley (1988)

continuing, decline in membership thereafter. Between 1960 and 1980 Protestant church membership fell from 16% of the population (aged fifteen and over) to 10%. The number of Catholics, however, fell much less while the number of Muslims has risen substantially. The latter increase is of course largely due to migration from Pakistan and Bangladesh, while Catholic exceptionalism too may be due to migration: the influx of Catholic migrants from the Republic of Ireland may have masked a decline among British-born Catholics.

These figures of Church membership are very different from our survey data. Our survey estimates may properly be regarded as measures of religious self-image or identity, and they have a somewhat similar relation to church membership as party identification figures have to political party membership. Thus Brierley's figures suggest that around 17% of the adult British population were Church members in 1985. Our data on the other hand yield a proportion of 67% who regarded themselves as belonging to a particular religion. Even if we exclude the complete non-attenders, our proportion falls only to 42%.

Different definitions, then, yield very different pictures of religion in contemporary Britain. The Churches' own membership records give a picture of a rather secular society with low levels of church membership; our religious self-image measure suggests that our society is not so secular after all. Both measures, however, show a marked decline. Thus the church membership figures indicate a fall from 16% to 10% in the proportion of Protestants between 1960 and 1985, while our religious identity measure suggests a fall from 67% to 31% between 1964 and 1987.[5]

Given our findings that nonreligious people are more likely to vote Labour, these changes suggest that Labour will have benefited from the decline of religion. Following the same procedure as with social class, we estimate that, taken on its own, the decline in religion will have led to a 4.0 point decline in the Conservatives' share and a 4.1 point increase in Labour's.

Region

Turning next to region, table 13.3 shows that the regional trends have been much more modest than the trends in the sizes of the classes or the religious groups.[6] The more Labour-inclined territories of Scotland, Wales and the North made up a minority of the population even in 1961. By 1987 the figure had shrunk slightly from 43% to 40%. Our survey estimates are, not perhaps surprisingly given our sampling procedure, closely in line with the official figures. And they suggest that the changing regional distribution will have had very little impact on the parties' share of the vote. It is unlikely that they have changed any party's share of the vote by more than 0.1 points.

TABLE 13.3 Regional Trends

	1951	1961	1971	1981	1987
Scotland	10.4	10.1	9.6	9.5	9.2
Wales	5.3	5.1	5.0	5.1	5.1
England:					
North	NA	27.6	27.0	26.4	25.9
Midlands	NA	18.6	19.3	19.9	20.1
South	NA	38.5	39.1	39.0	39.6
		99.9%	100.0%	99.9%	99.9%
G.B. (000's)	48,917	51,380	54,369	54,814	55,355

Source: Regional Trends

Education

Changes in class structure, religious membership and identity, and in regional distribution are largely autonomous of government action. Other social trends may have more to do with government action and may be more reversible. This is clearest in the case of education where the Robbins Report of 1963 led to the creation of new universities, and where the raising of the school-leaving age to 16 in 1974 boosted the numbers taking the public examinations of O-level and CSE. And while popular pressure will probably prevent any government from overtly reversing these particular changes, there can be no doubt that educational opportunities are to some extent under government control.[7]

Official data on the education of the population are surprisingly scarce. The best official series comes from the General Household Survey, and this is shown in table 13.4.[8]

Table 13.4 shows changes over the short period from 1972 to 1987 that are as striking as those in church membership. Other survey evidence suggests that there had been rather rapid change over the preceding twenty years as

TABLE 13.4 Qualifications of the Adult Population

Highest qualification	1972	1981	1987
Degree	3	7	10
Higher education below degree	5	9	12
A-level or equivalent	3	6	9
O-level or equivalent	10	13	20
CSE, grades 2–5, etc.	9	12	12
Foreign and other	3	4	3
No qualification	68	50	34
	101%	101%	100%
N	23,163	11,425	15,637

Source: General Household Survey

well (Halsey, Heath and Ridge 1980). In absolute numbers, the most dramatic change comes in the proportion of the population with no qualifications, which halved in fifteen years. More relevant however to understanding political change is the proportion of graduates, and while this trebled over the period covered by table 13.4, the absolute numbers still remain rather small.[9]

Despite the rapid change in the educational qualifications of the electorate, it is likely that its effect on politics has been rather small. As we saw in chapter 6, higher education is distinctively associated with voting for the Liberals, but our procedure suggests that the Liberal/Alliance will have gained only around 0.8 points from the expansion of higher education.

Housing

The 1960s saw a major change in the housing market too. Table 13.5 looks at the trends in housing tenure.[10] As we can see, the proportion of owner-occupiers doubled between 1951 and 1986, with particularly rapid expansion between 1961 and 1971. This increase occurred largely at the expense of private renting. As Papadakis and Taylor-Gooby (1987) have argued, this change can largely be explained by the massive state subsidies which local-authority housing and owner-occupation (through tax relief on mortgage interest) have received. While the Conservative legislation on council house sales has led to a 5 point reduction in local authority housing between 1981 and 1986, this has merely undone the expansion of the previous twenty years. The net change in council housing over the period covered by the election studies is therefore effectively zero.[12]

The analyses of chapter 8 should lead us to be particularly cautious about causal interpretations of the association between housing and vote. The short-run political consequences of buying a council house seem to be rather small, although the long-run consequences may well be larger. However, if we follow the same procedure as in estimating the effects of the other social

TABLE 13.5 Housing Tenure in Great
Britain 1951–86

	1951	1961	1971	1981	1986
Owned	31	39	50	56	63
Council	17	27	31	31	26
Other	52	33	19	13	11
	100%	99%	100%	100%	100%

Source: Taylor-Gooby

changes, we arrive at estimates of a 4.6 point increase for the Conservatives
and a 5.0 point decrease for Labour.

Trade Unions

Trends in trade union membership also have some parallels with council
housing. Union density (actual membership as a percentage of potential
membership) showed an increase during the 1960s (largely due to the spread
of white-collar unionism), and has fallen back in the 1980s.[12]

TABLE 13.6 Trade Union Membership (UK)

	1951	1961	1971	1981	1984
Actual membership (000's)	9,530	9,916	11,135	12,106	11,086
Potential membership	21,177	22,527	22,884	24,551	24,194
Density %	45.0	44.0	48.7	49.3	45.8

Source: Price and Bain (1988), table 4.11

Problems of causality are likely to be as serious, or perhaps even more
serious, in the case of trade union membership and vote as they are in the
case of housing. However, given that the net change over the period as a
whole has been rather small, our procedure suggests that the effect will have
been very small, amounting perhaps to a 0.4 point drop in Labour's share.
We can therefore effectively ignore trade union membership as a source of
change.

Ethnicity

The final major social change which we should note is migration from the
New Commonwealth and Pakistan. Figures on ethnic groups in Britain are
particularly scanty. For recent years, the official Labour Force Survey gives
good estimates of the size of the different ethnic minorities, but for the earlier
years the more questionable Census statistics on birthplace have to be used.[13]

TABLE 13.7 Ethnicity

	% of total population of Great Britain				
	1951	1961	1971	1981	1987
West Indian	0.04	0.4	1.0	1.0	0.9
Indian	NA	NA	0.7	1.4	1.4
Pakistani/Bangladeshi	NA	NA	0.3	0.6	0.9
African	NA	NA	0.1	0.1	0.2
Mixed	NA	NA	NA	0.4	0.5
Other	NA	NA	0.4	0.4	0.6
All minorities	0.4	1.0	2.5	3.9	4.6

Sources: Peach et al (1988), Shaw (1988), Haskey (1988), Coleman (1983)

Table 13.7 shows the rapid growth of the ethnic minority population in the 1960s and 1970s, with the earlier arrival of West Indians and the later arrivals of Indians and, later still, of people from Pakistan and Bangladesh. These official estimates cover the population of all ages. Given the rather youthful age structure of the ethnic minority population, they will form a rather smaller proportion of the eligible electorate. There is also substantial evidence that eligible members of the ethnic minorities (due perhaps to language difficulties, political alienation, or fears of harassment) are less likely to register as electors (Anwar 1986). We must therefore expect to find a rather lower proportion of ethnic minorities in our sample than the 4.5% of table 13.7. Our election study figure for 1987 was 3.2%, and this cannot be far from the true figure for registered electors from the ethnic minorities.

We did of course find a specially strong association between ethnicity and vote, but because it is a strong association affecting only a small minority, its overall impact is likely to have been rather small. We estimate that it may have given Labour one extra point.

We thus have two changes which appear to have worked in the Conservatives' favour (and to a lesser extent the centre parties' favour)—the expansion of the salariat and the expansion of owner-occupation. We have two cases where there is little change and hence where the impact is likely to be rather neutral—region and trade union membership. We have one change which is likely to operate to the advantage of the centre parties—higher education. And we have two changes which are likely to have worked to the advantage of the Labour party—migration from the New Commonwealth and Pakistan, and the decline of religion.[14] Table 13.8 summarizes our estimates of the gains and losses to the parties arising from these social changes.

TABLE 13.8 The Hypothetical Effects of Social Change 1964–87

	Share of the vote		
Source of change	Conservative	Liberal/ Alliance	Labour
Class	+ 3.8	+ 0.7	− 4.5
Housing	+ 4.6	+ 0.6	− 5.0
Region	− 0.1	+ 0.1	− 0.1
T.U. membership	+ 0.5	− 0.1	− 0.4
Higher education	− 0.4	+ 0.8	− 0.5
Ethnicity	− 0.7	− 0.3	+ 1.0
Religion	− 4.0	+ 0.1	+ 4.1
Combined effects of class, housing, religion, ethnicity and education	+ 2.7	+ 1.8	− 4.0

Source: 1964 and 1987 cross-section surveys

The combined effects of social change

The analyses we have conducted so far in this chapter take each variable one at a time, and of course we need to conduct a more elaborate, but arithmetically quite straightforward, multivariate analysis to calculate the *combined* effect of the social changes on the parties' shares of the vote. The increase in owner-occupation, for example, would to some extent have been associated with the expansion of the salariat, and so their effects would not be cumulative. We cannot therefore read off the overall effects by summing these individual ones.

To simplify the calculations, we ignore region and union membership since the net changes have been so small. We therefore carry out a multivariate analysis of changes in higher education, religion, ethnicity, housing tenure and social class, and the results are shown in the bottom row of table 13.8. The results indicate a rather modest increase of 2.7 points in the Conservative share of the vote, a 4.0 point decline in Labour's, and a 1.8 increase in the Liberal/Alliance share.

These estimates of the consequences of social change are rather less than those which we have reached in earlier publications, or indeed than those which Franklin independently reached using somewhat different methods. The main reason for the discrepancy is of course the introduction of religion into the analysis. The decline of religion has counteracted the expansion of the salariat and the spread of owner-occupation. Social change has not been uniformly working against the Labour party.

We can also use this method to estimate the impact of social change on class voting. One common theory is that the spread of owner-occupation within the working class will have increased the proportion of working-class Conservatives, while the growth of the new middle class will have increased the proportion of middle-class socialists. The consequence of these changes within the classes, it is alleged, will have been to bring the classes closer together in their voting behaviour—in other words to produce class dealignment.

Our calculations suggest otherwise. The expansion of home-ownership and of higher education, together with the decline in religion, suggest that the classes should have diverged not converged in their political behaviour. Thus Conservative voting should have increased by two points in the salariat but decreased by one point in the working class.

This rather surprising result is easily understandable once we check on the scale of the social changes within the classes. What we find is that home-ownership has spread substantially in the salariat as well as in the working class, while religion has declined even faster in the working class than it did in the salariat. Social change therefore does not necessarily produce class dealignment after all, at least over the 1964–1987 period. It might be a different story of course over the next twenty-five years since the expansion of home-ownership in the salariat and the decline of religion in the working class will necessarily slow down as they approach the 'ceiling' and 'floor' respectively.

Before placing too much weight on the results of these analyses, however, we must look carefully at the limitations and the pitfalls involved in our method.

The general problem, of course, is that of drawing causal inferences from cross-sectional data. Chapter 8 demonstrated some of these problems in the cases of council house purchase and share purchase. As we saw, while individual home-owners were certainly more likely to vote Conservative than were council tenants, it was far from clear that expanding home ownership expands Conservative voting; it may simply redistribute voters into different housing categories. People who were already inclined to the Conservatives may take the opportunity to purchase their council houses, and the net impact on the Conservative share of the vote may thus be zero. Just as the welfare and creative occupations may be a sanctuary for radicals, rather than a cause of their radicalism, so owner-occupation may be a sanctuary for individualists, rather than a cause of individualism. The expansion of home-ownership may therefore simply give more individualists the opportunity to realize their ambitions rather than increase the total number of individualists in the society.

This argument applies not only to the expansion of home-ownership but, to a greater or lesser degree, to almost all the other social changes mentioned above. Consider, for example, the changing shape of the class structure itself. The expansion of the salariat and the contraction of the working class mean that there has been a surplus of upward mobility over downward in Britain during the last quarter-century. However, as Butler and Stokes showed, people whose parents had supported the Conservative party were more likely to be upwardly mobile than were people whose parents had supported the Labour or Liberal parties. Once again, it was the Conservative-inclined who were more likely to take advantage of the new opportunities. This finding still holds true. Thus in 1987, 67% of respondents from working-class Conservative backgrounds had been upwardly mobile compared with 50% from working-class Labour backgrounds. In this way, a process of selective mobility is involved with the expansion of the salariat, just as it is with the expansion of home-ownership.

The same kind of process may apply even to the decline of religion. Thus the decline of church attendance might conceivably be due to new leisure opportunities (perhaps through the increased ownership of private cars) tempting some people away from church on Sundays. The people who availed themselves of these new leisure opportunities might have been those who were already more inclined to have doubts about their religion. The new leisure opportunities might thus reduce church attendance without affecting religious commitment.

A possible view, then, of the impact of social change would be that it simply redistributes individuals according to their prior political values and identities and has no causal consequence at all for the parties' electoral fortunes. There is surely some truth in this view, but we doubt if it is the whole story. Again, the case of social mobility is quite convincing. While a Conservative family background increases the probability of upward mobility, the majority of the upwardly mobile in fact come from Labour backgrounds. And these upwardly mobile people from Labour backgrounds are more likely to defect from Labour than are those who remained behind in the working class.

In short, both processes are likely to be at work. There is an element of selective mobility but there also seems to be an element of political conversion as well. It may well be, too, that selective mobility occurs in the short-run while political conversion occurs over a rather longer time-scale. Short-run panel data generally show that selective mobility is the dominant process, while the main evidence for political conversion comes from longer-run data such as that on social mobility.

It is probably wise to assume, therefore, that our individual analyses of the changing class structure and so on overestimate the impact, particularly the short-run impact, of each social change. However, since we have a number of contradictory trends, the true combined long-run effects may not be all that different from our estimate in table 13.8.[15]

Political change

While there have been some important social changes over the past twenty-five years, political changes may have been even more important. Our period has seen the extension of the franchise, increased numbers of Liberal candidates, the formation (and more recently demise) of the SDP, changed tactical considerations, and changed ideological positions held by the Labour and Conservative parties. In all of these respects there are changed political circumstances facing the elector.

The extension of the franchise

The extension of the franchise in 1968 to 18–20 year olds is a political change that is surely irreversible in the forseeable future. Given the small proportion of the electorate which this group makes up, its potential for political effect is bound to be small, however.

The young elector tends to be rather less interested in politics, somewhat less likely to turn out and vote, less committed to any political party, and somewhat more volatile.[16] These seem to be features which are characteristic of young voters at all elections.

TABLE 13.9 The Voting Behaviour of 18–20 year-olds and of Older Voters

	Conservative	Labour	Other		
1970	33	56	12	101%	(86)
	47	45	7	99%	(1363)
February 1974	26	44	30	100%	(61)
	38	41	21	100%	(2009)
October 1974	29	46	25	100%	(80)
	36	42	21	99%	(1868)
1979	50	40	10	100%	(50)
	47	38	16	101%	(1554)
1983	42	36	22	100%	(182)
	45	29	26	100%	(3004)
1987	38	40	23	101%	(133)
	44	31	25	100%	(3047)

Note: The first row for each year shows the vote of 18–20 year olds. The second row shows the figures for voters aged 21 and over.
Source: British Election Cross-Section Surveys

The political preferences of young voters have also tended to be somewhat to the left of the average voter. As we can see from table 13.9, Labour has always fared slightly better, and the Conservatives usually worse, among the 18–20 year olds than they have among the other, older voters. In several years the differences are small and, given the small numbers of 18–20 year olds in the sample, are non-significant. But the overall pattern is clear and reasonably consistent.

However, a small effect that affects a small number of electors is not going to have much impact on the overall election result. To estimate the net impact of extending the franchise to 18–20 year olds is very straightforward: we can simply exclude them from the figures. And when we do so, we find that their absence would have cost Labour 0.4 points from their 1987 share of the vote.

The changing number of Liberal candidates

If extending the franchise has had a marginal impact, the changes in the number of Liberal candidates is perhaps the most major change, social or political, that we shall find. We have already seen that the changing opportunities to vote Liberal could well explain the increase in volatility and the decline in class voting since 1964; it is even more likely that Liberal interventions can explain a substantial part of the change in the parties' shares of the vote.

TABLE 13.10 Liberal/Alliance Candidates in Great Britain

	Liberal/ Alliance candidates	Liberal/ Alliance share of total vote	Average Liberal/ Alliance vote per candidate
1945	306	9.2	18.6
1950	475	9.3	11.8
1951	109	2.6	14.7
1955	110	2.8	15.1
1959	216	6.0	16.9
1964	365	11.4	18.5
1966	311	8.6	16.1
1970	332	7.6	13.5
February 1974	517	19.8	23.6
October 1974	619	18.8	18.9
1979	577	14.1	14.9
1983	633	26.0	26.0
1987	633	23.1	23.1

Source: Butler and Butler (1986); table 1.1

Table 13.10 shows the changing number of Liberal candidates over the postwar period, the total share of the vote which they obtained, and their vote per candidate.

As we can see, the Liberals obtained only 11% of the vote in Britain in 1964 but 18% per candidate. And this suggests that up to 7 of the 12-point increase in the Liberal share of the vote between 1964 and 1987 can be ascribed to the increased number of Liberal candidates.

We might expect this to be something of an overestimate, since in 1964 the Liberals did not contest a random selection of seats but concentrated their efforts on more middle-class Conservative-held ones. If we control for social class, housing, religion and higher education as we did when assessing the impact of social change, our estimate of the effect still reaches 6.7 points however.[17]

Given the more working-class character of the seats which the Liberals failed to contest in 1964, it follows that these gains will have come disproportionately at Labour expense. We estimate that these Liberal interventions will have cost Labour 4.3 points and the Conservatives 2.4 points.

Tactical voting

The changing tactical situation (which will itself necessarily be a consequence of other changes) can also account for a small part of the overall change. Tactical voting can be seen as a kind of bonus to a party which has done well. It cannot on its own explain why a party's share of the vote should have increased. But if a party's share does increase for other reasons, it will tend to magnify the improvement.

TABLE 13.11 The Changing Tactical Situation

	Number of seats where		
There was no Liberal/Alliance candidate	Liberal/Alliance was 3rd or lower	Conservatives were 3rd or lower	Labour were 3rd or lower
1964	255	299	14	52
1987	0	349	45	251

Sources: Craig (1983); Times (1987)

Table 13.11 shows the changing tactical situation.[18] As we can see, in 1964 the Liberals were very likely to be in third place even when they did contest seats. They would therefore have been a net loser of tactical votes, and would probably have lost them roughly equally to Labour and the Conservatives.

In 1987 the Liberal/SDP Alliance was still in third place in over half the seats. But in 1987 unlike 1964 it was a beneficiary of tactical voting from Labour supporters, since Labour was now in third place in 251 seats compared with only 52 in 1964. As we saw in chapter 4, the Alliance's gains from tactical voting in 1987 almost balanced its losses, while the Conservatives were the main net beneficiaries of tactical voting, being the party that was least likely to be in third place.

TABLE 13.12 Net Tactical Gains and Losses

	% of total vote			
	Conservative	Labour	Liberal/Alliance	Other
1964	+0.6	+0.6	−1.0	−0.2
1987	+1.0	0.0	−0.4	−0.6
Difference	+0.4	−0.6	+0.6	−0.4

Sources: 1964 British Election cross-section survey and table 4.1

Table 13.12 shows our estimates of the gains and losses in 1964 and 1987, and the difference between them represents the contribution which the tactical bonuses (and penalties) have made to the change in the parties' fortunes. The figures for 1987 have been calculated directly from table 4.1, while we have had to make some informed guesses about the figures for 1964. The various pieces of evidence from chapter 4 suggested that a party loses around 10% of its support through tactical voting in constituencies where it had been in third place or lower at the previous election.[19] Given that the Liberals actually gained 11.4% of the vote in 1964 and 8.6% in 1966, this suggests that the Liberals may have lost around one percentage point overall (i.e. 10% of 10%). The other minor parties would also have suffered for the same reason, and we have made a small allowance for this. We have then divided the gains equally between between the Conservative and Labour parties.

These figures are clearly rather approximate, but their order of magnitude is surely about right. If the *total* amount of tactical voting was only 6% in 1987, and was less than this in 1964, then the *net* effects must have been rather small. Our conclusion, then, is that the Conservatives and the Alliance have won rather small bonuses over the 1964–87 period, while Labour and the other parties have received rather small penalties.

These effects are of course eminently reversible. If the Liberal Democrats are seen by the electorate to have significantly less chance of winning seats than the Alliance had in 1983 or 1987, the centre could easily return to the situation of being a net loser.

The formation of the SDP

It is quite likely that the formation of the SDP in 1981 also helped to boost the fortunes of the centre. In *How Britain Votes* we showed that there were some differences between SDP and Liberal identifiers in their recruitment and attitudes, and we inferred that the formation of the SDP might therefore have won votes for the centre that the Liberals on their own would not have gained. Thus in 1983 the SDP was relatively more likely to have recruited voters from Labour than from the Conservatives, and their identifiers were correspondingly somewhat to the left of Liberal identifiers. (As we emphasized in *How Britain Votes*, however, this evidence cannot be conclusive of causality.)

We can check our 1983 results against the 1987 data. What we find is that the differences between SDP and Liberal identifiers were rather smaller in 1987 than they had been in 1983. Thus in 1983 we found that the SDP recruited two former Labour voters for each recruit from the Conservatives whereas the Liberals drew more equally from the two main parties. But in 1987 the Liberal and SDP patterns of recruitment had tended to converge considerably. It is quite possible then that the boost which the centre received in 1983 from the formation of the SDP was a rather temporary one.

Estimating the remaining size of this boost (if any) in 1987 is rather more speculative than our previous exercises. We cannot use the kind of simulation that we used for estimating the impact of social change or of Liberal interventions. However, we do have measures of SDP supporters' feelings towards the other parties, and we can use these to make some estimates.

First of all we should note that only 5% of our total sample actually identified with the SDP, compared with 11% for the Liberals. Table 13.13 then looks at the feelings of SDP identifiers towards the other main parties.

TABLE 13.13 The Feelings of SDP Identifiers towards the Other Parties

	%	
Felt more favourable to the Liberals than to any other party	54	(94)
Felt more favourable to Labour than to any other party	1	(2)
Felt more favourable to the Conservatives than to any other party	6	(10)
Felt equally favourable to the Liberals and the Conservatives	15	(27)
Felt equally favourable to the Liberals and Labour	19	(33)
Felt equally favourable to all three parties	5	(9)
	100	(175)

We see from table 13.13 that a clear majority (54%) of SDP identifiers in 1987 preferred the Liberals to any other party, while there were very small numbers who preferred either Labour or the Conservatives. This leaves 39% who were indifferent between the Liberals and one or more of the other parties. It is possible that some of these groups at the bottom of table 13.13 would not have voted for the Liberals on their own if the SDP had not been formed. If we divide them evenly, we get an overall figure of 73% of SDP identifiers going to the Liberals (i.e. 54% plus half of 15% plus half of 19% plus one third of 5%), 12% going to Labour, and 15% going to the Conservatives. Given that 5% of the sample were SDP identifiers, this suggests that the centre vote would have been around one point lower in 1987 without the SDP.

Estimating the electoral consequences of the formation of the SDP from this kind of data (or indeed from any data) is particularly hazardous. People's feelings towards other parties will have been affected by the very processes which we are investigating, such as the formation of the SDP, and cannot therefore really tell us what would have happened if the process in question had not actually occurred. They are perhaps a better basis for estimating what the effects of the demise of the SDP might be.

It is also rather difficult to disentangle the effects of the formation of the SDP from the other political factors which gave rise to its formation, such as Labour's move to the left. We move on to consider this next.

Policy changes

As we have seen in chapters 11 and 12, studying the effects of policy changes is also very difficult. Voters' attitudes towards the issues are not independent of the parties' policy stances. Attitudes are not fixed or autonomous of the political process.

On purely theoretical, rational choice grounds we would of course expect that, if the Labour and Conservative parties move away from the centre, then centrist voters will be more inclined to defect to centrist parties such as the Liberals (or perhaps the Nationalists as a protest). Party identification theory on the other hand suggests that, if a party moves its policy position, it will to some extent carry its supporters with it. Unfortunately, party identification theory does not provide any precise way of calculating estimates, whereas rational choice theory does have the advantage of enabling us to formulate precise models.[20] Our best hope, therefore, is to adopt a rational choice approach while recognizing that it will overestimate the electoral consequences of policy change.

Let us begin by assuming that voters vote for the party which comes closest to their own position on the issues. As we described in chapter 11, we have information from the 1987 survey on where the voters themselves stood, and where they believed the parties to stand, on the issues of nationalization and privatization, unemployment and inflation, taxation and government spending, nuclear weapons, and law and order. Our measurements took the form of eleven-point scales.

TABLE 13.14 Perceived Distances between the Parties and the Average Respondent

	The average respondent's position	Distance between the average respondent and the Conservative party	Distance between the average respondent and the Alliance	Distance between the average respondent and the Labour party
Nuclear weapons	5.2	−2.9	0.2	3.1
Unemployment and inflation ·	3.5	−2.9	−0.4	1.1
Taxation and health and Social Services	4.5	−2.7	0.0	1.4
Nationalization and privatization	6.4	−2.8	0.8	3.4
Law and order	7.7	0.2	1.4	2.1
Overall	27.1	−11.1	2.0	11.1
N (minimum)	3634	3518	3080	3439

Source: 1987 cross-section survey

Table 13.14 shows the position of the average voter and the distance between the average voter and the parties on these five issues. One striking feature of this table is that, overall, Labour and Conservative were almost equidistant from the average voter with the Alliance position being very much closer to the average.[21] (We also asked our respondents to make global judgements of whether the parties were "extreme" or "moderate" and very similar proportions said that the Conservative and Labour parties were extreme—47% for the Conservatives and 49% for Labour). Of course, these overall distances from the average voter are made up in rather different ways:

Labour was perceived to be particularly far away from the average voter on defence and nationalization but relatively close on social services and unemployment. The Conservatives on the other hand were perceived to be quite a long way from the average voter on all issues except law and order.

Let us next assume that the voter chooses the party to which he or she comes closest. Following the usual rational choice theory, we assume that anyone to the left of (or at the same point as) the Labour position will vote Labour while anyone to the right of (or at the same point as) the Conservative position will vote Conservative. We further assume that people in between vote for whichever of Labour, Conservative or the Alliance they lie closest to. Following our evidence in chapter 11, we do not take account of the importance which people attach to the various issues but simply calculate the overall distances. Thus issues like law and order, on which the three parties are perceived to be close together, will have less weight in the overall calculation of distance than will issues like nationalization and defence on which the perceived gaps between the parties are much greater.[22]

If people had behaved according to these assumptions, we estimate that 28.4% would have voted Labour, 28.9% would have voted for the Alliance, and 42.6% would have voted for the Conservatives.[23] We should note that one important reason why Labour does rather poorly according to this model is that the Alliance position was closer to Labour's than it was to the Conservatives' position, thus leaving the Conservatives with a larger territory over which to gather votes.

Our next step is to calculate what effects the ideological polarization between the Labour and Conservative parties might have had on the vote. What we can do is to estimate what the parties' shares of the votes would have been had Labour and Conservative taken more centrist positions.

This exercise must have a somewhat arbitrary character as we do not have any measurements of where the parties stood on these issues in the 1970s before they became polarized. We must also remember that this model assumes that positions on the five scales are the only factors that influence voting. The various omitted factors mean that the model will overestimate the impact of issues (as will the problem of the causal relations between attitudes and party identification). We can use the model therefore only to suggest what is the *maximum* impact which a change of policy would have on the vote.

We can now employ this model to look at the hypothetical question of what would have happened if Labour had for example adopted a more centrist position on nuclear defence. The actual Labour position in 1987 on nuclear weapons was of course seen as well to the left of centre. The model suggests that if they had moved halfway towards the Alliance, then they would have been expected to increase their share of the vote by around 2%.

Similarly with nationalization, a move halfway towards the Alliance position would, according to our model, have brought Labour an extra 2% of the vote. Furthermore, if Labour moved towards the centre on both issues, the gains would be cumulative and the model predicts an extra 4%, the gains to Labour coming of course at the Alliance's expense.

Note that it is the presence of the Alliance to the left of centre that limits Labour's gains. If the Alliance or Liberal Democrats were now to move to the right of centre, that in itself would, on the assumptions of our model, boost Labour's fortunes and reduce the Conservatives'. A crucial point, then, in understanding the operation of a rational choice model is that a party's fortunes depend not on its absolute position but on its position *relative to other parties.*

The same sort of calculations can of course be applied to the Conservative party: if we assume that the Conservative party moves back towards the centre to the same extent as we assumed for the Labour party, we obtain rather similar estimates for the electoral consequences.

We must emphasize that we do not have comparable data from the 1970s on the parties' positions and so cannot make any precise calculations about the distances they have moved. However, it is surely wise to assume that there has been some substantial ideological polarization between the parties. The evidence of table 3.1 points rather clearly in this direction. It is also quite likely that the electorate believed that the Conservative party, and not just the Labour party, had moved away from the centre.[24]

We must emphasize that the estimates we have made follow from a strict application of a rational choice model, and make no allowance for party identification and the processes of attitude change described in chapter 12. We would be wise to assume from the evidence of chapters 3 and 12 that both "bottom up" and "top down" processes have been at work. It follows from this that we should make some allowance for the electoral consequences of the Labour and Conservative moves away from the centre, and that that allowance should probably be rather less than the estimates derived from our rational choice model above. Let us suggest that these moves away from the centre cost the Labour and Conservative parties two points each, the Alliance thus gaining four points.

The combined impact of social and political change

Table 13.15 summarizes these various social and political sources of change and their possible impacts on the parties. Taken together, they would appear to suggest that Labour's share will have fallen overall by fifteen points and the Conservative's share by two points, while the Liberal/Alliance share will have risen by around fourteen points. These overall figures are not a long way from the actual changes which the parties have experienced over this period. Since our estimates of social and political change are based on survey data, we must also use survey estimates of the actual changes in the parties' shares of the total vote.[25]

Our estimates of the social and political components of electoral change necessarily have a somewhat speculative character, most obviously in the case of ideological polarization. The combined estimate does however seem to be of the right order of magnitude. Furthermore, the gaps between the combined estimate and the actual change also seem quite plausible.

These gaps can be thought of as measuring short-run political factors such as the competence of the party, its record in government, and so on. It is clear that these short-run fluctuations can be quite considerable. For example,

TABLE 13.15 The Effects of Social and Political Change 1964–87

	share of the vote		
	Conservative	Liberal/Alliance	Labour
Social change	+2.7	+1.8	−4.0
Extension of the franchise	−0.3	+0.4	−0.1
Liberal candidates	−2.4	+6.7	−4.3
Tactical voting	+0.4	−0.4	−0.6
Formation of the SDP	−0.7	+1.3	−0.6
Ideological polarization	−2.0	+4.0	−2.0
Total predicted	−2.3	+13.8	−11.6
Actual change	+1.7	+12.8	−15.3

Source: models based on 1964 and 1987 cross-section surveys

between 1966 and 1970 Labour lost 5 points and yet there were no major changes over that period in the number of Liberal candidates, the parties' ideological positions, and so on.

We should also note that the gaps in table 13.15 between the combined estimate and the actual change reflect *differences* between 1964 and 1987 in the competence and record of the parties. They suggest that the Conservatives under Mrs Thatcher in 1987 scored four points higher than they had done under Sir Alec Douglas-Home in 1964, while Labour fared about four points worse under Mr Kinnock than it had done under Mr Wilson.

As we have noted, the various processes incorporated in table 13.15 have varying degrees of reversibility. Social change is probably the least reversible; judgements of competence are probably the most easily reversible. If we assume that the extension of the franchise and the presence of Liberal candidates in all constituencies are permanent elements of the political marketplace whereas the other changes (such as the tactical bonuses and ideological polarization) are reversible, then table 13.15 suggests that Labour's natural level of support is now around 8 points lower than its 1964 level, the Liberal's is 8 points up and the Conservatives' is roughly the same.

Of course, the political marketplace could change again if there were to be Green candidates in most constituencies. The evidence of chapter 12 suggested that a Green party which campaigned on the protection of the countryside would particularly threaten the Liberals, and to a lesser extent the Conservatives, while a Green party which emphasized nuclear issues would threaten the Labour party more.

The political future will therefore depend on the deliberate strategies pursued by the parties. While in retrospect we can see that the SDP failed to break the mould of British politics, it is not implausible to suggest that the mould had already been changed once when the Liberals chose to become a national force in 1974 and had been changed again when the Labour and

Conservative parties moved away from the centre. It will no doubt be changed again at the next election. In understanding political change it is crucial, we believe, to recognize how the mould has differed from election to election.

Notes

[1] Table 13.1 is taken from Heath and McDonald (1987), which derives from Routh (1980), Routh (1987), Price and Bain (1988) and Bain, Bacon and Pimlott (1972). These sources in turn derive from the Census.

[2] The particular procedure we use for constructing social class (namely classifying economically active married women according to their own occupation rather than the head of household's occupation) produces a slightly smaller working class than alternative procedures, but the direction and scale of the change is very similar whichever procedure is used. Thus our procedure produces a fall in the working class from 51% in 1964 to 36% in 1987 whereas the head of household procedure yields a fall from 51% to 37%. These changes may be compared with a fall in the number of manual workers in the labour force from 58% in 1961 to 45% in 1981.

[3] Following a helpful suggestion from Crewe (1987) we have changed our procedure from that adopted in *How Britain Votes*. Instead of applying the 1964 conditional probabilities to the actual 1987 frequencies, we have followed the reverse procedure and applied the 1987 conditional probabilities to the 1964 frequencies. This has the advantage, inter alia, that the estimates of the conditional probabilities will be based on larger cell frequencies. It also means that our results are not affected by the intervention of Liberal candidates, and so we avoid the problem of double counting.

[4] In table 13.2 the Anglicans include the Church of England, Church in Wales and Scottish Episcopalian. The Nonconformists include Baptists, Methodists, Presbyterian (excluding Church of Scotland), and members of the Congregational Churches (now the United Reformed Church). In the case of Catholics the figures are based on the numbers of communicants.

[5] We should note that the rate of decline is rather faster according to the survey data than the Church membership data, and we should bear in mind the possibility that the procedural changes introduced in the 1974 British Election Survey may have exaggerated the survey trend. Still, the different measures all agree that the trend has been sharply downwards. And we would not be too far out if we concluded that both Protestant members and identifiers had halved in number.

[6] The official regional classification was changed in 1965. *Regional Trends* has published figures using the new classification for 1961 but not for 1951. Published figures for 1951 are not therefore comparable with the later figures, and have been excluded from table 13.3.

[7] Perhaps the clearest example of this is the failure of governments to expand selective secondary education in line with the number of school-age children in the late 1950s, leading to a decline in the proportion attending selective secondary school. See Halsey, Heath and Ridge (1980).

[8]The General Household Surveys are representative samples of the Great Britain population. The 1972 figures given in table 13.4 cover persons aged 15 or over not in full-time education. Those for 1981 and 1986/87 cover economically active persons aged 25–69 not in full-time education.

The GHS includes professional qualifications of degree-level along with degrees themselves. We have not followed this practice in our treatment of the BES data. We have also included foreign degrees along with British degrees. The reason for our procedure is that we believe that it is people's experience within the educational institution, rather than the qualification they receive, that is relevant for understanding their political attitudes and behaviour. We would not expect people with professional, degree-level qualifications to have had the same institutional experiences as the people who have gained degrees, and we would not therefore expect them to have the same political attitudes.

[9]Our survey estimates tally closely with these official ones. People who are not in the labour market tend to have somewhat fewer or lower qualifications than those who are economically active, and so our estimates of the electorate's qualifications are somewhat lower than those of table 13.4 which are based on the economically active population. However, if we calculate our figures on the same basis as those of table 13.4 the differences are within sampling error.

[10]The figures used in table 13.5 have been derived by Peter Taylor-Gooby from *Social Trends*, which in turn takes its figures from the General Household Survey.

[11]A very similar pattern is shown by our survey estimates, although our data seem to exaggerate the extent of change. Thus our 1964 estimates are closely in line with expectations, but by 1987 we have rather too many owner-occupiers in our survey (70% compared with the official estimate of 63% for 1986). We need to bear this in mind when estimating the political consequences of the housing changes.

[12]The official figures derive from trade union records. It is interesting to note that our survey estimates are substantially lower than the official ones. If we calculate potential membership in the same way as the official sources (that is, employees plus the unemployed), we obtain a figure of 36% compared with the official 45%. One possible explanation for the discrepancy is that of response bias in our survey: as we have seen our survey rather overestimates the proportion of owner-occupiers (and exaggerates the growth of owner-occupation), and so conversely it would not be surprising to find that we have underestimated trade union members (and have exaggerated the decline in membership). Of course, another possibility is that trade unions inflate their membership numbers.

[13]In table 8.7 East African Asians have been combined with Indians. The figures for 1981 and 1987 derive from the Labour Force Survey and are taken from Haskey (1988). The figures for 1951, 1961 and 1971 are derived from the Census. Peach et al (1988) have made estimates for these years for the West Indian Ethnic population; Shaw (1988) has made estimates for the total ethnic minority population; and Coleman (1983) has made estimates for all groups in 1971. The figures for all ethnic minorities refer to non-white ethnic

COMPONENTS OF CHANGE   223

minorities. There are of course large ethnic minorities in Britain of Irish, Polish, Cypriot origin and so on which are not covered by these figures. [14] There have of course been other changes too, such as the spread of share ownership, rising living standards, increasing unemployment and increasing inequality. The evidence we reviewed in chapters 8, 9 and 10 suggested that their electoral consequences will have been rather small. We should also note that there have been important changes in women's participation in the labour market. We would not therefore wish to claim that our analysis is exhaustive, although we suspect that the introduction of further social changes will have rather little impact on the results of the multivariate analysis (see below).

We have also excluded changes in attitudes (for example towards public ownership) from our analysis. While the timing of the shift to the right in 1979 cannot be explained by social change, the overall changes in attitudes between 1964 and 1987 would appear to be broadly in line with the changes in social structure, and there is therefore a serious risk of double counting if we include both changes in attitudes and changes in social structure.

[15] We should also note that our survey estimates of the changes in religion and in housing tenure are probably overestimates, but since they have opposite political consequences these errors too are likely to cancel out.

[16] For example, of electors aged 18–20 in 1983, 63% reported in 1987 that they had voted (or abstained) in the same way at both elections, compared with 70% of older electors. Because of the small numbers in the panel study, these figures are based on recall data from the 1987 cross-section survey. They are unadjusted and therefore not comparable with the figures reported in chapter 2. For a detailed analysis of young voters see Brown 1989.

[17] Our estimate of the effect of Liberal candidates is based on the same general methods as in assessing the political consequences of social change. Thus we take the 1964 conditional probabilities in seats which the Liberals did contest and calculate what they would have obtained given the actual distribution of class, housing, religion and education in the seats which they did not contest. It should be noted that we do not take into account any contextual effects in assessing the impact of Liberal candidates, and it is likely that contextual effects will reduce our estimate somewhat.

[18] The numbers do not add up to the number of constituencies in Britain (618 in 1964 and 633 in 1987) because there were constituencies where Plaid Cymru or the SNP were in first or second place. (Also, in Rhondda East in 1964 the Communist Party pushed the Conservatives into third place in a seat which the Liberals did not contest.)

[19] From table 4.4 we can calculate that tactical voting was thirteen points higher in seats where one's preferred party had been in third place or worse at the previous election. And from table 4.5 we see that in 1987 the actual Liberal vote of Liberal identifiers was nine points less in Conservative/Labour seats, while the actual Labour vote of Labour identifiers was twelve points lower in Conservative/Alliance seats. These estimates are consistent with the overall estimate of 6% tactical voters in 1987, since a party will have fewer of its identifiers in seats where it came third. In other words,

a party does not lose 10% of its *total* support through tactical voting but rather 10% of its support *in the seats where it came third or lower*.

[20] Butler and Stokes of course used the concept of generation to model change from a party identification perspective. We would not wish to discount their strategy entirely, but there can be little doubt that ideological changes tend to operate across-the-board affecting all generations to more or less the same extent. See Crewe 1974, Abramson 1978).

[21] While the distributions of respondents on the original scales tend to be skewed and/or peaked round particular values, the overall distribution on the summated scale is much closer to a normal distribution. In particular, the average and the median have the same value.

[22] This does not solve the problem of weighting, since our results will still be dependent on the number and type of issues which we include.

[23] In reaching this estimate we have excluded nonvoters and voters for the minor parties from the analysis. In other words, we have applied the model to the members of the sample who reported voting for Labour, Conservative or Alliance. This procedure gets us somewhat closer to the actual election result than does our previous method, described in *How Britain Votes*. However, we should note that our estimates are vulnerable to the assumptions which we make about missing data. In particular, many respondents were ignorant about the Alliance position on one or more issues but were happy to place the Labour and Conservative parties on the scales. We have assumed that it is not rational for such people to vote for the Alliance, even if their own position on the scales is identical to that which other respondents gave to the Alliance. Accordingly, we assume that the closest party to these respondents is either the Labour or the Conservative party. This assumption reduces our estimate of the Alliance share of the vote.

[24] Questions on whether the parties were extreme or moderate were asked in October 1974, 1979 and 1983. There was in fact rather more change in perceptions of the Conservative party than there were of the Labour party, 42% saying that the Conservative party was extreme in 1974, 49% in 1983 and 47% in 1987, whereas the figure for the Labour party was 49% in all three years. However, we should note that respondents were offered five options in 1974 but only three in 1983 and 1987 and this methodological change is likely to have affected the trends. In particular, with only three options the respondents will be more likely to use the centre option.

[25] We are indebted to Ivor Crewe for pointing this out. See Crewe (1987).

Appendix I

The British Election Surveys 1963–1987

The British Election Surveys constitute the longest academic series of nationally representative probability sample surveys in this country. They have taken place immediately after every General Election since 1964, giving a total of eight so far. There have also been two nonelection year surveys (in 1963 and 1969), a postal referendum study in 1975, additional Scottish studies in 1974 and 1979, an additional Welsh study in 1979 and a campaign study in 1987.

The series was originated by David Butler (Nuffield College, Oxford) and Donald Stokes (University of Michigan), who continued to direct the studies until 1970. The series then passed on to Ivor Crewe, Bo Sarlvik and James Alt at the University of Essex (later joined by David Robertson) who organized the two 1974 surveys and the 1979 one. The 1983 and 1987 studies were directed by Anthony Heath (Jesus and Nuffield Colleges, Oxford), Roger Jowell (SCPR), John Curtice (Universities of Liverpool and Strathclyde), Julia Field (SCPR), together with Sharon Witherspoon (SCPR) in 1987.

Nuffield College found the bulk of the funds for the initial fieldwork of the Butler and Stokes' surveys. The Economic and Social Research Council (previously the Social Science Research Council) then became the major funding agency, wholly supporting the Essex surveys. The 1983 study was jointly funded by the Economic and Social Research Council, Pergamon Press and Jesus College, Oxford while the 1987 study was jointly funded by the ESRC, Pergamon Press and the Sainsbury Trusts, who generously allowed the British Social Attitudes Survey to join forces with the Election Study.

Broadly speaking, the aim of the Election Studies series has been to explore the changing determinants of electoral behaviour in contemporary Britain.

Initially it was modelled on the work of the Michigan school of political science in the USA (of which Donald Stokes was a member) and shared the Michigan interest in socialization and partisan identification as major and stable influences on electoral behaviour. Since then, other interests have come to the fore reflecting developments in academic political science (such as the rise of rational choice theories) and changes in the political context.

Despite the different interests of the three research groups, there has been substantial continuity and a common core of questions has been asked in each of the surveys. Thus there have almost always been questions, first, on electoral behaviour itself (turnout, party choice, and timing of the vote decision); second, on political perceptions and identification (perceived difference between the parties, political interest and party identification); third, on social and political attitudes; fourth, on subjective social class and political antecedents; and fifth on objective biographical data (education, housing tenure, trade union membership, occupation, religion, age, sex and marital status). There is broad agreement from the political science community that this common core of questions is an essential component of the past series of Election Studies and of any future ones.

Taken in conjunction with the sets of questions unique to each of the individual surveys (most notably those concerning topical political issues), this common core makes the Election Studies a particularly rich series of data sets, valuable both for cross-sectional and time-series analyses. It is particularly outstanding for the detail of the occupational information. This usually covers the respondent's spouse and father, as well as the respondent him/herself, and is coded to the Office of Population Censuses and Surveys system of occupation groups (from which can be derived social class, socio-economic group and other classifications). The Election Studies are unique in having such detailed data going back in a continuous series to 1963.

The sample sizes of the cross-section Election Surveys have varied from under 2000 to nearly 4000. They have been designed to yield representative cross-sections of the electorate in England, Wales and Scotland (south of the Caledonian Canal). Northern Ireland has always been excluded. Many of the surveys have also included a substantial panel element composed of respondents who had been interviewed in one or more previous surveys.

The series began in 1963 with a stratified random sample of 2009 respondents drawn from the current electoral registers of 80 constituencies in Britain.[1] In 1964 such respondents as could be traced and contacted from the 1963 list were reinterviewed yielding 1481 completed panel interviews. Ageing, death and migration necessarily made these surviving panel members unrepresentative of the electorate, so new names were also drawn from the new registers in the same 80 constituencies. When appropriately weighted, these two elements give a representative cross-section of the electorate in 1964. (Note, however, that panel members who had moved from their original addresses were excluded from the cross-section, producing a sample size smaller than the total number of interviews conducted.)

This pattern, with variations, was followed up to and including 1979. Diagram I.1A and table I.2A describe the structure of the panels and cross-sections in detail.[2] Table I.3A gives the response rates. It will be seen that there was no panel study between 1979 and 1983, due to lack of funding, while in 1987 the panel and cross-section surveys were completely independent, just as they were in February 1974, rather than combined as they had been in 1966 or 1979.

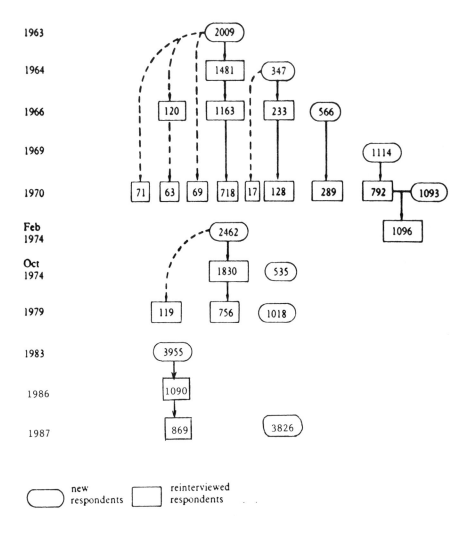

DIAGRAM I.1A. Election Study Interviews

TABLE I.2A Sample Size

		Electorate sample
1963	Electorate: new respondents 2009	2009
1964	Electorate: new respondents 347; from 1963 electorate 1422	1769
	1963–64 panel 1481 (59 no longer at sample address and therefore not included in 1964 electorate sample)	
1966	Electorate: new respondents 566; from 1963 and 1964 electorates 1308	1874
	1963–64–66 panel 1163 (165 no longer at sample address; part of panel but not 1966 electorate sample)	
	1963–66 panel 1283 (166 no longer at sample address; part of panel but not 1966 electorate sample)	
	1964–66 panel 1360 (192 no longer at sample address; part of panel but not 1966 electorate sample)	
1969	Electorate: new respondents 1114	1114
1970	Electorate: new respondents 1093; from 1969 electorate 750	1843
	1963–64–66–70 panel 718	
	1963–64–70 panel 787	
	1963–66–70 panel 781	
	1963–70 panel 921 not included in 1970 electorate sample	
	1964–66–70 panel 831	
	1964–70 panel 915	
	1966–70 panel 1107	
	1969–70 panel 792 (42 no longer at sample address and therefore not included in 1970 electorate sample)	
Feb 1974	Electorate: new respondents 2462	2462
	1969–70–Feb 1974 panel 1096 (not included in Feb 1974 electorate sample)	
Oct 1974	Electorate: new respondents 535; from Feb 1974 electorate 1830	2365
1979	Electorate: new respondents 1018; from Feb 1974 electorate 875	1893
	Feb 1974–79 panel 866	
	Oct 1974–79 panel 765	
	Feb 1974–Oct 1974–79 panel 756	
1983	Electorate: new respondents 3955	3955
1987	Electorate: new respondents 3826	3826
	1983–86 panel 1090	
	1983–86–87 panel 869	

TABLE I.3A Response Rates in Cross-Section Surveys 1963–87

	1963	1964	1966	1969	1970	Feb 1974	Oct 1974	1979	1983	1987
Percentage response rate	79.4	68.3	69.9	78.2	69.7	75.8	73.7	60.9	72.4	70.0

Notes

[1]The names drawn from the electoral register were used to obtain a sample of households rather than individuals. The aim was to secure a sampling frame closer to the register on which the 1964 election would be fought rather than the already out of date 1963 register.

[2]Sources for diagram I.1A and tables I.2A and I.3A are as follows: for the 1963–1970 surveys they are *Study of Political Change in Britain 1963–1970*, Volume 1: Introduction and Codebook, Volume II: Questionnaire and Notes; *Political Change in Britain 1969–1970*: codebooks and questionnaire; and Butler and Stokes (1974). Figures for the 1970 electorate sample and 1969–1970 panel sample are taken from the relevant codebook. (The codebooks and questionnaires were made available by the Inter-University Consortium for Political and Social Research, Ann Arbor, Michigan.)

For the 1974–1979 surveys the sources were *British Election Study at the University of Essex Technical Paper 1980:1* and the codebooks for the British Election Study 1969-February 1974 Panel Sample, the February 1974 Cross-section, and the October 1974 Cross-section. (These codebooks were made available by the Economic and Social Research Council Data Archive at the University of Essex.)

These sources do not always tally exactly with other published figures, but the discrepancies are all very minor.

Appendix II

Technical Details of the 1987 Surveys

The Cross-Section Survey

The survey was designed to yield a representative sample of eligible voters living in private households in Great Britain. It is not a random sample of all resident adults, but only of those on the electoral register and eligible to vote in the General Election of June 1987.

As with previous surveys in the election study series, electors living in Northern Ireland and the Scottish Highlands and Islands were excluded from the sampling frame; the former because its party composition and particular concerns would have required a separately-designed study, and the latter because the small and scattered population could not be interviewed cost-effectively.

A three-stage selection procedure was used. First, a sample of 250 constituencies was selected, with probability proportionate to size of electorate. Before selection, the constituencies were ranked by percentage of households that were owner-occupied and stratified within population density bands (persons per hectare) within Registrar General's Standard Regions. In order to make the strata fairly equal in size, the population density banding varied according to the standard region.

Second, all polling districts within the selected constituencies were ordered in a logical sequence associated with the alphabetic or numeric labelling system used within the constituency. Any polling district with fewer than 500 electors was combined with the one following it in this (circular) list, to form one unit. In the course of selecting constituencies, a random elector had been picked. The polling district within which the preselected elector lived was the selected polling district, giving selection probabilities proportionate to the electorate.

Third, within each of the 250 selected polling districts, a systematic random sample of 24 electors was selected with equal probability. Any of the selected electors who were ineligible to vote in the General Election (peers and those whose eighteenth birthday took place after June 7th) were replaced with an eligible elector (selected by means of a random number table).

Overall, a sample of 6000 names was thus selected. In two cases, despite repeated efforts on the part of both SCPR and OPCS to obtain the current electoral registers, they were not available. Hence, registers compiled in winter 1985–86 were used. In all other cases, registers compiled in winter 1986–87 were used.

A small-scale pretest of the questionnaire was carried out shortly after the announcement of the election. Four interviewers carried out 45 interviews. They were briefed beforehand and debriefed afterwards by the research team.

Fieldwork for the survey began on 23 June, before which all interviewers were personally briefed by SCPR researchers working on the project (Roger Jowell, Sharon Witherspoon and Julia Field). A few supplementary briefings were later led by experienced regional field supervisors. In all, 221 SCPR interviewers worked on the survey.

Some potential respondents who had been difficult to locate, or had moved, or had refused, or had broken appointments, were re-issued to interviewers (usually interviewers who had not made the initial calls) during the later phases of fieldwork. The names of 97 movers were reissued and in 67 cases an interview was obtained. Some 645 names were reissued for other reasons; in these cases 172 productive interviews were obtained. In all, response was raised by just over 3% by reissuing names. The final response rate was 70%.

A total of 61% of the interviews were obtained by the end of July 1987 and 93% by the end of August. A further 5.5% were conducted after that, mainly recalls on respondents who were unable or unwilling to be interviewed earlier.

The response breakdown is shown in table II.1A.

TABLE II.1A BES Cross-Section: Response Summary

	N	%	%
NAMES ISSUED:	6000	100.0	
Addresses out-of-scope			
(empty, demolished, no trace)	8	0.1	
Named person:			
dead	66	1.1	
emigrated	25	0.4	
under age	4	0.*	
mover-address unknown	313	5.2	
untraceable	121	2.0	

[*Continued next page*

TABLE II.1A—Continued

	N	%	%
TOTAL FOUND OR ASSUMED TO BE OUT OF SCOPE OR UNTRACEABLE	537	9.0	
TOTAL IN-SCOPE	5463	91.0	100.0
Interview obtained	3826	63.8	70.0
Of which:			
with self-completion	3415	56.9	62.5
without self-completion	411	6.9	7.5
Interview not obtained	1637	27.3	30.0
Of which:			
refusal	1017	17.0	18.6
refusal by someone else in h/h (proxy)	137	2.3	2.5
broken appointment	72	1.2	1.3
refusal to office	5	0.*	0.*
not contacted—never in	137	2.3	2.5
senile/incapacitated	102	1.7	1.9
away or in hospital	79	1.3	1.4
ill at home	29	0.5	0.5
Other (incl. complete refusal of information at address)	59	1.0	1.1

The self-completion supplement

Following the model of the British Social Attitudes Series, we designed a self-completion supplement which we invited all respondents to complete on their own after the interview and return either via an interviewer collection or by post. In all 89% of the respondents completed and returned the supplement.

The 1983–87 panel study

A subsample of the 1983 election study respondents was selected for a panel to be reinterviewed twice. The first interview was to provide measures of change before the 1987 election, and the second reinterview was to provide measures after the election. The sample was designed to achieve a panel of 800 respondents who would be interviewed on all three occasions. Since the major purpose of the panel was to understand change, the questionnaires consisted largely of exact replications of questions asked in the 1983 survey. However, in order to maintain respondent interest and cooperation, some new material was introduced.

Of the 250 constituencies in the 1983 BES, 115 were selected for the panel: 27 constituencies had already been used in a previous follow-up study of the 1983 BES respondents and were therefore deleted from the list of constituencies to be used in drawing the panel sample. The selection of constituencies for the panel was then made on a systematic random basis independently within the strata used for drawing the original 250 constituencies for the 1983 sample. The 1983 list of constituencies had originally been stratified by region (11 regions) and density (3 density bands) giving a total of 32 strata (there being no high density constituencies in East Anglia). For drawing the panel constituencies, however, ten of these strata were grouped into pairs. This was because a proportionate distribution would have resulted in no selections in a stratum (as in the case with the high density band in Wales) or because the purposive selection of 27 polling districts for the previous follow-up study had left insufficient polling districts to use for the panel.

After deletion of the 1983 unproductives and those unwilling to be reinterviewed, 1634 respondents' names and addresses were issued to interviewers. The first round of fieldwork took place in November/December 1986. A total of 1090 productive interviews were achieved, an overall response of 67%. Much of the non-response was caused by difficulty in locating respondents who had moved between 1983 and 1986; 40% of non-response at this stage was attributable to the failure to establish the new addresses of movers. A further 10% of non-response resulted from the death or emigration of respondents.

Post-election fieldwork began on 22 June. Some 91% of interviews were achieved within 7 weeks of the election and almost all the remainder completed by the end of August: 1020 addresses were issued to interviewers, the remaining 70 having said at wave 1 that they were unwilling to be reinterviewed. In all, 869 productive interviews were achieved. Of the 1634 names originally issued, therefore, 54% completed the final wave of interviews. It may be noted that in previous BES panel studies over comparable timespans 58% of the original names survived over the 1966–70 period, 58% over the 1970-February 1974 period, and 41% over the October 1974–1979 period.

The response breakdown of the two waves of the panel is shown in table II.2A.

TABLE II.2A BES Panel: Response Summary

	Round one			Round two		
	No.	%	%	No.	%	%
NAMES ISSUED	1634	100		1020	100	
Addresses out of scope (empty, demolished, no trace)	11	0.7		—	—	
Named person:						
dead	42	2.6		5	0.5	
emigrated	9	0.6		3	0.3	
mover—address unknown	172	10.5		4	0.4	
untraceable	27	1.6		3	0.3	
TOTAL FOUND OR ASSUMED TO BE OUT OF SCOPE OR UNTRACEABLE	261	16.0		15	1.5	
TOTAL IN SCOPE	1373	84.0	100.0	1005	98.5	100.0
Interview obtained	1090	66.7	79.4	869	85.2	86.5
(but unwilling for further interview)	(70)					
Interview not obtained	283	17.3	20.6	136	13.3	13.5
Of which:						
Refusal	150	9.2	10.9	66	6.5	6.6
Refusal by someone else in h/h (proxy)	18	1.1	1.3	6	0.6	0.6
Broken appointment	15	0.9	1.1	14	1.4	1.4
Not contacted—mover, address known but unable to follow up	16	1.0	1.2	1	0.1	0.1
Not contacted—never in	41	2.5	3.0	19	1.9	1.9
Senile/incapacitated	10	0.6	0.7	2	0.2	0.2
Away or in hospital	15	0.9	1.1	10	1.0	1.0
Ill at home	11	0.7	0.8	8	0.8	0.8
Other (inc. complete refusal of information at address)	7	0.4	0.5	10	1.0	1.0

Appendix III

Components of Nonresponse Bias in the British Election Surveys

Graham Farrant and Colm O'Muircheartaigh
Joint Centre for Survey Methods

This report addresses the issue of nonresponse in the British Election Surveys. Whereas all survey data are affected by nonresponse, in general the extent to which it is possible to determine the characteristics of the nonrespondents is limited by the absence of data about them at the household or individual level. Thus where any analysis of nonresponse is reported at all it consists only of comparing the profile of respondents to a particular survey with the known (or assumed) profile of the population from which the sample was drawn. There are of course serious limitations on the information available about the population—in terms both of variables available and of the reference period. In the absence of population data the profile of a survey with a large sample base (such as the General Household Survey) is sometimes used as a standard. In the present case there are however some additional possibilities of learning about the nonrespondents.

In the 1987 election survey each respondent was asked to complete, after the face-to-face interview, a self-completion booklet which was to be returned separately. By examining the characteristics of those who did not return the self-completion booklet we may obtain some insight into the nature (or correlates) of nonresponse. The 1983 election survey provides information of a different kind. There was a panel element in the survey, in that a subsample of 1983 respondents was selected for continued study in 1986 and 1987. The record of responses for these subsequent approaches provides an indication

235

of population groups for which attrition is a particularly serious problem. In addition to these special features both data sets provide an opportunity to carry out the standard comparisons with available profiles of the general population relating to the time of the surveys.

The kinds of information provided by these analyses differ; one set of analyses relates to the propensity to return self-completion supplements, another to the propensity to remain as a respondent in a (multi-wave) panel survey, and the third to the propensity to respond to a cross-sectional survey. Though there is no available empirical evidence to suggest that the characteristics of these different types of nonresponse should be related, the election surveys provide a body of data on which all the analyses can be performed.

The samples on which the analyses are based are described briefly in table III.1A below.

TABLE III.1A Sample Size and Response: 1987 and 1983 BES Surveys

	Issued sample (in scope)	Respondents	Response rate %
1987 BES:			
Full survey	5463	3826	70.0
Self-completion supplement	3826	3415	89.3
1983 BES			
Full survey	5463	3955	72.4

Comparison of 1987 survey respondents with the general population in 1987

There are limited possibilities for assessing the representativeness of the 1987 BES respondents in terms of the general population in 1987. Figures for age and sex are available from the OPCS mid-1987 Monitor, and for economic activity and socio-economic group from the 1987 General Household Survey, although this survey is also subject to potential nonresponse bias. Moreover, we should note that these general population estimates, unlike the British Election Survey, include people who have not actually registered as electors. The discrepancies between the British Election Survey and the population estimates might therefore be due to nonregistration rather than to nonresponse bias.

Table III.2A gives the proportions for age, sex, economic activity and vote in the three categories: general population, all survey respondents, and all self-completion respondents.

TABLE III.2A Comparing Two Respondent Samples with Population Profile

| | | 1987 BES respondents: | |
	OPCS Mid-87 Monitor	All	Self-completion only
Category	%	%	%
Male	48.0	48.0	48.5
Female	52.0	52.0	51.5
N		3826	3415
Age			
18–24	15.0	12.9	12.9
25–34	18.7	17.9	17.9
35–59	39.1	42.7	43.0
60–74	18.7	19.6	20.1
75 +	8.8	6.9	6.1
N		3795	3392
Economic activity	(GHS)		
Working	57.3	55.6	56.2
Waiting to take up work	0.5	0.5	0.5
Unemployed	5.1	5.5	5.3
Permanently unable to work	2.3	2.7	2.6
Looking after home	14.3	15.4	15.2
Retired	17.1	17.3	17.1
Student	2.0	1.5	1.6
YTS/else	1.5	1.5	1.5
	100.1%	100%	100%
N	20,504	3826	3415
	Actual Election result (GB)		
Vote in 1987			
Conservative	43.3	43.9	43.5
Labour	31.5	31.2	30.7
Alliance	23.1	23.5	24.5
Other	2.1	1.4	1.4
	100.0%	99.9%	100.1%
N	31,799,271	3204	2897

Comparison with the OPCS data shows no bias in distribution by sex. All five age subgroups showed a degree of initial nonresponse bias in the 1987 sample. For those over 35, nonresponse to the self-completion supplement compounded the effect, i.e. the additional nonresponse exacerbated the bias already present as a result of the initial nonresponse to the 1987 survey.

For the variable economic activity, however, the reverse appears to be the case. Those groups initially under- and over-represented in the original survey sample become rather more accurately represented (in relative terms) among respondents to the self-completion supplement.

We can also compare the BES survey respondents with the official figures for turnout and vote. The official figures here do of course take as their baseline registered electors. The figures for vote are shown in table III.2A, and the samples correspond quite closely to the actual election result. There are, however, much larger discrepancies between the sample and official figures for turnout. These are discussed in full in Swaddle and Heath (1989).

Self-completion responses in the 1987 BES

The purpose of this analysis is to examine the correlates of nonresponse to the self-completion supplement to the 1987 BES. The first objective is to identify any differences in propensity to complete the supplement; the second is to determine whether any differential nonresponse should be taken into account in analysing variables based on the self-completion supplement. In assessing the impact of the nonresponse the size of the nonresponding group—in this case only 10.7% of the eligible group—must of course be taken into account.

Seventeen variables from the main survey were chosen to cover broad demographic and socio-economic categorizations of respondents and to make it possible to consider possible relationships between these variables and the responses to the political/attitudinal questions. The variables were:

Demographic/life-cycle: Age, sex, ethnicity, marital status, economic activity;
Socio-economic: Social class, educational qualifications, housing tenure, age on leaving school, telephone in accommodation;
Political/attitudinal: Voting in 1987, 1983 and 1979; party identification, willingness to re-interview, attitude towards nationalization and privatization, attitude to election result.

There are a number of ways in which data on nonresponse can be presented, the appropriateness of which depend on the use to be made of the results. The simplest and most straightforward is to calculate the nonresponse rate (on the self-completion supplement) for each category of respondent to the interview. Having done this for each category of each of the seventeen variables above (61 categories in all), the eight categories with the highest and lowest nonresponse (non-return) rates are presented in table III.3A. The nonresponse rate may be interpreted as the propensity not to return the self-completion supplement.

TABLE III.3A 1987 BES Self-completion Supplement: Highest and Lowest Rates of Nonresponse

Category	Number interviewed	% of each category not responding
Unwilling to be re-interviewed	363	32.5
Nationalization: "cannot choose"	243	26.7
Non-white ethnicity	123	26.0
Aged 75 or over	263	20.9
Widowed	345	19.1
No political identification	523	17.3
Has no telephone	520	16.9
Did not vote, 1987	531	16.4
Willing to be re-interviewed	3463	8.5
Has educational qualification	2253	8.3
Salariat social class	990	8.1
Manual supervisor/technician	213	7.0
Liberal vote 1979	284	7.0
Alliance vote 1983	475	6.7
Liberal/SDP party identification	619	6.1
Alliance vote 1987	754	6.0

Note: Two other variable categories showed high rates of nonresponse; 'other' party vote in 1983, and other party vote in 1979. In both cases, however, the base for the percentage calculation was less than 50 cases.

The overall nonresponse rate for the whole sample was 10.7%; for individual categories the nonresponse rate varied from 6.0% to 32.5%. Among the eight categories with the highest nonresponse rates two different classes are worth considering—demographic and attitudinal. In demographic terms the old (75 and over), the widowed and the non-white were the poorest responders; in attitudinal terms the indications are that the indifferent were the most likely not to respond—those who could not choose either more or less nationalization, those with no political identification and those who did not vote in 1987. Among the groups with the lowest nonresponse the situation is dominated by Liberal/Alliance supporters (this may suggest that Liberal/ Alliance supporters are neither indifferent nor indecisive); in terms of socio-demographic characteristics the salariat, manual supervisors/ technicians and those with some educational qualifications exhibited the highest propensity to return the supplement.

The 'willing/unwilling to be re-interviewed' categories are included in the analysis as the response to this question would be used to determine whether an individual would be approached again if a further wave of interviewing were to be undertaken. The response thus relates to the issue of attrition in panel surveys.

A second way of looking at nonresponse is to compare the marginal distributions of important characteristics of the sample for respondents and for nonrespondents separately. Table III.4A below presents these distributions for age, marital status and attitude to nationalization.

TABLE III.4A Self-completion Supplement, Respondents and Nonrespondents: Age, Marital Status, and Attitude to Nationalization

	Self-completion respondents %	Self-completion nonrespondents %	All survey respondents %
Age			
18–24	12.9	13.2	12.9
25–34	17.9	17.9	17.9
35–59	43.0	39.2	42.7
60–74	20.1	16.1	19.6
75+	6.1	13.6	6.9
	100%	100%	100%
N	3392	403	3795
Marital status			
Married/as if	69.3	58.4	68.1
Widowed	8.2	16.1	9.0
Divorced/separated	4.9	4.6	4.9
Single	17.6	20.8	17.9
	100%	99.9%	99.9%
N	3415	409	3824
Attitude to nationalization			
More nationalization	16.4	15.2	16.3
No change	30.7	27.7	30.4
More privatization	47.7	40.9	46.9
Cannot choose	5.2	16.2	6.4
	100%	100%	100%
N	3412	401	3813

The distributions for respondents and nonrespondents differ substantially in a number of respects; this means that some categories of individuals account for a disproportionate share of the nonresponse. In particular, the over 75s comprise 14% of the nonrespondents, whereas they account for only 6% of the respondents. The widowed comprise 16% of the nonrespondents and only 8% of the respondents; conversely the married account for 58% of the nonrespondents and 69% of the respondents. Those who cannot choose a response to the nationalization question are also heavily over-represented among the nonrespondents—accounting for 16%—as against the respondents, of whom they account for only 5%.

The BES panel 1983–1987

It was envisaged at the time of the 1983 BES that a subsample of the respondents might be re-interviewed on later occasions, thus constituting a panel for the purposes of longitudinal analysis. A (nonprobability) sample of areas from the original sample was selected for inclusion in the panel. The potential panel therefore consisted of those respondents from the 1983 cross-section from these selected areas. Respondents in the cross-sectional sample for the 1983 BES had been asked at the time whether they would be willing to be re-interviewed at a later date. Those who had agreed were approached for interview in 1986 and (if they permitted it) again in 1987.

In evaluating the panel in terms of representativeness there are therefore six components to be examined. First, the nonresponse at the time of the 1983 survey; second, the extent to which the subsample of areas was unrepresentative; third, the loss due to the expressed unwillingness of 1983 respondents to be re-interviewed; fourth, the actual nonresponse in 1986; fifth, the loss due to the expressed unwillingness of the 1986 respondents to be re-interviewed again; and sixth, the actual nonresponse in 1987. The term used to describe the gradual loss of cases from a panel is *attrition*.

As with the analysis of nonresponse to the self-completion supplement in the 1987 BES, the aim of this analysis is to identify the extent, and the potential impact, of differential nonresponse (in this case, attrition) over the life of the panel, from the 1983 BES to the 1987 panel interviews.

The initial selection for the panel—the selection by area—resulted in a subsample which, for a number of demographic and attitudinal characteristics, was unrepresentative of the respondents in the original 1983 survey. This outcome is a consequence of the sampling process rather than of nonresponse. There are therefore two elements in the assessment of panel attrition.

The first of these examines the extent to which the panel has become unrepresentative of the original survey respondents. The reason for the differential attrition—whether it arises from the sampling process, or from nonresponse, or a combination of these—is not an issue in this case. If attrition—from whatever source—has changed the underlying composition of the panel so that the panel is no longer representative of the population, then this may have a bearing on the conclusions which might be drawn from the panel data.

The second element concerns the specific effects of panel nonresponse. Since the sample of areas selected was not representative of the areas in the original sample, the effects of the area selection must be excluded from any measurement of nonresponse. The subsample of respondents *after* the selection by area is therefore used as the benchmark from which to measure differential nonresponse. This analysis concentrates on panel attrition, the cumulative effect of successive approaches to the sample members. The purpose of this analysis is first to describe the extent of differential attrition in the panel and then to compare this with nonresponse to the self-completion supplement.

Tables III.5A shows the losses arising from nonresponse at each of these individual stages, as well as cumulatively from initial nonresponse up to and including the final round of panel interviews in 1987. Also shown is the cumulative rate of nonresponse in the panel, treating the initial survey

TABLE III.5A Respondents and Nonrespondents between 1983 and 1987

	Sample size at start of each stage	Non-respondents	% Non-response at each stage	Cumulative % non-response	Respondents
1983 cross-sectional survey	5463	1508	27.6	27.6	3955
Selected for panel	1820			35.0	
Selected for panel, unwilling to be re-interviewed		186	10.2		
Approached for interviewed in 1986	1634	544	33.3	56.6	1090
Interviewed in 1986, unwilling to be re-interviewed		70	6.4	59.5	
Approached for interview in 1987	1020	151	14.8	65.4	869

response as the base. It should be noted that the selection by areas reduced the size of the potential panel by 54%. This is not a nonresponse effect, and the impact of the area selection is therefore not taken into account in table III.5A.

Table III.5A provides a picture of the way in which the original sample selected for the 1983 BES was gradually eroded until only a minority of the selected individuals remained. Ignoring the selection of the sample of areas only 34.6% of those who might have been respondents at the final stage of the panel actually responded. The loss of sample members started with the nonresponse to the initial cross-sectional survey in 1983—a 28% nonresponse rate. Of the remaining 72% one in ten refused to give permission for a further visit by an interviewer, reducing the potential pool to 65% of the original sample. There was then a 33% nonresponse rate on the occasion of the 1986 interviews; part of this was of course due to non-contacts which would not apply in a cross-sectional survey such as failure to trace people who had moved, for example. Of the 44% who had survived up to this stage a further 6% refused permission to be approached again. At the final stage (the 1987 interviews) one in seven of the remainder did not respond. This gave an overall nonresponse rate from start to finish of 65.4% or two out of every three selected eligible individuals.

It is possible, though not likely, that the nonresponse in the panel is such that it affects equally all the categories of individuals in the population, and that the representativeness of the observed sample is therefore unaffected. The extent to which the sample is representative of the population can only be checked for variables for which population data are available. It is of interest to see whether attrition of the sample causes the remaining sample to deviate further from the population structure. Table III.6A below shows the position for age and sex.

TABLE III.6A Sex and Age in 1983: Comparison of 1981 Census Data with Respondents at Five Stages of the Panel

	1981 Census	1983 cross-section	Selected by area	Willing to reinterview	Took part in 86 panel	Took part in 87 panel
Male	48.0	47.3	47.1	48.5	49.4	51.2
Female	52.0	52.7	52.9	51.5	50.6	48.8
N	—	3955	1820	1634	1090	869
Age						
18–24	14.0	14.3	15.1	15.6	13.8	13.4
25–34	19.0	18.9	18.6	19.6	20.2	20.7
35–59	39.0	42.0	41.3	41.9	44.8	45.2
60–74	19.0	18.7	18.7	17.8	17.0	16.3
75+	8.0	6.2	6.2	5.2	4.3	4.3
N	—	3935	1811	1627	1081	863

TABLE III.7A Population Categories Experiencing the Largest Degree of Change in Proportional Size: 1983 to 1987 Panel

Most under-represented Categories	1983 all respondents %	Selected by area %	Willing to reinterview %	Took part in 86 panel %	Took part in 87 panel %
Has no telephone	18.5 (728)	17.5 (317)	16.1 (262)	13.6 (147)	11.8 (102)
Nationalization: "cannot choose"	11.5 (451)	11.1 (201)	9.4 (153)	8.1 (88)	7.5 (65)
Aged 75+	6.2 (245)	6.2 (113)	5.2 (84)	4.3 (46)	4.3 (37)
Local authority housing tenure	26.2 (1026)	23.3 (420)	22.0 (356)	20.7 (224)	18.3 (158)
Private rented housing tenure	8.2 (320)	8.3 (150)	7.8 (126)	6.4 (69)	5.8 (50)
Widowed	8.2 (323)	7.9 (143)	7.0 (115)	6.4 (70)	6.2 (54)
Labour vote in 1983	24.3 (937)	21.7 (384)	21.4 (341)	20.4 (218)	18.6 (158)
Most over-represented:					
Liberal vote in 1979	8.5 (328)	9.3 (164)	9.9 (157)	10.9 (115)	12.1 (102)
Petty bourgeoisie	7.7 (277)	8.5 (140)	8.2 (122)	9.0 (90)	9.4 (75)
Salariat social class	26.3 (942)	27.1 (446)	28.3 (420)	29.4 (294)	31.9 (255)
Nationalization: "privatize more"	37.6 (1482)	39.2 (711)	40.9 (668)	42.2 (459)	45.5 (395)
Conservative vote in 1983	37.1 (1432)	39.8 (705)	40.3 (644)	41.5 (443)	43.4 (369)
Has educational qualification	53.7 (2116)	56.0 (1015)	58.2 (948)	60.4 (655)	62.6 (542)
Owner-occupier housing tenure	65.7 (2574)	68.4 (1234)	70.3 (1139)	72.9 (788)	75.9 (656)

The sex distribution of the respondents to the 1983 survey was in close agreement with the population figures for the 1981 Census. The area selection had little effect, but from the point of asking for agreement to a further interview through the final approach in 1987 the proportion of men in the sample increased and the proportion of women decreased with the larger part of the change coming between the 1986 and 1987 interviews. The age distribution for the 1983 respondents differs from the population figures by under-representing the old and over-representing the 35–59 group. This imbalance is exacerbated by each subsequent approach, with the major change coming between 1983 and 1986.

For variables where no population data are available it is still possible to examine the way in which the sample composition changes from the 1983 respondents to the 1987 respondents. Though such changes do not necessarily reflect departures of the sample structure from the population structure (since we do not know the population structure), the balance of probability lies with this interpretation.

Table III.7A presents the categories whose proportional size is most affected during the life of the panel. The effect can come about in two ways: if the category suffers from a disproportionately high rate of nonresponse then it will become gradually under-represented in the panel; alternatively, if the category has a disproportionately low rate of nonresponse (high rate of response) it will become over-represented in the panel. In this analysis it is the differential rate of nonresponse that is relevant and not the overall rate of nonresponse, which is given in table III.5A.

The most affected category is households without a telephone (remember that this means they were without a telephone in 1983—all categories in this analysis are defined according to the 1983 responses). Such households represented 18.5% of the 1983 respondents; of the 1987 panel respondents they comprised only 11.8%. Those who answered 'cannot choose' to the question on nationalization also suffered from considerable attrition during the course of the panel—from 11.5% in 1983 to only 7.5% in 1987. The other categories whose representation was diluted were the old (although there may have been some real mortality here), the widowed, those with local authority or private rented housing, and those who voted Labour in 1983. In the case of Labour vote and local authority housing a substantial part of the effect was due to the selection of areas.

The characteristics of the categories whose representation increased during the life of the panel were generally those complementary to the under-represented categories. The owner-occupiers, the salariat and the petty bourgeoisie, and those who voted Conservative in 1983 increased their proportional representation in the sample. Those who wanted more privatization in 1983 also increased their representation, as did those who voted Liberal in 1979.

Table III.7A shows the way in which the change in representation came about. The first change (from 'all 1983 respondents' to the 'selected areas') arises from the design and not from individual decisions of the respondents. The other three changes all result from respondent decisions.

The overall pattern is strikingly consistent. With only two minor exceptions the stages have a cumulative effect—each stage reinforces the effects of
the previous stages. By coincidence this is true even of the selection of areas
where the choice was determined by extraneous factors. The overall effect
however is to make the final panel sample in 1987 very different in
composition from the 1983 cross-sectional sample.

In most cases the largest impact on the composition of the sample arose
between obtaining the consent of the 1983 respondent to a further visit by
the interviewer and the actual survey in 1986. This is not surprising since
there is a three-year interval between these two stages. It is noticeable,
however, that in some cases the biggest change is between the 1986 and 1987
surveys.

Table III.8A summarizes the position in terms of the panel nonresponse
itself (i.e. excluding the effect of selecting the areas). The overall panel
nonresponse rate was 52.3% (a little over half of those who responded to the
1983 survey and who were selected for the panel failed to respond in 1987).
The eight most affected categories and the seven least affected are shown. For
four of the categories more than two thirds of those eligible did not respond
in 1987; at the other extreme, of those who voted Liberal in 1979, almost

TABLE III.8A Panel Nonresponse from 1983 (Area-Selected Sample) to 1987: Highest
and Lowest Rates of Nonresponse

Category	Overall nonresponse at 1987 panel stage
	%
ALL RESPONDENTS	52.3
Has no telephone	67.8
Nationalization: "cannot choose"	67.7
Aged 75 and over	67.3
Private rented accommodation	66.7
Retired	62.5
Local authority accommodation	62.4
Widowed	62.2
Did not vote, 1983	61.8
	%
Owner-occupier	46.8
Has educational qualification	46.6
Petty bourgeoisie	46.4
Alliance vote, 1983	45.5
Nationalization: "privatize more"	44.4
Salariat	42.8
Liberal vote, 1979	37.8

two thirds *did* respond. The categories in this table are not the same as those in the previous table because the effect of the area selected is excluded.

Comparing nonresponse to the panel with nonresponse to the self-completion supplement

In comparing the panel nonresponse with the nonresponse to the self-completion supplement the effect of the area selection on the sample should be excluded from consideration. Nonresponse for the panel is therefore measured using the sample of selected areas as the base. Fifteen variables were available with which to compare the effect of nonresponse to the self-completion supplement with its effect on the panel between 1983 and 1987. These are the variables listed on page 238 above with the exception of willingness to reinterview and voting in 1987. These variables contained 54 respondent categories, 4 of which contained too few cases (in one or both samples) to be reliably compared. Thus there were in all 50 categories where the comparison was meaningful.

To obtain a general impression of the nonresponse in the two situations we defined two outcomes for respondent categories: over-representation and under-representation. In both the panel and the self-completion analyses these outcomes were defined by category levels of nonresponse which were, respectively, either above average or below average.

Twenty-two of the 50 respondent categories were found to be under-represented, as a result of (high) differential nonresponse, in both the panel and in the self-completion respondents. Twenty categories were over-represented in both. Thus 42 of 50 respondent categories showed the same pattern of differential nonresponse in the panel and for the self-completion supplement.

TABLE III.9A Outcome of Differential Nonresponse for 50 Categorizations of Respondent: 1983 and 1987 BES

NUMBER OF CATEGORIZATIONS:

		1983 BES: Panel members in 1987	
		Over-represented	Under-represented
1987 BES: self-completion respondents	Over-represented	20	7
	Under-represented	1	22

The same consistency was apparent when severity of nonresponse was taken into account: seven of the 10 categories which were *most* underrepresented in the self-completion supplement—that is, had the highest levels of nonresponse—were also among the 10 most under-represented categories in the panel. These were:

Aged 75 or over,
Widowed,
Did not vote in 1983,
No telephone,
Didn't care about election result,
Local authority tenure,
Said 'cannot choose' to the question on nationalization.

Eight of the 50 respondent categories showed different outcomes in the two situations. We have not identified any clear pattern to these inconsistent categories.

Conclusions

The principal feature of the analysis is that there is a high level of consistency in the results. We can build up an interesting composite picture of the good and poor respondent. Neither of these composites represents a real individual or set of individuals; the sizes of the samples with which we are dealing makes it impossible to examine such groups directly. A more complex analysis than that carried out here would be necessary to investigate this further. An artificial profile of nonresponse prone groups can be constructed, however, by combining the characteristics that are shown to be severally related to a propensity not to respond.

The elderly widowed phoneless without strong opinions on political issues will have a high propensity not to cooperate in surveys. The middle-aged (35–59) middle class who voted for the Liberals or the Alliance will tend to respond to our approaches.

Our investigation of nonresponse to the self-completion supplement to the 1987 BES suggests that though the nonrespondents did differ in many respects from the respondents the nonresponse rate was sufficiently low to make these differences inconsequential for most analyses. For the 1983–86–87 BES panel, on the other hand, the rate of attrition and the differences between continuing and lost panel members were such that great care should be taken in generalizing the results of the panel data.

However, we should note that the problems with the panel may be more serious in the case of frequency distributions than in the case of the relationships between variables. Compare, for example, the frequency distributions of vote in 1983 reported by the 3955 original respondents and the distribution reported (in 1983) by the 869 respondents who survived till the final panel wave of 1987. The 95% confidence intervals, calculated from the 1983 reports, are also shown. We can see that the percentages for the surviving panel respondents lie well outside the 95% confidence interval calculated from the original 1983 sample.

TABLE III.10A Frequency Distribution of 1983 Vote

	1983% respondents %	1983 95% confidence interval	1987% panel respondents %
Conservative	36.2	±1.5	42.5
Labour	23.7	±1.4	18.2
Liberal/Alliance	19.9	±1.3	22.4
Other	1.2	±0.3	1.3
Did not vote	16.7	±1.2	13.6
Refused, etc.	2.3	±0.5	2.1
	100.0%		100.1%
N	3955		869

Relationship between Vote in 1979 and Vote in 1983: Log Odds Ratios

	1983 respondents	1983 95% confidence interval	1987 panel respondents
Con:Lab	5.4	±0.4	5.3
Con:Lib	3.6	±0.4	3.8
Lib:Lab	4.3	±0.7	3.8
Con:DNV	2.3	±0.3	1.8
Lib:DNV	2.8	±0.4	3.0
Lab:DNV	2.6	±0.3	2.4

If, however, we consider the relationship between (reported) 1979 and 1983 vote and calculate the symmetrical log odds ratios, we see that the surviving panel respondents more closely resemble the original 1983 sample. The log odds ratios calculated from the reports of the surviving 869 respondents lie well within the 95% confidence intervals in most cases.

The fact that one analysis of relationships is well-behaved does not of course imply that this will be true for all such analyses, and we would stress the need for caution in generalizing the results of the panel data.

SOCIAL AND COMMUNITY PLANNING RESEARCH
and
THE UNIVERSITY OF OXFORD. NUFFIELD COLLEGE

Head Office
35 Northampton Square,
London, EC1V 0AX.
Telephone· 01-250 1866

P.934

June 1987

BRITISH GENERAL ELECTION STUDY 1987

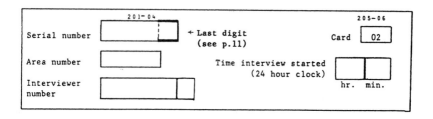

	201-04			205-06
Serial number		← Last digit (see p.11)	Card	02
Area number		Time interview started (24 hour clock)		
Interviewer number			hr.	min.

QUESTIONNAIRE CONTENTS

		Col./ Code	Skip to
	I. POLITICAL INTEREST		
	ASK ALL		
1.	Would you say you cared a good deal which Party won the recent general election or that you didn't care very much which Party won?	207	
	Cared a good deal	1	
	Didn't care very much	2	
2.	During the election campaign:	208	
a)	Did you watch or listen to any Party election broadcasts on television or radio? Yes	1	
	No	2	
b)	Did you read any newspaper articles about the election campaign?	209	
	Yes	1 →	c)
	No	2 →	d)
	IF YES (CODE 1) AT b		
c)	Which <u>daily morning</u> paper did you read most? **PROBE IF NECESSARY:**	210-11	
	Which one did you <u>rely</u> on most for news about the election campaign? (Scottish) Daily Express	01	
	Daily Mail	02	
	CODE ONE ONLY Daily Mirror/Record	03	
	Daily Star	04	
	The Sun	05	
	Today	06	
	Daily Telegraph	07	
	Financial Times	08	
	The Guardian	09	
	The Independent	10	
	The Times	11	
	Morning Star	12	
	London Daily News	13	
	Other Scottish/Welsh/regional or local <u>daily morning</u> paper (SPECIFY)		
	_____	96	
	Other (SPECIFY) _____	97	
	ASK ALL	212	
d)	Did you go to hear any candidate at a political meeting? Yes	1	
	No	2	
e)	Did you do any canvassing or other work for a candidate? Yes	213	
		1	
	No	2	
f)	Did you have any political Party's poster in a window? <u>INCLUDE CAR WINDOW IF MENTIONED</u>	214	
	Yes	1	
	No	2	

		Col./Code	Skip to

ASK ALL

.a) Did a canvasser from any Party call at your home to talk to you during the election campaign?

		215	
Yes		1 →	b)
No		2 →	Q.4

IF YES (CODE 1) AT a .

b) From which Party or Parties?

CODE ALL THAT APPLY.

DO NOT PROMPT.

IF "ALL OF THEM", PROBE FOR WHICH. IF CANNOT DISTINGUISH, CODE DON'T KNOW.

Other (SPECIFY) _____

	Col./Code	Skip
Conservative	1	216
Labour	2	217
SDP or Liberal or Alliance	3	218
(Scotland) Scottish National	6	219
(Wales) Plaid Cymru	7	220
The Green Party	8	221
	7	222
Don't know/Can't remember any	8	223 224 225

ASK ALL

. Do you know whether the Alliance candidate in your constituency was a Liberal or a Social Democrat?

		226
Yes, Liberal		1
Yes, SDP		2
No, don't remember		4

.a) Which do you think would generally be better for Britain nowadays ... READ OUT ...

	227	
... to have a government formed by one political party on its own,	1 →	Q.6
or - to have a government formed by two political parties together - in coalition?	2 →	b)
(Don't know)	8 →	Q.6

IF TWO PARTIES/COALITION (CODE 2) AT a

b) Which of these Party groupings do you think would provide the best government for Britain ... READ OUT ...

	228	
... Conservative and Alliance,	1	
or - Labour and Alliance,	2	Q.6
or - Conservative and Labour,	3	
or - some other grouping?	4 →	c)
(Don't know)	8 →	Q.6

IF OTHER GROUPING (CODE 4) AT b

c) Which grouping is that?   WRITE IN

	229-30

	231-32	SPARE

	Col./ Code	Skip to

II. VOTING/PARTY PREFERENCE

ASK ALL

6.a) Talking to people about the general election, we have found that a lot of people didn't manage to vote. How about you - did you manage to vote in the general election?

		Col./Code	Skip to
		2 3 3	
Yes, voted		1 →	Q.7
No		2 →	b)

IF NO (CODE 2) AT a , ASK b) AND c)

b) Why was that?
   PROBE FULLY FOR REASONS WHY RESPONDENT DIDN'T VOTE.
   RECORD VERBATIM.

	Col./Code
	2 3 4 – 3 5
	2 3 6 – 3 7
	2 3 8 – 3 9
	2 4 0 – 4 1
	2 4 2 – 4 3

c) Suppose you <u>had</u> voted: Which Party would you have been most likely to vote for?   DO NOT PROMPT.

IF NONE/DON'T KNOW, PROBE BEFORE CODING:
Which Party would you <u>most like</u> to have won in your constituency?

	Col./Code	Skip to
	2 4 4 – 4 5	
Conservative	01	
Labour	02	
SDP or Liberal or Alliance	03	
Scottish National	06	Q.10
Plaid Cymru	07	
The Green Party	08	
Other (SPECIFY) _____	97	
None/Don't know (AFTER PROBE)	98	

ASK ALL WHO VOTED (CODE 1) AT Q.6a

7. How long ago did you decide that you would definitely vote the way you did: was it...
   ... READ OUT ...

	Col./Code
	2 4 6
... a long time ago,	1
sometime last year,	2
sometime this year,	3
or - during the election campaign?	4
(Don't know)	8

	Col./ Code	Skip to

<u>ASK ALL WHO VOTED (CODE 1) AT Q.6a</u>

8.a)   Which Party did you vote for in the general election?
<u>DO NOT PROMPT.   CODE IN COLUMN a BELOW.</u>

<u>ASK ALL EXCEPT CODES 95 OR 98 AT a.</u>
<u>OTHERS GO TO Q.9</u>

b)   Was there any time during the general election campaign
     when you <u>seriously thought</u> you might vote for another
     Party?   <u>IF YES</u>:   Which Party?
     <u>DO NOT PROMPT - BUT SEE INSTRUCTION BOX.</u>
     <u>ONE CODE IN COLUMN b BELOW - IF MORE THAN ONE PARTY, RING CODE 96</u>

c)   If the voting paper had required you to give <u>two</u> votes, in
     order of preference, which Party would you have put as your
     second choice?
     <u>DO NOT PROMPT - BUT SEE INSTRUCTION BOX.</u>
     <u>ONE CODE IN COLUMN c.</u>

> If respondent voted SDP or Liberal or Alliance
> (Code 03 at a), then code 03 is **not** allowed at
> b) or c).
> <u>EXPLAIN IF NECESSARY</u>:   "They did not stand
> against each other, so is there any other party
> (you seriously thought about/that you would put
> as second choice)?"

	a) Voted <u>for</u>	b) Thought <u>about</u>	c) 2nd <u>Vote</u>
	247-48	249-50	251-52
Conservative	01	01	01
Labour	02	02	02
SDP or Liberal or Alliance	03	03	03
Scottish National	06	06	06
Plaid Cymru	07	07	07
The Green Party	08	08	08
Other (SPECIFY) a) _____	97	-	-
b) _____	-	97	-
c) _____	-	-	97
Refused to disclose voting	95 →Q9	-	-
More than one other Party thought about	-	96	-
No/none	-	90	90
Don't know	98 →Q9	98	98

	Col./Code	Skip to

<u>ASK ALL WHO VOTED (CODE 1 AT Q.6a)</u>

<u>CARD A</u>

9.a) Which one of the reasons on this card comes <u>closest</u> to the main reason you voted for the Party you chose?

2 5 3

I always vote that way — 1

I thought it was the best Party — 2   } Q.10

I really preferred another Party but it had no chance of winning in this constituency — 3 → b

Other (SPECIFY) _____ — 7 → c

None of these/Don't know — 8 → Q.10

<u>IF CODE 3 AT a</u>   2 5 4 – 5 5

b) Which was the Party you really preferred?   <u>DO NOT PROMPT</u>

Conservative — 01

Labour — 02

SDP or Liberal or Alliance — 03

Scottish National — 06   } Q.10

Plaid Cymru — 07

The Green Party — 08

Other (SPECIFY) _____ — 97

<u>IF 'OTHER' (CODE 7) AT a</u>

c) May I just check, would you have preferred to vote for a different Party from the one you did vote for?   <u>IF YES</u>: Which Party?   <u>DO NOT PROMPT</u>

2 5 6 – 5 7

Yes –   Conservative — 01

Labour — 02

SDP or Liberal or Alliance — 03

Scottish National — 06

Plaid Cymru — 07

The Green Party — 08

Other (SPECIFY) _____ — 97

No – no other party preferred — 90

2 5 8 – 5 9   SPARE

		Col./ Code	Skip to

ASK ALL

10.a) Thinking back to Election Day, do you remember
which Party you thought would win <u>this constituency</u>?
IF YES: Which Party?   <u>DO NOT PROMPT</u>

260-61

	Col./Code
Conservative	01
Labour	02
SDP or Liberal or Alliance	03
Scottish National	06
Plaid Cymru	07
The Green Party	08
Other Party (SPECIFY) _____	97
Didn't think/don't remember/don't know	98

b) And on Election Day, do you remember which Party
you thought would win the most seats <u>nationally</u>?
IF YES: Which Party?   <u>DO NOT PROMPT - BUT PROBE</u>
<u>FOR "MOST SEATS" IF NECESSARY.</u>

262-63

	Col./Code
Conservative	01
Labour	02
SDP or Liberal or Alliance	03
Scottish National	06
Plaid Cymru	07
The Green Party	08
Other Party (SPECIFY) _____	97
(Expected no winner)	90
Didn't think/don't remember/don't know	98

11. Some people say that we should change the voting
system to allow smaller political parties to get
a fairer share of MPs.   Others say that we should
keep the voting system as it is to produce effective
government.   Which view comes <u>closer</u> to your own
... <u>READ OUT</u> ...

264

<u>IF ASKED, THIS REFERS</u>   ... that we should change the voting system, | 1
<u>TO 'PROPORTIONAL</u>
<u>REPRESENTATION'</u>   or - keep it as it is? | 2

(Don't know) | 8

		Col./ Code	Skip to

ASK ALL

12.a) Generally speaking, do you think of yourself
as Conservative, Labour, Liberal, Social Democrat,
(IF SCOTLAND: Nationalist/IF WALES: Plaid Cymru),
or what?

IF "ALLIANCE", PROBE: Liberal or Social Democrat?
ONE CODE IN COLUMN a)

IF NONE/DON'T KNOW (CODE 90 OR 98)

b) Do you **generally** think of yourself
as a little closer to one of the
Parties than the others? IF YES: Which Party?   a)   b)
IF "ALLIANCE", PROBE: Liberal or
Social Democrat?   265-66   267-68

ONE CODE IN COLUMN b)

	a)	b)	Skip
Conservative	01	01	
Labour	02	02	
Liberal	04	04	
Social Democrat	05	05	
Alliance (AFTER PROBE)	03	03	c)
Scottish Nationalist	06	06	
Plaid Cymru	07	07	
The Green Party	08	08	

Other (SPECIFY) a) _____   97   -

        b) _____   -   97

	a)	b)	
None/No	90	90	Q.13
Don't know	98	98	

IF PARTY CODED AT a OR b)   269

c) Would you call yourself very strong ...   Very strong   1
(QUOTE PARTY AT a OR b), fairly strong
or not very strong?   Fairly strong   2

                                            Not very strong   3

                                              (Don't know)   8

ASK ALL

CARD B

13. Please choose a phrase from this card to say how you feel about
... READ OUT ...

	Strong- ly in favour	In favour	Neither in favour nor against	Against	Strongly against	(DK/ Can't say)	
a) .. the Conserva- tive Party?	1	2	3	4	5	8	270
b) .. the Labour Party?	1	2	3	4	5	8	271
c) .. the Social Demo- cratic Party?	1	2	3	4	5	8	272
d) .. the Liberal Party?	1	2	3	4	5	8	273
IF SCOTLAND							
e) .. the Scottish Nationalist Party?	1	2	3	4	5	8	274
IF WALES							
f) .. Plaid Cymru?	1	2	3	4	5	8	275

		Col./ Code	Skip to

ASK ALL

14.a) Generally speaking, do you think of the <u>Liberal Party</u> as being closer to the Conservative Party or closer to the Labour Party?   <u>RECORD IN COLUMN a)</u>

b) And the <u>Social Democratic Party</u>, would you say it was closer to the Conservative Party or closer to the Labour Party?   <u>RECORD IN COLUMN b)</u>

	a) Liberal	b) SDP
	2 7 6	2 7 7
Closer to Conservatives	1	1
Closer to Labour	2	2
No difference/neither	3	3
Don't know	8	8

c) Considering everything the Liberal and Social Democratic Parties stand for, would you say that ... <u>READ OUT</u> ...

	2 7 8
... there is a great difference between them,	1
some difference,	2
or - not much difference?	3
(Don't know)	8

d) Now, considering everything the Conservative and Labour Parties stand for, would you say that ... <u>READ OUT</u> ...

	2 7 9
... there is a great difference between them,	1
some difference,	2
or - not much difference?	3
(Don't know)	8

e) Do you think there is <u>more</u> difference now between the Conservative and Labour Parties than there was at the <u>1983</u> election, <u>less</u> difference or about the <u>same</u> amount?

	2 8 0
More now	1
Same	2
Less now	3
Don't know	8

CARD 03   3 0 5 - 0 6

		Col./ Code	Skip to

15.a) INTERVIEWER: REFER TO Q.8a (VOTE IN 1987)

- **WRITE IN**   PARTY VOTED FOR [   ]   3 0 7
  OR
- **CODE**   Did not vote/refused voting information/don't know vote   2   Q.19

IF PARTY WRITTEN IN AT a)

b) You said you voted _____ . (PARTY AT a) in the   3 0 8 - 1 0
1987 general election. Can you say a bit about <u>why</u> you
decided to vote for the _____ (PARTY AT A)?   3 1 1 - 1 3

PROBE FULLY FOR REASONS.   CODE VERBATIM.

3 1 4 - 1 6

3 1 7 - 1 9

3 2 0 - 2 2

3 2 3 - 2 5

3 2 6 - 2 8

3 2 9 - 3 1

3 3 2 - 3 4

3 3 5 - 3 7

3 3 8 - 4 0

3 4 1 4 2   SPARE

**IF PARTY AT Q.15a IS CONSERVATIVE, OR LABOUR, OR LIBERAL OR SDP
OR ALLIANCE, ASK Q.16**

OTHERS GO TO Q. 19   3 4 3

16.a) Have you ever voted for any party <u>other</u> than the
_____ (PARTY AT Q.15a) in any <u>general</u>   Yes   1 →   b)
election since 1964?   No other Party voted for 2 }
IF ASKED, INCLUDES 1964   Not voted in election (since 1964) 3 } Q.18

IF YES AT a, RING CODE **X** FOR PARTY AT Q.15a,   Don't
AND ASK b) ABOUT THE **OTHER** TWO PARTIES.   (Not asked) Yes No   know

b)i) 'Have you ever voted <u>Conservative</u> in
a general election since 1964?   X   1   2   8   3 4 4

ii) Have you ever voted <u>Labour</u> in a general
election since 1964?   X   1   2   8   3 4 5

iii) Have you ever voted <u>Liberal</u> or <u>SDP</u> or
<u>Alliance</u> in a general election since
1964?   X   1   2   8   3 4 6

	Skip to	Col./ Code

THIS PAGE IS FOR PEOPLE WHO HAVE VOTED FOR MORE THAN ONE MAJOR U.K. PARTY SINCE 1964

IF **ANY** 'YES' (CODE 1s) AT Q.16b, ASK Q.17 ABOUT
EACH PARTY CODED 1

347-48

349-50

IF THERE ARE **NO** CODE 1s AT Q.16b, GO TO Q.18

351-52

IF **CONSERVATIVE PARTY** EVER VOTED FOR (CODE 1 AT b.i)

17.a) You say you have voted <u>Conservative</u> in a general election since 1964. Why do you <u>not</u> support the Conservative Party nowadays?

PROBE FULLY.   RECORD VERBATIM.

353-54

355-56

357-58

359-60

361-62

363-64

365-66

IF **LABOUR PARTY** EVER VOTED FOR (CODE 1 AT b.ii)

367-68

b) You say you have voted <u>Labour</u> in a general election since 1964. Why do you <u>not</u> support the Labour Party nowadays?

PROBE FULLY.   RECORD VERBATIM.

369-70

371-72

NOW GO TO Q.19

373-74

375-76

377-78

379-80

407-08

409-10

411-12

IF **LIBERAL/SDP/ALLIANCE** EVER VOTED FOR (CODE 1 AT b.iii)

413-14

c) You say you have voted (<u>Liberal/SDP/Alliance</u>) in a general election since 1964. Why do you <u>not</u> support the Alliance nowadays?

PROBE FULLY.   RECORD VERBATIM.

415-16

417-18

419-20

421-22

423-24

425-26

427-28

429-30

431-32

	Col./ Code	Skip to

THIS PAGE (AND FACING PAGE) IS FOR FIRST-TIME VOTERS AND PEOPLE WHO HAVE VOTED FOR THE SAME MAJOR U.K. PARTY SINCE 1964 — 433-38 / SPARE

18. **INTERVIEWER:** ENTER LAST DIGIT OF SERIAL NUMBER AND REFER TO PARTY AT Q.15a — 439 / 440

- IF CONSERVATIVE VOTER **AND** LAST DIGIT IS: 1, 2, 3, 4, 5, 6 or 7 — 1 — a)
  OR 8, 9, 0 — 2 — c)

  - IF LABOUR VOTER **AND** LAST DIGIT IS: 1, 2, 3, 4, 5, 6 or 7 — 3 — b)
    OR 8, 9, 0 — 4 — c)

    - IF SDP, LIBERAL OR ALLIANCE VOTER **AND** LAST DIGIT IS: 1, 2, 3, 4 or 5 — 5 — a)
      OR 6, 7, 8, 9 or 0 — 6 — b)

a) I want to ask you about <u>one</u> of the parties you have not supported in a general election. Why would you say you do <u>not</u> support the Labour Party? IF NECESSARY: What do you dislike about it?

PROBE FULLY AND RECORD VERBATIM.

441-43

444-46

447-49

450-52

453-55

456-58

459-61

462-64

465-67

468-70

NOW GO TO Q.19

	Col./ Code	Skip to

18.b) I want to ask you about <u>one</u> of the parties you have not supported in a general election. Why would you say you do <u>not</u> support the Conservative Party? <u>IF NECESSARY</u>: What do you dislike about it?

PROBE FULLY AND RECORD VERBATIM.

	Col./Code
	441-43
	444-46
	447-49
	450-52
	453-55
	456-58
	459-61
	462-64
	465-67
	468-70

NOW GO TO Q.19

c) I want to ask you about <u>one</u> of the parties you have not supported in a general election. Why would you say you do <u>not</u> support the Alliance? <u>IF NECESSARY</u>: What do you dislike about it?

PROBE FULLY AND RECORD VERBATIM.

	Col./Code
	441-43
	444-46
	447-49
	450-52
	453-55
	456-58
	459-61
	462-64
	465-67
	468-70

NOW GO TO Q.19 | 471-80 | SPARE |

					Col./ Code	Skip to

PARTY/LEADERSHIP IMAGES

CARD 05 | 5 0 5 - 0 6

ASK ALL

19.a)

i) On the whole, would you describe the Conservative Party nowadays as ... READ OUT ...

ii) And the Labour Party nowadays, is it ... READ OUT ...

iii) And the SDP/Liberal Alliance, is it ... READ OUT ...
RECORD IN APPROPRIATE COLUMN

	i) Conservative	ii) Labour	iii) Alliance
	5 0 7	5 0 8	5 0 9
.. extreme,	1	1	1
or - moderate?	2	2	2
(Neither or both)	3	3	3
(Don't know)	8	8	8

b)

i) And would you describe the Conservative Party nowadays as ... READ OUT ...

ii) And the Labour Party nowadays, is it ... READ OUT ...

iii) And the Alliance, is it ... READ OUT ...
RECORD IN APPROPRIATE COLUMN

	Conservative	Labour	Alliance
	5 1 0	5 1 1	5 1 2
.. united,	1	1	1
or - divided?	2	2	2
(Neither or both)	3	3	3
(Don't know)	8	8	8

c)

i) On the whole, would you describe the Conservative Party as ... READ OUT ...

ii) And the Labour Party, is it ... READ OUT ...

iii) And the Alliance, is it ... READ OUT ...
RECORD IN APPROPRIATE COLUMN

	Conservative	Labour	Alliance
	5 1 3	5 1 4	5 1 5
.. good for one class,	1	1	1
or - good for all classes?	2	2	2
(Neither or both)	3	3	3
(Don't know)	8	8	8

d)

i) And on the whole, would you describe the Conservative Party nowadays as ... READ OUT ...

ii) And the Labour Party, is it ... READ OUT ...

iii) And the Alliance, is it... READ OUT ...
RECORD IN APPROPRIATE COLUMN

	Conservative	Labour	Alliance
	5 1 6	5 1 7	5 1 8
.. capable of being a strong government,	1	1	1
or - not capable of being a strong government?	2	2	2
(Neither or both)	3	3	3
(Don't know)	8	8	8

e)

i) And on the whole, would you describe the Conservative Party nowadays as ... READ OUT ...

ii) And the Labour Party, is it ... READ OUT ...

iii) And the Alliance, is it ... READ OUT ...
RECORD IN APPROPRIATE COLUMN

	Conservative	Labour	Alliance
	5 1 9	5 2 0	5 2 1
.. caring,	1	1	1
or - uncaring?	2	2	2
(Neither or both)	3	3	3
(Don't know)	8	8	8

				Col./Code	Skip to

ASK ALL

19.f)

i) And would you describe the Conservative Party nowadays as ... READ OUT ...

ii) And the Labour Party is it ... READ OUT ...

iii) And the Alliance, is it ... READ OUT ... RECORD IN APPROPRIATE COLUMN

	i) Conservative	ii) Labour	iii) Alliance
	5 2 2	5 2 3	5 2 4
.. likely to unite the nation,	1	1	1
or - divide the nation?	2	2	2
(Neither or both)	3	3	3
(Don't know)	8	8	8

5 2 5-2 9   SPARE

---

20. Now some similar questions, but this time about some of the main party leaders.

a) i) Would you describe Mrs Thatcher as ... READ OUT ...

	i) Mrs Thatcher	ii) Mr Kinnock	iii) Dr Owen	iv) Mr Steel
	5 3 0	5 3 1	5 3 2	5 3 3
.. good at getting things done,	1	1	1	1
or - bad at getting things done?	2	2	2	2
(Neither or both)	3	3	3	3
(Don't know)	8	8	8	8

ii-iv) REPEAT ai) FOR OTHER THREE LEADERS IN TURN, CODING IN APPROPRIATE COLUMNS

b) i) And would you describe Mrs Thatcher as ... READ OUT ...

	i) Mrs Thatcher	ii) Mr Kinnock	iii) Dr Owen	iv) Mr Steel
	5 3 4	5 3 5	5 3 6	5 3 7
.. extreme,	1	1	1	1
or - moderate?	2	2	2	2
(Neither or both)	3	3	3	3
(Don't know)	8	8	8	8

ii-iv) REPEAT bi) FOR OTHER THREE LEADERS IN TURN, CODING IN APPROPRIATE COLUMNS

c) i) And, on the whole, would you say Mrs Thatcher ... READ OUT ...

	i) Mrs Thatcher	ii) Mr Kinnock	ii) Dr Owen	iv) Mr Steel
	5 3 8	5 3 9	5 4 0	5 4 1
.. looks after one class,	1	1	1	1
or - looks after all classes?	2	2	2	2
(Neither or both)	3	3	3	3
(Don't know)	8	8	8	8

ii-iv) REPEAT ci) FOR OTHER THREE LEADERS IN TURN, CODING IN APPROPRIATE COLUMNS

(Q.20 continues overleaf)

- 15 -

				Col./ Code	Skip to

20d) i) And would you describe <u>Mrs Thatcher</u> as ... <u>READ OUT</u> ...

	i) Mrs Thatcher	ii) Mr Kinnock	iii) Dr Owen	iv) Mr Steel
	5 4 2	5 4 3	5 4 4	5 4 5
... capable of being a strong leader,	1	1	1	1
or - not capable of being a strong leader?	2	2	2	2
(Neither or both)	3	3	3	3
(Don't know)	8	8	8	8

ii-iv) <u>REPEAT d i) FOR OTHER THREE LEADERS IN TURN, CODING IN APPROPRIATE COLUMNS</u>

e) i) And, on the whole, would you describe Mrs Thatcher as ... <u>READ OUT</u> ...

	i) Mrs Thatcher	ii) Mr Kinnock	iii) Dr Owen	iv) Mr Steel
	5 4 6	5 4 7	5 4 8	5 4 9
... caring,	1	1	1	1
or - uncaring?	2	2	2	2
(Neither or both)	3	3	3	3
(Don't know)	8	8	8	8

ii-iv) <u>REPEAT e i) FOR OTHER THREE LEADERS IN TURN, CODING IN APPROPRIATE COLUMNS</u>

f) i) And would you describe <u>Mrs Thatcher</u> as ... <u>READ OUT</u> ...

	i) Mrs Thatcher	ii) Mr Kinnock	iii) Dr Owen	iv) Mr Steel
	5 5 0	5 5 1	5 5 2	5 5 3
... likely to unite the nation,	1	1	1	1
or - divide the nation?	2	2	2	2
(Neither or both)	3	3	3	3
(Don't know)	8	8	8	8

ii-iv) <u>REPEAT f i) FOR OTHER THREE LEADERS IN TURN, CODING IN APPROPRIATE COLUMNS</u>

g) i) And, on the whole, would you describe Mrs Thatcher as ... <u>READ OUT</u> ...

	i) Mrs Thatcher	ii) Mr Kinnock	iii) Dr Owen	iv) Mr Steel
	5 5 4	5 5 5	5 5 6	5 5 7
... likeable as a person,	1	1	1	1
or - not likeable as a person?	2	2	2	2
(Neither or both)	3	3	3	3
(Don't know)	8	8	8	8

ii-iv) <u>REPEAT g i) FOR OTHER THREE LEADERS IN TURN, CODING IN APPROPRIATE COLUMNS</u>

5 5 8-5 9   SPARE

		Col./ Code	Skip to

CAMPAIGN ISSUES & IDEOLOGY

<u>ASK ALL</u>

21. During the election, a lot of issues were mentioned as being important for the sake of the country.

	a) Britain 560-66	b) You and your Family 567-73

a) <u>SHUFFLE CARDS</u> (RANDOMLY SHUFFLED)

Thinking back to the election, which <u>three</u> of these issues would you say were the most important issues <u>facing Britain</u>? First tell me the <u>most</u> important, and then the <u>second</u> most important, and then the third.

INTERVIEWER: WRITE 1, 2 AND 3 IN THE APPROPRIATE BOXES IN COLUMN a

b) <u>SHUFFLE CARDS</u> (RANDOMLY SHUFFLED)

And which three of these were the most important issues facing <u>you and your family</u>? Again start with the <u>most</u> important, and then the <u>second</u> and then the <u>third</u>.
INTERVIEWER: WRITE 1, 2 AND 3 IN THE APPROPRIATE BOXES IN COLUMN b.

	a)	b)
Prices	☐	☐
Unemployment	☐	☐
Taxes	☐	☐
Health and social services	☐	☐
Crime	☐	☐
Education	☐	☐
Defence	☐	☐

ASK ALL

CARD C

22.a) Since the last general election in June 1983, would you say that <u>prices</u> have increased or fallen? Please choose a phrase from the card.

REPEAT FOR ITEMS b)-g) BELOW

		Increased a lot	Increased a little	Stayed the same	Fallen a little	Fallen a lot	(Don't know)	
	... (PRICES)	1	2	3	4	5	8	574
b)	What about unemployment?	1	2	3	4	5	8	575
c)	Taxes?	1	2	3	4	5	8	576
d)	The standard of the health and social services?	1	2	3	4	5	8	577
e)	Crime?	1	2	3	4	5	8	578
f)	The quality of education?	1	2	3	4 .	5	8	579
g)	Britains safety from the threat of war?	1	2	3	4	5	8	580

CARD 06 6 0 5 — 0 6

Defence

<table>
<tr><td>OFFICE
USE
6 0 7</td></tr>
</table>

ASK ALL
SCALE CARD 1 AND GIVE PENCIL

23.

Please look at this card.

Some people feel that government should <u>get rid of all nuclear weapons in Britain without delay</u>. These people would put themselves in **Box A**. (POINT)

Other people feel that government should <u>increase nuclear weapons in Britain without delay</u>. These people would put themselves in **Box K**. (POINT)

And other people have views somewhere <u>in-between,</u> along here ... (<u>POINT LEFT A-F)</u> or along here (<u>POINT RIGHT K-F)</u>.

IF NECESSARY, EXPLAIN AGAIN.

a) In the first row of boxes, please tick whichever box comes closest to <u>your own</u> views about nuclear weapons in Britain.

Now where do you think the Conservative and Labour Parties stand:

b) First the Conservative Party. In the next row of boxes, please tick whichever box you think comes closest to the views of the <u>Conservative Party</u>?

c) Now in the next row please tick whichever box you think comes closest to the views of the <u>Labour Party</u>?

d) And finally, please tick whichever box you think comes closest to the views of the <u>SDP/Liberal/ Alliance</u>?

e) Now please tell me the letters of the boxes you ticked: in the first row? The second row? The third row? The fourth row? RING CODES IN GRID AS APPROPRIATE

e) CODING: RING ONE IN EACH COLUMN

	a) Own views	b) Conser- vative	c) Labour	d) Alliance	
	608-09	610-11	612-13	614-15	
A =	01	01	01	01	= A
B =	02	02	02	02	= B
C =	03	03	03	03	= C
D =	04	04	04	04	= D
E =	05	05	05	05	= E
F =	06	06	06	06	= F
G =	07	07	07	07	= G
H =	08	08	08	08	= H
I =	09	09	09	09	= I
J =	10	10	10	10	= J
K =	11	11	11	11	= K
Left of A =	95	95	95	95	= Left of A
Right of K =	96	96	96	96	= Right of K
Don't know =	98	98	98	98	= Don't know

INTERVIEWER: You may change any code already ringed if, on reflection, a respondent wants to change his or her mind. Ensure that final entries are clear on grid and on scale card. If asked you may confirm that letter **F** is the middle box.

Get rid   **OFFICE USE ONLY**   Increase

A	B	C	D	E	F	G	H	I	J	K

			Col./Code	Skip to

ASK ALL

24.a) Do you think Britain should continue to be a member of the EEC - the Common Market - or should it withdraw?   CODE IN COLUMN a

b) And do you think Britain should continue to be a member of NATO - the North Atlantic Treaty Organisation - or should it withdraw? CODE IN COLUMN b

	a) EEC 616	b) NATO 617
Continue	1	1
Withdraw	2	2

25.a) Do you think that the siting of American nuclear missiles in Britain makes Britain a safer or a less safe place to live?   CODE IN COLUMN a

b) And do you think that having our own independent nuclear missiles makes Britain a safer or a less safe place to live?   CODE IN COLUMN b

	a) American nuclear missiles 618	b) Own nuclear missiles 619
Safer	1	1
Less safe	2	2
(Don't know)	8	8

CARD D

26. Please use this card to say whether you think the government should or should not do each of the following things, or doesn't it matter either way?

... READ OUT a-b BELOW AND CODE FOR EACH

	Definitely should	Probably should	Doesn't matter either way	Probably should not	Definitely should not	(Don't know)	
a) ... Pull British troops out of Northern Ireland immediately?	1	2	3	4	5	8	620
b) ... Spend less on defence?	1	2	3	4	5	8	621

CARD E

27. Which of these statements comes closest to what you yourself feel should be done?   If you don't have an opinion just say so.

	622
Britain should keep her own nuclear weapons, independent of other countries	1
Britain should have nuclear weapons only as part of a Western defence system	2
Britain should have nothing to do with nuclear weapons under any circumstances	3
(No opinion/Don't know)	8

	623-26	SPARE

Unemployment & Inflation

SCALE CARD 2

28.

> Please look at this card.
>
> Some people feel that getting people back to work should be the government's top priority. These people would put themselves in **Box A**. (POINT)
>
> Other people feel that keeping prices down should be the government's top priority. These people would put themselves in **Box K**. (POINT)
>
> And other people have views somewhere in-between, along here (POINT LEFT A-F) or along here (POINT RIGHT K-F).

a) In the first row of boxes, please tick whichever box comes closest to your own views about unemployment and inflation.

Now where do you think the Conservative and Labour Parties stand:

e) CODING: RING ONE IN EACH COLUMN

b) First the Conservative Party. In the next row of boxes, please tick whichever box you think comes closest to the views of the Conservative Party?

c) Now in the next row please tick whichever box you think comes closest to the views of the Labour Party?

d) And finally, please tick whichever box you think comes closest to the views of the SDP/Liberal/ Alliance?

e) Now please tell me the letters of the boxes you ticked: in the first row? The second row? The third row? The fourth row? RING CODES IN GRID AS APPROPRIATE

	a) Own views	b) Conservative	c) Labour	d) Alliance	
	6 2 7 - 2 8	6 2 9 - 3 0	6 3 1 - 3 2	6 3 3 - 3 4	
A =	01	01	01	01	= A
B =	02	02	02	02	= B
C =	03	03	03	03	= C
D =	04	04	04	04	= D
E =	05	05	05	05	= E
F =	06	06	06	06	= F
G =	07	07	07	07	= G
H =	08	08	08	08	= H
I =	09	09	09	09	= I
J =	10	10	10	10	= J
K =	11	11	11	11	= K
Left of A =	95	95	95	95	= Left of A
Right of K =	96	96	96	96	= Right of
Don't know =	98	98	98	98	= Don't kno

> INTERVIEWER: You may change any code already ringed if, on reflection, a respondent wants to change his or her mind. Ensure that final entries are clear on grid and on scale card. If asked you may confirm that letter F is the middle box.

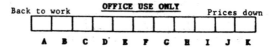

Back to work   **OFFICE USE ONLY**   Prices down   6 3 5 - 3 8   SPARE

A   B   C   D   E   F   G   H   I   J   K

Taxation and Government Services

SCALE CARD 3

29.

> Please look at this card.
>
> Some people feel that government should put up taxes a lot and spend much more on health and social services.   These people would put themselves in **Box A**. (POINT)
>
> Other people feel that government should cut taxes a lot and spend much less on health and social services.   These people would put themselves in **Box K**. (POINT)
>
> And other people have views somewhere in-between, along here (POINT LEFT A-F) or along here (POINT RIGHT K-F).

a) In the first row of boxes, please tick whichever box comes closest to your own views about taxes and government spending?

Now where do you think the Conservative and Labour Parties stand:

b) First the Conservative Party. In the next row of boxes, please tick whichever box you think comes closest to the views of the Conservative Party?

c) Now in the next row please tick whichever box you think comes closest to the views of the Labour Party?

d) And finally, please tick whichever box you think comes closest to the views of the SDP/Liberal/ Alliance?

e) Now please tell me the letters of the boxes you ticked: in the first row? The second row?   The third row?   The fourth row? RING CODES IN GRID AS APPROPRIATE

e) CODING: RING ONE IN EACH COLUMN

	a) Own views	b) Conservative	c) Labour	d) Alliance	
	6 3 9 - 4 0	6 4 1 - 4 2	6 4 3 - 4 4	6 4 5 - 4 6	
A =	01	01	01	01	= A
B =	02	02	02	02	= B
C =	03	03	03	03	= C
D =	04	04	04	04	= D
E =	05	05	05	05	= E
F =	06	06	06	06	= F
G =	07	07	07	07	= G
H =	08	08	08	08	= H
I =	09	09	09	09	= I
J =	10	10	10	10	= J
K =	11	11	11	11	= K
Left of A =	95	95	95	95	= Left of A
Right of K =	96	96	96	96	= Right of K
Don't know =	98	98	98	98	= Don't know

> INTERVIEWER: You may change any code already ringed if, on reflection, a respondent wants to change his or her mind.   Ensure that final entries are clear on grid and on scale card.   If asked you may confirm that letter F is the middle box.

Services up   **OFFICE USE ONLY**   Taxes down   SPARE 6 4 7 - 5 0

A   B   C   D   E   F   G   H   I   J   K

		Col./Code	Skip to

CARD F

30. Using this card, please say whether you agree or disagree with each of these statements, or say if you are not sure either way ...
READ OUT a-d AND CODE FOR EACH

		Strongly agree	Agree	Not sure either way	Dis-agree	Strongly disagree	(Don't know)	
a)	... When someone is unemployed, it's usually his or her own fault?	1	2	3	4	5	8	651
b)	... The government should spend more money to create jobs?	1	2	3	4	5	8	652
c)	... Much of our unemployment has been caused by trade unions?	1	2	3	4	5	8	653
d)	... Too many people these days like to rely on government handouts?	1	2	3	4	5	8	654

CARD G

31. Just to clarify your views, suppose the government had to choose between the three options on this card.   Which do you think it should choose?

655

Reduce taxes and spend <u>less</u> on health, education and social benefits	1
Keep taxes and spending on these services at the <u>same</u> level as now	2
Increase taxes and spend <u>more</u> on health, education and social benefits	3
(None)	4
(Don't know)	8

CARD H

32. And suppose your <u>local council</u> had to choose between the three options on this card.   Which do you think it should choose?

656

Reduce rates and spend <u>less</u> on local services	1
Keep rates and spending on local services at the <u>same</u> level as now	2
Increase rates and spend <u>more</u> on local services	3
(None)	4
(Don't know)	8

CARD I

33. Please use this card to say whether you think the government <u>should</u> or <u>should not</u> do the following things, or. doesn't it matter either way?
READ OUT a-f BELOW AND CODE FOR EACH

		Defin-itely should	Prob-ably should	Doesn't matter either way	Prob-ably should not	Defin-itely should not	(Don't know)	
a)	... get rid of private education in Britain?	1	2	3	4	5	8	657
b)	... spend more money to get rid of poverty?	1	2	3	4	5	8	658
c)	... encourage the growth of private medicine?	1	2	3	4	5	8	659
d)	... put more money into the National Health Service?	1	2	3	4	5	8	660
e)	... spend more money on education?	1	2	3	4	5	8	661
f)	... reduce government spending generally?	1	2	3	4	5	8	662

Nationalisation

SCALE CARD 4

4.

> Please look at this card.
>
> Some people feel that the government should <u>nationalise many more private companies</u>. These people would put themselves in **Box A**. (POINT)
>
> Other people feel that government should <u>sell off many more nationalised industries</u>. These people would put themselves in **Box K**. (POINT)
>
> And other people have views somewhere <u>in-between</u>, along here (POINT LEFT A-F) or along here (POINT RIGHT K-F).

a)   In the first row of boxes, please tick
     whichever box comes closest to <u>your own</u>
     views about nationalisation and privatisation.

Now where do you think the
Conservative and Labour Parties
stand:

b)   First the Conservative Party.
     In the next row of boxes, please
     tick whichever box you think
     comes closest to the views of
     the <u>Conservative Party</u>?

c)   Now in the next row please
     tick whichever box you think
     comes closest to the views
     of the <u>Labour Party</u>?

d)   And finally, please tick
     whichever box you think
     comes closest to the views
     of the <u>SDP/Liberal/
     Alliance</u>?

e)   Now please tell me the
     letters of the boxes you
     ticked: in the first row?
     The second row?   The
     third row?   The fourth
     row?
     RING CODES IN GRID
     AS APPROPRIATE

e) CODING: RING ONE IN EACH COLUMN

	a) Own views	b) Conservative	c) Labour	d) Alliance	
	663-64	665-66	667-68	669-70	
A =	01	01	01	01	= A
B =	02	02	02	02	= B
C =	03	03	03	03	= C
D =	04	04	04	04	= D
E =	05	05	05	05	= E
F =	06	06	06	06	= F
G =	07	07	07	07	= G
H =	08	08	08	08	= H
I =	09	09	09	09	= I
J =	10	10	10	10	= J
K =	11	11	11	11	= K
Left of A =	95	95	95	95	= Left of A
Right of K =	96	96	96	96	= Right of K
Don't know =	98	98	98	98	= Don't know

> INTERVIEWER: You may change any code already ringed if, on reflection, a respondent wants to change his or her mind. Ensure that final entries are clear on grid and on scale card. If asked you may confirm that letter F is the middle box.

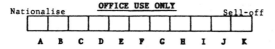

Nationalise   **OFFICE USE ONLY**   Sell-off   SPARE   671-80

A   B   C   D   E   F   G   H   I   J   K

Redistribution

SCALE CARD 5

O.U.O.
CARD 06
705-06

35.

> Please look at this card.
>
> Some people feel that government should <u>make much greater efforts to make people's incomes more equal</u>.   These people would put themselves in **Box A**. (POINT)
>
> Other people feel that government should <u>be much less concerned about how equal people's incomes are</u>.   These people would put themselves in **Box K**.   (POINT)
>
> And other people have views somewhere <u>in-between</u>, along here (<u>POINT LEFT A-F</u>) or along here (<u>POINT RIGHT K-F</u>).

a)   In the first row of boxes, please tick whichever box comes closest to <u>your own</u> views about redistributing income

Now where do you think the Conservative and Labour Parties stand:

b)   First the Conservative Party. In the next row of boxes, please tick whichever box you think comes closest to the views of the Conservative Party?

c)   Now in the next row please tick whichever box you think comes closest to the views of the Labour Party?

d)   And finally, please tick whichever box you think comes closest to the views of the SDP/Liberal/ Alliance?

e)   Now please tell me the letters of the boxes you ticked: in the first row? The second row?   The third row?   The fourth row? RING CODES IN GRID AS APPROPRIATE

e) CODING: RING ONE IN EACH COLUMN

	a) Own views 707-08	b) Conservative 709-10	c) Labour 711-12	d) Alliance 713-14	
A =	01	01	01	01	= A
B =	02	02	02	02	= B
C =	03	03	03	03	= C
D =	04	04	04	04	= D
E =	05	05	05	05	= E
F =	06	06	06	06	= F
G =	07	07	07	07	= G
H =	08	08	08	08	= H
I =	09	09	09	09	= I
J =	10	10	10	10	= J
K =	11	11	11	11	= K
Left of A =	95	95	95	95	= Left of A
Right of K =	96	96	96	96	= Right of K
Don't know =	98	98	98	98	= Don't know

> <u>INTERVIEWER</u>:   You may change any code already ringed if, on reflection, a respondent wants to change his or her mind.   Ensure that final entries are clear on grid and on scale card.   If asked you may confirm that letter **F** is the middle box.

Make incomes more equal   **OFFICE USE ONLY**   Less concerned about equal incomes

A   B   C   D   E   F   G   H   I   J   K

SPARE
715-18

		Col./Code	Skip to

36.a) Just to make sure about your views, are you generally in favour of ... READ OUT ...   `719`

... more <u>nationalisation</u> of companies by government,   1 ⎫
more <u>privatisation</u> of companies by government,   2 ⎬   b
or - should things be left as they are now?   3 ⎫
Other (SPECIFY) _____   7 ⎬   Q.37
(Don't know)   8 ⎭

IF MORE NATIONALISATION OR PRIVATISATION (CODES 1 OR 2 AT a)   `720`

b) A <u>lot</u> more (nationalisation)/(privatisation) or a <u>little</u> more?

A lot more   1
A little more   2
Don't know   8

ASK ALL
CARD I AGAIN

37. Using this card, do you think the government <u>should</u> or <u>should not</u> do the following, or doesn't it matter either way?

READ OUT AND CODE a-b

	Defin-itely should	Prob-ably should	Dosn't matter either way	Prob-ably should not	Defin-itely should not	Don't know	
a) ... introduce stricter laws to regulate the activities of trade unions?	1	2	3	4	5	8	`721`
b) ... give workers more say in running the places where they work?	1	2	3	4	5	8	`722`

CARD J

38. And still using the card, please say whether you agree or disagree with each of these statements, or say if you are not sure either way.
... READ OUT a-d AND CODE FOR EACH

	Strongly agree	Agree	Not sure either way	Dis-agree	Strongly disagree	(Don't know)	
a) ... High income tax makes people less willing to work hard?	1	2	3	4	5	8	`723`
b) ... Income and wealth should be redistributed towards ordinary working people?	1	2	3	4	5	8	`724`
c) ... It is better for Britain when trade unions have little power?	1	2	3	4	5	8	`725`
d) ... The government should give more aid to poor countries in Africa and Asia?	1	2	3	4	5	8	`726`

Law and Order

SCALE CARD 6

39.

> Please look at this card.
>
> Some people feel that <u>protecting civil rights is more important than cutting crime</u>. These people would put themselves in **Box A**. (POINT)
>
> Other people feel that <u>cutting crime is more important than protecting civil rights</u>. These people would put themselves in **Box K**. (POINT)
>
> And other people have views somewhere <u>in-between</u>, along here (POINT LEFT <u>A-F</u>) or along here (POINT RIGHT K-F)

a) In the first row of boxes, please tick whichever box comes closest to <u>your own</u> views about law and order?

Now where do you think the Conservative and Labour Parties stand:

b) First the Conservative Party. In the next row of boxes, please tick whichever box you think comes closest to the views of the <u>Conservative Party</u>?

c) Now in the next row please tick whichever box you think comes closest to the views of the <u>Labour Party</u>?

d) And finally, please tick whichever box you think comes closest to the views of the <u>SDP/Liberal/ Alliance</u>?

e) Now please tell me the <u>letters</u> of the boxes you ticked: in the first row? The second row? The third row? The fourth row?
RING CODES IN GRID AS APPROPRIATE

e) CODING: RING ONE IN EACH COLUMN

	a) Own views	b) Conservative	c) Labour	d) Alliance	
	727-28	729-30	731-32	733-34	
A =	01	01	01	01	= A
B =	02	02	02	02	= B
C =	03	03	03	03	= C
D =	04	04	04	04	= D
E =	05	05	05	05	= E
F =	06	06	06	06	= F
G =	07	07	07	07	= G
H =	08	08	08	08	= H
I =	09	09	09	09	= I
J =	10	10	10	10	= J
K =	11	11	11	11	= K
Left of A =	95	95	95	95	= Left of
Right of K =	96	96	96	96	= Right of
Don't know =	98	98	98	98	= Don't kn

> INTERVIEWER: You may change any code already ringed if, on reflection, a respondent wants to change his or her mind. Ensure that final entries are clear on grid and on scale card. If asked you may confirm that letter F is the middle box.

Protect rights

OFFICE USE ONLY

Cut crime

SPARE 735-3

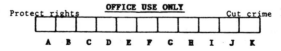

A   B   C   D   E   F   G   H   I   J   K

Welfare

SCALE CARD 7

40.

> Please look at this card.
>
> Some people feel that <u>the poor in Britain are entitled to more help from government</u>.   These people would put themselves in **Box A**.   (POINT)
>
> Other people feel that <u>the poor in Britain should get less help from government and do more to help themselves</u>.   These people would put themselves in **Box K**.   (POINT)
>
> And other people have views somewhere <u>in-between,</u> along here (POINT LEFT A-F) or along here (POINT RIGHT K-F)

a)   In the first row of boxes, please tick whichever box comes closest to <u>your own</u> views about government help for the poor?

		a) Own views	b) Conser-vative	c) Labour	d) Alliance	
	Now where do you think the Conservative and Labour Parties stand:	e) CODING: RING ONE IN EACH COLUMN				
		738-39	740-41	742-43	744-45	
b)	First the Conservative Party. In the next row of boxes, please tick whichever box you think comes closest to the views of the <u>Conservative Party</u>?	A = 01	01	01	01	= A
		B = 02	02	02	02	= B
		C = 03	03	03	03	= C
c)	Now in the next row please tick whichever box you think comes closest to the views of the <u>Labour Party</u>?	D = 04	04	04	04	= D
		E = 05	05	05	05	= E
		F = 06	06	06	06	= F
d)	And finally, please tick whichever box you think comes closest to the views of the <u>SDP/Liberal/ Alliance</u>?	G = 07	07	07	07	= G
		H = 08	08	08	08	= H
		I = 09	09	09	09	= I
		J = 10	10	10	10	= J
e)	Now please tell me the letters of the boxes you ticked: in the first row? The second row? The third row? The fourth row? RING CODES IN GRID AS APPROPRIATE	K = 11	11	11	11	= K
		Left of A = 95	95	95	95	= Left of A
		Right of K = 96	96	96	96	= Right of K
		Don't know = 98	98	98	98	= Don't know

> INTERVIEWER: You may change any code already ringed if, on reflection, a respondent wants to change his or her mind.   Ensure that final entries are clear on grid and on scale card.   If asked you may confirm that letter F is the middle box.

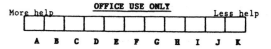

More help   **OFFICE USE ONLY**   Less help   SPARE 746-49

A   B   C   D   E   F   G   H   I   J   K

	Col./Code	Skip to

OTHER ISSUES

<u>ASK a) IN SCOTLAND AND ENGLAND ONLY</u>

<u>IN WALES, GO TO b)</u>

41.a) An issue in Scotland is the question of an elected Assembly - a special parliament for Scotland dealing with Scottish affairs. Which of these statements comes closest to your view ... READ OUT ...

750

... Scotland should become completely independent, — 1

or - there should be an elected assembly for Scotland, — 2

or - some other way should be found to make sure the needs of Scotland are better understood by the government in London, — 3

or - keep the governing of Scotland much as it has been? — 4   Q.42

Other (SPECIFY) _____

_____ — 7

(Don't know) — 8

<u>ASK IN WALES ONLY</u>

b) An issue in Wales is the question of an elected Assembly - a special parliament for Wales dealing with Welsh affairs. Which of these statements comes closest to your view ... READ OUT ...

751

... Wales should become completely independent, — 1

or - there should be an elected assembly for Wales, — 2

or - some other way should be found to make sure the needs of Wales are better understood by the government in London, — 3

or - keep the governing of Wales much as it has been? — 4

Other (SPECIFY) _____

_____ — 7

(Don't know) — 8

<u>ASK ALL</u>   752

42.a) Do you think that <u>local councils</u> ought to be controlled by <u>central government</u> more, less or about the same amount as now?

More — 1
Less — 2
About the same — 3
(Don't know) — 8

b) And do you think the <u>level of rates</u> should be up to the local council to decide, or should central government have the final say?   753

Local council — 1
Central government — 2
(Don't know) — 8

		Col./ Code	Skip to

CARD K

3. And now I want to ask about some changes that have been happening in Britain over the years. For each one I read out, please use this card to say whether you think it has gone too far or not gone far enough.

READ OUT a)-o) AND CODE FOR EACH

		Gone much too far	Gone too far	About right	Not gone far enough	Not gone nearly far enough	(Don't know)	
a)	First the welfare benefits that are available to people today?	1	2	3	4	5	8	7 5 4
b)	How about attempts to give equal opportunities to women in Britain?	1	2	3	4	5	8	7 5 5
c)	The right to show nudity and sex in films and magazines?	1	2	3	4	5	8	7 5 6
d)	The building of nuclear power stations?	1	2	3	4	5	8	7 5 7
e)	The right to have protest marches and demonstrations?	1	2	3	4	5	8	7 5 8
f)	Attempts to give equal opportunities to black people and Asians in Britain?	1	2	3	4	5	8	7 5 9
g)	Allowing the sale of council houses to tenants?	1	2	3	4	5	8	7 6 0
h)	The movement towards comprehensive schooling?	1	2	3	4	5	8	7 6 1
i)	Immigration into Britain?	1	2	3	4	5	8	7 6 2
j)	The availability of abortion on the National Health Service?	1	2	3	4	5	8	7 6 3
k)	Building new houses in country areas?	1	2	3	4	5	8	7 6 4
l)	Attempts to give equal opportunities to homosexuals - that is, gays and lesbians?	1	2	3	4	5	8	7 6 5
m)	Privatisation of industries?	1	2	3	4	5	8	7 6 6
n)	Spending by local councils?	1	2	3	4	5	8	7 6 7
o)	Laws controlling trade unions?	1	2	3	4	5	8	7 6 8

		Col./ Code	Skip to

ASK ALL   769

44.a) Do you ever think of yourself as belonging to any particular class?   Yes, middle class   1 } Q.45
IF YES: Which class is that?   Yes, working class   2 }

Yes, other (SPECIFY IN FULL) _____

_____   3 }
No   4 } b)
Don't know   8 }

IF OTHER, OR NO, OR DON'T KNOW (CODES 3, 4 OR 8 AT a)   770

b) Most people say they belong either to the middle class or the working class. If you had to make a choice, would you call yourself ... READ OUT ...
- ... middle class, 1
- or - working class? 2
- (Refused) 6
- (Don't know) 8

ASK ALL   771

45.a) On the whole, do you think there is bound to be some conflict between different social classes, or do you think they can get along together without any conflict?
- Bound to be conflict 1 → b)
- Can get along 2 } Q.46
- Don't know 8 }

IF BOUND TO BE CONFLICT (CODE 1 AT a)   772

b) A lot of conflict or just a little?
- A lot of conflict 1
- Just a little 2
- (Don't know) 8

V. BACKGROUND & CLASSIFICATION

ASK ALL

Now some questions about yourself and your background.

46.a) Do you remember which Party your father usually voted for when you were growing up? ONE CODE IN COLUMN a

b) And your mother? ONE CODE IN COLUMN b   DO NOT PROMPT

	a) Father	b) Mother
	773-74	775-76
Conservative	01	01
Labour	02	02
Liberal	04	04
Scottish National	06	06
Plaid Cymru	07	07
Other (SPECIFY) a) _____	97	-
b) _____	-	97
Varied	96	96
Not applicable/Not brought up in Britain	94	94
Refused to disclose voting	95	95
Did not vote	90	90
Can't remember/Don't know	98	98

		Col./ Code	Skip to

47. Thinking back to when you were aged about 14, what job did your **father** have then? <u>GET AS MUCH DETAIL AS POSSIBLE. PROBE FULLY.</u>

   777

   1

(IF NO DETAILS CAN BE OBTAINED, RING CODE →

AND WRITE IN REASON: _____)

   778 →

a) What was the name or title of his job? _____

   705- 06 CARD 07

   _____

O.U.O.

   _____

O.C.   807-11

b) What kind of work did he do most of the time in that job?
IF RELEVANT: What materials/machinery did he use? _____

   812-13

   _____

E.S.   814-15

   _____

S.E.G.   816-17

c) What training or qualifications were needed for the job at that time?

   _____

SC/NM.M   818-19

   _____

SIC   820-21

   _____

H-G

SPARE 822-23

d) Did he supervise or was he responsible for the work
of any other people?   <u>IF YES</u>: About how many?

Yes: <u>WRITE IN NO.</u>:

No: <u>RING</u>:   0000

   824-27

   828

e) Was he ... <u>READ OUT</u> ...   ... an employee,   1

or - self-employed?   2

f) What did (his employer) (<u>IF SELF-EMPLOYED</u>: he)
make or do? _____

   _____

g) Roughly how many people were employed at the
place where he worked?
<u>PROBE AS NECESSARY</u>

   829

	Code
No other employees	6
Fewer than 10	1
10-24	2
25-99	3
100-499	4
500 or more	5

<u>ASK ALL</u>

48. And where were you living at that time, when **you** were 14?
<u>PROBE AS NECESSARY</u>: What town or village or city were you
living in then?
<u>PROBE FOR VILLAGE/TOWN/CITY **AND** COUNTY.</u>
<u>IF NOT IN U.K. GET NAME OF COUNTRY</u>

   O.U.O.
   830-31

TOWN/VILLAGE/CITY _____

COUNTY _____

(IF NECESSARY) COUNTRY _____

	Col./ Code	Skip to

ASK ALL

CARD L

O.U.O.   8 3 2 - 4 2

49.a) Which of these descriptions applies to what you were doing
last week, that is, in the seven days ending last Sunday?
PROBE: Any others?   CODE ALL THAT APPLY IN COLUMN I

A B C
D E F
G H J
K L

IF ONLY ONE CODE AT I, TRANSFER IT TO COLUMN II
IF MORE THAN ONE AT I, TRANSFER HIGHEST ON LIST TO II

		COL I	COL II ECONOMIC POSITION

8 4 3 - 4 4

In full-time education (not paid for by employer, including on vacation)	A	01 →	Q.51
On government training/employment scheme (e.g. Community Programme, Youth Training Scheme, etc)	B	02 →	b)
In paid work (or away temporarily) for at least 10 hours in the week	C	03	} c)
Waiting to take up paid work already accepted	D	04	
Unemployed and registered at a benefit office	E	05	
Unemployed, not registered, but actively looking for a job	F	06	
Unemployed, wanting a job (of at least 10 hrs per week) but not actively looking for a job	G	07	} b)
Permanently sick or disabled	H	08	
Wholly retired from work	J	09	
Looking after the home	K	10	
Doing something else (SPECIFY) _____	L	11	

IF CODE 02, OR 05-11 AT a

8 4 5

b) How long ago did you last have a paid job
(other than the government scheme you
mentioned) of at least 10 hours a week,
excluding Saturday or holiday jobs?

Within past 12 months	1	
Over 1-5 years ago	2	
Over 5-10 years ago	3	} c)
Over 10-20 years ago	4	
Over 20 years ago	5	
Never had paid job of 10+ hrs a week	6	→ Q.51

IF EVER HAD JOB (CODES 03-04 AT a OR CODES 1-5 AT b)

8 4 6

c) Are you now a member of a trade union or
staff association?   PROBE AS NECESSARY

Yes: trade union	1	} Q.50
Yes: staff association	2	
No	3	→ d)

IF NO AT c

d) Have you ever been a member of a trade
union or staff association?   PROBE AS
NECESSARY

8 4 7

Yes: trade union	1
Yes: staff association	2
No	3

	Col./ Code	Skip to

REFER TO ECONOMIC POSITION OF RESPONDENT (OPPOSITE):

- IF IN <u>PAID WORK</u> NOW (CODE 03 AT Q.49a), ASK ABOUT <u>PRESENT</u> JOB

  O.U.O.

- IF WAITING TO TAKE UP PAID WORK (CODE 04 AT Q.49a), ASK ABOUT
  FUTURE JOB

  O.C. 848-52

- IF NOT NOW WORKING BUT HAS EVER HAD JOB (CODES 1-5 AT Q.49b), ASK
  ABOUT <u>LAST</u> JOB.

  853-54

50.   Now I want to ask you about your (present/future/last) job.
      CHANGE TENSES FOR (BRACKETED) WORDS AS APPROPRIATE

      E.S.
      855-56

a)   What (is) your job?   <u>PROBE AS NECESSARY</u>:

      S.E.G.

      What (is) the name or title of the job? _____

      857-58

      _____

      SC/NM.M
      859-60

b)   What kind of work (do) you do most of the time? <u>IF RELEVANT</u>:   What
      materials/machinery (do) you use? _____

      SIC
      861-62

      _____

      H-G

c)   What training or qualifications (are) needed for that job? _____

      SPARE 863-64

      _____

d)   (Do) you supervise or (are) you responsible for the
      work of any other people?   <u>IF YES</u>: How many?

                        Yes: WRITE IN NO.:   [   ][   ][   ]

      865-6.8

                        No: RING: 0000

      869

e)   Can I just check: (are) you ... <u>READ OUT</u> ...   ... an employee,   1   f)
                                        or - self-employed?   2   g)

      IF EMPLOYEE (CODE 1) AT e

      CARD M   870

                                   Private firm or company   1

      f) Which of the types of organisation on   Nationalised industry/
          this card (do) you work for?   public corporation   2

          <u>PRIORITY CODE</u>   Local Authority/Local Education Authority   3

                                      Health authority /hospital   4

                                   Central Government/Civil Service   5

                                              Charity or trust   6

      Other (SPECIFY) _____   7

      ASK ALL
g)   What (does) your employer (<u>IF SELF-EMPLOYED</u>: you) make or do at the
      place where you usually (work)?   <u>IF FARM, GIVE NO. OF ACRES</u>

      871

h)   Including yourself, how many people (are)   (No employees)   6
      employed at the place you usually (work) from?   Under 10   1
      <u>IF SELF-EMPLOYED</u>: (Do) you have any employees?   10-24   2
      <u>IF YES</u>: How many?   25-99   3
                                                             100-499   4
                                                          500 or more   5

      872

i)   (Is) the job ... <u>READ OUT</u> ...   ... full-time (30+ hours per week)   1
                                       or - part-time (10-29 hours per week)   2

	Col./ Code	Skip to

ASK ALL

873-74 SPARE

51.a) At present are you ... <u>READ OUT</u> ...

PRIORITY CODE

875

... married, 1 ⎫
or - living as married, 2 ⎭ b)

or widowed, 3 ⎫
divorced or separated, 4 ⎬ Q.53
or - not married? 5 ⎭

IF MARRIED OR LIVING AS MARRIED (CODES 1 OR 2 AT a)
CARD N

b) Which of these descriptions applied to what your (husband/wife/partner) was doing last week, that is the seven days ending last Sunday? PROBE: Any others? CODE ALL THAT APPLY IN COL. I

IF ONLY ONE CODE AT I, TRANSFER IT TO COL. II   COL | COL II
IF MORE THAN ONE AT I, TRANSFER HIGHEST ON LIST TO II   I | ECONOMIC POSITION

876-77

In full-time education (not paid for by employer, including on vacation) A | 01 → Q.53

On government training/employment scheme (e.g. Community Programme, Youth Training Scheme etc.) B | 02 → c)

In paid work (or away temporarily) for at least 10 hours in the week C | 03 ⎫
Waiting to take up paid work already accepted D | 04 ⎭ d)

Unemployed and registered at a benefit office E | 05 ⎫
Unemployed, <u>not</u> registered, but actively looking for a job F | 06 ⎪
Unemployed, wanting a job (of at least 10 hrs per week), but not actively looking for a job G | 07 ⎬ c)
Permanently sick or disabled H | 08 ⎪
Wholly retired from work J | 09 ⎪
Looking after the home K | 10 ⎭

Doing something else (SPECIFY) _____ L | 11

878-80 SPARE

IF CODE 02, OR 05-11 AT b

OUO 907-17
A B C
D E F
G H J
K L

c) How long ago did your (husband/wife/partner) last have a paid job (other than the government scheme you mentioned) of at least 10 hours a week?

918

Within past 12 months 1 ⎫
Over 1-5 years ago 2 ⎪
Over 5-10 years ago 3 ⎬ d)
Over 10-20 years ago 4 ⎪
Over 20 years ago 5 ⎭
Never had paid job of 10+ hours a week 6 → Q.53

IF EVER HAD JOB (CODES 03-04 AT b OR CODES 1-5 AT c)

919

d) Is your (husband/wife/partner) now, or has (he/she) ever been, a member of a trade union?
<u>PROBE AS NECESSARY</u>

Yes - now 1
Yes - used to be 2
No 3
Don't know 8

REFER TO ECONOMIC POSITION OF SPOUSE/PARTNER (OPPOSITE):

- IF IN PAID WORK NOW (CODE 03 AT Q.51b), ASK ABOUT <u>PRESENT</u> JOB
- IF WAITING TO TAKE UP PAID WORK (CODE 04 AT Q.51b), ASK ABOUT <u>FUTURE</u> JOB
- IF NOT NOW WORKING BUT HAS EVER HAD PAID JOB (CODES 1-5 AT Q.51c) ASK ABOUT <u>LAST</u> JOB

52.   Now I want to ask you about your (husband's/wife's/partner's) job.   <u>CHANGE TENSES FOR (BRACKETED) WORDS AS APPROPRIATE</u>

a)   What (is) the name or title of that job? _____

_____

b)   What kind of work (does) he/she do most of the time?   <u>IF RELEVANT:</u>
What materials/machinery (does) he/she use?   _____

_____

c)   What training or qualifications (are) needed
for the job?   _____

_____

d)   (Does) he/she supervise or (is) he/she responsible
for the work of any other people?   <u>IF YES:</u> How many?

Yes: WRITE IN:

No: RING: 0000

e)   (Is) he/she ... <u>READ OUT</u> ...   ... an employee,   1   f)
                                            or - self-employed?   2   g)

<u>IF EMPLOYEE (CODE 1) AT e</u>
CARD O
                                            Private firm or company   1
f)   Which of the types of organisation   Nationalised industry/public
on this card (does) (he/she)   corporation   2
work for?   Local Authority/Local Education
<u>PRIORITY CODE</u>   Authority   3
                                        Health Authority/NHS hospital   4
                                    Central Government/Civil Service   5
                                                Charity or trust   6

Other (SPECIFY) _____   7

<u>ASK ALL</u>
g)   What (does) the employer (<u>IF SELF-EMPLOYED</u> : he/she) make or do at
the place where he/she usually (works)?   <u>IF FARM GIVE NO. OF ACRES</u>

_____

h)   Including him/herself, roughly how many people
(are) employed at the place where he/she usually   (No employees)   6
(works) (from)?   <u>IF SELF EMPLOYED:</u> Do you have   Under 10   1
any employees?   <u>IF YES:</u> How many?   10-24   2
                                                        25-99   3
                                                      100-499   4
                                                  500 or more   5

i)   (Is) the job ... <u>READ OUT</u> ...   ... full-time (30 hours + per week)   1
                              or - part-time (10-29 hours per week)?   2

Col./Code	Skip to
O.U.O.	
O.C.	920-24
	925-26
E.S.	927-28
S.E.G.	929-30
SC/M.NM	931-32
SIC	933-34
H-G	
935-38	
939	
940	
941	
942	
943-45	SPARE

		Col./ Code	Skip to

<u>ASK ALL</u>

946

53.a) Compared with British families in general, would you say your household's income is ... <u>READ OUT</u> ...

... far below average, — 1
below average, — 2
average, — 3
above average, — 4
or-far above average? — 5
(Don't know) — 8

b) Do you, or does anyone in your household, own or have the use of a car or a van?

<u>IF YES, PROBE:</u> One car/van or more than one?

947
Yes - one — 1
Yes - two or more — 2
No — 3

c) Are you, or is anyone in your household, covered by a private health insurance scheme that allows you to get private medical treatment?

<u>IF YES, PROBE:</u> Through a group (e.g. employer/ trade union) or as an individual?

948
Yes - through group — 1
Yes - individually — 2
No — 3
Don't know — 8

<u>CARD P</u>

d) Do you (or your husband/wife/partner) own, or have you ever bought, shares in any of these recently privatised companies?

<u>PROBE FOR CORRECT CATEGORY</u>

949
Yes - have shares now — 1
Yes - bought but none owned now — 2
No - never bought any — 3
(IF VOLUNTEERED: Applied for shares but none allocated) — 4
Don't know — 8

e) And do you (or your husband/wife/partner) own any <u>other</u> shares quoted on the stock exchange, including unit trusts?

950
Yes — 1
No — 2

<u>ASK ALL</u>

54.a) Do you have any children, including step-children or others in your care (living here or away from home) who are: ... <u>READ OUT</u> ...

i) ... aged under 16?   IF YES: WRITE IN NUMBER [ ]   951-52
IF NO: RING CODE   None   90

ii) ... aged 16 or over and still in full-time education?   IF YES: WRITE IN NUMBER [ ]   953-54
IF NO: RING CODE   None   90

<u>ASK ALL</u>

955

b) Have you ever sent - or are you considering sending - any children in your care to a private (fee-paying) primary or secondary school in Britain?

<u>PROBE FOR CORRECT CATEGORY</u>

Yes - in the past — 1
Yes - now — 2
Yes - considering — 3
No — 4

956   SPARE

	Col./Code	Skip to

ASK ALL

55. How old were you when you completed your
continuous full-time education?

WRITE IN AGE: ☐☐   9 5 7–5 8

OR CODE: Had no school-
ing at all   00

ASK ALL

CARD Q

56. Have you passed any exams or got any of
the qualifications on this card?

IF YES: Which ones? Any others?   No qualification   00   9 5 9–6 0

CODE ALL THAT APPLY   BRITISH EXAMS/QUALIFICATIONS CSE Grades 2-5   01   9 6 1–6 2

CSE Grade 1 ⎫
GCE 'O' level ⎬   02   9 6 3–6 4
School certificate ⎪
Scottish (SCE) Ordinary/lower ⎭

GCE 'A' level/'S' level ⎫
Higher certificate ⎬   03   9 6 5–6 6
Scottish (SCE) Higher ⎭

Recognised trade apprenticeship completed   05   9 6 7–6 8

RSA/other clerical, commercial qualification   06   9 6 9–7 0

City & Guilds Certificate - Craft/Intermediate/Ordinary/Part I   07   9 7 1–7 2

City & Guilds Certificate - Advanced/Final/Part II or Part III   08   9 7 3–7 4

City & Guilds Certificate - Full technological   09   9 7 5–7 6

BEC/TEC General/Ordinary National Certificate (ONC) or Diploma (OND)   10   9 7 7–7 8

BEC/TEC Higher/Higher National Certificate (HNC) or Diploma (HND)   11   9 7 9–8 0

Teachers training qualification   12   100 7–0 8

Nursing qualification   13   100 9–1 0

Other technical, professional or business qualification/certificate   14   101 1–1 2

University or CNAA degree or diploma   15   101 3–1 4

Other British qualification: (SPECIFY) _____   97   101 5–1 6

OVERSEAS EXAMS/QUALIFICATIONS: Overseas school-leaving
exam/certificate   91   101 7–1 8

Degree   92   101 9–2 0

Other(post-school) exam/qualification(SPECIFY) _____   97   102 1–2 2

---

57. ASK ALL

Did you go to a private, fee-paying primary   1 0 2 3
or secondary school in Britain?

IF YES: At primary level, secondary level, or both?

Yes - primary level   1
Yes - secondary level   2
Yes - both   3
No - neither   4

			Col./ Code	Skip to

INTERVIEWER:

58.a) CODE FROM OBSERVATION FOR ALL RESPONDENTS:

	Col./Code
	1 0 2 4
White/European	1
Indian/East African Asian/Pakistani/Bangladeshi/Sri Lankan	2
Black/African/West Indian	3
Other (inc. Chinese)	4

b) RECORD RESPONDENT'S SEX:

	Col./Code
	1 0 2 5
Male	1
Female	2

c) ASK: What was your age last birthday?   WRITE IN: [ ] Years   1.0 2 6-2 7

ASK ALL

59.a) Do you regard yourself as belonging to any particular religion?

IF YES: Which one?

PROBE FOR DENOMINATION   **Christian:**

	Col./Code	Skip to
	1 0 2 8-2 9	
No religion	00 →	Q.60
No denomination	01	
Roman Catholic	02	
Church of England/Wales, Anglican, Episcopal	03	
Church of Scotland/Presbyterian	04	
Methodist	05	
Baptist	06	
United Reform Church (URC), Congregational	07	b)
Other Christian (SPECIFY) _____	08	
Non-Christian: Jew	12	
Hindu	13	
Islam/Moslem	14	
Sikh	15	
Buddhist	16	
Other Non-Christian (SPECIFY) _____	97	

IF ANY RELIGION NAMED (CODES 01-97 AT a)

b) Apart from special occasions, such as weddings, funerals, baptisms and so on, how often nowadays do you attend services or meetings connected with your religion?

PROBE AS NECESSARY

	Col./Code
	1 0 3 0
Once a week or more	1
Several times a month	2
Less often but at least once a month	3
Several times a year	4
At least once a year	5
Less often than once a year	6
Varies/Don't know	7
Never/practically never	8

		Col./ Code	Skip to
	INTERVIEWER : FOR ALL RESPONDENTS:	1 0 3 1⁴3 2	
60.a)	CODE WHETHER ACCOMMODATION IS ... ... Private household,	A →	b)
	or Institution (SPECIFY TYPE) _____	01 →	Q.63
	IF PRIVATE HOUSEHOLD (CODE A)		
	b) Do you - your household - own or rent this (house/flat/accommodation)?		
	OWNING INCLUDES WITH MORTGAGE OWNS House	02 ⎱	c)
	or	03 ⎰	
	CO-OWNS Flat/maisonette		
	IF RENTED : From whom? RENTS FROM Local Authority - house	04 ⎫	
	Local Authority - flat/maisonette	05	
	Housing Association	06 ⎬	e)
	Private company/landlord	07	
	Other (SPECIFY) _____	97 ⎭	
	IF OWNS (CODE 02 OR 03 AT b)	1 0 3 3	
	c) Have you ever been a local authority tenant? Yes	1	d)
	No	2	Q.62
	IF YES (CODE 1 AT c)	1 0 3 4	
	d) Were you a local authority tenant in this (house/flat/accommodation) before your household purchased it? Yes	1	f)
	No	2	e)
	IF CURRENTLY RENTING (CODES 04-97 AT b) OR NO (CODE 2 AT d)	1 0 3 5	
	e) Have you ever bought a council house or flat that you were living in? Yes	1	f)
	No	2	Q.61
	IF YES AT d) OR e)		
	f) When did you buy accommodation from a council? WRITE IN: 19 [Year □□]	1 0 3 6 - 3 7	
	OR		
	Don't know/Can't		
	CODE: remember	98	
	IF CURRENTLY RENTS FROM LOCAL AUTHORITY (CODES 04 OR 05 AT Q.60b)		
	OTHERS GO TO Q.62		
61.	How likely is it that your household will try to buy this house/flat from the local council in the next 5 years or so; would you say ... READ OUT ...	1 0 3 8	
	... very likely,	1	
	quite likely,	2	
	not likely,	3	
	or definitely not?	4	
	(Negotiations already started)	5	
	(Don't know)	8	

		Col./ Code	Skip to

ASK ALL IN PRIVATE HOUSEHOLDS (CODE A AT Q.60a)

62. In whose name is this (house/flat/accommodation) owned or rented?

	Col./Code	
	1039	
Respondent and/or spouse only	1	
Parent or parent-in-law	2	
Other (SPECIFY IN FULL) _____	7	

ASK ALL

CARD R

63. Which of these is the <u>main</u> source of income for you (and your husband/wife/partner) at present?

ONE CODE ONLY

	Code	
	1040-41	
Earnings from employment (own or spouse/partner's)	01	
Occupational pension(s) - from previous employer(s)	02	
State retirement or widow's pension(s)	03	
Unemployment benefit	04	
Supplementary benefit	05	
Invalidity, sickness or disabled pension or benefit(s)	06	
Other state benefit (SPECIFY) _____	07	
Interest from savings or investments	08	
Student grant	09	
Dependent on parents/other relatives	10	
Other main source (SPECIFY) _____	97	

CARD S

64. And which of the letters on this card represents the <u>total</u> income of your household from <u>all</u> sources, before tax?

NB: INCLUDES INCOME FROM EARNINGS, BENEFITS, SAVINGS ETC.

ONE CODE ONLY

	House- hold Income	
	1042-43	
X =	01	
P =	02	
Q =	03	
R =	04	
T =	05	
S =	06	
O =	07	
K =	08	
L =	09	
B =	10	
Z =	11	
M =	12	

		Col./ Code	Skip to

65.a) May I just check, thinking back to the last general election - that is the one in 1983 - do you remember which Party you voted for then, or perhaps you didn't vote in that election?
DO NOT PROMPT. CODE IN COLUMN a BELOW

ASK b UNLESS REFUSED/NOT ELIGIBLE (CODES 95 OR 94 AT a)

b) And what about the election before that - that is the one in 1979. Do you remember which Party you voted for then, or perhaps you didn't vote in that election?
DO NOT PROMPT - CODE IN COLUMN b
(IF 'ALLIANCE' OR 'SDP' NAMED, EXPLAIN: "They did not exist as such in 1979", BUT STILL DO NOT PROMPT.)

	a) 1983		b) 1979
	1044-45		1046-47
Conservative	01	b)	01
Labour	02	b)	02
SDP or Liberal or Alliance	03	b)	-
Liberal	-	b)	04
Scottish National	06	b)	06
Plaid Cymru	07	b)	07
The Ecology (Green) Party	08	b)	08
Other (SPECIFY) ______	97	b)	97
Refused to disclose voting	95	→ Q.66	95
Did not vote	90	→ b)	90
Not eligible/Too young to vote	94	→ Q.66	94
Don't remember	98	→ b)	98

ASK ALL

66.a) Where were you living at the time of the June 1979 general election? Can you give me the full postal address?
PROBE AS NECESSARY TO GET STREET ADDRESS, INCLUDING POSTCODE IF POSSIBLE. SEE INSTRUCTIONS FOR EXPLANATION.

		1048
RECORD ON P.2 (BOTTOM) OF ARF - NOT HERE - AND CODE:	Address recorded: (if same as now, write "same" on ARF)	1
Address not recorded (SPECIFY WHY) ______		2

b) And how long have you lived at your present address?
PROBE FOR BEST ESTIMATE

		1049-50
WRITE IN NUMBER OF YEARS:	☐☐	
OR CODE:	Less than 1 year	96

c) And how long have you lived in this neighbourhood?
DO NOT DEFINE 'NEIGHBOURHOOD' - LET RESPONDENT DEFINE.
PROBE FOR BEST ESTIMATE

		1051-52
WRITE IN NUMBER OF YEARS:	☐☐	
OR CODE:	Less than 1 year	96

			Col./ Code	Skip to

67.a) **Are you a member of a political Party?**
       IF YES, PROBE: Which one?   DO NOT PROMPT   No: Not member   `1 0 5 3-5 4` 00 ⎫
       INCLUDE PEOPLE WHO HAVE TEMPORARILY   Yes: - Conservative   01 ⎬ Q.68
       NOT PAID SUBS BUT INTEND TO.
                                                              - Labour   02 → b)
                                                              - Liberal   04 ⎫
                                                      - Social Democratic   05 ⎪
                                                      - Scottish National   06 ⎬ Q.68
                                                          - Plaid Cymru   07 ⎪
       Other (SPECIFY) _____   97 ⎭

       IF 'LABOUR' (CODE 02 AT a)   `1 0 5 5`

       b) **Are you a member of the Labour Party through a**
           trade union or did you join as an individual   Individual   1
           member?   IF 'BOTH', RING CODE 1 ONLY   through TU   2

        ASK ALL
68.   **Finally about politics, do you feel that any of the**   No: No party   `1 0 5 6-5 7` 00
        political parties in Britain properly represent   Yes: Conservative   01
        the views of people like you?
        IF YES: Which one?   Labour   02
        DO NOT PROMPT BUT
        IF "ALLIANCE" PROBE: Liberal   04
                                                                      SDP   05
        Liberal or Social Democrat or Alliance?   Alliance (AFTER PROBE)   03
                                                           Scottish National   06
                                                               Plaid Cymru   07
                                                           The Green party   08
        Other Party (SPECIFY) _____   97

69.a)   **Is there a telephone in (your part of)**   Yes   `1 0 5 8` 1 → c)
        this accommodation?   No   2 → b)

        IF NO AT a   `1 0 5 9`

        b) **Do you have easy access to a 'phone where you can**   Yes - home   1 ⎫
            receive incoming calls? IF YES, ASK: Is this a   Yes - work   2 ⎬ c)
            home or a work number? IF BOTH, CODE HOME ONLY   No   3 → Q.70

        IF YES AT a OR b

        c) A few interviews on any survey are checked by a
            supervisor to make sure that people are satisfied
            or if something needs clarifying. In case my   `1 0 6 0`
            supervisor needs to contact you it would be helpful
            if we could have your telephone number.   Number given   1
        RECORD TEL. NO. ON ARF - NOT HERE - AND CODE: Number refused   2

        ASK ALL
70.   **When the next general election comes round - which**   `1 0 6 1`
        is likely to be in 4 or 5 years' time - there may
        be another survey like this one. Would you be   Yes, willing   1 → Q.71
        willing to take part in it again?   No, not willing   2 → Q.72

	Col./ Code	Skip to

IF WILLING AT Q.70

71.   Suppose we call on you at this address after the next
election and for some reason cannot get in touch with
you. Is there another address or 'phone number you
could give us of someone who would know your whereabouts?
IF NECESSARY, PROMPT: Perhaps the address of a friend
or relative who is unlikely to move?

RECORD 'STABLE ADDRESS' ON ARF (D) - NOT HERE
AND CODE:

	Col./Code
	1 0 6 2
Another address/tel. no. given	1
No other address/tel. no. given	2

INTERVIEWER TO COMPLETE ABOUT SELF-COMPLETION QUESTIONNAIRE:

1 0 6 3

72.a) Was it ...   ... filled in immediately after interview

<u>ONE CODE ONLY</u>   in interviewer's presence,   1

            or - <u>left behind</u> to be filled in after interview?   2

Other (SPECIFY) _____   7

1 0 6 4

b) Was (is) it ... ... returned by interviewer with this questionnaire,   1

                (planned to be) collected by interviewer,   2

            or - (planned to be) posted back by respondent?   3

INTERVIEWER: 1 0 6 5 - 68

Time interview   24 hour clock   Minutes   1 0 6 9 - 7 1
completed   **DURATION OF**
                          INTERVIEW

                      DAY   MONTH   YEAR
       DATE OF INTERVIEW   8 7   1 0 7 2 - 7 7

Interviewer   Interviewer
Signature: _____   Number

1 0 7 8 - 80   SPARE

**THANK RESPONDENT FOR HIS OR HER HELP. REMEMBER TO MAKE
ARRANGEMENTS FOR SELF-COMPLETION QUESTIONNAIRE, AND TO
CHECK ARF FOR ALL DETAILS.**

SOCIAL AND COMMUNITY PLANNING RESEARCH
and
THE UNIVERSITY OF OXFORD. NUFFIELD COLLEGE

Head Office
35 Northampton Square,
London, EC1V 0AX.
Telephone· 01-250 1866

BRITISH GENERAL ELECTION STUDY 1987   P.934

SELF-COMPLETION QUESTIONNAIRE

```
OFFICE USE ONLY:
                   Area no.
Interviewer to   ┌───┬───┬───┐
       enter:    └───┴───┴───┘
              Serial No.
              ┌───┬───┬───┐
              └───┴───┴───┘
Rec.     Interviewer no.
┌───┐    ┌───┬───┬───┬───┐
└───┘    └───┴───┴───┴───┘
 11.07
```

To the selected respondent:

• Thank you very much for agreeing to take part in this important study of
  the British general election.   This study is the eighth in the series
  of election studies which have taken place after every British general
  election since 1964.   The study consists of an interview and this self-
  completion questionnaire.

• Completing the questionnaire.   The questions inside cover a wide range
  of subjects, but each one can be answered simply by placing a tick (√)
  or writing a number in one or more of the boxes provided.   No special
  knowledge is needed: we are sure that everyone will be able to offer
  an opinion on all questions.   And we want all people to take part, not
  just those with strong views or particular viewpoints.   The questionnaire should not take long to complete, and we hope you will find it
  interesting and enjoyable.   It should be completed only by the person
  interviewed about the election by our interviewer.   And, of course,
  your participation will be treated as confidential and anonymous.

• Returning the questionnaire.   Your interviewer will arrange with you
  the most convenient way of returning the questionnaire.   If the interviewer has arranged to call back for it, please complete it and keep it
  safely until then.   If not, please complete it and post it back to us
  in the pre-paid addressed envelope as soon as you possibly can.

Thank you for your help.

*Social and Community Planning Research is an independent social research
institute registered as a charitable trust.   Its projects are funded
by government departments, local authorities, universities and founda-
tions to provide information on social issues in Britain.   This study
has been funded mainly by the Sainsbury Charitable Trusts, with
contributions from the Economic and Social Research Council, Pergamon
Press, and the Universities of Oxford and Newcastle.   Please contact us
if you require further information.*

	OFFICE USE ONLY

1. Listed below are some things people have said make them proud of Britain. Please write a '1' in the box next to the thing that makes you feel proudest of Britain. Then write a '2' in the box next to the thing that makes you feel next proudest of Britain and '3' next to the third thing.

WRITE 1, 2, 3 IN ORDER IN THE BOXES

British scientific achievements ☐	11.08
The British Parliament ☐	11.09
British sporting achievements ☐	11.10
The British monarchy ☐	11.11
British theatre and the arts ☐	11.12
British economic achievements ☐	11.13
The British health and welfare system ☐	11.14

OR TICK

None of these make me proud of Britain ☐	11.15

2. All in all, how well or badly do you think the system of democracy in Britain works these days?

PLEASE TICK ONE BOX

(✓)

It works well and needs no changes ☐₁	11.16
It works well and needs some changes ☐₂	
It does not work well and needs a lot of changes ☐₃	
It does not work well and needs to be completely changed ☐₄	

3. How much do you trust British governments of _any_ political party to place the needs of the nation above the interests of their own political party?

PLEASE TICK ONE BOX

(✓)

Just about always ☐₁	11.17
Most of the time ☐₂	
Only some of the time ☐₃	
Almost never ☐₄	

Please continue .....

4.a) How much do you trust British police not
to bend the rules in trying to get a
conviction?

OFFICE
USE
ONLY

PLEASE TICK ONE BOX

(✓)

Just about always	1
Most of the time	2
Only some of the time	3
Almost never	4

11.18

b) And how much do you trust top civil servants
to stand firm against a minister who wants to
provide false information to parliament?

PLEASE TICK ONE BOX

(✓)

Just about always	1
Most of the time	2
Only some of the time	3
Almost never	4

11.19

5. There are some people whose views are considered
extreme by the majority.

Think of people who want to overthrow the government
by revolution. Do you think such people should be
allowed to ...

PLEASE TICK ONE BOX
ON EACH LINE

Should it be allowed?

	Definitely	Probably	Probably not	Definitely not	
a) ... hold public meetings to express their views?	1	2	3	4	11.20
b) ... teach 15 year olds in schools?	1	2	3	4	11.21
c) ... publish books expressing their views?	1	2	3	4	11.22

Please continue .....

6.a) Suppose a law was being considered by Parliament
which you thought was really unjust and harmful.
Which, if any, of the following things do you think
people ought to do?

PLEASE TICK ONE BOX
ON EACH LINE

People ought to ...	Yes	No	
Contact their MP?	1	2	11.23
Sign a petition?	1	2	11.24
Go on a demonstration?	1	2	11.25
Join a protest group?	1	2	11.26

b) And which of these things have you ever done?

PLEASE TICK ONE BOX
ON EACH LINE

Have you ever ...	Yes	No	
Contacted your MP?	1	2	11.27
Signed a petition?	1	2	11.28
Gone on a demonstration?	1	2	11.29
Joined a protest group?	1	2	11.30

7. Please tick one box to show which of these two
statements comes closest to your views?

PLEASE TICK
ONE BOX   OR

	(✓)	
Politicians should spend more time listening to the views of ordinary people	1	11.31
Politicians should rely more on their own judgement, instead of on public opinion	2	

8. And please tick one box to show which of these
statements comes closest to your views?

PLEASE TICK
ONE BOX

In a general election ...

	(✓)	
... it's not really worth voting	1	11.32
... people should vote only if they care who wins	2	
... it is everyone's duty to vote	3	

Please continue 11.33-35

OFFICE
USE
ONLY

9.   Please tick one box for *each* statement to show how
     much you agree or disagree with it.

PLEASE TICK ONE BOX
ON EACH LINE

	Agree strongly	Agree	Neither agree nor disagree	Disagree	Disagree strongly	OFFICE USE ONLY
a) Differences in social position between people are acceptable because they show what people have made out of their chances.	1	2	3	4	5	11.36
b) Voting is the only way people like me can have any say about how the government runs things.	1	2	3	4	5	11.37
c) Only if differences in income and social position are large enough is there an incentive for individual effort.	1	2	3	4	5	11.38
d) People like me have no say in what the government does.	1	2	3	4	5	11.39
e) All in all, I think social differences in this country are fair.	1	2	3	4	5	11.40
f) Sometimes politics and government seem so complicated that a person like me cannot really understand what is going on.	1	2	3	4	5	11.41
g) It doesn't really matter which Party is in power, in the end things go on much the same.	1	2	3	4	5	11.42
h) Parties are only interested in people's votes, not in their opinions.	1	2	3	4	5	11.43

Please continue .....

		OFFICE USE ONLY

10. Do you think that trade unions in this country have too much power or too little power?

PLEASE TICK ONE BOX

(✓)

Far too much power	1
Too much power	2
About the right amount of power	3
Too little power	4
Far too little power	5

11.44

11. How about business and industry? Do they have too much power or too little power?

PLEASE TICK ONE BOX

(✓)

Far too much power	1
Too much power	2
About the right amount of power	3
Too little power	4
Far too little power	5

11.45

12. And what about the government, does it have too much power or too little power?

PLEASE TICK ONE BOX

(✓)

Far too much power	1
Too much power	2
About the right amount of power	3
Too little power	4
Far too little power	5

11.46

13. Between 1983 and 1987, how well or badly do you think the Conservative government handled each of the following issues?

PLEASE TICK ONE BOX ON EACH LINE

	Very well	Fairly well	Not very well	Not at all well	
a. Prices?	1	2	3	4	11.47
b. Unemployment?	1	2	3	4	11.48
c. Taxes?	1	2	3	4	11.49
d. Health and social services?	1	2	3	4	11.50
e. Crime?	1	2	3	4	11.51
f. Education?	1	2	3	4	11.52
g. Defence?	1	2	3	4	11.53

Please continue .....

11.54-55

14.   Some people say that British governments nowadays –
of <u>whichever</u> Party – can actually do very little to
change things.   Others say they can do quite a bit.
Do you think that British governments nowadays can
do very little or quite a bit ...

PLEASE TICK ONE BOX   **Very**   **Quite**
ON EACH LINE   **little**   **a bit**

a. ... to keep prices down?   ☐₁   ☐₂   11.56

b. ... to reduce unemployment?   ☐₁   ☐₂   11.57

c. ... to reduce taxes?   ☐₁   ☐₂   11.58

d. ... to improve the health and social services?   ☐₁   ☐₂   11.59

e. ... to reduce crime?   ☐₁   ☐₂   11.60

f. ... to improve the quality of education?   ☐₁   ☐₂   11.61

g. ... to improve Britain's safety from the threat of war?   ☐₁   ☐₂   11.62

15.a) Which of these three possible solutions
to Britain's electricity needs would you
favour most?

*PLEASE
TICK
ONE
BOX*   (✓)

We should make do with the power stations we have already   ☐₁

We should build more coal-fuelled power stations   ☐₂   11.63

We should build more nuclear power stations   ☐₃

b) As far as **nuclear** power stations are
concerned, which of these statements
comes closest to your own feelings?

*PLEASE
TICK
ONE
BOX*   (✓)

They create very serious risks for the future   ☐₁

They create quite serious risks for the future   ☐₂
                                                                  11.64
They create only slight risks for the future   ☐₃

They create hardly any risks for the future   ☐₄

Please continue .....

16.a) Which one of these two statements comes
       closest to your own views?

       PLEASE TICK   Industry should be prevented from causing damage to   (✓)
       ONE BOX   the countryside, even if this sometimes leads to   ☐₁
                                                              higher prices

               OR   11.65

                         Industry should keep prices down, even if this   ☐
                             sometimes causes damage to the countryside   ☐₂

   b) And which of these two statements comes
       closest to your own views?

       PLEASE TICK   The countryside should be protected from development,   (✓)
       ONE BOX   even if this sometimes leads to fewer new jobs   ☐₁

               OR   11.66

                         New jobs should be created, even if this sometimes   ☐
                             causes damage to the countryside   ☐₂

17.   Please tick one box on each line to show
       how you feel about ...

PLEASE TICK ONE BOX ON EACH LINE	It should be stopped altogether	It should be dis- couraged	Don't mind one way or the other	It should be encour -aged	
a) ... Increasing the amount of countryside being farmed?	☐₁	☐₂	☐₃	☐₄	11.67
b) ... Building new housing in country areas?	☐₁	☐₂	☐₃	☐₄	11.68
c) ... Putting the needs of farmers before protection of wildlife?	☐₁	☐₂	☐₃	☐₄	11.69

18.   Which, if either, of these two statements comes
       closest to your opinion on British nuclear weapons?

       PLEASE TICK   Britain should rid itself of nuclear weapons,   (✓)
       ONE BOX   while persuading others to do the same   ☐₁

               OR   11.70

                         Britain should keep its nuclear weapons until   ☐
                             we persuade others to reduce theirs   ☐₂

                                              Please continue 11.71-72

19.a) Please tick one box to show which <u>best</u> describes
the sort of work you do.

(If you are not working now, please tick a box to
show what you did in your <u>last</u> job.)

PLEASE TICK ONE BOX

(✓)

Farmer or farm manager ☐ 0 1

Farm worker ☐ 0 2

Skilled manual work (for example: plumber, electrician,
fitter, train driver, cook, hairdresser) ☐ 0 3

Semi-skilled or unskilled manual work (for example: machine
operator, assembler, postman, waitress, cleaner, labourer) ☐ 0 4

11.73-74

Professional or technical work (for example: doctor,
accountant, school teacher, social worker, computer programmer) ☐ 0 5

Manager or administrator (for example: company director, manager,
executive officer, local authority officer) ☐ 0 6

Clerical (for example: clerk, secretary, telephone operator) ☐ 0 7

Sales (for example: commercial traveller, shop assistant) ☐ 0 8

Other (Please describe) _____ ☐ 9 7

(Never had a job) ☐ 9 0

b) Are you self-employed or do you work for
someone else as an employee?

(If you are not working now, please answer about
your <u>last</u> job)

PLEASE TICK ONE BOX

(✓)

Self-employed ☐ 1

Employee ☐ 2

11.75

(Never had a job) ☐ 3

c) As your position at work, are you (or were you) ...

(✓)

*PLEASE TICK
ONE BOX*

... a supervisor or foreman of manual workers, ☐ 1

a supervisor of non-manual workers, ☐ 2

11.76

or - <u>not</u> a supervisor or foreman? ☐ 3

(Never had a job) ☐ 4

Please continue .....

20.a) And now please tell us about your **first** job -
       please tick one box to show which best describes
       the sort of work you did in your **first** job.

       (Even if you are still in your first job, please
       tick one box)   (✓)

       PLEASE TICK ONE BOX   **Farmer or farm manager**   [0 1]

                                                      Farm worker   [0 2]

                 Skilled manual work (for example: plumber, electrician,
                              fitter, train driver, cook, hairdresser)   [0 3]
       Semi-skilled or unskilled manual work (for example: machine
           operator, assembler, postman, waitress, cleaner, labourer)   [0 4]

                                                                                        11.77-78

                      Professional or technical work (for example: doctor,
         accountant, school teacher, social worker, computer programmer)   [0 5]
       Manager or administrator (for example: company director, manager,
                         executive officer, local authority officer)   [0 6]

             Clerical (for example: clerk, secretary, telephone operator)   [0 7]

             Sales (for example: commercial traveller, shop assistant)   [0 8]

       Other (Please describe) _____ _____   [9 7]

                                                  (Never had a job)   [9 0]

    b) Were you self-employed or did you work
        for someone else as an employee?   (✓)
        (Please tell us about your **first** job)   Self-employed   [1]
        PLEASE TICK ONE BOX   11.79
                                                        Employee   [2]

                                                  (Never had a job)   [3]

    c) As your position at work, were you . . .   (✓)
        PLEASE TICK   . . . a supervisor or foreman of manual workers,   [1]
        ONE BOX
                            a supervisor of non-manual workers,   [2]
                                                                                        11.80
                            or ~ **not** a supervisor or foreman?   [3]

                                                  (Never had a job)   [4]

                                      Please continue .....   CARD 12

21. Please *tick one box for each statement* below to
    show how much you agree or disagree with it.

		Agree strongly	Agree	Neither agree nor disagree	Dis- agree	Disagree strongly	
a.	Government should redistribute income from the better-off to those who are less well off.	□₁	□₂	□₃	□₄	□₅	12.07
b.	Big business benefits owners at the expense of workers.	□₁	□₂	□₃	□₄	□₅	12.08
c.	Too many people these days like to rely on government handouts.	□₁	□₂	□₃	□₄	□₅	12.09
d.	Ordinary working people do not get their fair share of the nation's wealth.	□₁	□₂	□₃	□₄	□₅	12.10
e.	Many people who get social security don't really deserve any help.	□₁	□₂	□₃	□₄	□₅	12.11
f.	When someone is unemployed it's usually his or her own fault.	□₁	□₂	□₃	□₄	□₅	12.12
g.	There is one law for the rich and one for the poor.	□₁	□₂	□₃	□₄	□₅	12.13
h.	The welfare state makes people nowadays less willing to look after themselves.	□₁	□₂	□₃	□₄	□₅	12.14

Please continue .....

THE 1987 QUESTIONNAIRES AND SCALE CARDS   305

OFFICE
USE
ONLY

PLEASE TICK ONE BOX
FOR EACH STATEMENT

	Agree strongly	Agree	Neither agree nor disagree	Dis- agree	Disagree strongly	
i. If welfare benefits weren't so generous, people would learn to stand on their own two feet.	1	2	3	4	5	12.15
j. Full cooperation in firms is impossible because workers and management are really on opposite sides.	1	2	3	4	5	12.16
k. Young people today don't have enough respect for traditional British values.	1	2	3	4	5	12.17
l. People who break the law should be given stiffer sentences.	1	2	3	4	5	12.18
m. Management will always try to get the better of employees if it gets the change.	1	2	3	4	5	12.19
n. For some crimes, the death penalty is the most appropriate sentence.	1	2	3	4	5	12.20
o. Schools should teach children to obey authority.	1	2	3	4	5	12.21
p. The law should always be obeyed, even if a particular law is wrong.	1	2	3	4	5	12.22
q. Censorship of films and magazines is necessary to uphold moral standards.	1	2	3	4	5	12.23

Please continue 12.24-25

22. Please think of the <u>two</u> people you discussed politics
with most often, during the election campaign.

Please answer a, b and c below about:
- the <u>first</u> person, that is the person you
discussed politics with most often
- the <u>second</u> person, the person you discussed
politics with next most often
- IF YOU <u>NEVER</u> DISCUSSED POLITICS WITH ANYBODY,
PLEASE TICK THIS BOX ⟶ ☐₁
AND GO TO Q.23 (page 13)

12.26

a) What relationship is this person to you?

	First person	Second person
TICK ONE BOX ONLY FOR THE FIRST PERSON, AND ONE BOX ONLY FOR THE SECOND PERSON	Husband/wife/partner ☐₁	☐₁
	Other family member in your household ☐₂	☐₂
	Other family member <u>not</u> in your household ☐₃	☐₃
	Co-worker ☐₄	☐₄
	Neighbour ☐₅	☐₅
	Friend other than co-worker or neighbour ☐₆	☐₆

12.27 /
12.28

---

b) As far as you know, does this person think
of himself or herself as ...

	First person	Second person
TICK ONE BOX ONLY FOR THE FIRST PERSON AND ONE BOX ONLY FOR THE SECOND PERSON	... Conservative ☐₀₁	☐₀₁
	Labour ☐₀₂	☐₀₂
	SDP or Liberal or Alliance ☐₀₃	☐₀₃
	Scottish National ☐₀₆	☐₀₆
	Plaid Cymru ☐₀₇	☐₀₇
	The Green Party ☐₀₈	☐₀₈
or - something else? (PLEASE STATE) _____	☐₉₇	
_____		☐₉₇

12.29-30
12.31-32

---

c) And does this person live in ...

	First person	Second person
TICK ONE BOX ONLY FOR THE FIRST PERSON AND ONE BOX ONLY FOR THE SECOND PERSON	... the same household as you, ☐₁	☐₁
	the same street, ☐₂	☐₂
	the same neighbourhood, ☐₃	☐₃
	the same town or borough, ☐₄	☐₄
	the same city or county, ☐₅	☐₅
	or - live further away? ☐₆	☐₆

12.33 /
12.34

Please continue .....

12.35

23.   Some people say that all political parties look
       after certain groups and are not so concerned
       about others.

How closely do you think the <u>Conservative Party</u>
looks after the interests of ...

PLEASE TICK ONE BOX
ON EACH LINE

	Very closely	Fairly closely	Not very closely	Not at all closely	
a. ... working class people?	☐₁	☐₂	☐₃	☐₄	12.36
b. ... middle class people?	☐₁	☐₂	☐₃	☐₄	12.37
c. ... unemployed people?	☐₁	☐₂	☐₃	☐₄	12.38
d. ... big business?	☐₁	☐₂	☐₃	☐₄	12.39
e. ... trade unions?	☐₁	☐₂	☐₃	☐₄	12.40
f. ... black people and Asians in Britain?	☐₁	☐₂	☐₃	☐₄	12.41
g. ... homosexuals, that is gays and lesbians?	☐₁	☐₂	☐₃	☐₄	12.42

24.   And the <u>Labour Party</u> - how closely do you think
       the Labour Party looks after the interests of ...

PLEASE TICK ONE BOX
ON EACH LINE

	Very closely	Fairly closely	Not very closely	Not at all closely	
a. ... working class people?	☐₁	☐₂	☐₃	☐₄	12.43
b. ... middle class people?	☐₁	☐₂	☐₃	☐₄	12.44
c. ... unemployed people?	☐₁	☐₂	☐₃	☐₄	12.45
d. ... big business?	☐₁	☐₂	☐₃	☐₄	12.46
e. ... trade unions?	☐₁	☐₂	☐₃	☐₄	12.47
f. ... black people and Asians in Britain?	☐₁	☐₂	☐₃	☐₄	12.48
g. ... homosexuals, that is gays and lesbians?	☐₁	☐₂	☐₃	☐₄	12.49

Please continue .....

25. And the SDP/Liberal Alliance - how closely
     does it look after the interests of ...

PLEASE TICK ONE BOX   Very   Fairly   Not very   Not at all
ON EACH LINE   closely   closely   closely   closely

a. ... working class people?   ☐₁   ☐₂   ☐₃   ☐₄   12.50

b. ... middle class people?   ☐₁   ☐₂   ☐₃   ☐₄   12.51

c. ... unemployed people?   ☐₁   ☐₂   ☐₃   ☐₄   12.52

d. ... big business?   ☐₁   ☐₂   ☐₃   ☐₄   12.53

e. ... trade unions?   ☐₁   ☐₂   ☐₃   ☐₄   12.54

f. ... black people and Asians
    in Britain?   ☐₁   ☐₂   ☐₃   ☐₄   12.55

g. ... homosexuals, that is gays
    and lesbians?   ☐₁   ☐₂   ☐₃   ☐₄   12.56

26. Which one of these types of school did you last
     attend full-time?   (✓)

PLEASE TICK ONE BOX -   None - never attended any school ☐₉₀
DO NOT INCLUDE COLLEGE
OR UNIVERSITY   Primary or Elementary school   ☐₀₁

Secondary school in England or Wales:

                                       Secondary modern   ☐₀₂   12.57-58

                     Comprehensive (inc. sixth-form college) ☐₀₃

                                         Grammar school   ☐₀₄

                                           Direct grant   ☐₀₅

          Independent fee-paying (e.g. private or 'public') ☐₀₆

                                       Technical school   ☐₀₇

Secondary school in Scotland:

                                       Junior secondary   ☐₀₈

                     Comprehensive (inc. sixth-form college) ☐₀₉

                        Senior secondary (6-year selective) ☐₁₀

                              Grant-aided (direct grant) ☐₁₁

                          Independent fee-paying (private) ☐₁₂

Other school in the UK   ☐₉₇
(PLEASE DESCRIBE) _____

                                       School outside UK: ☐₉₈

                              Please continue .....

27.a) To help us plan better in future, please tell
us about <u>how long</u> it took you to complete this
questionnaire?

PLEASE TICK ONE BOX

(✓)

Less than 15 minutes ☐ 1

Between 15 and 20 minutes ☐ 2

Between 20 and 30 minutes ☐ 3

Between 30 and 45 minutes ☐ 4

Between 45 and 60 minutes ☐ 5

Over one hour ☐ 6

12.59

b) And on what <u>date</u> did you fill in the questionnaire?

PLEASE WRITE IN: DAY _____

12.60-

MONTH _____

12.62-6

THANK YOU VERY MUCH FOR YOUR HELP!

12.64-8

Please keep the completed questionnaire for the interviewer
if he or she has arranged to call for it.   Otherwise,
please post it <u>as soon as possible</u> in the pre-paid,
addressed envelope provided.

OFFICE USE ONLY:

P.934/X
Summer 1987

Serial No.

SCALE CARDS 1-7

SOCIAL AND COMMUNITY PLANNING RESEARCH
and
THE UNIVERSITY OF OXFORD. NUFFIELD COLLEGE

BRITISH GENERAL ELECTION STUDY 1987

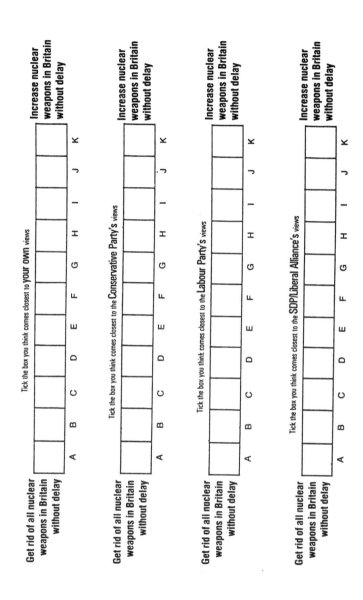

Tick the box you think comes closest to **your own** views

Get rid of all nuclear weapons in Britain without delay

A B C D E F G H I J K

Increase nuclear weapons in Britain without delay

Tick the box you think comes closest to the **Conservative Party's** views

Get rid of all nuclear weapons in Britain without delay

A B C D E F G H I J K

Increase nuclear weapons in Britain without delay

Tick the box you think comes closest to the **Labour Party's** views

Get rid of all nuclear weapons in Britain without delay

A B C D E F G H I J K

Increase nuclear weapons in Britain without delay

Tick the box you think comes closest to the **SDP/Liberal Alliance's** views

Get rid of all nuclear weapons in Britain without delay

A B C D E F G H I J K

Increase nuclear weapons in Britain without delay

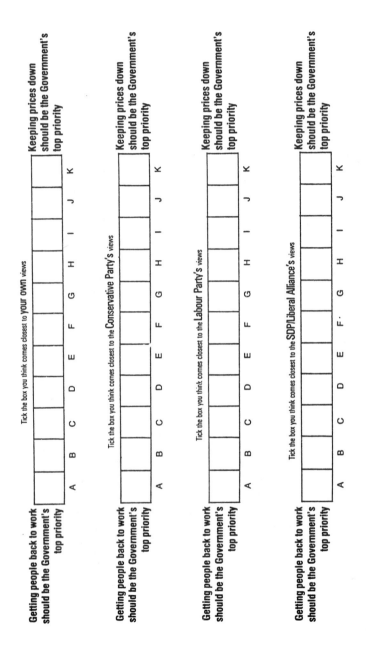

Tick the box you think comes closest to **your own** views

Getting people back to work should be the Government's top priority

A   B   C   D   E   F   G   H   I   J   K

Keeping prices down should be the Government's top priority

Tick the box you think comes closest to the **Conservative Party's** views

Getting people back to work should be the Government's top priority

A   B   C   D   E   F   G   H   I   J   K

Keeping prices down should be the Government's top priority

Tick the box you think comes closest to the **Labour Party's** views

Getting people back to work should be the Government's top priority

A   B   C   D   E   F   G   H   I   J   K

Keeping prices down should be the Government's top priority

Tick the box you think comes closest to the **SDP/Liberal Alliance's** views

Getting people back to work should be the Government's top priority

A   B   C   D   E   F.   G   H   I   J   K

Keeping prices down should be the Government's top priority

Scale 2
Q.28

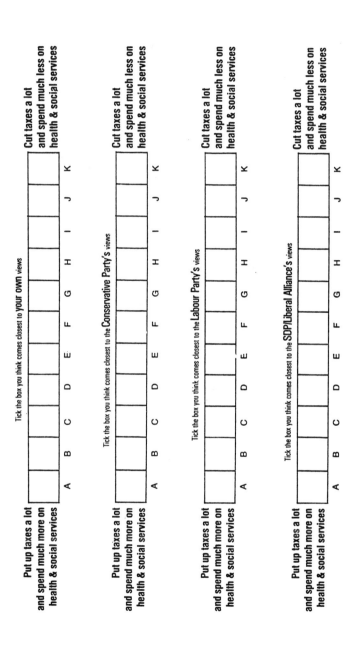

Tick the box you think comes closest to your own views

Put up taxes a lot and spend much more on health & social services   A B C D E F G H I J K   Cut taxes a lot and spend much less on health & social services

Tick the box you think comes closest to the Conservative Party's views

Put up taxes a lot and spend much more on health & social services   A B C D E F G H I J K   Cut taxes a lot and spend much less on health & social services

Tick the box you think comes closest to the Labour Party's views

Put up taxes a lot and spend much more on health & social services   A B C D E F G H I J K   Cut taxes a lot and spend much less on health & social services

Tick the box you think comes closest to the SDP/Liberal Alliance's views

Put up taxes a lot and spend much more on health & social services   A B C D E F G H I J K   Cut taxes a lot and spend much less on health & social services

Scale 3
Q.29

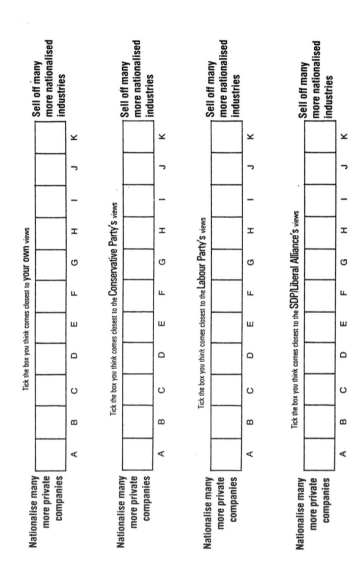

Scale 4
Q.34

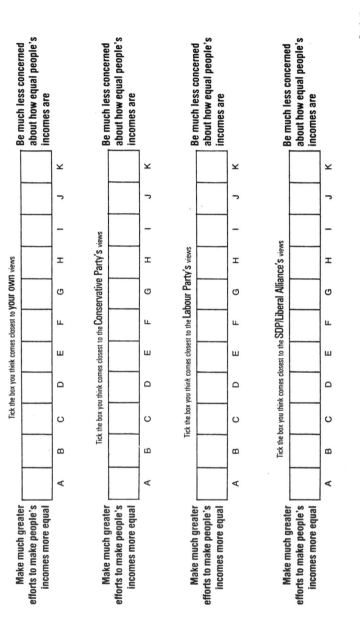

Tick the box you think comes closest to **your own** views

Make much greater efforts to make people's incomes more equal

A B C D E F G H I J K

Be much less concerned about how equal people's incomes are

Tick the box you think comes closest to the **Conservative Party's** views

Make much greater efforts to make people's incomes more equal

A B C D E F G H I J K

Be much less concerned about how equal people's incomes are

Tick the box you think comes closest to the **Labour Party's** views

Make much greater efforts to make people's incomes more equal

A B C D E F G H I J K

Be much less concerned about how equal people's incomes are

Tick the box you think comes closest to the **SDP/Liberal Alliance's** views

Make much greater efforts to make people's incomes more equal

A B C D E F G H I J K

Be much less concerned about how equal people's incomes are

Scale 5
Q.35

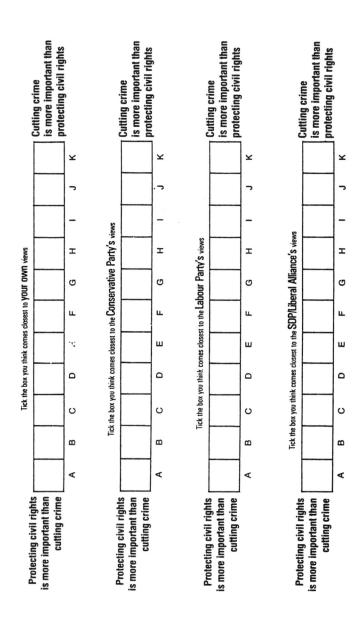

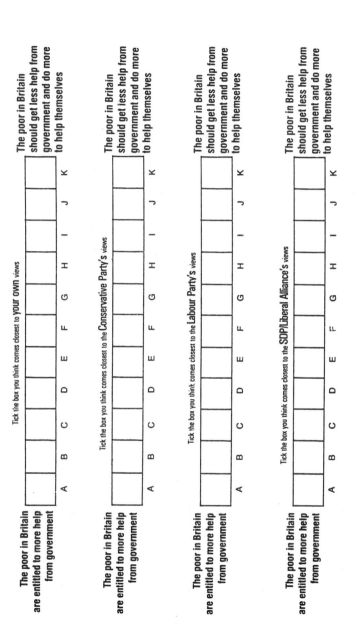

Scale 7
Q.40

Bibliography

Abercrombie N and Warde A (1988) *Contemporary British Society*, Cambridge: Polity Press.

Abramson P R (1972) Intergenerational social mobility and partisan choice, *American Political Science Review* **66**, 1291–1294.

Abramson P R (1978) Generational replacement and partisan dealignment in Britain and the United States, *British Journal of Political Science* **8**, 505–9.

Abrams M, Rose R and Hinden R (1960) *Must Labour Lose?* Harmondsworth, Middlesex: Penguin.

Aish A-M (1989) Environmentally-related attitudes: measurement and dimensionality, Report for the Survey Methods Centre, London: SCPR.

Aldrich J H and Nelson F D (1984) *Linear Probability, Logit and Probit Models*, Beverly Hills: Sage.

Alford R R (1962) A suggested index of the association of social class and voting, *Public Opinion Quarterly* **26**, 417–425.

Alt J (1979) *The Politics of Economic Decline*, Cambridge: Cambridge University Press.

Alt J (1984) Dealignment and the dynamics of partisanship in Britain, in Dalton R J, Flanagan S C and Beck P A (eds) *Electoral Change in Advanced Industrial Democracies*, Princeton: Princeton University Press.

Alt J and Turner J (1982) The case of the silk-stocking socialists and the calculating children of the middle class, *British Journal of Political Science* **12**, 273–90.

Anwar M (1986) *Race and Politics*, London: Tavistock.

Bain G S, Bacon R and Pimlott J (1972) The labour force, in A H Halsey (ed) *Trends in British Society since 1900*, London: Macmillan.

Bakke E W (1933) *The Unemployed Man*, London: Nisbet.

Bean C and Symons J (1990) Ten years of Mrs T, Centre for Labour Economics, LSE, discussion paper no 370.

Belknap G and Campbell A (1952) Political party identification and attitudes toward foreign policy, *Public Opinion Quarterly* **15**, 601–23.

Bishop G F, Tuchfarber A J and Oldendick R W (1978) The nagging question of question wording, *American Journal of Political Science* 22, 250–69.

Bochel J M and Denver D T (1970) Religion and voting: a critical review and new analysis, *Political Studies* 18, 205–219.

Brierley P (1988) Religion, in A H Halsey (ed) *British Social Trends since 1900*, London: Macmillan.

Brint S (1984) "New-class" and cumulative trend explanations of the liberal political attitudes of professionals, *American Journal of Sociology* 90, 30–69.

Brown A (1989) *The Young Voter*, M Sc Thesis, University of Oxford.

Budge I, Crewe I and Farlie D (eds) (1976) *Party Identification and Beyond*, New York: Wiley.

Bürklin W (1981) Die Grunen und die 'Neue Politik', *Politische Vierteljahresschrift* 22, 359–382.

Bürklin W P (1985) The split between the established and the non-established left in Germany, *European Journal of Political Research* 13, 283–93.

Bürklin W P (1987) Governing left parties frustrating the radical nonestablished Left: the rise and inevitable decline of the Greens, *European Sociological Review* 3, 109–126.

Butler D (1989) *British General Elections since 1945*, Oxford: Basil Blackwell.

Butler D and Butler G (1986) *British Political Facts 1900–1985*, London: Macmillan.

Butler D and Kavanagh D (1984) *The British General Election of 1983*, London: Macmillan.

Butler D and Kavanagh D (1988) *The British General Election of 1987*, London: Macmillan.

Butler D and Stokes D (1969) *Political Change in Britain*, London: Macmillan.

Butler D and Stokes D (1974) *Political Change in Britain*, revised edition, London: Macmillan

Cain B (1978) Strategic voting in Britain, *American Journal of Political Science* 22, 639–55.

Campbell A, Converse P E, Miller W E and Stokes D E (1960) *The American Voter*, New York: Wiley. Abridged edition 1964.

Capdevielle J and Dupoirier E (1981) L'effet patrimoine, in J Capdevielle et al, *France de Gauche vote à Droite*, Paris: Presses de la FNSP, 169–230.

Cautrès B (1989) L'effet chomage, in Charlot M (ed) *L'Effet Thatcher*, Paris: Economica.

Central Statistical Office (1989a) *Social Trends: 1989 edition*, London: HMSO.

Central Statistical Office (1989b) *Economic Trends: 1989 edition*, London: HMSO.

Charlot M (1975) The ideological distance between the two major parties in Britain, *European Journal of Political Research* 3, 173–80.

Charlot M (1985) The ethnic minorities' vote, in A Ranney (ed) *Britain at the Polls 1983*, Durham, North Carolina: Duke University Press, 139–154.

Charlot M (1989) Un effet patrimoine? in M Charlot (ed) *L'Effet Thatcher*, Paris: Economica.

Coleman D (1983) The demography of ethnic minorities, in Kirkwood K, Herbertson M A and Parkes A S (eds) *Biosocial Aspects of Ethnic Minorities*, Journal of Biosocial Science, Supplement No 8.

Converse P (1964) The nature of belief systems in mass publics, in D Apter (ed) *Ideology and Discontent*, New York: Free Press.

Cotgrove S and Duff A (1980) Environmentalism, middle class radicalism and politics, *Sociological Review* 28, 333–51.

Coutts K and Godley W (1989) The British economy under Mrs Thatcher, *Political Quarterly* 60, 137–151.

Cox D R (1970) *The Analysis of Binary Data*, London: Methuen.

Craig F W S (1981) *British Electoral Facts 1832–1980*, Chichester: Parliamentary Reference Service.

Craig F W S (1988) *Britain Votes 4: British Parliamentary Election Results 1983–87*, Aldershot: Gower.

Crewe I (1973) The politics of "affluent" and "traditional" workers in Britain: an aggregate data analysis, *British Journal of Political Science* 3, 29–52.

Crewe I (1974) Do Butler and Stokes really explain political change in Britain? *European Journal of Political Research* 2, 47–92.

Crewe I (1981) Why the Conservatives won, in Penniman H (ed) *Britain at the Polls, 1979*, Washington: American Enterprise Institute for Public Policy.

Crewe I (1984) The electorate: partisan dealignment ten years on, in Berrington H (ed) *Change in British Politics*, London: Frank Cass.

Crewe I (1985) Great Britain, in Crewe I and Denver D (eds) *Electoral Change in Western Democracies: Patterns and Sources of Electoral Volatility*, London: Croom Helm, 100–150.

Crewe I (1986) On the death and resurrection of class voting: some comments on *How Britain Votes*, *Political Studies* 34, 620–638.

Crewe I (1987) A new class of politics?, *Guardian* 15 June 1987.

Crewe I, Fox A and Alt J (1977) Non-voting in British General Elections: 1966-October 1974, in C Crouch (ed) *British Political Sociology Yearbook, vol 3: Participation in Politics*, London: Croom Helm, 38–109.

Crewe I, Sarlvik, B and Alt, J (1977) Partisan dealignment in Britain 1964–1974, *British Journal of Political Science* 7, 129–190.

Crewe I and Searing D D (1988) Mrs Thatcher's Crusade: Conservatism in Britain, 1972–1986, in Cooper B, Kornberg A and Mishler W (eds) *The Resurgence of Conservatism in Anglo-American Democracies*, Durham: Duke University Press.

Curtice J (1986) Political partisanship, in Jowell R, Witherspoon S and Brook L (eds) *British Social Attitudes: The 1986 Report*, Aldershot: Gower.

Dahrendorf R (1988) Changing social attitudes under Mrs Thatcher, in Skidelsky R (ed) *Thatcherism*, London: Chatto and Windus.

Dalton R J (1988) *Citizen Politics in Western Democracies: Public Opinion in the United States, Great Britain, West Germany and France*, Chatham, New Jersey: Chatham House Publishers.

Dalton R J, Flanagan S C and Beck P A (1984) *Electoral Change in Advanced Industrial Societies: Realignment or Dealignment?* Princeton: Princeton University Press.

Davis J A (1986) British and American attitudes: similarities and contrasts, in Jowell R, Witherspoon S and Brook L (eds) *British Social Attitudes: the 1986 Report*, Aldershot: Gower.

Dilnot A W and Stark G K (1986) The poverty trap, tax cuts and the reform of social security, *Fiscal Studies* 7:1–10.

Downs A (1957) *An Economic Theory of Democracy*, New York: Harper and Row.

Dunleavy P (1979) The urban basis of political alignment: social class, domestic property ownership, and state intervention in consumption processes, *British Journal of Political Science* 9, 409–443.

Dunleavy P (1980a) The political implications of sectoral cleavages and the growth of state employment: Part 1, the analysis of production cleavages, *Political Studies* 28, 364–383.

Dunleavy P (1980b) The political implications of sectoral cleavages and the growth of state employment: part 2, cleavage structures and political alignment, *Political Studies* 28, 527–549.

Dunleavy P (1984) Voting and the electorate, in Drucker H et al (eds) *Developments in British Politics* (revised edition), London: Macmillan.

Dunleavy P (1987) Class dealignment revisited: why odds ratios give odd results, *West European Politics* 10, 400–419.

Dunleavy P and Husbands C T (1985) *British Democracy at the Crossroads: Voting and Party Competition in the 1980s*, London: Allen and Unwin.

Eijk C van der, and Niemoller B (1979) Recall accuracy and its determinants, *Acta Politica* 14, 289–342.

Elias P (1990) Growth and decline in trade union membership in Great Britain: evidence from work histories, SCELI Working Paper 16, Nuffield College, Oxford: ESRC/SCELI.

Elliott B, McCrone D and Bechhofer F (1988) Anxieties and ambitions: the petit bourgeoisie and the New Right in Britain, in Rose D (ed) *Social Stratification and Economic Change*, London: Hutchinson.

Evans G and Durant J (1989) Understanding of science in Britain and the USA, in Jowell R, Witherspoon S and Brook L (eds) *British Social Attitudes: Special International Report*, Aldershot: Gower.

Evans G, Heath A and Payne C (1989) Modelling trends in the class/party relationship 1964–1987 using log-linear analysis, paper presented at ECPR workshop, Paris, 10–15 April 1989.

Fair R C (1978) The effect of economic events on votes for the president, *Review of Economics and Statistics* 60, 159–73.

Fienberg S E (1980) *The Analysis of Cross-Classified Categorical Data*, 2nd ed, Cambridge, Mass: MIT Press.

Fiorina M (1981) *Retrospective Voting in American National Elections*, New Haven: Yale University Press.

Fishman N and Shaw A (1989) The tactical voting campaign, in I Crewe and M Harrop (eds), *Political Communication: The British General Election of 1987*, Cambridge: CUP.

Forrest R and Murie A (1984) Residualisation and council housing: aspects of changing social relations of housing tenure, *Journal of Social Policy* 12, 453–68.

Franklin M (1985) *The Decline of Class Voting in Britain*, Oxford: Clarendon Press.

Franklin M (1987) The Falklands factor, *Contemporary Record*, autumn 1987.

Franklin M and Page E C (1984) A critique of the consumption cleavage approach in British voting studies, *Political Studies* 32, 521–36.

Frey B and Garbers H (1971) Politico-Econometrics: on estimation in political economy, *Political Studies* 19, 317.

Galbraith J W and Rae N C (1989) A test of the importance of tactical voting: Great Britain 1987, *British Journal of Political Science* 19, 126–136.

Gallie D (1978) *In Search of the New Working Class*, Cambridge: Cambridge University Press.

Gallie D (1989) Trade union allegiance and decline in British Urban Labour markets, SCELI working paper 9, Nuffield College, Oxford: ESRC/SCELI.

Gamble A (1987) Crawling from the wreckage, *Marxism Today*, July 1987, 12–17.

Garnsey E (1975) Occupational structure in industrialized societies: some notes on the convergence thesis in the light of Soviet experience, *Sociology* 9, 437–458.

Goldthorpe J H, Lockwood D, Bechhofer F and Platt J (1968) *The Affluent Worker: Political Attitudes and Behaviour*, Cambridge: Cambridge University Press.

Goldthorpe J H (1980) *Social Mobility and Class Structure in Britain*, Oxford: Clarendon Press.

Goldthorpe J H (1982) On the service class, its formation and future, in Giddens A and Mackenzie G (eds) *Social Class and the Division of Labour*, Cambridge: Cambridge University Press.

Goldthorpe J H (1987) *Social Mobility and Class Structure in Modern Britain*, 2nd edition, Oxford: Clarendon Press.

Goldthorpe J H and Payne C D (1986) Trends in intergenerational class mobility in England and Wales 1972–1983, *Sociology* 20, 1–24.

Goodhart C A E and Bhansali R H (1970) Political economy, *Political Studies* 18, 43–106.

Gorz A (1976) Technology, technicians and class struggle, in Gorz A (ed) *The Division of Labour: The Labour Process and Class Struggle in Modern Capitalism*, Brighton: Harvester.

de Graaf N D and Ultee W (1987) Intergenerationele mobiliteit en politieke verhoudingen, *Acta Politica* 22, 3–37.

Haberman S J (1982) Analysis of dispersion of multinomial responses, *Journal of the American Statistical Association* 77, 568–580.

Hall S (1979) The Great Moving Right Show, *Marxism Today* 23 (January 1979): 14–20.

Hall S (1985) Authoritarian populism: a reply to Jessop et al, *New Left Review* 151, 115–124.

Halsey A H, Heath A F and Ridge J M (1980) *Origins and Destinations: Family, Class and Education in Modern Britain*, Oxford: Clarendon Press.

Harris R and Seldon A (1987) *Welfare Without the State: A Quarter-Century of Suppressed Public Choice*, London: Institute of Economic Affairs.

Harrop M (1980) The urban basis of political alignment, a comment, *British Journal of Political Science* 10, 388–398.

Harrop M and Miller W L (1987) *Elections and Voters: A Comparative Introduction*, London: Macmillan.

Haskey J (1988) The ethnic minority populations of Great Britain: their size and characteristics, *Population Trends* 54, 29–31.

Heath A F (1981) *Social Mobility*, Glasgow: Collins

Heath A F (1986) Do people have consistent attitudes? in Jowell R M, Witherspoon S and Brook L (eds) *British Social Attitudes: The 1986 Report*, Aldershot: Gower.

Heath A F (1990) The sociology of social class, in C G N Mascie-Taylor (ed) *The Biology of Social Class*, Oxford: Clarendon Press.

Heath A F (1990) Class and political partisanship, in Clark J, Mogdil S and Mogdil C (eds) *John Goldthorpe: Consensus and Controversy*, London: Falmer Press.

Heath A F and Clifford P (1990) Class inequalities in education in the twentieth century, *Journal of the Royal Statistical Society, series A* 153, 1–16.

Heath A F and Evans G (1988) Working-class Conservatives and middle-class socialists, in Jowell R, Witherspoon S and Brook L (eds) *British Social Attitudes: The 5th Report*, Aldershot: Gower.

Heath A F, Jowell R M and Curtice J K (1985) *How Britain Votes*, Oxford: Pergamon.

Heath A F, Jowell R M and Curtice J K (1986) Understanding electoral change in Britain, *Parliamentary Affairs* 39, 150–64.

Heath A F, Jowell R M and Curtice J K (1987) Trendless fluctuation: a reply to Crewe, *Political Studies* 35, 256–277.

Heath A F, Jowell R M and Curtice J K (1988) Class dealignment and the explanation of political change: a reply to Dunleavy, *West European Politics* 11, 146–8.

Heath A F and McDonald S-K (1987) Social change and the future of the Left, *Political Quarterly* 58, 364–377.

Heath A F and McDonald S-K (1988) The demise of party identification theory? *Electoral Studies* 7, 95–107.

Heath A F and Topf R (1986) Educational expansion and political change in Britain: 1964–1983, *European Journal of Political Research* 14, 543–567.

Heath A F, Jowell R M, Curtice J K and Evans G (1990) The rise of the new political agenda? *European Sociological Review* 6, 31–48.

Himmelweit H T, Jaeger, M and Stockdale J (1978) Memory for past vote: implications of a study of bias in recall, *British Journal of Political Science* 8, 365–76.

Himmelweit H T, Humphreys P, and Jaeger M (1985) *How Voters Decide* (revised edition), Milton Keynes: Open University Press.

Hope K (1975) Crewe's test of the embourgeoisement thesis, *British Journal of Political Science* 5, 256–8.

Hornsby-Smith M P and Lee R M (1979) *Roman Catholic Opinion*, Guildford: University of Surrey.

Hornsby-Smith M P (1987) *Roman Catholics in England*, Cambridge: Cambridge University Press.

Inglehart R (1971) The silent revolution in Europe: intergenerational change in post-industrial societies, *American Political Science Review* 65, 991–1017.
Inglehart R (1977) *The Silent Revolution: Changing Values and Political Styles among Western Publics*, Princeton: Princeton University Press.
Inglehart R (1981) Post-materialism in an environment of insecurity, *American Political Science Review* 75, 880–900.
Inglehart R and Rabier J-R (1986) Political realignment in advanced industrial society: from class-based politics to quality-of-life politics, *Government and Opposition* 21, 456–79.
Jahoda M, Lazarsfeld P F and Zeisel H (1933) *Die Arbeitslosen von Marienthal*, English edition London: Tavistock, 1973.
Jessop B, Bonnett K, Bromley S and Ling T (1984) Authoritarian populism, two nations and Thatcherism, *New Left Review* 147, 32–60.
Jessop B, Bonnett K, Bromley S and Ling T (1985) Thatcherism and the politics of hegemony: a reply to Stuart Hall, *New Left Review* 153, 87–101.
Johnston R (1983) The neighbourhood effect won't go away: observations on the electoral geography of England in the light of Dunleavy's critique, *Geoforum* 14, 161–68
Johnston R J, Pattie C J and Allsopp J G (1988) *A Nation Dividing? The Electoral Map of Great Britain 1979–87*, Harlow: Longman.
Kavanagh D (1987) *Thatcherism and British Politics*, Oxford: OUP.
Kavanagh D (1990) Ideology, sociology and Labour's strategy, in Clark J, Mogdil S and Mogdil C (eds) *John Goldthorpe: Consensus and Controversy*, London: Falmer Press.
Kelley J and McAllister I (1987) Social context and electoral behaviour in Britain, *American Journal of Political Science* 31, 564–586.
Kiewiet D R (1983) *Macro-economics and Micro-politics: The Electoral Effects of Economic Issues*, Chicago: University of Chicago Press.
Kinder D R and Kiewiet D R (1981) Sociotropic politics: the American case, *British Journal of Political Science* 11, 129–161.
Korpi W (1972) Some problems in the measurement of class voting, *American Journal of Sociology* 78, 627–42.
Kramer G H (1971) Short-term fluctuations in U.S. voting behaviour, 1896–1964, *American Political Science Review* 65, 131–43.
Kramer G H (1983) The ecological fallacy revisited: aggregate- versus individual-level findings on economics and elections and sociotropic voting, *American Political Science Review* 77, 92–111.
Kriesi H (1989) New social movements and the new class in the Netherlands, *American Journal of Sociology* 94, 1078–1116.
Laver M (1984) On party policy, polarisation and the breaking of moulds: the 1983 British party manifestos in context, *Parliamentary Affairs* 37, 33–39.
Layard R and Nickell S (1989) The Thatcher Miracle? Centre for Labour Economics, LSE, discussion paper no 343. (A shortened version is published in the *American Economic Review (papers and proceedings)* 79, 215–219.)
Liem R and Liem J H (1988) Psychological effects of unemployment on workers and their families, *Journal of Social Issues* 44, 87–105.
Lievesley D and Waterton F (1985) Measuring individual attitude change,

in Jowell R and Witherspoon S (eds) *British Social Attitudes: The 1985 Report*, Aldershot: Gower.

Lipset S M (1981) *Political Man: The Social Bases of Politics*, expanded edition, Baltimore: Johns Hopkins University Press.

Lipsey D, Shaw A and Willman J (1989) *Labour's Electoral Challenge*, Fabian Research Series 352, London: Fabian Society.

McAdams J (1987) Testing the theory of the new class, *The Sociological Quarterly* 28, 23–49.

McPherson A and Willms J D (1987) Equalisation and improvement: some effects of comprehensive reorganisation in Scotland, *Sociology* 21, 509–539.

Mallet S (1963) *The New Working Class*, Paris: Editions du Seuil.

Markus G (1988) The impact of personal and national economic conditions on the Presidential vote: a pooled cross-sectional analysis, *American Journal of Political Science* 32, 137–154.

Marshall G, Newby H, Rose D and Vogler C (1988) *Social Class in Modern Britain*, London: Hutchinson.

Marshall G, Rose D, Newby H and Vogler C (1988b) Political quiescence among the unemployed in modern Britain, in Rose D (ed) *Social Stratification and Economic Change*, London: Hutchinson.

Miller W L (1978) Social class and party choice in England: a new analysis, *British Journal of Political Science* 8, 257–74.

Miller W L (1980) What was the profit in following the crowd? The effectiveness of party strategies on immigration and devolution, *British Journal of Political Science* 10, 15–38.

Miller W L and Raab G (1977) The religious alignment at English elections between 1918 and 1970, *Political Studies* 25, 227–251.

Miller W L, Tagg S and Britto K (1986) Partisanship and party preference in government and opposition: the mid-term perspective, *Electoral Studies* 5, 31–46.

Morris C N and Preston I (1986) Taxes, benefits and the distribution of income 1968–83, *Fiscal Studies* 7, 18–27.

Mosteller F (1968) Association and estimation in contingency tables, *Journal of the American Statistical Association* 63:1–28.

Moyser G (1978) The political organisation of the middle class: the case of the Church of England, in Garrard J et al (eds) *The Middle Class in Politics*, Farnborough: Saxon House.

Nickell S J (1980) A picture of male unemployment in Britain, *Economic Journal* 90, 776–794.

Norpoth H (1987) The Falklands War and government popularity in Britain: rally without consequence or surge without decline? *Electoral Studies* 6, 3–16.

Norris P (1990) Thatcher's enterprise society and electoral change, *West European Politics* 13, 63–78.

Office of Population Censuses and Surveys (1970) *Classification of Occupations 1970*, London: HMSO.

Office of Population Censuses and Surveys (1980) *Classification of Occupations 1980*, London: HMSO.

Papadakis E and Taylor-Gooby P (1987) *The Private Provision of Public Welfare*, Brighton:Wheatsheaf Books.

Parkin F (1968) *Middle Class Radicalism: The Social Bases of the British Campaign for Nuclear Disarmament*, Manchester: Manchester University Press.
Peach C, Robinson V, Maxted J and Chance J (1988) Immigration and ethnicity, in A H Halsey (ed) *British Social Trends Since 1900*, London: Macmillan.
Pedersen M N (1979) The dynamics of European party systems: changing patterns of electoral volatility, *European Journal of Political Research* 7, 1–27.
Pedersen M N (1983) Changing patterns of electoral volatility in European party systems, 1948–1977: explorations in explanation, in Daalder H and Mair P (eds) *Western European Party Systems: Continuity and Change*, Beverly Hills: Sage
Pierce J and Rose D (1974) Non-attitudes and American public opinion, *American Political Science Review* 68, 626–49.
Price R and Bain G S (1988) The labour force, in A H Halsey (ed) *British Social Trends Since 1900*, London: Macmillan.
Przeworski A and Sprague J (1986) *Paper Stones: A History of Electoral Socialism*, Chicago: University of Chicago Press.
Rallings C S (1975) Two types of middle-class Labour voter? *British Journal of Political Science* 5, 107–128.
Rentoul J (1989) *Me and Mine*, London: Unwin Hyman.
Robertson D (1984) *Class and the British Electorate*, Oxford: Basil Blackwell.
Robertson D (1987) Britain, Australia, New Zealand and the United States 1946–1981: an initial comparative analysis, in Budge I, Robertson D and Hearl D (eds) *Ideology, Strategy and Party Change: Spatial Analyses of Post-War Election Programmes in 19 Democracies*, Cambridge: Cambridge University Press.
Rose R and McAllister J (1986) *Voters Begin to Choose: From Closed Class to Open Elections in Britain*, London: Sage
Routh G (1980) *Occupation and Pay in Great Britain 1906–79*, London: Macmillan.
Routh G (1987) *Occupations of the People of Great Britain, 1801–1981*, London: Macmillan.
Royal Commission on the Distribution of Income and Wealth (1976–9) London: HMSO.
Rubinstein W D (1986) *Wealth and Inequality in Britain*, London: Faber and Faber.
Runciman W G (1966) *Relative Deprivation and Social Justice*, London: Routledge and Kegan Paul.
Sanders D, Ward H and Marsh D (with D Fletcher) (1987) Government popularity and the Falklands War: a reassessment, *British Journal of Political Science* 17, 281–314.
Sarlvik B and Crewe I (1983) *Decade of Dealignment*, Cambridge: Cambridge University Press.
Schlozman K and Verba S (1979) *Injury to Insult*, Cambridge, Mass: Harvard University Press.
Shaw C (1988) Latest estimates of ethnic minority populations, *Population Trends* 51, 5–8.

Sobel M E (1981) Diagonal mobility models: a substantively motivated class of designs for the analysis of mobility effects, *American Sociological Review* **46**, 893–906.

Sobel M E (1985) Social mobility and fertility revisited: some new models for the analysis of the mobility effects hypothesis, *American Sociological Review* **50**, 699–712.

Soltow L (1968) Long-run changes in British income inequality, *Economic History Review* **21**, 17–29.

Stigler G J (1973) General economic conditions and national elections, *American Economic Review* **63** (part 2), 161–167.

Stouffer S A, Suchman E A, DeVinney L C, Star S A and Williams R M Jr (1949) *The American Soldier I: Adjustment During Army Life*, Princeton: Princeton University Press.

Studlar D (1974) British public opinion, colour issues, and Enoch Powell: a longitudinal analysis, *British Journal of Political Science* **4**, 371–82.

Studlar D (1978) Policy voting in Britain: the coloured immigration issue in the 1964, 1966 and 1970 General Elections, *American Political Science Review* **72**, 46–64.

Sullivan J L, Piereson J E and Marcus G E (1978) Ideological constraint in the mass public: a methodological critique and some new findings, *American Journal of Political Science* **22**, 233–49.

Swaddle K and Heath A F (1989) Official and reported turnout in the British General Election of 1987, *British Journal of Political Science* **19**, 537–570.

Taylor S and Payne C (1973) Features of electoral behaviour at by-elections, in Cook C and Ramsden J (eds) *By-Elections in British Politics*, London: Macmillan.

Thompson K (1974) Church of England Bishops as an elite, in Stanworth P and Giddens A (eds) *Elites and Power in British Society*, Cambridge: Cambridge University Press.

Touraine A (1966) *La Conscience Ouvriere*, Paris: Editions du Seuil.

Tufte E R (1975) Determinants of the outcomes of midterm Congressional elections, *American Political Science Review* **69**, 812–826.

Vickers J and Yarrow G (1988) *Privatization: An Economic Analysis*, Cambridge, Mass: MIT Press.

Wald K D (1983) *Crosses on the Ballot: Patterns of British Voter Alignment since 1885*, Princeton, NJ: Princeton University Press.

Waterton J and Lievesley D (1987) Attrition in a panel study of attitudes, *Journal of Official Statistics* **3**, 267–282.

Weakliem D (1989) Class and party in Britain, 1964–83, *Sociology* **23**, 285–297.

Webb P (1987) Union, party and class in Britain: the changing electoral relationship, 1964–1983, *Politics* **7**, 15–21.

Weir B T (1975) The distortion of voter recall, *American Journal of Political Science* **59**, 53–62.

Index

Coleman, D   208, 222
Common Market, attitudes to   36, 37, 39, 40, 47
Concentration, index of   37
Conditioning in panel studies   30, 122
Consumption cleavages   103
Converse, P   11, 45
Cotgrove, S   93
Council house
  purchase   126–130, 133–5
  sales   120
Countryside
  attitudes to   188–92, 194
  scale   116, 117, 188–9, 197–8
Coutts, K   144
Craig, F W S   2, 214
Crewe, I   3, 4, 9, 10, 11, 12, 16, 17, 19, 22, 25, 29, 62, 63, 78, 81, 87, 102, 103, 104, 107, 136, 166, 170, 171, 172, 184, 190, 221, 224
Curtice, J   4, 9, 63, 65, 66, 90, 172, 196, 202

Dahrendorf, R   172
Dalton, R J   5, 6, 12, 186
Davis, J A   147
Dealignment
  class   62–84, 103, 209–10
  partisan   62
Death penalty, attitudes to   41, 48, 174, 177, 195
Defence, attitudes to   39, 46
Denver, D T   99
Diamond Commission   156
Difference between the parties   33–4, 49, 180–2
Dilnot, A W   170
Dissimilarity, index of   29
Downs, A   6, 172
Duff, A   93
Dunleavy, P   5, 62, 92, 100, 102, 103, 104, 110
Dupoirier, E   121
Durant, J   147

Economic Trends   144, 156, 157
Education
  and attitudes   174–5, 183, 189
  expansion   205–6
  and vote   90–2, 94, 95, 97, 98, 100, 115, 209
Eijk, C van der   30
Electoral Register   165
Elias, P   106
Elliott, B   66
Embourgeoisement   168–9, 170

Empire, attitudes to   41, 48
Equal opportunities for women, attitudes to   174, 177
Equal opportunities for blacks, attitudes to   174, 177, 195
Ethnicity
  size of ethnic groups   207–8, 222
  and vote   86, 112–3, 209
Evans, G   66, 74, 147, 196

Fair, R C   154
Family Expenditure Survey   169
Farlie, D   12
Farrant, G   235
Father's class see Social origins
Fienberg, S E   22, 36
Fiorina, M   12, 145
Fishman, N   53
Flanagan, S C   12
Flow of the vote   18, 19, 29, 30, 152
Fluidity   21–5, 117
Mr Foot   35
Foreign aid, attitudes to   174, 177, 195
Forrest, R   130
Fox, A   19, 166
Franchise extension   30, 79, 211–2
Franklin, M   3, 32, 33, 38, 43, 49, 51, 62, 63, 78, 99, 154, 202
Free Market Right   177–9
Frey, B   154

Galbraith, J W   53, 54
Gallie, D   100, 106
Gallup   34, 73, 74, 172
Gamble, A   122
Garbers, H   154
Garnsey, E   202
Gender and attitudes   174–5, 183, 189
General Household Survey   130, 205–6, 222
Godley, W   144
Goldthorpe, J H   63, 64, 66, 78, 170
Goodhart, C A E   7, 154
Gorz, A   100
Government responsibilities, perceptions of   146–7
Government spending, attitudes to   39, 42, 46, 48
de Graaf, N D   99
Green issues, attitudes to   188

Haberman, S J   37
Hall   8, 171, 172, 195
Halsey, A H   206, 221
Harris, R   184